THE REMINISCENCES OF
Rear Admiral Neil M. Stevenson
Chaplain Corps, U.S. Navy (Retired)

INTERVIEWED BY
Paul Stillwell

U.S. Naval Institute • Annapolis, Maryland

Copyright © 1998

Preface

This oral history originated with a request from the Chaplain Resource Board that the Naval Institute do an oral history with Chaplain Stevenson as a supplement to the CRB's own ongoing historical program. Because the Naval Institute's collection comprises primarily line officers, the memoir of a staff corps officer, specifically a Chief of Chaplains, is a welcome addition.

In telling the story of his life and naval career, Chaplain Stevenson made it clear that he wanted to contribute more than just a collection of sea stories about various incidents in his career. There are some sea stories, to be sure, but the main focus is on issues. He uses numerous examples from his experience to illustrate the implementation of those issues.

Included among the issues were the following:

>The need for Navy chaplains to master the concept of institutional ministry, rather than limiting themselves to parish ministry

>The vital necessity of sea duty in the background and makeup of a Navy chaplain

>The importance of planning, programming, and budgeting for religious resources on the basis of demonstrated requirements, rather than the previous practice of depending on paternalism from the line community

>The need for casualty assistance calls to be command functions rather than just chaplain responsibilities

>The role of the Chaplain Corps in the Vietnam War

>The need for open channels of communication between chaplains and the commands and major claimants they serve

>Serving the needs of all individuals in a command, rather than just those of specific faith groups

>Promotion in the Chaplain Corps should be on the basis of demonstrated merit and potential, not on any quota system for faith groups

>The division of labor between the Chief of Chaplains and his deputy

>The need for acceptance of increased responsibility by those chaplains highest in the hierarchical structure

>The integration of minorities into the Chaplain Corps as a whole

>Meeting the varied needs of Navy and Marine Corps families

>The establishment of the religious program specialist (RP) enlisted rating in the mid-1970s

>The value of postgraduate education and other advanced training for members of the Chaplain Corps

In the course of remembering his career, Chaplain Stevenson speaks of dozens of his fellow chaplains, in a variety of contexts. The most impressive word portrait is a fascinating description of the personality and working style of Rear Admiral John J. O'Connor, Chief of Chaplains in the late 1970s. Chaplain Stevenson worked in the front office for a year and thus had a firsthand perspective on Chaplain O'Connor's style, impact, and achievements.

In the course of moving from the initial raw transcript of the oral interviews to this final version, both Chaplain Stevenson and I have done considerable editing in the interests of accuracy, smoothness, and clarity. A few sections have been rearranged in sequence in order to facilitate a chronological approach to his career. Further, I have inserted footnotes to provide further information for readers who use the volume. In going through the entire process of editing and footnoting, Chaplain Stevenson has been most cooperative. The result is a final version that has been considerably enhanced over that in the raw initial transcripts. In addition, he has pulled from his files a number of documents that relate to the subjects discussed in the interviews. These documents are included as appendices at the end of the volume.

Ms. Ann Hassinger of the Naval Institute's history division has made a significant contribution through her diligence in the overall process of printing, proofreading, and overseeing the binding of the completed volumes.

                                                          Paul Stillwell
Director, History Division
U.S. Naval Institute
August 1998

REAR ADMIRAL NEIL MACGILL STEVENSON
CHAPLAIN CORPS
UNITED STATES NAVY (RETIRED)

Personal Data

Born: 26 December 1930, Brooklyn, New York

Parents: Margaret MacGill Stevenson, born 1903, Greenoch, Scotland
Henry Stevenson, born 1889, Belfast, Ireland

Married: 3 July 1953 to Georgia Diane Neal

Children: Heather, born 3 August 1954
Holly, born 14 August 1957
Heidi, born 3 May 1960

Ordained: 25 November 1955, by New York Presbytery of United Presbyterian Church, North America Brooklyn, New York

Education

Bachelor of arts in history and psychology, Tarkio College, Tarkio, Missouri, 1952
Master of divinity, Pittsburgh Theological Seminary, Pittsburgh, Pennsylvania, 1955
Master of theology, Princeton Theological Seminary, Princeton, New Jersey, 1968

Dates of Rank

Lieutenant (junior grade): 1 December 1955
Lieutenant: 1 December 1956
Lieutenant Commander: 1 September 1962
Commander: 1 March 1967
Captain: 1 July 1973
Rear Admiral: 1 October 1980

Chronological Transcript of Service

April 1957-May 1957	Student, Chaplain School, Newport, Rhode Island
June 1957-June 1958	Naval Training Center, Great Lakes, Illinois
June 1958-September 1960	Staff, Commander Destroyer Squadron Ten
September 1960-November 1962	Naval Station, Newport, Rhode Island
December 1962-November 1964	USS Saratoga (CVA-60)
December 1964-August 1967	Naval Air Station, Glenview, Illinois
September 1967-May 1968	Student, Postgraduate School, Princeton Theological Seminary

June 1968-July 1969	Staff, Commander Third Marine Amphibious Force, South Vietnam
August 1969-August 1972	Chaplains Division, Bureau of Naval Personnel, Arlington, Virginia
September 1972-June 1973	Student, Chaplain School (Advanced Course) Newport, Rhode Island
June 1973-June 1976	Senior Chaplain, Naval Training Center, Orlando, Florida
June 1976-July 1977	Chaplains Division, Bureau of Naval Personnel, Arlington, Virginia
June 1977-June 1980	Fleet Chaplain, Pacific Fleet/Chaplain, Naval Logistics Command Pacific Fleet, Pearl Harbor, Hawaii
July 1980-July 1983	Deputy Chief of Chaplains
August 1983-August 1985	Chief of Chaplains

Awards

Distinguished Service Medal
Meritorious Service Medal
Legion of Merit with combat V
Armed Forces Expeditionary Medal
Vietnam Service Medal
Republic of Vietnam Meritorious Unit Citation
Vietnam Campaign Medal

Civilian Career

January 1956-March 1957	Pastor, Mission Creek United Presbyterian Church, Summerfield, Kansas
October 1985-September 1995	Pastor, Williamsburg Presbyterian Church, Williamsburg, Virginia

Authorization

The U.S. Naval Institute is hereby authorized to make available to individuals, libraries, and other repositories of its choosing the transcripts of seven oral history interviews concerning the life and naval career of the undersigned. The interviews were recorded on 10 February 1988, 11 February 1988, 22 November 1988, 17 April 1989, 18 September 1989, 16 November 1989, and 1 March 1990 in collaboration with Paul Stillwell for the U.S. Naval Institute.

The undersigned does hereby release and assign to the U.S. Naval Institute the rights and title to these interviews, with the exception that the undersigned retains the right to use the material for his own purposes, as he sees fit. The copyright in both the oral and transcribed versions shall be the sole property of the U.S. Naval Institute. The tape recordings of the interviews are and will remain the property of the U.S. Naval Institute.

Signed and sealed this 12th day of October 1997.

Neil M. Stevenson
Rear Admiral, Chaplain Corps, USN (Ret.)

Interview Number 1 with Rear Admiral Neil M. Stevenson, Chaplain Corps, U.S. Navy (Retired)

Place: National Naval Medical Center, Bethesda, Maryland

Date: Wednesday, 10 February 1988

Interviewer: Paul Stillwell

Q: Admiral, to begin at the beginning could you start, please, by telling something about your early years, your parents, and your home life.

Admiral Stevenson: I was born in Brooklyn, New York, in an area called Fort Hamilton. My father had come from Belfast, Ireland, in 1921, and my mother had come from Greenock, Scotland, in 1923. I think they got married in 1927. My father was a bricklayer, and my mother worked for a Wall Street concern. The Depression in 1929 brought about my mother's unemployment by 1930, and I was born in December of 1930. I think my birth had something to do with the Depression.*

Q: How long did the family live in the New York area?

Admiral Stevenson: My mother still lives in Manhasset, Long Island. The family lived in Brooklyn the whole time I was home and for some years afterward. My father died in 1956, and my mother moved to Long Island in 1967.

Q: Where did you go to school?

Admiral Stevenson: I went to the local schools: Public School 127, Public School 104, and Fort Hamilton High School. There was quite a contrast in those schools, as I look back on them now. P.S. 127 covered kindergarten through sixth grade, and it was really a rather

---

* Following the crash of the New York Stock Exchange in late October 1929, the United States was plunged into the Great Depression, from which it did not recover until the nation geared up for World War II at the beginning of the 1940s. The Depression was marked by high unemployment and many business failures.

exclusive school for a public school. It was an extremely neighborhood school and all that kind of thing. I went to P.S. 104 for the seventh and eighth grades. That was my introduction into the broader world of what I suppose most people assume New York schools to be like.

Q: What do you mean by that?

Admiral Stevenson: Well, it took in a much larger neighborhood and a much broader spectrum of ethnic backgrounds. It was a school where you had to contend with some fistfights and things like that once in a while. Such things were not part of the first six grades. It was a tougher neighborhood, I guess you'd say.

Q: What sort of an economic effect did the Depression have on your family's standards?

Admiral Stevenson: When I got older, I could recognize how disastrous it was, but I don't remember having any awareness of the impact it was having on my folks as I grew up. I know that all building projects ended, so nobody needed any bricklayers. My father was involved in seeking work in all kinds of jobs. He worked as a longshoreman for a while; he worked in this, that, and everything else to keep the family going. In fact, during World War II, I remember Dad worked in a shipyard because of the lack of bricklaying in New York.

My mother worked also, and they both worked extremely hard to keep my sister and me in that same neighborhood and that same school system. The school system had advantages--especially in P.S. 127 and high school--because our neighborhood, which you'd call a poor neighborhood, was adjacent to a very rich neighborhood. That offered a great advantage to all of us in our schooling and in our social lives.

Q: You rubbed shoulders with them and got some advantages.

Admiral Stevenson: Yes, we got a lot of advantages. I was in high school from 1945 to 1949, and we lived in a neighborhood where I think the rent was $32.00 or $35.00 a month for the four-room apartment that we lived in. We walked everywhere in those days, and to walk to Fort Hamilton High School, you walked past two-family dwellings. Then you walked past an area of one-family houses that weren't even attached to each other. That was pretty fancy stuff. The homes along the Narrows, by the high school, sold for $50,000 to $100,000. They were very elaborate homes. We all went to that same high school. As my father would say, "This is a great country!" It was a great advantage to get the same education that the students from these more well-to-do homes were getting.

Most of the guys and gals in my immediate neighborhood were children of parents who had come from the old country. The parents of most of the guys and gals from the better neighborhoods had been in America for generations. Maybe it was the age group, but I don't recall anybody in grade school talking about college. The majority of the people we went to high school with talked in terms of college and made a college education sound like a norm. It wasn't the norm for those of us who lived in apartment houses.

Q: How good a student were you?

Admiral Stevenson: I was a fair-to-middle student. I guess I did pretty well, although I did not do well in seventh and eighth grade. I didn't do well at P.S. 104 at all. In fact, my mother was suspicious of my high school grades, because I went from being a mediocre student in grade school to doing rather well in high school. I think it had to do with growing up. It had to do with the environment of the freedom of high school, of choosing classes, of moving around, of different kinds of faculty.

We drove by P.S. 104 one time when my middle daughter was a young child. I pointed out the fact that her father had gone to school there. She looked at it and said, "That's not a school; that's a prison." It had fences like prisons, and the boys all marched in single file in one door, and the girls all marched in single file through a different door. It was a very, very rigid kind of environment.

Neil M. Stevenson #1 - 4

Q: What do you recall about your religious upbringing?

Admiral Stevenson: The Presbyterian Church was the closest Protestant church that was within walking distance, and so that's basically why I'm Presbyterian. Nobody had a car or any money for carfare. In those days, people literally had their choice between having a couple of cents to put in the collection plate and money to pay for carfare, so you went to the church that was nearby.

Q: How active were your parents in the church?

Admiral Stevenson: Just fairly active. There were a lot of people in our neighborhood who became active in the church after World War II that had not been active in the church during the Depression years. They they did not feel that they could be active in a church financially. And if they couldn't really put money in the collection plate, they weren't going to go to church. I think my parents and a lot of the people in our neighborhood were in that category.

One of the joys of my life was the fact that I served on active duty in the Navy with one rabbi and, let's see, I think five or six Catholic priests who were from the same neighborhood. We didn't necessarily know of each other when we were growing up, but got to meet each other in the Navy. Rabbi Nisson Shulman grew up in our neighborhood. Eddie Fallon, who was known as Buddy Fallon in the neighborhood, was a World War II hero as a glider pilot in the Army in World War II. Eddie Fallon was one of the priests from the neighborhood. Al Sullivan, Franciscan whom I served with in the Navy, is from the neighborhood. Bob Ecker was one of the young priests at Our Lady of Angels parish. And Jim Boyd had grown up in Bay Ridge, Brooklyn.

So it was a predominantly Catholic neighborhood, and we were involved with Catholic friends. It was the St. Anselm's area there, and I played on St. Anselm's baseball team for a period of time as an additional ballplayer brought in from the neighborhood. The priest at St. Anselm's in those days was called "Old Father Smith," and the curate was called "Young Father Smith." (I was recently told that the bishop of those years enjoyed assigning priests by name.) But my father, being from the north of Ireland, thought that my playing ball for St. Anselm's was a miracle.

In large measure, I think Dad had left Ireland because after his experiences in World War I, he could not abide the atmosphere that, unfortunately, still exists in that country. He was a machine gunner in The Welsh Regiment. Dad served in Mesopotamia from 1914 to 1919, and he was loyal to the crown. He used to talk about the unreasonable hatred between people of the same language and the same culture and the same religion. But my father was indeed impressed with America and with the fact that a Protestant kid could find himself on third base on St. Anselm's ball team, even though I was a ringer. That's the kind of neighborhood it was, though; people took care of each other.

The jobs I got when I was in high school, I got largely through the influence of my Catholic friends. There was a man in our block that I suppose some people would call a ward heeler. I don't really remember that he had that much connection with political parties, or anything like that, but Mr. Forsyth was very active in St. Anselm's. When it came time for the kids in the neighborhood to get jobs, and so forth, Mr. Forsyth was always good to say, you know, "Don't forget Neil," and things like that.

Q: Did the family finances allow you to get to Ebbets Field once in a while?[*]

Admiral Stevenson: Yes, we used to get there every once in a while. My father and my mother were both great Dodger fans, as we all were. Everybody in Brooklyn in those days had two religions, his religious faith and the Dodgers. In fact, it was a real shock, later in life, to realize how much we were tied up--we literally lived and died with the Dodgers.

Q: The '40s were glory years for them.

Admiral Stevenson: Well, those of us who were born in 1930 were old enough to remember how they got the name "Bums." The Dodgers were not a good team in the '30s.

---

[*] Ebbets Field was the home of baseball's Brooklyn Dodgers from 1913 to 1957.

In the '40s, they started coming on with this theme of "Wait till next year." That's when they would come close to winning but not quite make it.[*]

I'd say 10 to 15 times a year we'd hop on the bus and go out to Ebbets Field and see a game. I have a lot of great memories from those years. I can name all of the Brooklyn Dodgers of the '40s and the early '50s, but I can't tell you who plays for the Dodgers today. In fact, in 1955 my father was very, very ill, and my mother used to give Dad a little brandy every once in a while to keep him alive to see the Dodgers win the World Series. The Dodgers won the World Series in October of '55.[†] Dad died in January of '56.

Q: What were some of the hobbies and extracurricular activities you were involved in as a boy?

Admiral Stevenson: Well, my hobby was the street, as it was for everybody else. Brooklyn was really a fabulous place to grow up, although everybody thinks he grew up in a wonderful place. My wife grew up on a farm, and I hear her talk about how exciting it was to grow up on a farm. She had all these animals around, her own horse, and all this sort of stuff. But to grow up in Brooklyn in those days, the street was the world and the activities went on constantly. There were stick ball games, two or three a day; in the evening you played caught-caught-ring-a-levio. So you ran the neighborhood. If there weren't enough guys to play stick ball, you played box ball. If there weren't enough guys to play box ball, you played stoop ball. It all had to do with playing ball constantly.

If you had a few cents, you could get on a trolley car or a subway, and all the museums, all the parks, all of New York was available to you. There were great libraries in the neighborhood. There were few, if any, times when you were bored or you were without companionship, because all you had to do was go out in the street. Even when you were a little kid, there were guys who came around with a truck that had a carousel on it. A penny

---

[*] The Brooklyn Dodgers won National League pennants in 1941, 1947, and 1949; in 1946 the Dodgers tied for the league lead during the regular season but lost in a playoff. They lost in all three World Series appearances in the 1940s.
[†] The 1955 World Series was the only one the Brooklyn Dodgers won; the team moved to Los Angeles after the 1957 season.

bought a ride on that merry-go-round, so you didn't even have to go anywhere to get to the merry-go-round.

Q: Great sense of community, it sounds like.

Admiral Stevenson: Yes, and a tremendous, tremendous appreciation for things ethnic. The ethnicity of things was an order unto itself, which is now humorous, but for some reason we thought that's the way things were. If we had a <u>weltanschauung</u>--if we had a world view, that's what we thought of the world. For example, we really thought to have a fruit store you had to be Italian; to have a delicatessen you had to be Norwegian; to have a butcher shop you had to be German. I mean, it sounds ridiculous now, but back then when you went to a good butcher shop, you just assumed that it was a German butcher shop.

People were very ethnic-conscious, and people referred to each other in ethnic terms. I was referred to as a Scottie, because the assumption was that my parents were from Scotland, even though my father was from Ireland. We used to tease; we used to tell ethnic jokes. I don't recall any real controversy over that. They were told on the radio, too, on shows like "Can You Top This?"

Q: Was there any bigotry on the basis of ethnic background?

Admiral Stevenson: Yes, I think there was probably a lot of bigotry around. I'm not so sure that we were all aware of it, so maybe we were part of the bigotry. One case might be that people in the neighborhood were upset because a member of their family was marrying outside the religion. To be very honest with you, that could sometimes be the fact that an Irish Catholic was marrying an Italian Catholic. I mean, that's, really the way it was. It had a lot of humor to it.

One of my memories from childhood is a time I was sitting on the front stoop with my dad. The man who owned the apartment houses around there was an old Irishman who had never married. And he owned about four or five of the six family apartment houses on the block, and he lived in our building. His name was Patrick Flanagan, and he was a real recluse. Every morning he got up, got dressed up, went to Mass at St. Anselm's, and then came back and got in his overalls for the rest of the day. He lived in the basement, where the coal for the furnace was stored. Well, he was telling my father that it was unfortunate, since I was a fairly good student, that I wasn't able to go to Catholic parochial school, where the sisters would give me a good education. And my father, who was from Ireland, responded by saying he thought Neil was getting a very good education in the public school, because most of the teachers were Jewish.

So that just sort of pictures of what the neighborhood was like. People had an appreciation for what other people in the neighborhood were able to do, and yet at the same time, there was something about you should stay with your own kind, whatever your own kind was. Yet you could end up playing ball for the Catholic school like I was.

Everybody in the neighborhood worked, so I got my first job when I was 11 years old. That would have been in 1942. Mr. Eisler, a Jewish gentleman, ran the neighborhood drugstore. He had a dog in the drugstore--a bulldog. So he hired a kid to walk the bulldog at 7:00 and 10:00 at night, to deliver the prescriptions throughout the neighborhood in the evenings, and to sweep out the store. I did it six nights a week from 7:00 till 10:00, and I got paid three bucks per week. It was really a great job. It was a big deal.

Q: I would think it was a challenge to get your homework done around that schedule.

Admiral Stevenson: Well, I don't really recall us doing an awful lot of homework.

Q: What were your ambitions in those years?

Admiral Stevenson: Oh, I don't know. I suppose to play ball. Everybody in the neighborhood was going to be a big ball player. They may have talked occasionally about doing something else, but I think in those early years everybody was going to be a ball player.

Q: When you got in with this Fort Hamilton crowd, did that influence you toward college?

Admiral Stevenson: Yes, that influenced me towards college, and the church influenced me towards college, because I was very active in the youth group at the church. The emphasis in the youth group in those days was on vocation: "What are you going to do with your life? What skills do you have? How does the Lord want to use you?" Programmatically, that was what the Westminster Fellowship was all about.

The role models in the church were the people who were the sponsors of the youth groups and so forth. In the main, these were people who had been to college. And the Presbyterian Church itself had been college-oriented, had founded colleges like Princeton throughout the early American society. Again, the emphasis in the church was not only what college are you going to go to, but what Presbyterian college are you going to go to. This was the same as for my Catholic buddies. For them in those days it was, "What Catholic college are you going to go to?"

Q: What were the choices that you faced when you graduated from high school?

Admiral Stevenson: Well, I didn't think I had a lot of college opportunity available to me. There were a couple things going on then. First of all, for me to go to college really meant a change, being from a family that came from the old country. When I would talk about going to college, my father used to say, "Well, this is a wonderful country that you can even think about these things." My parents were willing to help me as best they could, but there certainly wasn't much financial help available.

I don't know if you know anything about bricklaying, but bricklaying is one of those jobs where the hourly wage looks rather high. But in a city like New York there are an awful lot of times when, even if you wanted to lay brick, you're not allowed to lay brick--when the weather is too cold for the cement, when it's raining, when it's snowing. So the annual wages, I don't think, were very great. As I said, my parents did other jobs to keep us all going, but there just wasn't any financial support for a college education around the house.

I was not the kind of student that was going to get any big scholarship. The competition to go to college in 1949 was pretty keen, because even in the high school we had GIs, and the GI Bill had rightly set things up for them.[*] It was probably one of the greatest pieces of legislation we ever had in this country. So the colleges were filled with GIs, and GIs had their financial backing from the government.

My college dream became a reality for me through some good fortune. I was sent as a delegate to a Presbyterian youth convention, which took place at a small school called Tarkio College in Tarkio, Missouri. In the summer in 1948, at this youth convention, I was playing softball, and I met the president of the college, a tremendous gentleman named Dr. M. Earle Collins. After the softball game, he talked to me about going to college, about finances, and said that if I went to Tarkio College, there would be a small scholarship and the guarantee of a job.

I went back to Brooklyn and announced to everybody I was going to Missouri. I think my parents were pretty skeptical that I could make it. I think my mother was much more attuned to the difficulties of financing a college education than my father was. My mother thought that if I was even going to try college, I should try to get into Brooklyn College or CCNY.[†] But I had no desire at all to ride a subway to school. If I had stayed in New York, I really think I'd have ended up working and not going to college.

Q: Missouri must have sounded like the far hinterlands.

Admiral Stevenson: Well, it did, but, you see, I always wanted to live in America. Again, I had grown up in a world in which everybody was identified by ethnic group. People would say "Well, we saw you took the Italian girl home from high school the other night after the dance." That was a normal kind of conversation in Brooklyn, but for me it was kind of an exciting thing to think about going where I thought America really was, out there in the

---

[*] The GI Bill, officially the Servicemen's Readjustment Act of 1944, provided educational assistance and other benefits to all veterans honorably discharged with six or more months of active service after 16 September 1940.
[†] CCNY--City College of New York.

Midwest. Also, as a city kid, I was kind of intrigued with the idea of going out into rural territory. Believe me, you won't find anything more rural than Tarkio, Missouri.

Q: Was that trip out there to the youth conference your first real time away from home?

Admiral Stevenson: I'd been on a couple of youth retreats for a week, church-sponsored things. But, yes, that was the first time I'd crossed a multitude of states and done things like that. My folks didn't have a car, because they couldn't afford one, and because you didn't need one in Brooklyn.

The youth sponsors for the presbytery were a gentleman named Ray Schember and his wife, Alice, who had no children of their own. They drove their car and took us out to this convention and brought us back. They were great role models and a positive influence on us. Ray had been a first lieutenant in World War II and had gotten shot up. He was, and still is, quite an influence on young people. It was interesting that when I got to college, he decided that he would go into the ministry. He left New York and went to Muskingum, another one of those Presbyterian colleges. He and I ended up in the seminary together for a year or so.

One of my great memories is that through the kindness of these same friends, I got as far as Wisconsin when I was going to start college a year later. The Schembers took me to the 1949 youth convention. I knew that the college would have representation at that year's youth conference, which was up in Lake Geneva. Once I got there, I scouted out the Tarkio crowd and paid my mileage to ride the college station wagon down to Missouri. I had to be there, I think, 15 days before college started to get my work assignments.

The college president's daughter was one of the delegates to the convention, and so we dropped her off at the college manse at Tarkio. It was getting late in the day when we got there, and Dr. and Mrs. Collins came out and invited us to stay for a cookout-- hamburgers and watermelon and so forth. In those days--at least where I came from--one did not make long-distance telephone calls without some kind of an emergency. It was either the next day or the day after when I got a phone call from my parents in New York. They wanted to know if I had arrived safe and sound and what was happening.

Nonchalantly, I informed my father that I had arrived in the college station wagon, had had diner at the college president's home, and all was okay. I can remember that my father said just, "It's a wonderful country." I appreciate now what Dad was saying more than I did then.

Q: You said you had a job at Tarkio. What did you do to support yourself there?

Admiral Stevenson: Well, a lot of us in that college had jobs. We did everything. We mowed the lawns, and we stoked furnaces, and we cleaned dormitories. There were about ten of us who had to show up before school started to start our work. D. B. Lindsay was the college engineer. He told us all what we were to do every day. I remember one morning he asked if any of us knew how to hang wallpaper. The guy standing next to me said, "Raise your hand."

I said, "I don't know how to hang wallpaper."

He said, "But I do, and the two of us can work together." So I ended up working for about a month hanging wallpaper. I think that's a pretty typical experience of guys who went to school in those days.

Q: Did you encounter any culture shock in this new environment?

Admiral Stevenson: Yes. I want to tell you something about the great contrast between having lived in Yew York all those years and then getting out to the Midwest. I guess New York was more or less like growing up in Europe, and the Midwest was certainly totally different. It took me a while to adjust to midwestern ways and midwestern food. For instance, now that they have pizza in Missouri, people don't realize that in the early 1950s pizza was a New York thing. You couldn't find any pizza in Missouri!

Q: What were some of the other adjustments?

Admiral Stevenson: Oh, well, it was difficult to learn to dress down. When I was a kid, you went to high school in coat and tie, and that was expected in a public high school. You were there for business, and therefore, you would wear a coat and tie. When I went to college, of course, nobody wore a coat. I used to get teased, because all I had were coats and ties. It took me a while to finally buy a pair of jeans and a sport shirt.

Q: And you were dating Americans instead of Europeans.

Admiral Stevenson: I was dating Americans instead of Europeans. In fact, one of the things my wife and I tease about is the fact that I went to college so that I could marry an American.

The athletic programs in the college in those days were totally dominated by the GI's. An interesting lesson from that era was that most of the 18- and 19-year-olds could not compete in athletics with 25- and 26-year-olds.

Q: So you didn't.

Admiral Stevenson: So we didn't, except I did play baseball. And I had the good fortune of going through college in three years that way, because I went to summer school.

Q: You and I discussed earlier that I, also, went to a small religious school there in Missouri. I know we had heavy emphasis on religion courses and compulsory weekly chapel services and so forth. Was it that way, also, at Tarkio?

Admiral Stevenson: I think we were required to take only two religious courses in our entire time at college. There was a requirement for daily chapel, but I think only one or two of those chapel services was of an actual religious nature. The other chapel services were pretty much taken up by what would be called student activities: papers given by different literary societies on the campus and skits and things like that. But you're right, there was a chapel at 9:00--something every day. Attendance was taken, and everybody was required to be there. I don't recall it being considered anything but a norm, and so nobody was very rebellious about it.

The campus life was your entire social life. I fell in love with Diane right after I got on the campus.* So we went together the whole time we were in college, which meant we ate together in the refectory every day. We went together to all the dances, all the plays, all the athletic events. Everybody on the campus was more or less expected to participate in all campus activities. So Diane and I have reflected that one of the things we really enjoyed about the Navy years was that same atmosphere of expectation that you are part of a community, and you enjoy being a total part of whatever the community's involved with. I know some people find that restrictive, or a burden, but from the background of our school years it was a joy; it wasn't a burden.

Q: Where did your future wife come from?

Admiral Stevenson: Her dad rented a farm five miles outside town. Diane's folks were not too keen about me, and I don't blame them. I don't think it's the most thrilling thing in the world to hear that your daughter is dating a guy from Brooklyn who is contemplating going to seminary. I don't think they struggled to send their only daughter off to college in hopes that she'd marry some guy from the East who was going to seminary.

Q: What was the concern about seminary?

Admiral Stevenson: Well, I think the concern was that they probably wanted their daughter to marry somebody who had a little more of a financially secure future than a Presbyterian minister. Would you want your daughter to have to put up with what "people" thought was the life of a minister's wife in those days? And, I guess, in some respects people in the Midwest placed certain expectations and demands on a minister's wife. I don't recall us spending a lot of time thinking about it, but I know that it was a concern to Diane's folks, and I can appreciate how it would be.

---

* Her maiden name was Georgia Diane Neal.

They lived on a farm that had only recently gotten electricity. Up through high school years my wife rode a horse to school. The last mile to get to the farm was a dirt road that turned to mud with the slightest rain. Of course, as a city kid, I didn't know how to handle mud. Every time I tried to drive that road, I usually put the car in a ditch. When this happened, my future father-in-law--a very, very quiet man--would be awakened late at night, and I mean anything past 9:00 at night was late to Homer. Then he'd have to come down and get the tractor and put chains around the front of my jalopy and haul me out of the mud. I don't think those things thrilled him as a father, but he'd do anything for his daughter.

Q: Well, I hope he relented at some point.

Admiral Stevenson: Oh, he relented a great deal. I just get a big kick out of remembering what a shock it must have been for them that of all the guys on campus, Diane dragged this Brooklynite home.

Q: I think you mentioned to me previously that your future wife was the homecoming queen.

Admiral Stevenson: My Diane was homecoming queen, and I voted against her. I didn't want to share her with the rest of the campus. I think I persuaded my roommate to vote against her, and I voted against her, and I think we were the only two votes that were against her.

Q: In retrospect, how would you evaluate the quality of your education at Tarkio College?

Admiral Stevenson: Well, in retrospect, I rate it extremely high. I think everybody that goes to college thinks that he was there when the very best of the faculty was there.[*] It was

---

[*] During Stevenson's years as an undergraduate, Tarkio College had about 200-220 students and 20-23 faculty members at a given time.

an intimate faculty; we visited them in their homes. You know, there was no question that we were all known by name. The faculty was available to us. As I look back on it now, I say to myself, "Good Lord, those people were available to us constantly in academic functions and in social functions." They took a great personal interest in where we were going to go. Everybody who was in my class who wanted to go to graduate school, got into graduate school. And they went where they wanted to go: Ohio State, the University of Colorado, Princeton. Five of us went from the class to the Pittsburgh-Xenia Theological Seminary at the same time. So I look back on it as a fabulous education.

Q: How early did you decide on the ministry as a career?

Admiral Stevenson: Well, I had had the role model from the pastors in Brooklyn, and I think it was because of the vocational emphasis of the whole church structure. I don't think any male in those days went off to college from a Presbyterian church without being conscious of the fact that he had to make a decision as to whether or not he was going into the ministry.

At the end of World War II, with the natural emphasis of vocations in the church, there was a real pressure on young people; at least we thought there was a real pressure. This was a new world; World War II had been won, and there was a multitude of things that dedicated people had to get done for God and country in this world. There was a legitimate sense of patriotism as well as responsibility--Marshall Plan, United Nations, etc.* The idea was to get things done.

So I would say the majority of the people of my age group that I was dealing with were really asking themselves, "What talents have I been given and how does God want me to use them in this world?" The things I had tried out seemed to reinforce going to seminary. My majors in college were psychology and history, which seemed to fit. Of course, the minute you showed any interest in the seminary, you were immediately

---

* At the Harvard University commencement in 1947, Secretary of State George C. Marshall made an address in which he outlined a plan for the economic rebuilding of war-ravaged Europe. Congress passed the European Recovery Act, and the program of American support came to be known as the Marshall Plan. The United Nations was founded in 1945, at the end of World War II.

counseled not to take religion courses. They wanted to be sure that you had an education in other things. The assumption was that if you went to the seminary, you'd get all the religion stuff you need, so don't spend precious college dollars to get any of those subjects. That is still good advice.

Q: Was there a conscious decision at some point to go into the ministry, or did you just follow this path that seemed to be laid out?

Admiral Stevenson: I followed the path. I had lots of experiences with members of my family that really thought that seminary was a waste of time. If you'd been the lucky one in the family to get an education, you ought to do something with it other than go into the ministry. Basically, it just flowed in that direction. I remember when I got to the seminary that first year--probably because I did not want to study as hard as they wanted me to study--spending a lot of time trying to think that maybe I could do something else, and maybe I ought to get out of there and do something else.

Q: Did you have any role models or strong influences at Tarkio?

Admiral Stevenson: Lots of them. I've already mentioned the college president, Dr. Collins, who was a tremendous influence on me. Our psychology and philosophy professor, Dr. R. W. George, is known, I think, to all graduates of those days as a tremendous influence on all of us. Our religion professor, Dr. Al Martin, is one of those quiet and unknown geniuses who had a tremendous influence on us. He was a man who had studied under Karl Barth in Europe.[*] Unfortunately, Dr. Martin never published, and it's hard to think of somebody of his academic ability who never published. I think he read and spoke seven or eight languages. He was intimately involved in constant correspondence with Karl Barth and other theologians like Hans Kuhn. And here he was out in this little college in Missouri. In later years I asked him why he never published. He said that he was either so

---

[*] Karl Barth (1886-1968) was a Swiss Protestant Reformed theologian and educator. He was a champion of a dialectic theology and the author of a number of books.

busy reading, or that he recognized in his readings that about anything he could publish had already been written, so he didn't do any writing himself. He was a very interesting gentleman.

Q: Do you have any more memories of Tarkio before we get you to the seminary?

Admiral Stevenson: Well, no, except to say that it was just absolutely unbelievable. Those were three fabulous years. Diane and I met each other, and I got an education that was seemingly not available. I was introduced to a whole different culture. I ended up working on farms and things like that that were not part of my background. And I ended up graduating with honors, no less. It meant a real difference in my entire life.

Q: Was Pittsburgh Theological Center the natural progression in the Presbyterian Church?

Admiral Stevenson: Yes, it was. I didn't know it when I was growing up as a kid, but there were three Presbyterian denominations in the United States. The church I had gone to in Brooklyn was in the smallest denomination. It was the United Presbyterian Church of North America. There were five colleges of that denomination and only one seminary. That turned out to be Pittsburgh-Xenia Theological Seminary, which is now known as Pittsburgh Theological Seminary. And I'm sure they would want me to let you know that it's the oldest Presbyterian seminary in the United States. It's older than Princeton Theological Seminary.

Q: What sort of financial assistance did you get to go there?

Admiral Stevenson: Well, the seminary in those days was very generous. The tuition was minimal, so you could handle the fees if you could handle the room and board expenses and the costs for books, and so forth. My first year in seminary was the greatest financial difficulty of my life. If I had not lucked out and had a job as a waiter in what they called the eating club, to pay for my food, I would not have made it that year. That was really a very thin year for me in every way.

I had worked at the college the summer before I went to the seminary. I had enough money to get home to New York on a bus, and I ended up with almost $100.00 when I got to the Pittsburgh seminary. When I left Brooklyn to go to the seminary, my Catholic neighbors gave me about 40 or 45 bucks that they had put together. I think Mr. Flanagan, the landlord, probably contributed half of that collection. And a memory that's most important to me is that something similar happened a dozen or so times after that. There were times when I would be visiting Brooklyn, and Mr. Flanagan would put a rumpled-up $20.00 bill in a very dirty envelope that had been down by the coal bin in the basement, where he lived, for God knows how long. If we were in a car, he'd be standing out on the stoop waiting for us to leave. As the car was pulling away from the curb, he would throw the money in the window.

People in Brooklyn did things like that. When somebody needed two bucks, he ended up getting five bucks. It was that kind of neighborhood.

Q: What highlights do you recall from your seminary years?

Admiral Stevenson: Well, my first year in seminary was a terrible year. I had graduated from college cum laudé, but the seminary was a completely different atmosphere, a completely different world. I was back in the city, for one thing. Besides that, I am not a good linguist, and during your first year in seminary you're introduced to Greek and Hebrew. I flunked Greek, which is not the way to become a Presbyterian minister. Diane was teaching school in Iowa, and I was in Pittsburgh. We were married a year later, in July 1953. From September 1952 to May 1953 was a very long year. I can't say I really enjoyed seminary that year.

Q: How readily did you take to the religion courses?

Admiral Stevenson: I took rather well to the courses, outside of the language courses. Eventually I passed the famous Greek placement exam, which moved you from Greek grammar in exegesis.* I think I passed those examinations because members of the faculty were lenient enough to think that Stevenson might be okay, even though he would never be a Hebrew or Greek scholar.

Q: Did you have any self-doubts during that year?

Admiral Stevenson: Oh, yes--that whole year! I don't think I was the only one, but it certainly was a year that had something to do with my joining the Navy. It was a year in which I kept saying to myself, "If you're flunking Greek, why don't you join the Army and go to Korea and do something worthwhile? How will I ever get my degree in theology with this hangup on language?" I remember a funny story about my how my Greek was, although it wasn't funny the day it happened. I was called on one day to read in class, and the professor critiqued me by saying, "If any Greek had ever been from Brooklyn, he would read Greek that way." He didn't know I was from Brooklyn, but that's how badly I was doing.

When I went to grade school, the New York school system was experimenting. For instance, they were spelling light, L-I-T-E, and not teaching phonetics, etc. So one of the handicaps, if you want to call it that, that I had coming from Brooklyn was that I was not familiar with grammar and phonetics. That doesn't help you when you're dealing with foreign languages. In Brooklyn we had to pass regents' exams at the conclusion of each major subject studied, so I think I got a good education. Yet when I went to the Midwest to college and was asked in an English composition class to diagram a sentence, I couldn't. I didn't know how to parse a sentence. Midwesterners learned how to diagram and parse sentences, but to my knowledge we never spent any time with it in the Brooklyn schools.

Q: Was there some point in Pittsburgh that you turned the corner and began feeling comfortable with it?

---

* Exegesis is an explanation or critical interpretation of a text.

Admiral Stevenson: Yes, I turned the corner when I got married. When you talk about an influence on someone's life, anyone would tell you that the great influence on my life was and is Diane. We got married in the summer of 1953, and that's been my life. I graduated in '55. I graduated from seminary in November rather than in May, because I had to make up for the time I had spent nonproductively in the Greek grammar courses.

Q: And it was literally all Greek to you.

Admiral Stevenson: It was all Greek to me. Interestingly, though, I ended up with high grades in exegesis. And, of course, once you get into exegetical studies, all the commentaries and so forth are open and available to you. So one of Dr. Taylor's worst Greek students turned out to be at least a passing exegetical student.

Q: How did you get involved with the Navy? What led to that decision?

Admiral Stevenson: Well, I thought about that in many ways. Several role models and examples come into that. First of all, as I mentioned, my father was in the British Army in the First World War from 1914 to 1919. He served the majority of that time in Mesopotamia, which is where the war between Iran and Iraq is now being fought.[*] I wish now that I had had enough sense when I was a kid to ask my dad more questions about more things, but I guess a lot of guys feel that way.

But, anyway, my father used to tease me about the Navy when I was a kid. He would say, "It's not like the Army; if you join the Navy, you'll have a warm bed, and you'll have hot meals, so the place to be is the Navy." Also, living there in Brooklyn, on the

---

[*] The war began in September 1980, when Iraqi forces invaded Iran. It became essentially a stalemate and ended with a cease-fire in August 1988.

Narrows, we sometimes got to see the U.S. Fleet. I remember visiting the Brooklyn Navy Yard and touring the USS Helena when she was being built prior to World War II.*

One of the men who worked in the Brooklyn Navy Yard was a Navy chief petty officer called Pappy Pryor, who lived next door. He was a great man in our neighborhood for helping the kids throw footballs and stuff like that. He and his young bride of those years had a little baby. I understand that he ended up after World War II being a warrant officer.

Chief Pryor would have been an influence, because my father always used to point to him and talk about serving your country. I don't think people understand, but if you grew up in a "British family," and grew up in those years of World War II, you knew you had an obligation to serve your country. And the feeling was, "When you serve, you ought to join the Navy."

All those associations made me think that the Navy was pretty fabulous, so I always thought in terms of the Navy. Then, when I married Diane, her cousin was married to a naval aviator, Dusty Rhoades.† Dusty was a really great guy, and just hearing him tell about the Navy interested me. Of course, being somewhat of a maverick added to my interest in the Navy rather than a parish.

Q: What do you mean by being a maverick?

Admiral Stevenson: Well, I never felt part of the seminary. I had a strong feeling in college that I was part of a college family. But from day one until I graduated--and I think the faculty agreed with this--I never really seemed to fit the mold of the seminary. Most of the guys in the seminary came from rural or white-collar backgrounds.‡ There weren't too many blue-collar kids in the seminary. Seminarians had dads who were either bankers or farmers. There weren't very many bricklayers' kids in the seminary.

---

* The light cruiser Helena (CL-50) was launched 27 August 1939 at the New York Navy Yard and commissioned 18 September that same year. For the memoir of one of her first crew members, see the Naval Institute oral history of Captain Franklin F. Shellenbarger.
† Commander Everett A. Rhoades, USN.
‡ All candidates for the bachelor of divinity were male in those days, and only males were eligible for ordination as teaching elders.

Q: Did you have doctrinal differences?

Admiral Stevenson: No, I don't think I had doctrinal differences. I think I had life-style differences. I know that I used to laugh that there were seminarians who prayed for Diane and me because we went to dances. It seemed rather humorous to us. Being married, we lived off-campus. In order to support us, I worked in the railroad yards at night as a produce inspector. Quite frankly, I felt closer to the guys in the railroad yards, who were really a bunch of characters, than I did the seminarians.

Q: You must have been a source of some amusement to the railroad yard guys.

Admiral Stevenson: Well, the railroad guys didn't know that I was going to the seminary. I was just a kid who was going to school, and there were lots of schools in Pittsburgh. That job was another lucky break.

I really don't know; I may have also been somewhat rebellious. I was behind the eight ball with my problems in Greek, so from the first year in the seminary I was not going to be able to compete for any scholastic prizes. So there was some sense in which the seminary was an endurance contest, and there were some in those days who also referred to Pittsburgh-Xenia Seminary as a school for masochists. I mean, it had a very, very good and demanding faculty. There were members of the faculty who were very opposed to any of the students being married. If you were really dedicated, you wouldn't get married. You'd just be a student.

I'd just have to tell you I was never that comfortable in that environment.

Q: What was involved in the process of applying for the Navy's Chaplain Corps and being accepted?

Admiral Stevenson: I joined the Navy during my senior year in the seminary. It was a matter of going to the recruiting station in Pittsburgh and following the laborious procedures--medical, paperwork, etc.--and obtaining the ecclesiastical endorsement of my denomination. Joining the Navy was--and ought to be--the same for a chaplain as any other candidate, except for the additional requirement for the endorsement of one's faith group.

Q: How did the church in Summerfield, Kansas, fit into the whole sequence of your experience?

Admiral Stevenson: Well, that was another one of those quirks in life. When I was in college, one of my fellow students was a guy named Joe Barr. Joe Barr came from a very prominent, influential family in Nebraska. His father, Everett Barr, was a well-known man in the United Presbyterian Church. He was a great soil conservation leader and was a very strong man in the Republican Party. His brother-in-law was Senator Wherry, who was a very conservative Republican.[*]

Joe Barr invited me to go home the first Thanksgiving I was in college, in 1949. The school was going to be closed, so Joe invited me to go to Nebraska with him to work a little bit around the farm. They were very gracious and not only gave me a room and fed me, they also paid me for what little work I did around the farm. I'd shoveled coal and snow in Brooklyn, and I learned how to shovel wheat, or whatever it was they wanted, in Nebraska. I don't think I was any big help, but at the end of the four days, I remember Mr. Barr gave me $20.00. Fabulous!

Then, in 1953, when I completed my first year in the seminary, I was required to intern in a church for the summer. You did what was called your field work. The rural church in Mission Creek, Nebraska, needed a student for the summer. The local post office was Summerfield, Kansas, just across the border. Since I knew Mr. Barr, they said, "Fine." So Neil got to go out to Nebraska for the summer. I was only 100 miles from Tarkio, where Diane's folks lived. Diane and I got married in July, and our first home was the parsonage in Mission Creek, Nebraska.

---

[*] Kenneth S. Wherry served as a U.S. Senator from Nebraska from 1943 until his death in 1951. Wherry Housing for military families was named for him.

In 1955, when I graduated from the seminary, the Presbyterian endorsing agent told me that I would be going to chaplain school and Navy duty. Diane and I went to New York, where I was ordained in my home church to be a chaplain in the Navy. In the meantime, I called the endorsing agent in Pittsburgh, and he said, "Well, I don't know if the Navy's going to want you at this time or not." I suddenly realized that I wouldn't be going into the Navy as soon as I expected. To make a long story short, I went to the Mission Creek church with the understanding that if and when the Navy called me, I was going into the Navy.

Q: That was probably useful background before going in.

Admiral Stevenson: Yes, it was extremely good. Fifty percent of the parishioners were graduates of Tarkio College, so it was a great place to break in. I don't know how helpful I was to the Mission Creek Church. It was a dual parish, Mission Creek and Barneston. They were great people, and they let me do the studying I needed to do to put homilies together. During that time, in February 1956, I was commissioned in the Navy and became part of the reserve unit in Lincoln, Nebraska.

I went to the mailbox one day in early 1957, and there was a set of orders to active duty. I was ordered to report to chaplain school on 1 April 1957. Wonderful! I told the church authorities that I would be leaving for the Navy, and they were very gracious about it. In the meantime, my mother-in-law, Juanita Neal, died unexpectedly and threw us into a total spin. She got ill one day with an earache, and a week later she was gone. Our Heather was two years old by that time, and Diane was pregnant with Holly. It was not the best time in the world for a set of orders to come.

Because Diane's dad was all alone on the farm, I got some pickup trucks and moved what furniture we had over to the farm. The idea was that when I went to chaplain school, Diane would stay with her dad. He needed her, and she needed a place to stay, because the orders said that no dependents were to come to Newport. It was a very emotional time for us as a family. I was leaving my wife and daughter Heather, whom I'd never been separated from before. I was a typical civilian.

One thing you had to do in those days before you went on active duty was to go to a naval command and take a pre-reporting physical. I went to Fort Omaha in Omaha, Nebraska, and I took a physical. I was a very skinny guy in those days, and after the checkup, a chief petty officer said to me, "You flunked your physical. You can't go on active duty."

I had given up my job at the church, and so I was in a tenuous situation. I said to him, "Well, that can't be."

He said, "Well, I'm sorry. You're too skinny." He stamped "disqualified," or some such thing on my orders. I was in a state of shock. I drove about halfway from Omaha to the farm in Missouri, and I just didn't know what to do. I was going home to tell my wife, "I don't have a job, and the Navy won't take me."

You know, sometimes in life you have to be part dumb and part bold. I stopped at a gas station phone booth and called the Chief of Chaplains' office in Washington. I got a wonderful man on the phone. He was Admiral George Rosso, serving as what we would call today the Deputy of the Chief of Chaplains.[*] I found out later that his nickname was "The Iron Duke," that he had piercing blue eyes, that he was a New Yorker, and that he didn't really believe in fooling around with naive or idiotic people.

Anyway, I got him on the phone, and I never will forget it. To me it was one of the greatest times of my military career. In what I'm sure was a voice of panic, I explained the situation to him. In a very direct, very calm voice, this priest said over the phone, "Chaplain, do you have your orders?"

I said, "Yes, sir, they're out in the car. I'm in a phone booth."

He said, "Chaplain, go get your orders." (It was like he was instructing a rookie, and I was a rookie.)

I went out to the car, found the orders, and came back into the phone booth. I said, "I have my orders, and they've stamped . . ."

He said, "Be quiet. Just shut up, just shut up." He said, "Now start reading your orders to me."

---

[*] Rear Admiral George A. Rosso, CHC, USN. Admiral Rosso later served as the Chief of Chaplains from June 1958 to June 1963.

I was still trying to tell him, "Well, but they put this stamp on."

And he was telling me, "Shut up and read your orders."

I finally got the point, and I read about the first two sentences of the orders: "On or about 1 April 1957, report to Naval Chaplain School," and so forth. When I finished reading that, this kind, thoughtful, direct gentleman said to me, "Now, chaplain, do you understand what you read?"

I said, "Yes, sir."

He said, "Then why don't you do what you just read?"

That was the end of the conversation. I felt very strange driving out of the driveway a couple of days later for Newport, Rhode Island, with a set of orders with this "disqualified" stamp on them. Recently a young friend of mine joined the Navy and reported to chaplains school. I was telling him how naive I was back then. I was so naive that when I got to Newport I didn't go to the base and spend a free night in the BOQ.[*] I went to a motel and spent money I really didn't have, because my orders said 1 April, and I wasn't going to report on 31 March. When I reported, a wonderful chaplain--one of the best chaplains the Navy ever had, Chaplain Merle Young--was the officer in charge of the school.[†] He greeted me, and he said, "Well, we've been wondering just how skinny you were."

Q: What are your recollections of chaplain school?

Admiral Stevenson: I thought chaplain school was pretty great. I think one of the advantages I had in the Chaplain Corps was that I was back with Catholics and clergy of other faith groups. For me that was a comfortable environment.

Q: Brooklyn again.

---

[*] BOQ--bachelor officers' quarters.
[†] Captain Merle N. Young, CHC, USN. His oral history is in the series conducted by the Navy's Chaplain Corps.

Admiral Stevenson: It was kind of like being in Brooklyn again; that's right. That had a great deal to do with my career. I was surprised all through my career with the number of my Protestant colleagues who had never been associated with rabbis and priests. I had grown up in a pluralistic environment, so I was back in an environment that was very comfortable.

Q: What does the school do to turn an ordained minister into a Navy chaplain.

Admiral Stevenson: Well, one would hope they do a lot better today than they did in those days. For one thing, they instructed us on the history of the Chaplain Corps. I think that was very important to give us a sense of joining a community that had an inheritance to it. We were still very much taken with the model of the World War II chaplain and what the World War II chaplain had accomplished. By the way, every day I get to look out my office window at the College of William and Mary, where the World War II Navy chaplain school was located.[*] They turned out 2,000 chaplains in that short period of time, and those people were capable of meeting the needs of Navy and Marine Corps personnel.

During our training, they put us through military drill. They sent us over to try to save the "Buttercup," and it sank.[†] They tried every way they could just to familiarize us with the life of the Navy.

One thing that happened when I was in chaplain school was not part of the curriculum, but it was a very important part of the experience. A member of our class received word that his son was going to have a tonsillectomy operation. That introduced us to the fact that he was not going to be allowed to go home for his son's operation. That was a very, very valid learning experience, the first time we realized what would happen when we had emergencies in our own families. We had come as civilian pastors from an environment in which a man was expected to be home when his child was being born or receiving surgery. We needed to be introduced to the realities of Navy life, in which we

---

[*] Williamsburg Presbyterian Church, which Stevenson served as pastor at the time of the interview, is across the street from William and Mary.
[†] "Buttercup" is the nickname for a damage control training device designed to teach the skills needed to control shipboard flooding.

would be counseling sailors who, because of the needs of the service, would not be going home for their children being born.

The chaplains got two months of training to make the transition from civilian pastor to Navy chaplain. Quite frankly, I think it takes almost five years to make that transition. But they did a good job of trying to do it to us in two months.

We didn't know how to salute; we didn't know how to wear a uniform. I remember getting together with a classmate trying to find out how to put a cover on our cap. We went down to Oberhardt's Uniform Shop in Newport. Herb Epstein, the man who sold us the uniforms, was Max Oberhardt's son in law. Herb became an unofficial instructor for us. I mean, he was the one who said, "Well, you know, you guys are worried about this. This'll happen and that'll happen," and so forth. Things turned out just about the way he predicted.

The school was good, and some of those friendships have remained over the years.

Q: Were there any other Navy-related lessons you learned, things about dealing with sailors specifically?

Admiral Stevenson: Well, we went out to sea for a day and found out we could get seasick. It was a tutorial system; we were trained by chaplains to be chaplains. We had an athletic program to make sure we stayed in shape, running and playing ball, faculty involvement, etc.

Q: How did your first assignment come about after chaplain school?

Admiral Stevenson: A chaplain came up from the detailer's office in Washington and interviewed all of us. We also filled out preference cards while we were at school. During the last two weeks of school, we were given our orders. In those days they sent you from chaplain school to shore duty, where you would be under the influence of other chaplains for nine months to a year. Then they sent you to sea duty. That was of great advantage to all of us. Unfortunately, they're not able to follow that policy these days.

Q: What has made the change since then?

Admiral Stevenson: One thing is economics. They're not going to give you two or three sets of orders in one year--orders to chaplain school, orders to shore duty, and then another set to sea duty. That's very expensive. And the second fact is that in today's Navy you've got to make your mark quickly. In an attrition environment, you need that sea duty fitness report in your service jacket.

Q: Why were you sent to Great Lakes specifically?

Admiral Stevenson: I think I was ordered to Great Lakes because that was the closest command to my family and my furniture. Perhaps I went to Great Lakes because Diane was seven months pregnant. I'm speculating on their thinking. And maybe a jaygee would do the least harm under the supervision of some of the more experienced chaplains there.[*] For whatever reason, it turned out to be a golden opportunity. For a year I really received a tremendous indoctrination into the Navy.

Q: It would be helpful for you to recount that, please.

Admiral Stevenson: Well, shortly after I reported, Chaplain Bob Schwyhart reported in as the senior chaplain.[†] He has one of the great records in the history of the Chaplain Corps. He had been in chaplaincy before World War II. He was a man not only of great experience, but also a man of great patience.

    Elizabeth Schwyhart took seriously the indoctrination of chaplains' wives. I suppose today they would refer to Mrs. Schwyhart as a lady of the old school. Mrs. Schwyhart's brother had been in charge of the chaplain school in World War II, Chaplain Neyman.[‡] Mrs. Schwyhart knew what was expected of chaplains and of chaplains' wives. And, thank

---

[*] Jaygee--lieutenant (junior grade).
[†] Captain Robert M. Schwyhart, CHC, USN. His oral history is in the series conducted by the Navy's Chaplain Corps.
[‡] Captain Clinton A. Neyman, CHC, USN.

God, they, in a very nice way, demanded the protocol and everything that went with being a naval officer in those days. You were not to be seen without your gray gloves; you made your calls, and calls were returned. If you needed to be told something, there was no hesitancy about telling you what was expected.

The Schwyharts entertained the chaplains in their home and exemplified the norms of Navy life and social etiquette. You know, one of the transitions from pastor to chaplain, from civilian to naval officer, was being taught that an invitation to someone's home did not include your children. I'm serious. Pastors think that if they're invited, the whole family's invited, all the kids and so forth. Well, that was not true in the Navy. And Mrs. Schwyhart made it <u>extremely</u> <u>clear</u> that when you were invited, your kids were not invited.

I laugh today because I notice it among my civilian friends in the parish. There's almost an assumption among the clergy that if they have to go to a social event to which their children are not invited, that some loving lady in the parish will gladly babysit their kids for free. Well, Mrs. Schwyhart was teaching great lessons. Her lesson is still valid today for chaplains and their families: everybody else hires a babysitter; you hire a babysitter. Chaplains must meet the social requirements of naval officers, not ministers. They are paid as naval officers. May there never be a 10% discount mentality associated with naval chaplains. By commission and ordination they ought to pay more than their share.

Interview Number 2 with Rear Admiral Neil M. Stevenson, Chaplain Corps, U.S. Navy (Retired)

Place: National Naval Medical Center, Bethesda, Maryland

Date: Thursday, 11 February 1988

Interviewer: Paul Stillwell

Q: It's good to see you again this morning, Admiral. When we stopped yesterday, we were talking about your time at Great Lakes.

Admiral Stevenson: At Great Lakes worship services were conducted in drill halls with compulsory attendance by recruits. The average divine service had 1,000 recruits, half of them coughing, sitting on folding chairs, while you were trying to establish a worship atmosphere. You tried to have a homily that could be heard and would grab their attention.

One of the greatest illustrations I ever heard came from a sermon by Carroll Chambliss, in which he illustrated to the recruits that our generation certainly had made its mistakes, and the expression for it was "You dropped the ball."[*] But that if you dropped the ball, at least you could pick it up and maybe catch the guy going into second base. Whereas, in the vernacular of that day, 1957, their problems were illustrated by saying, "The cookie crumbled." And when a cookie crumbled, that was it!

I've told Carroll for years that I never exactly knew what he meant, but it was a big hit with all the recruits.

Q: What were your specific duties in relation to the recruits?

Admiral Stevenson: I was assigned with the other junior chaplains to Recruit Training Command. Besides providing for divine services and standing the duty about every fourth night--delivering death messages and so forth--we had office hours for counseling recruits.

---

[*] Lieutenant (junior grade) Carroll R. Chambliss, CHC, USN.

There was a process in those days in which every man who came to recruit training was interviewed by a chaplain. So in that year I became totally familiar with young adults, their problems, the whole counseling spectrum.

In those days the Navy still had a program of character-education lectures. Each chaplain would be teaching one or two character-education classes a day. If one can find a copy of that material, he will find it is extremely dated. Later, in the early 1970s, I had the training desk in the Chief of Chaplains' office when there was some insistence from the Congress that those materials be eliminated. So I had the opportunity to review what remained of that material to make sure that it was eliminated. It was really interesting for me to observe at that time what a time piece those lectures were in regards to the '50s. The materials were structured on natural law, etc.

Q: Did they have to do with current events from the '50s?

Admiral Stevenson: No, more of the ethos of the '50s. For instance, we did not have as broad an understanding of race relations, interfaith marriages, and interracial marriages, etc., as we had gained since the '60s and the '70s.

Q: Chaplain Chambliss is a black man. What was the status of black chaplains at that time?

Admiral Stevenson: I believe we had only two black chaplains on active duty in those days. The Chamblisses--not only Carroll but his wife Chris--just fit in so well and seemed like such a perfect part of our Chaplain Corps and our Navy that I'm not so sure that the rest of us were aware of how few black chaplains were on active duty. The Chamblisses were at Great Lakes when I reported. Carroll had served on enlisted duty in a portion of World War II, so he certainly knew more about the Navy than I did.

Q: That, of course, was a consciousness-raising era. That was the time of the Little Rock riots, and so forth, on school desegregation, so it was coming more and more to a national focus.[*]

Admiral Stevenson: Yes, President Truman had integrated the armed forces in the 1940s.[†]

Q: What were the sorts of problems that the recruits brought to you in these counseling sessions?

Admiral Stevenson: Oh, recruits in those days brought every conceivable problem in the world to the chaplain. The greatest advantage that the chaplain has ever had is the fact that whether parents are faithful to their religious disciplines or not, when their children are going into the Navy, they have a habit of reminding them that, "If you have a problem, go see the chaplain." In a way, it's a compliment to the Chaplain Corps, but it's also a tremendous advantage to the chaplain. Everybody came to the chaplain, and when the chaplain couldn't assist directly, he would be a referral service to others in the system who could provide.

A young man would have pneumonia, and he wouldn't really want to tell his company commander, because he didn't want to fall behind. So I would simply talk to the young man for a while and convince him that he ought to get over to medical and get treatment. Or a recruit would have girlfriend problems back home. In those years of the draft, some recruits were married and were having marital problems. And, needless to say, most of them had financial problems. Recruits were hardly paid at all in the economy of those days. They had problems with homesickness; they had problems with adjusting to the culture shock of recruit training, Navy life, and there were always a few real bizarre

---

[*] In the fall of 1957 President Dwight D. Eisenhower used federal troops to enforce school desegregation in Little Rock, Arkansas.
[†] On 26 July 1948, President Harry S Truman issued Executive Order 9981, which said, "It is hereby declared that there shall be equality of treatment and opportunity for all persons in the armed services without regard to race, color, religion, or national origin."

circumstances. You know, the recruit who had fallen in love and decided he wanted to get married on his one six-hour liberty into the city of Chicago, and things of that nature.

Q: What could you offer to the fellow who was homesick?

Admiral Stevenson: Just being available to listen. Like most homesickness, it resolves itself when you share the problem with another, because talking it out makes you feel more at home. We reminded them that they had signed an obligation. We asked them why they joined the Navy. That would bring to mind that maybe there weren't any jobs at home, or it was time to get away from parents, or they had dropped out of school. Once you found out a recruit had dropped out of school, you knew he was very much in danger of dropping out of the Navy.

The character education classes added motivational-type presentations to our counseling. It was felt in those days that this kind of information was owed to recruits to educate them about the big world that they were going into. Another kind of a fatherly role.

Some of these things could be bizarre. I had the duty one time, and I got called over to recruit training because a mother and a stepfather had traveled hundreds of miles to come to the command and convince the command not to discharge this lady's son from the Navy. He had been caught stealing in recruit training and was being discharged. While this was all being discussed with JAG officers and the officer of the day, the boy's stepfather pleaded with me as the chaplain that we had to keep this young man in the Navy because he was so disruptive on the family.[*] The stepfather claimed that the boy had stolen his mother's wedding ring and hocked it.

Q: How was that one resolved? Do you recall?

Admiral Stevenson: He did not stay in the Navy.

---

[*] JAG--Judge Advocate General, in other words, a Navy legal specialist.

Q: How did you deal with all the disparate denominational needs and backgrounds of these recruits? Did you have sort of a homogenized presentation?

Admiral Stevenson: We were very parochial. This was another situation in which we were not aware of how ineffective we were. We operated within denominational boxes. We were not really conscious, in my opinion, of the disservice we were to those of other faith groups, or to those of no faith group. Today's chaplain does a much, much better job than we did in those days.

Q: Are there other examples you might cite of progress that has been made since that time in the Chaplain Corps?

Admiral Stevenson: Oh, I think the progress in regards to minorities is a whole different world than it was in those days. I mean, it would be hard to make comparisons when you look at some of the things that have happened in society and church in the United States since those days; when you look at the ecumenical movement. Things do change and do change for the better. I would have to say over my 29 years in the Navy, I definitely think things have gotten better for people and the Navy.

A lot of it was that we were not even sensitive to what the problems were. Our world was largely confined to three office signs: Catholic, Protestant, and Jew. Such logos may have solved the problem for the chaplains who sat behind them, but they were not solving the problem for the people in need who came and had to make a choice as to which door, if any, they were going to open. So I feel very strongly that an improvement is that today's chaplain's office has an open sign on that says, "Chaplain." Today's chaplain is of such stature that she or he, on hearing the need of the individual, will make the right decision, either to provide for that individual or to facilitate the person being referred to a source where the individual's needs will be met. Provide or facilitate, but in any and all situations the chaplain can be proactive and helpful.

Q: Did you make a specific effort to keep up with progress in your own denomination?

Admiral Stevenson: Keeping up with one's own denomination is not that difficult. I think you're always conscious of your own roots. And in the case of a Presbyterian, wherever you're stationed, you're invited to that area's presbytery meetings; you're hearing from your faith group's endorsing agent; your family's affiliated with the local Presbyterian Church, so I don't think that's a problem at all.

In order for a chaplain to be a professional, one of the absolute requirements is that he has to be secure in his own identity and aware of his own role. You have to be so comfortable with who you are and what you are that you don't have to be defensive. You can be open to everybody. Your personhood and your religious affiliation are not threatened by anyone or anything. You are a professional, and, therefore, you're able to help other people. If you have a defensive posture and your whole approach to your religion is apologetic, then you're not doing anybody any good. Defensiveness does happen in religion, and it's an occupational hazard with clergy. I think a certain degree of seminary training is defensive, i.e., how to have answers for all other religious faiths in the world. Chaplains really don't need that.

Q: How much religion per se got into your sermons, and how much of it was an extension of the character-education program?

Admiral Stevenson: The question mixes apples and oranges. Preaching the gospel is <u>not</u> a moral lecture. In my own case, my seminary emphasized that preaching was expository, and that was all I ever used the whole time I was in the Navy. That's what I use in the parish now.

Let me put it this way: there are things, in my opinion, that one would never use in a Navy environment in a homily. For instance, if I believe in baptism by sprinkling, I would never preach on the reasons why I, personally, believe that sprinkling is a legitimate form of baptism. The reason it would be ridiculous to do that is that some people in the chapel might be Baptists who believe in immersion. There's no need to deal with that kind of doctrinal-type stuff. For me, the homily is supposed to take some portion of the word of

God, whether it's from the lectionary or from a text one has chosen outside the lectionary, and exposit the meaning and significance of that passage historically and apply it to people's lives in the now.

I would go further and say that is why I would never speak publicly regarding birth control or abortion. The subjects are for private discussions, not for one-sided public proclamations. I think the vast majority of chaplains would say the same thing. I also know my strongly held views on this did not always go over well with senior officers who thought the chaplain should echo their view of morality. It's difficult for some folks to understand that a chaplain is not simply a moralist with a pocket full of absolutes.

Q: Is there anything else to recall about that Great Lakes experience?

Admiral Stevenson: No, it was just a very good way for me to get my feet on the ground in the naval service.

Q: Then it was on to sea duty.

Admiral Stevenson: Then it was on to sea duty.

We knew that in somewhere between nine months and a year we were going to get orders to sea duty. Again I was very fortunate. I got orders back to Newport, Rhode Island, to Destroyer Squadron Ten--Lightning Ten. The hardest part of that was finding a place to live. Newport wasn't an easy place to find a place to live in those days. We went back and found a little cramped place.

In that destroyer squadron I was introduced to the real Navy--a very important part of any chaplain's career. I discovered years later just how important shipboard duty is for a chaplain when I became a supervisory chaplain and had a couple of chaplains working for me who had not been to sea in ships. There's a world of difference between a chaplain who has served in a ship and a chaplain who has not. I mean, the earlier in your career you can get that ship, the better off you are.

Q: What advantages does that bring?

Admiral Stevenson: I think that it's only when you get into a ship that you really understand the chain of command. Chain of command outside of a ship is sort of a management system, but in a ship it's a reality. It's a visible reality every moment of the day.

As a chaplain you become totally familiar with the life of a sailor, not in some mockup ship at Great Lakes, but the reality of the frustrations of maintaining ships, operating ships. The reality is that the day does not end at 5:00 o'clock, or 6:00 o'clock, but it goes around 24 hours a day. The real Navy is made up of, in the best sense of the word, workaholics.

I don't think any shore duty, or even overseas duty, would make you conscious of what the real Navy is like. The Navy has its origins at sea and brings them to land. The risk factors on human lives, the introduction to people being lost at sea, blown off a carrier deck and lost, etc. The sea as adversary, etc.

Q: The reality of deployments, separations.

Admiral Stevenson: The reality of deployments, the reality of not going ashore in your own home port because some equipment has broken down.

No, I don't think that a chaplain can really counsel effectively unless he has been there himself. I go back to that basic counseling situation of the Navy. You know the old expression regarding children being conceived and born. You have to be there for the laying of the keel but not for the launching. A way of measuring the transformation of a civilian clergyman into a Navy chaplain is when one recognizes the needs of the Navy--the fact that dads can't always be there when babies are born. Again, it sounds impossible in a civilian frame of reference. But once you've put in your tour of sea duty, it's understandable.

Q: How does one chaplain go about serving all the ships in a squadron?

Admiral Stevenson: How many hours have we got for this? [Laughter]

Okay, for a chaplain even to go to destroyer duty is a culture shock. It was that for me. You have come from a busy parish situation, and you have come from a recruit training command, where you had an office and where you had counseling situations and you were teaching courses, and so forth. Then you get on a destroyer, where you find that there is no office space. The majority of the counseling is going to be done in what they call "the ministry of presence," which basically means you're walking around, climbing up and down ladders, you're running into people who say just, "Hey, Chaplain, I need to talk to you about this." So you grab a corner someplace, or you step into a gun mount or passageway to have some privacy. That's an entirely different world.

In those days the chaplain was kept busier--I guess that's the right word--in port than at sea because he was largely confined to the one ship at sea. We continued to have character-education lectures, and we'd give them on the mess decks, as we would normally have divine services on the 01 or in the mess decks.* It was really a ministry of getting to know absolutely everybody. I must say that there were times when I was bored, and I did my share of reading, because everybody else was so tied up. Or the sea conditions were such that one wasn't getting around very much in the North Atlantic.

In 1958 they had really just started helo-hopping. In fact, my predecessor had always moved from ship to ship by highline, and I moved from ship to ship mostly by helicopters. In those days we were totally unprepared for helicopter transfers. I remember the first time I made a helicopter transfer, the XO went back to the fantail with me, and he said, "They'll lower this harness and you put it around you either frontwards or backwards. We'll see when it gets here which way it is." Because he didn't know and I didn't know how to get into the harness. Kind of awkward when you get hooked up the wrong way.

In the helicopter they used in those days, you came up through the deck of the helicopter, and the hatch would be hanging down. Normally you ended up getting your head cracked as you were getting in and out, because you didn't wear a helmet. It was easier to get out of a helicopter, though. You just sort of sat on the hatch, and when the

---

* Decks above the ship's main deck have zeroes preceding them. In ascending order they are 01, 02, 03, etc. "Mess deck" is the term for the area where enlisted crew members eat. In more recent years it has come to be known officially as the "enlisted dining facility."

hatch opened up you dropped out in the arms, as it were, of the friendly confines of the horse collar.*

Q: How much movement did you do from ship to ship?

Admiral Stevenson: Well, it depended on circumstances: where we were, what the operations were, and the sea state. We didn't do nearly as much in those days as the chaplains do today. We're talking about a period of time in which helicopters did not fly after sundown. The big joke on the ASW aircraft carriers was that the helicopter pilots knew all the movies because they were able to be in the wardroom every night.†

Q: I think you told me yesterday when the recorder wasn't running that the chaplain moved with the movies, too, so you saw the same movies every place you went.

Admiral Stevenson: I remember one Christmas in that squadron when I moved from ship to ship every day, and the same movie went with me every day.

It was a great adjustment for me. Again, I'm grateful to all those shipmates who educated me on what the requirements of my job were. Chaplains were also heavily involved in those days in arranging tours during port visits.

One of the really exciting and fun things for me in those days, when we were deployed, was finding a Catholic priest to celebrate Mass. When you'd chop to the Sixth Fleet, you received from the Sixth Fleet chaplain a list of civilian priests that you might find in the ports of the Med.‡ You'd get off the ship and go hunting for this church or this abbey. You encountered the language problem while trying to find it. Then you were sometimes debating what price would be paid for a priest to come and say Mass on your ships. Sometimes the remuneration included a can of coffee or things like that.

---

* The horse collar is a doughnut-like device that goes under the armpits of the person being raised and lowered. It is attached to a wire that is winched up as the passenger is raised from the deck of the ship.
† ASW--antisubmarine warfare.
‡ "Chop" is short for change operational control. Med--Mediterranean Sea.

But one of the great concepts of ministry in destroyers was the recognition that you were to be available and visible to everyone in the squadron. How you made yourself available and visible to them and got from ship to ship was a major problem. At one time I had 11 destroyers, and another time I had 8 destroyers. One time, quite humorously, I had two destroyers in the Mediterranean and four destroyers in the Pacific, and I think two others somewhere else. That was a highly impossible situation.

Q: Did you wind up then going to ships in other squadrons or organizations that were in the vicinity?

Admiral Stevenson: Yes, the chaplain on the staff of SOPA saw to that.[*] When I first went to Destroyer Squadron Ten, we deployed a week or ten days after I reported. We were to be on a four-month cruise to the Mediterranean. It ended up being a round-the-world cruise, so I very quickly learned that one has to adapt to the contingencies of the service. I was riding a ship in the Mediterranean when the word came from our commodore that I had my choice: I could stay with the ships that were staying in the Mediterranean, or I could proceed with the ship that I happened to be riding at that time. She and three of the other ships were scheduled to escort the USS Essex through the Suez Canal and to the Pacific. We had arrived during the Lebanon crisis in 1958, and then we escorted the Essex around to the Quemoy-Matsu situation.[†]

Q: What was the ship you went around in?

---

[*] SOPA--senior officer present afloat.
[†] On 15 July 1958, in response to a request from the President of Lebanon, the Sixth Fleet landed U.S. Marines at Beirut because the nation was threatened by civil war and foreign invasion. On 23 August, Communist China began an intensive artillery bombardment of the offshore islands of Quemoy and Matsu, which were held by the Nationalist Chinese government. The Seventh Fleet escorted troop transports that carried forces to protect the two islands. The aircraft carrier Essex (CVA-9) supported both of these operations.

Admiral Stevenson: I was on the USS Hale (DD-642), if I remember correctly. We had in company with us the USS Forrest Sherman, which was our DesRon 10 flagship; the USS Charles Roan, and the USS Forrest Royal.*

The squadron commodore was one of the reasons that I stayed in the Navy. I went to destroyer duty thinking I'd serve my three years and return to a civilian parish. One of the great influences on me at that time was the commodore of DesRon 10, who was later selected for admiral, Robert Weeks.† You could not have a better role model than Commodore Weeks.

Q: What qualities in him did you admire?

Admiral Stevenson: Well, I observed that all the sailors in DesRon 10 had a great admiration and affection for Lightning Ten, which was the squadron identification. They had call signs in those days, and ComDesRon 10 had the best call sign in the entire fleet, "Cocktail Echo."

Commodore Weeks was looked upon as a man of great integrity. He exemplified what a naval officer ought to be--professional. He was a highly educated man. I always noticed that the sailors wanted to see ComDesRon 10 departing and arriving. He took his time saluting the ensign and addressing the quarterdeck. You know, everything was done the way it ought to be done. I later found out--did not know it in those days--that he had something to do with the Purple Code in World War II and had the reputation for being one of the great communicators in the history of the Navy.‡

Q: He was later Director of Naval Communications.§

---

* DesRon 10--Destroyer Squadron Ten.
† Captain Robert H. Weeks, USN. He was addressed by the title "commodore" because he commanded a multi-ship unit.
‡ Prior to World War II, U.S. codebreakers were able to break the Japanese Purple Code that was used for diplomatic messages.
§ As a rear admiral, Weeks served as Commander Naval Telecommunications Command from 1 July 1967 to 21 March 1968.

Admiral Stevenson: That's right.

Q: The attitude of line officers can make a tremendous difference on how well a chaplain is received. Did he set a good tone from the top?

Admiral Stevenson: Yes. One of the advantages that I had in my career was that I was ordered to a destroyer squadron where the chaplain was welcomed by the commodore. I called it the luck of the draw. I didn't run into, as some of my friends have told me they ran into, an atmosphere of, "Well, what are we going to do with you?"

I was welcomed to the squadron. When I reported to DesRon 10, they were having a series of inspections prior to deployment, and I was introduced during the critiques of these inspections in the various wardrooms. My predecessor evidently had very negative feelings about pinup pictures, and I was not aware of that. At one of these critiques, the commodore said, "We normally hear from the chaplain in regards to pinup pictures at this time. Does the new chaplain in the squadron have anything to say about the pinup pictures?"

Being caught off guard, but being a city kid, I responded by saying that I hadn't seen any yet, and I couldn't make a judgment until I had seen them, or something like that. That sort of broke the ice for me with the wardroom. Maybe the commodore thought that I needed that chance.

I can remember being absolutely fascinated, after a while, by the commodore's skill for getting me to different ships at different times when he thought maybe I might be somewhat helpful.

Q: Do you have any examples that you recall of that?

Admiral Stevenson: Well, a couple of things. I remember one thing that he taught me shortly after I joined the squadron was that I should get as many haircuts as I could get because a chaplain could learn an awful lot from a ship's barber. I assume that is still true.

There were ships in our squadron that were under heavy tensions. I think the commodore had enough confidence in me that he would order me to that ship, if for no other reason than to add another voice of conversation to the wardroom, or things of that nature.

I take it for granted now, but in those days it was a startling thing how different one ship could be from another ship, and not necessarily dependent on the leadership of that ship. It was almost as though certain attitudes were ingrained into the hull when that ship was built. In the 27 months that I was with the squadron, one of the most delightful ships to be in was the USS Forrest Royal. It was a happy, hard-working ship. You'd go to some other ships, and it would be just the opposite. I was in the squadron long enough that there were many changes of command. The new COs always made some difference, but still a ship is a ship is a ship.[*]

Q: Did you have a chance to defuse some of these tensions that you encountered?

Admiral Stevenson: I hope so. Let's put it the other way; I hope it didn't cause added tension. A chaplain is required to take a lot of teasing, and there were lots of practical jokes in those days.

Q: Such as?

Admiral Stevenson: Well, you've got to remember that we were living in the age of the draft, and we had a lot of officers who definitely were in the Navy only for their tour of duty.[†] It was a sort of a nonchalant atmosphere in those days in comparison to today's Navy. Lots of gags were pulled, and we had what I looked upon as real characters. Maybe it was that we were at sea long enough that we got desperate for things to do. For instance, an officer would finally be qualified to be officer of the deck under way, and the word would be passed by some of his shipmates that all hands were to put on life jackets.

---

[*] CO--commanding officer.
[†] Males in the United States were subject to conscription prior to the inauguration of the all-volunteer force in 1973. Many elected to enlist in the Navy rather than be drafted into the Army.

Four of these ships were <u>Fletcher</u>-class destroyers: <u>Abbott</u>, <u>Benham</u>, <u>Hunt</u>, and <u>Hale</u>.* Officers' country was up forward in these ships, and it was an open bay with curtains but no doors. I recall a situation on the USS <u>Hale</u>. The XO was a great guy, and the CO was very tense.† We had a navigator who used to annoy the commanding officer during star sights.‡ While he was reading stars, the navigator would recite, from beginning to end, "Twinkle, twinkle, little star, how I wonder . . ." He was reprimanded constantly by the old man for doing this silly stuff.

One day I was talking to crew members, maybe giving a character-education lecture, Bible study, or something on the fantail. The XO came back there and saw me, and he said, "What are you doing here?"

I said, "Giving this lecture." I kept giving the lecture, and the XO suddenly ran away. I couldn't figure out what the emergency was because he was really moving out. He called me in a little later to his stateroom and told me he had thought that I was lazy. Every day after lunch he had gone by my stateroom, and he thought I was in my bunk because he saw legs in there. What had happened was he'd come back on the fantail and realized that it couldn't be the chaplain in the bunk. So he had left the fantail and had run back to my stateroom to find out who was taking daily noon naps in the chaplain's bunk. It was actually the navigator.

The brilliant but sleepy navigator was Pete Gallagher, a graduate of the New York Maritime College at Fort Schuyler.§ Pete was a fellow New Yorker, and he was shrewd enough that he was always figuring out those kind of angles. He could get himself a good half-hour nap without anybody disturbing him because they thought it was the chaplain in the bunk.

Q: Are there any of the individual skippers that you especially remember?

---

* The USS <u>Fletcher</u> (DD-445) and her sisters comprised the largest class of destroyers ever built for the U.S. Navy. All told, there were 175 ships of the class, commissioned 1942-44. Characteristics as originally built: standard displacement of 2,050 tons, 376 feet long, and 40 feet in the beam; top speed of 37 knots. Each ship was armed with five 5-inch guns, ten 40-millimeter guns, and ten 21-inch torpedo tubes.
† XO--executive officer.
‡ Navigators typically take readings of azimuth and altitude of various stars in the morning and evening in order to do celestial navigation calculations to determine the ship's position.
§ Lieutenant (junior grade) Pete C. Gallagher, Jr., USNR.

Admiral Stevenson: In a 26-, 27-month period of time, we must be talking about, 22, 23 skippers. All were interesting gentlemen and all under a ton of pressure. Most of them were commanders, some of them lieutenant commanders.

I don't know if you want me to just name skippers or what. Ernie Hipp was a young commander whose change of command was in Yokosuka, Japan.[*] The first time he had to bring the ship in was at Midway. Midway is not the easiest place in the world to bring a ship in alongside the pier. He brought it in close enough that the boatswain's mate just leaned over and handed the lines across, cutting it pretty close.

There was one skipper who has a son, whom I assume is still in the Navy Chaplain Corps. There's an expression in Scripture: "As is his name, so is he." And Pleasant Murphy was a most pleasant skipper.[†] He commanded the USS Samuel B. Roberts when we were on an inland seas cruise. We were one of the squadrons deployed to the St. Lawrence River and the Great Lakes when President Eisenhower and Queen Elizabeth opened the St. Lawrence Seaway in 1959.[‡]

During the cruise, Captain Murphy asked me to conduct a memorial service for a sailor who had drowned in the Detroit River while the ship was under way. I naturally did so, but then the commodore--Captain Philip Hauck by this time--wanted me to get back to USS Forrest Sherman ASAP.[§] The plan called for me to jump off the flying bridge of the Samuel B. Roberts when she was going up in the lock at Sault Ste. Marie and run to the other lock in order to jump to Forrest Sherman as she was going down. The distance of the jump probably wasn't as far as I thought at the time, but it helps to be young and bold.

I was bold and rookie enough in those days too. I remember the commodore advising me not to tell folks I was from Brooklyn. He was trying to be nice and suggest I read his bio. It commenced by stating he was born in Sheepshead Bay, New York, a

---

[*] Commander Ernest C. Hipp, Jr., USN.
[†] Commander Pleasant L. Murphy, USN.
[‡] Dwight D. Eisenhower served as President of the United States from 20 January 1953 to 20 January 1961. Elizabeth II became Queen of the United Kingdom in 1952 and is still on the throne more than 40 years later.
[§] Captain Philip F. Hauck, USN.

section of Brooklyn. I told him I'd been to Sheepshead Bay, and I'd stick with Brooklyn. You're got to be naive to tell the commodore that.

Q: Do you remember any specific ports from that around-the-world tour?[*]

Admiral Stevenson: Well, I found out that the world is 72% water. In that round-the-world cruise, we stopped in San Juan for 24 hours. I was then riding a destroyer that had an evaporator problem, and we ended up in Roosey Roads.[†]

Then we stopped for refueling in the Azores. We had two or three days in Naples, and we went through the Suez Canal and did not go ashore again until we went in for some refitting in Subic Bay. We went out and operated and went into Yokosuka. Two of our ships returned to Newport via South Africa, and I stayed with the two ships that went to Pearl Harbor. From Pearl Harbor to San Diego. San Diego down around Panama, and then up to Gitmo for some exercises and back up to Newport, Rhode Island.[‡]

We had payday in Yokosuka, and we all went out and spent our money buying the kinds of things you could buy in those days. So when we got to Pearl Harbor, we were all broke. Nobody had any money whatsoever, so the chaplain had the joy of organizing softball tournaments. One of the few frustrations I had in those years was the fact that everybody wanted the chaplain to be an umpire. Of course, I wanted to play ball; I didn't want to be an umpire. But the chaplain has to be the umpire.

My introduction to tragedy in the Navy came on that cruise. We had just pulled out of Pearl Harbor heading for San Diego when we got the word that an Air Force plane had ditched in the Pacific, and we were to move out at rapid speed to see if we could rescue the pilot. I was riding the USS Hale, and, being a Fletcher, she could really crank up speed. At first she was ordered to follow in Forrest Sherman's wake, and then it was decided to let the Hale go off and do her thing.

---

[*] The USS Hale (DD-642) began this cruise on 23 July 1958, going through the Mediterranean, Suez Canal, India, and Japan. After transiting the Panama Canal, she returned to Newport on 24 November 1958.
[†] Roosevelt Roads Naval Station is on the east coast of Puerto Rico.
[‡] "Gitmo" is the nickname for Guantanamo Bay, Cuba.

We got to the location where the aviator had bailed out. He was dead. Two helicopters had come out from Kaneohe to be involved in the rescue operation.[*] One of the helicopters went over and lowered a crewman. And the crewman, as I best remember it, got the dead aviator into the harness and got him up in the helicopter. The helicopter left the crewman in the water for one of our boats to pick up. The helo then lowered the aviator's body onto the fantail of the Forrest Sherman. One of the helicopters--and I think it was the one that lowered the dead body--disintegrated just as it was pulling away. Just what happened, I don't know--whether the blades got out of sync or what, but it just blew up. The other helicopter said that it was low on fuel and it wanted to try to land on the fantail of either the Forrest Sherman or the Hale. Preparations were made: lowering gun mounts, getting fire equipment, etc.

After several tries, the aviator decided that he would rather ditch in the water than try to land on the fantail. There were no helicopter pads on destroyers in those days. And that's what happened. Remember, we had depth charge racks on the fantails in those days. Anyway, our boat had recovered the crewman from the helicopter that blew up because he had stayed in the water, and it also picked up the crew of the ditched helo. I believe two Marine aviators were lost, plus the Air Force aviator who had gone down in the beginning.

This was my first introduction to tragedy at sea, to the impact that it had on the crew, of how keyed up the crew was to be part of a rescue operation, and the frustration the entire crew felt about the loss of the aviators. We spent the entire night searching with searchlights and everything, trying to find the aviators or anything we could find. The next day we went back into Pearl Harbor to deliver the dead body and the crewmen. It was a very tragic situation, especially when we learned that the wife of one of the deceased helo pilots was having a baby at that time.

Q: How did you react?

Admiral Stevenson: Well, I hope that I was some help to other people. I know that other people were a tremendous help to me. It just was such a totally frustrating circumstance,

---

[*] Kaneohe is the site of a Marine Corps air station on the eastern side of Oahu, Hawaii.

and then, of course, in the years in the chaplaincy, I learned about an awful lot of frustrating, tragic circumstances, particularly in the world of naval aviation. By the way, grief equals anger, and anger equals depression. That's what we went through, but I didn't know about the grief cycle in those days.

Q: What did you do for the crew in a situation like that to help them get through it?

Admiral Stevenson: Well, I could probably do an awful lot better job now than I did that time.

It was mostly, again, the chaplain going around talking with folks. People asked those questions that we don't have ready answers for: why would God allow things like this to happen? What part does human decision-making play in tragedy? Plus our American habit of saying, "Let's nail whoever is responsible." We don't like to think about corporate fault. Everybody had a guilt feeling that we could have done something more than what we did. But we had responded to the realities of the circumstance, I think, as best as could be.

The Navy in those days had many World War II veterans. In all those kinds of circumstances, the stable members, if you want to call them that, were the mature World War II veterans. They had seen all manner of tragedy, and they were able to work with all of us on accepting the fact that tragedy was always around.

Later, in San Diego, and the ship I was riding, USS Hale, got hit by a yard oiler and had to stay for repairs. Our doctor was a young bachelor. He had been riding the USS Forrest Sherman, and the commodore surmised that the young bachelor would like to stay longer in San Diego and that the married chaplain would be very happy to get back to Newport, Rhode Island. Commodore Weeks made the wonderful decision that the chaplain would ride the USS Forrest Sherman, and the doctor would ride the USS Hale.

While in USS Forrest Sherman, on the way from Gitmo to Newport, Rhode Island, a young sailor asked to be baptized. He was the first man I baptized during my career as a Navy chaplain. I hope it was as memorable a sacrament for him as it is a memorable one for me.

Q: Probably so.

Admiral Stevenson: He had done some determined study during that cruise and wanted to be a member of the Christian faith. His wife was a devout Christian, and he wanted to be baptized on the cruise so that when he got back, he could greet his wife and tell her that he had been baptized.[*]

Q: What sorts of things did chaplains do for dependents back home during a long cruise like that?

Admiral Stevenson: Well, the dependents had many problems in those days. Financial problems were horrendous for enlisted personnel and their families. I'd have to look back at the record, but they certainly didn't make much money.[†] Marital conflicts were usually part of those financial tensions. Young couples didn't want to live with Mom and Dad but couldn't afford to live in Newport, Rhode Island. I would hear, "Chaplain, we can find a place to live in Fall River, Massachusetts, but I don't have any transportation." The sacrifice that sailors made to serve their country in those days was more extreme than people today might appreciate.

Q: Well, I don't think many dependent services were available then, either.

Admiral Stevenson: No, and the ones that were available were not sophisticated. The Navy Relief was doing an outstanding job in those days. The Red Cross was extremely reliable in regards to message traffic. But, no, it was not nearly as sophisticated, and the assumption was whether you came into the Navy because of the draft, or whether you

---

[*] The Forrest Sherman (DD-931) returned to Newport on 11 November 1958.
[†] In the pay tables that went into effect on 1 June 1958, a seaman (E-3) with over two years of service received $124.00 a month base pay, while a petty officer third class (E-4) with more than three years made $160.00. In addition to base pay, an enlisted sailor of any grade received $51.30 a month for housing allowance if he had no dependents or one dependent. Housing allowance was $77.10 a month with two dependents and $96.90 with more than two.

joined the Navy to see the world, you were supposed to take care of yourself. The ship came first, and the Navy would try to take care of its own.

The dependents were very good about helping each other. They didn't call it networking in those days, but the networking that they did was outstanding. My wife still talks about the way the commodore's wife kept in touch with people by phone. When there were social events, there was sort of the roundup, "Let's get the gals together." The chiefs' wives played a similar role with enlisted personnel, and the Navy wives' clubs offered great support. There were nurseries for babies in those days, but not day-care centers.

One of the strong influences on me was my very solid force chaplain. Again, a World War II veteran--what I suppose people would refer to as a hard-nosed four-striper. The DesLant chaplain was Art McQuaid, a Catholic priest from the Diocese of Boston.[*] We all thought the world of him. He really played the hard-nosed role. He made those kinds of demands. He had a chaplain who missed ship's movement and who got back early to Newport, Rhode Island, without his ship from the Caribbean. Art McQuaid saw to it that the chaplain had to live the next three or four weeks in the BOQ rather than with his family until the ships got back. It was an impressive, appropriate lesson to that chaplain and to all the rest of us. You weren't just a wandering entrepreneur on your own out there. You were a chaplain under authority!

Two stories. I got word one day that Chaplain McQuaid wanted me in his office. There were two kinds of office visits in those days: there were the office visits where you were invited to sit down, and the office visits where you were not invited to sit down. Once I got the word that Father McQuaid wanted to see me, I went directly to his office. I was not invited to sit down. He said that he thought that I was the type of chaplain who should be in the regular Navy, that it was time to apply for augmentation. I remember saying something to the effect that I really hadn't thought that through, and he indicated that he wasn't too interested in whether I had thought it through or not. He said that Chaplain Jim Seim in another destroyer squadron had been augmented into regular Navy, and I was to go

---

[*] DesLant--Destroyer Force Atlantic Fleet. Captain Arthur F. McQuaid, CHC, USN.

see Chaplain Seim.* I was to go look at the paperwork that Chaplain Seim had handed in, and that I was to hand in my paperwork to Chaplain McQuaid within the next week.

I explained that my ships were going out into the North Atlantic on an ASW exercise. And he said, "That's good. Just have it all prepared so that when your ship comes back, you can hand it to me."

Well, I did. I mean, I did what I was told to do, and I had not thought through whether I wanted to be in the regular Navy or whether I wanted to be augmented or anything. I did it, and I came back and I handed it in. Some months later I was called into my commodore's stateroom, and the commodore said, "Congratulations, you've been selected for augmentation. And we're going to have the ceremony this afternoon."

So on the 01 deck of the USS Forrest Sherman I was sworn into the regular Navy. It was memorable because the commodore stopped the ceremony, turned to one of the yeomen, and said, "I'm not going to go through this ceremony if we don't have a G-D Bible to do it with." The yeoman ran off and found a Bible. Then the commodore told me to put my hand on the Bible and raise my other hand, and I was sworn into the regular Navy.

Q: Who was he?

Admiral Stevenson: It was Commodore Phil Hauck, who committed suicide some years later while serving on the JCS.† Hauck had problems.

Q: Do you have any more good McQuaid stories?

Admiral Stevenson: Yes, and I can get sentimental about some of those stories. First of all, you've got to know what a tough, hard-nosed guy McQuaid was, or that's the role he played.

When I was getting close to my projected rotation date, the PRD, I received orders to the naval station, Newport, Rhode Island. We thought this was wonderful. We loved

---

* Lieutenant James E. Seim, CHC, USN.
† JCS--Joint Chiefs of Staff. Hauck died 6 November 1961 in Washington, D.C.

Newport, Rhode Island, and here I was going to go from the destroyer squadron to the base. Then Art McQuaid called me in and told me that my orders would stand, but it had been decided in Washington that the chaplains at the chaplains' school could fill in at the station chapel and gap the billet for about six months. So I was going to be extended in DesRon 10 beyond my PRD.

That meant I would be with the DesRon 10 for one more deployment to the Mediterranean. (For domestic reasons, it was said, my relief was not going to be able to show up on time.) I would have to be relieved in the Med instead of being relieved in Newport prior to deployment. That was a great disappointment, because Diane was pregnant with our third child. And Diane was just not very well. She really had some serious medical problems with her third pregnancy. Chaplain McQuaid said, "You know that orders are orders, and you're going, and that's what the Navy's all about, etc., etc. We'll take care of Diane." And they did, they did.

Art McQuaid really checked constantly on her health. I had a shipmate on the Roberts, Al Hennessey, who was engaged to a Navy nurse, later Jane Hennessey.[*] Jane was alerted through Father McQuaid and through Al. When Diane went to the Newport naval hospital, she was well cared for during that critical period. I found out what it's like to worry about a wife and a baby being born while on deployment.

We deployed in March, and Heidi was born in May. Because this is so typical of Navy families, I tell the story. First of all, Elbert Carpenter was a fellow chaplain who had been a classmate of mine at chaplain school.[†] He and his wife said that they would get Diane to the hospital. And Margaret would take care of our two daughters until my mother arrived from New York, and all that kind of loving support.

Diane went to the hospital on Mother's Day, 3 May 1960, and had Heidi that day. The ships had just pulled into Naples and Med-moored when I got the message that I had a daughter and that Diane was not doing well. I should have saved a copy of the message. It was from Chaplain McQuaid and said, "Baby girl," but didn't give me the name. "Diane not doing well, but do not take emergency leave until further message."

---

[*] Lieutenant Aloysius G. Hennessey, Jr., USN.
[†] Lieutenant Elbert N. Carpenter, CHC, USN.

So I went out walking up and down the pier in Naples. Lo and behold, I ran into a famous chaplain who was on the staff of MSTS, Roderic Lee Smith.* He was riding the USNS Upshur, which had just pulled in. He had been the chaplain at the Coast Guard Academy, and I had met him once before when I was in chaplain school. Once Roderic Lee heard my story, he stayed with me. He didn't go on liberty. He and I walked the living daylights out of that big, long pier in Naples until about 2:00 in the morning. Then a message came in that Diane was all right. Roderic Lee then returned to the Upshur, and he always claims that he had a lot to do with Heidi being born.

I was riding the Forrest Royal, and the next morning the ship pulled out. We went on independent steaming to the Bay of Biscay and visited La Pallice, where the German submarine pens had been in World War II, then to Bordeaux on a special assignment. So I did not find out that Heidi's name was Heidi until about three or four weeks after her birth because mail didn't catch up with us. When it caught up, I put the letters all in sequence to read what had happened. Chaplains and their spouses, under the leadership of Father McQuaid, took good care of Diane and Heidi. (By the way, as soon as Diane came home from the hospital, Heather had measles and Holly had chicken pox, which they traded off. This is the story of a Navy wife.)

Prior to the deployment, since I was going to shore duty, we had arranged to move to a little house in Portsmouth, Rhode Island. So while I was gone on that cruise, Diane had the baby and Diane moved to a different house. So when I did get relieved in September, I came back, and things were squared away.

Q: Sort of makes you feel you're not so indispensable after all.

Admiral Stevenson: True--if you are married to the right woman.

McQuaid was a great force chaplain. As I said, he was very demanding. He would check your ships to see whether or not sailors knew you. The word was if Art McQuaid came around your ship with you and the sailors weren't saying, "Hello, chaplain. Good

---

* MSTS--Military Sea Transportation Service. Captain Roderic Lee Smith, CHC, USN. His oral history is in the series conducted by the Navy's Chaplain Corps.

morning, chaplain," indicating that they knew who you were, you were in big trouble with Art McQuaid. He would question you concerning the names of people on your ships and officers in the wardroom, and things like that. He knew what he was doing.

Q: What else do you recall from your destroyer days?

Admiral Stevenson: Well, it's people that make the Navy. Some of those ships were so old, they literally kept them together with baling wire. Fletcher- and Gearing-class destroyers made up most of the squadron. The chief petty officers were the backbone of those ships. I mean, if a ship had good petty officers, it was a good ship.

Q: You were prohibited from being part of the war-fighting capability of the ship. How much did you learn about that ship's operations?

Admiral Stevenson: Oh, you learned constantly. I mean, what else is discussed anywhere you go in a ship except the ship, what's wrong with it, what needs to be fixed, or how it works and so forth.

I never had any problems with the non-combatant status for a chaplain. It just makes sense. But, sure, you learn a good deal about navigation--you learn about all kinds of things. As I said, if you didn't learn those things and you didn't interact with people, you'd really be bored. Consider how many times a day I'd make the rounds in a ship with 200 personnel. That's just the way it was.

I look back on that like I look back on a lot of Navy things. The Navy is made up of the shortest years and the longest days that you can ever experience. Some of those days seemed like years. They just didn't end. We had a lot of bad weather in the Atlantic. Off Quemoy-Matsu, we had a lot of bad weather. I remember one period of three days when we were not able to use a chair in the wardroom. We ate off paper plates, and we sat on the deck for three days in a row. You literally rolled out of your bunk. You're just out there hanging on. You get to the place where you realize that you've got to get yourself in better shape because your arms are hurting from spending so much time hanging on. Vic

Modeen, the ComDesRon 10 communicator, was the one who taught me to pull the springs of a bunk halfway out, throw the mattress in, and make a cocoon out of the mattress.* Then you crawled into the cocoon so that you could sort of sleep while you were being banged around.

An awful lot of our officers and enlisted personnel were certainly getting out of the Navy as soon as they were eligible, but they did their job while they were there. I'll bet they all look back on their duty with favor.

Q: How well attended were your worship services?

Admiral Stevenson: Well, divine services were attended by somewhere between 6 and 24, depending on what was going on, what the conditions were, and whether we were in port or at sea. That was for Protestants. Catholic attendance for Mass or rosary was higher. More wanted divine services at sea than when in port. But you'd still make the rounds to provide a service in each ship. And, as I said, one of my delights was to be able to find a Catholic priest somewhere and get him out to the ship for Mass--whether he was another Navy chaplain, or whether he was a civilian--in Spain or Italy or somewhere like that--who didn't speak English.

Q: Would the Catholic priest in those countries just have the service in Latin?

Admiral Stevenson: Yes, in those days. And we would have things rigged for the visiting chaplain. There's a painting around, done by an artist who joined us in that last cruise in the Mediterranean in 1960. It's a watercolor that was made on the Forrest Royal, with the DesRon 10 emblem on the gun barrels and showing a priest holding Catholic Mass.† You see prints of it in a lot of chaplains' offices. That was my ship, and the artist took photos of the service I conducted--but made me a priest for the painting.

---

* Lieutenant (junior grade) Victor D. Modeen, USN.
† The painting, done by artist Louis J. Kaep, appeared on the cover of the August 1969 issue of U.S. Naval Institute Proceedings. That issue contains an article titled "The Navy Chaplaincy," by Commander Robert H. Warren, CHC, USN.

It was just one of the things that was happening in those days, and you didn't pay a lot of attention to it.

As I say, there are a lot of things in the early part of your career, or anywhere in your career, that I guess you take for granted.

Q: What were the living conditions like on board those ships then?

Admiral Stevenson: I happened to be reading Boswell's Johnson one time in those days.* And I could relate to the fact that Samuel Johnson did not like ships or the sea. He defined a sailor, in his English dictionary, as a prisoner who added to his lot the danger of drowning. Habitability in Fletcher and Gearing-class destroyers was about like that. The only air-conditioners were in the wardroom, the chiefs' quarters, and the crew's mess. The crew often wanted to sleep on deck because compartments were just beastly hot, particularly when you went through the Suez Canal and down into the Gulf area.

There were no partitions in the heads. About once a year, a ship would have a dependents' cruise. The CO and many of the ship's company would get excited about having a dependents' cruise. Then you'd have to put up with the ten letters from parents who came on the cruise and wrote letters saying they never realized that their son was being forced to live in such awful conditions. They didn't know their sons had to sleep sandwich style with a bunk two and a half feet from the next bunk on top of him.

I remember many times at sea in the after officers' country, I'd see my shoes floating around because the water had come up over the deck plates and into the staterooms.

Q: A ship that was along on that Great Lakes cruise was relatively new but still had problems. That was the Willis A. Lee. What do you recall about her?

Admiral Stevenson: Well, I never was in Willis A. Lee, but I had friends who served in Willis A. Lee. She was known to have engineering problems from day one, and the sonar

---

* Scottish lawyer and author James Boswell was best known for his Life of Samuel Johnson, published in 1791. Johnson, who lived from 1709 to 1784, was an English lexicographer, critic, and conversationalist.

dome was either flooding or not flooding--I forget which. People used to talk about the "Lee that never went to sea."*

One advantage of being in a Fletcher-class destroyer in those days was that if you could keep it going, it was a great tribute. Very uncomfortable. All the officers were forward with just curtains in between staterooms. And then the chiefs were forward of the officers. So, I mean, they had really picked the most uncomfortable places for officers and chiefs.

One of the real hazards of sea duty in a Fletcher was the number of people who were burned by soup. The galley was on the main deck, and the food had to be carried forward and down two ladders to the mess deck. Every time you had soup, some mess cook would be burned while carrying a pot of soup. The ships just were not built for any kind of habitability whatsoever. I wonder, for instance, why they were designed with open bridges. But they had speed, and with the right engineering people they would really move out and do a job.

If I remember correctly, the Forrest Sherman was the first destroyer class built after World War II. And they built her with a 1,200-pound steam system, and that was a constant harangue. I know our engineering people worked around the clock keeping that 1,200-pound system going. I don't know what the complications were, but I know that the people in the ship's company were dedicated. There was a great deal of admiration, not only for the ship's crew but the engineering officer on the DesRon 10 staff. The first squadron engineer during my tour was a guy named Charlie Kent, and the second one was an officer named Ralph Hooton.†

Q: Any specific memories about the ports you hit during that cruise?

Admiral Stevenson: I remember in 1958 going into the Azores for refueling on that first cruise. It was the only time in my whole sea career that I actually saw people in a whale boat whaling, with honest-to-God old-fashioned harpoons. That was quite a sight.

---

* The Naval Institute's oral history collection contains the memoir of Vice Admiral Frederick Schneider, USN (Ret.), who was the first skipper of the USS Willis A. Lee (DL-4).
† Lieutenant Commander Charles J. Kent, Jr., USN; Lieutenant Commande Ralph L. Hooton, USN.

Subic Bay in 1958--Olongapo was a great disaster. We had several sailors debilitated in Olongapo. And Olongapo was a town with mud streets in 1958.

So much of that destroyer time was strictly sea time. When we weren't on deployment, we were constantly involved in Alfa and Bravo Group ASW exercises in the Atlantic with ships like the USS Leyte.

Christmas of '58 we were out, two VIPs came out for Christmas. One was Bishop Furlong of the Roman Catholic Church from New York.[*] He was in his 70s then, and the last word I have, Bishop Furlong is still living and he's over 100 now. The bishop looked and acted a lot like Cardinal Spellman.[†] The other VIP was a Dr. Creeger, who was associated with the General Commission on Chaplains.[‡] I don't remember the name of the admiral who commanded our task group in those days, but he thought that we could helo these gentlemen around.[§] When I looked at Bishop Furlong, I recommended that just the Catholic padre on the Leyte and myself make the rounds, rather than the VIPs. So they just stayed on the Leyte. They flew out to the Leyte, and they left from the Leyte.

The TV crew that came out from New York to cover the "Navy protecting the world" over Christmas was headed up by Harry Reasoner, who was a very young reporter in those days.[**] Later they sent us out the tape of what was on New York television regarding our efforts. There was great attention paid to the numbers of turkeys and pounds of potatoes that we ate on the aircraft carriers. Little about our mission. That told us something about the media.

Q: You went ashore after that duty with DesRon 10. You've described this pattern where you were sort of following an ordained path of following orders, not making choices. Did you get a choice about going to the naval station at Newport?

---

[*] Most Reverend Philip J. Furlong, Auxiliary Bishop of the Military Ordinariate.
[†] Francis J. Spellman had been archbishop of New York and military vicar of the armed forces since 1939. He was created a cardinal in 1946 and served in that capacity until his death in 1967.
[‡] Dr. Marion J. Creeger, executive secretary of the General Commission on Chaplains.
[§] The flag officer embarked in the Leyte that Christmas was Rear Admiral Reynold D. Hogle, USN, Commander Carrier Division 18.
[**] Harry Reasoner, who went on to have a distinguished career in broadcast journalism, was born in 1923. He was with CBS News from 1956 to 1970 and with ABC News from 1970 to 1978, when he returned to CBS.

Admiral Stevenson: No, not really. I went to Newport because I got a set of orders. The previous chaplain had left that billet six months prior to my reporting. I had the good fortune of arriving when everything was in a bit of a mess. The chapel fund was unreconcilable, the office disorganized, etc.

It was an interesting tour of duty, because it meant coming in and sort of straightening out the office and getting a chapel program under way. The people who attended that chapel, which was one of the ugliest the Navy ever had, were war college students.[*] They reported in the fall and departed in the spring. You had to rework the whole program each academic year.

I still had a civilian pastor's mentality, and I was trying to make that chapel program into a church program. If I received a set of orders to that billet today, my whole approach would be 180 degrees out from what I did in those days. I'd know it's a chapel, not a church.

Q: What were some of the things you did then that you would not now do?

Admiral Stevenson: Well, I largely targeted my work at the chapel rather than throughout the entire command. I had the mentality that my work was mostly in response to people who came to my office, or people who came to the chapel. Instead, I should have recognized that in an institutional ministry my job was to get my presence, and what I represented in ministry and religion, to all members of the command. That's a mistake young chaplains make, and it's a problem that some chaplains, unfortunately, never get over. They never realize that the job is broader than an office and a chapel. You don't run what we now call a command religious program just by having a good Protestant, Catholic, or Jewish chapel program. It's got to be broader than that.

Q: Did you try to rectify that later, when you were Chief of Chaplains?

---

[*] The Naval War College is located at Newport.

Admiral Stevenson: Yes, and with the help of staff and others, it was one of the main intentions of my time as Deputy Chief of Chaplains and Chief of Chaplains.

Q: Well, but one of the pleasant benefits of that time there was that you got to be with your growing family much more than you had before.

Admiral Stevenson: Yes. We rented a lovely little house in Portsmouth. In the neighborhood and in the command there was a true sense of community. We had a fabulous Navy social life in those days. The officers' club in Newport would bring in the big bands. We would enjoy big dinner parties and big dance bands--Duke Ellington's band and all those things.[*]

As far as my own growth as a chaplain was concerned, the chaplain school was there, so I got to teach a couple minor courses in the chaplain school. By doing that, I got to meet a lot of new chaplains coming on board in the Navy. I was under the influence, again, of role models like Chaplain Ed Slattery, who was officer in charge of the chaplain school, and he was the base chaplain.[†] Slattery was a very demanding senior chaplain and at the same time a most considerate gentleman.

I worked for, in those days, two senior chaplains. Chaplain Joe Gallagher was and remains a saint.[‡] Then a rough old cob came in, and I don't know if this kind of priest exists in the world anymore. He was the kind of priest that was seen in the movies of my childhood. Tom Reilly was a rough, gruff old-fashioned ultra-conservative from Jersey.[§] I think the fact that I had grown up in Brooklyn allowed me to enjoy and survive Tom. Chaplains like McQuaid and Slattery were demanding, but Tom was different. Tom scared people.

Q: Intimidating?

---

[*] Edward Kennedy Ellington (1899-1974) was a bandleader and composer, one of the most notable black musicians of the 20th century.
[†] Captain Edward A. Slattery, CHC, USN.
[‡] Commander Joseph P. Gallagher, CHC, USN.
[§] Commander Thomas H. Reilly, CHC, USN.

Admiral Stevenson: Yes, intimidating. I'll give you two stories. It happened that when Diane and I first invited him to come to dinner, it was the first of April. Tom's the only chaplain that ever scared Diane. She laughs about it now, but when Diane opened the door to greet my senior chaplain, big Tom said, "Well, by God, I almost didn't come! I figured it was just an April Fool's joke because it's taken you six weeks to invite me to dinner."

But he was the greatest storyteller and one of the finest writers that I ever knew in my life. He was an absolute delight, but a really rough, tough old cob. His conservatism was unreal. He refused to believe that Sputnik happened.[*] In Tom's opinion, it was a Russian fabrication. He honestly didn't believe Russians were smart enough to do a thing like that, and that was the end of that subject.

There are lots of Tom Reilly stories. Tom operated on the basis of paternalism. Tom was the chaplain who built the submarine chapel at Pearl Harbor during World War II. He called it St. Dismas's because he stole everything.[†] I mean, command didn't even want to know they had a new chapel. He would borrow Seabees and he would borrow equipment.[‡] He just built it. I think it came to the public works people's attention when he asked for a parking lot, and they asked what it was for. And he said, "For my chapel." That's the kind of guy he was.

Anyway, the old chapel up in Newport had been a gymnasium. The chapel was up on the second deck. The pews were second hand from Harvard seminary and were hard as rocks. It was a very ugly chapel, really.

Tom came into the office one day and said, "Stevenson, get ahold of somebody that can put pads on those pews." There were 100 pews. He said, "Those pews are too hard; we need pads." So I called around and got some guys to come down from Fall River, Massachusetts. I presented their estimate, which was about $700.00, to Tom, and Tom said, "Let's do it."

---

[*] On 4 October 1957, the Soviet Union launched Sputnik I, the first articial earth satellite. It caused great uproar in the United States, which had expected to be first in space.
[†] Dismas, a saint of the Roman Catholic church, was one of the thieves crucified with Christ.
[‡] Seabees is the name universally applied to members of the Navy's mobile construction battalions (CBs).

I remember asking where the money was coming from, because we didn't have any money in the chapel fund for it. Tom told me not to worry about it. So the pads came and were put in the chapel, and the bill went to the command. The next thing I knew, Tom and I were standing in front of an unhappy XO. The highly annoyed XO said, "Who approved this, and what funding line is this coming from?"

Standing in front of the XO with Tom, I got a sincere understanding of Tom's approach to the Navy. It was quite frightening. The first thing Tom did was to inform the XO that he was senior to the XO. [Laughter] That's not exactly the way to win an argument. Then the next thing he did was tell the XO that it was really none of the XO's business. Tom announced that the CO's wife was coming out of Mass one day and said, "Father, these pews are awfully hard. Can't you do something about getting some pads?" So he got some pads! He never checked with the XO about funds to buy the pads.

Q: But if he had asked, the answer would have been no.

Admiral Stevenson: If he'd asked, the answer would have been no. Never would have found $700.00. But, again, pretty bad experience. It was that mentality that came over from the parish--a cumshaw--chaplains not really being a part of the Navy system. Chapels were considered as a separate entity from command and were to be supported out of offerings in the chapel fund. Things that really over the years we've tried to correct. In my memory it's a humorous but miserable occasion

Q: I daresay he wasn't too liberal or too tolerant on religious doctrine, either.

Admiral Stevenson: No, but he recognized borders made for good friends. He was a great storyteller; he was a great writer, and you don't want to get me on too many Tom stories because there's just too many wild stories.

Q: Well, fling out another one or two, maybe.

Admiral Stevenson: Well, typical of Tom, he told Diane one day that it was her job to come up with an ideal birthday present for his sister. And everything Diane mentioned was unacceptable. His sister had lived in the family home in New Jersey and was a retired schoolteacher. Then Tom came in one day and said he had found a birthday present for his sister. He had been talking to the butcher at the commissary, and the butcher's dog had had pups and Tom had gotten one of the pups. So Tom was taking the dog down to Jersey to give to his spinster sister.

A few weeks later he got a letter from his brother, who was a lawyer in New Jersey, who said that the sister was on the horns of a dilemma. She had received this "wonderful gift" from her brother, the priest, but couldn't stand the dog. The dog was messing up the old family home. This was an old-fashioned Irish house in which the parlor was hardly ever used. It was just for really good company on Sunday afternoon. The dog would sneak into the parlor and do its business under an oil portrait of Monsignor Mike, who was Tom's uncle.

In response, Tom wrote a beautiful letter. I wish we had Xerox in those days and I could have made a copy of it. He wrote to his brother and sister, announcing that they had his permission to get rid of the dog. He also wrote that he had sympathy for the dog because there were many times when he was a curate serving in Uncle Mike's parish that he felt the same about Uncle Mike that the dog did.

Lots of Tom Reilly stories.

You know, if you look at every situation as a situation of growth and learning, Tom in his own way contributed as much to my growing and understanding of the Navy Chaplain Corps and its requirements as anyone. Tom thought the junior chaplain ought to do everything. You know, the senior chaplain just sort of sat in his office, and if it really got to crisis, you called on him. But the junior chaplain did all the admin; the junior chaplain kept both the Catholic and Protestant chapel fund books; the junior chaplain did all the counseling. I mean, it was a wild scene.

Q: You talked about his scrounging around for resources. Was that typical of Navy chaplains at that time?

Admiral Stevenson: Yes, horribly so. Office equipment, chapel equipment. I suppose that's why it became such an important distinction for me. At the present time, on a once-a-month basis, I still teach a course at the VA hospital chaplains' school at Hampton on the difference between institutional ministry and parish ministry.*

The mentality in that day, unfortunately, was that you were simply a clergyman who happened to be wearing a uniform. A disastrous mentality, really. There was no need for you to really learn the Navy system. You would be taken care of by paternalism. A great deal of what happened was not based on meeting the needs of people in the Navy, but simply whether or not the chaplain could form a relationship with command so that command would be paternalistic towards things religious. I'm sure that there are still those who would say, "Yes, but those relationships were so important," and so forth. They were and they are, except that those relationships were limited to being personal rather than professional. The king with his chaplain in the "castle" chapel is not a valid or adequate model for ministry in our Navy. The chaplain is there by the First Amendment to meet the needs of all.

We had in those days, in Newport, Rhode Island, two absolutely fabulous role models for a junior chaplain. They were the two chaplains at the Officer Candidate School, Father Bill Walsh and Chaplain Dave Humphreys.† The finest relationship between two chaplains working a total command situation would be Bill Walsh and Dave Humphreys. When I was leaving Newport, Rhode Island, I had orders to the USS Saratoga, and both Dave Humphreys and Bill Walsh had had carrier duty. I was a lieutenant; they were commanders in those days. They educated me on the kinds of programs that they had in carrier duty.

But when you talk about--this is before Vatican II--but when you talk about ecumenicity, there was a real example of ecumenicity coming out of the pragmatism of the needs of the Navy.‡ So that Bill Walsh and Dave had a lot to do with my career.

---

* VA--Veterans Administration.
† Commander William J. Walsh, CHC, USN; Commander David M. Humphreys, CHC, USN.
‡ Vatican Council II was convened in October 1962 at the Vatican City by Pope John XXXII. It was attended by more than 2,500 Roman Catholic bishops and nearly 50 observer delegates from other Christian churches. It met in four annual sessions, concluding in December 1965. Vatican II revised some aspects of the church's organization and discipline and laid the groundwork for the establishment of Christian unity.

Q: In what ways?

Admiral Stevenson: Well, when I was later at Naval Air Station, Glenview, Illinois, Bill Walsh was the senior chaplain up at Great Lakes. The senior chaplain at Great Lakes could easily forget about the chaplain down at Glenview, but if anybody was coming from the Chief of Chaplains' office or anything like that, Bill would see to it that I was invited up and made part of the situation.

Q: When you're at a base like the one in Newport, do you get involved at all in being an enforcer of morals or a setter of standards, or what have you?

Admiral Stevenson: Good question. I wish I had a ready answer. On the enforcement business, no, I don't see it on the basis of the enforcement. Again, it's amazing in a few years what a different world it was in those days. For instance, when you talk about enforcement, let me mention spouse abuse, although in those days the term "spouse abuse" wasn't used. In dealing with a situation that involved, say, a sailor beating his wife, you worked with security and you worked with the XO. And one case that I remember, the answer was to respond to the abused wife's plea and the sailor's willingness to go back to sea duty. She felt that while he was on sea duty, they lived together fairly well. When he was on shore duty, he drank too much and beat her up too much and so forth. I know we were not as sensitive to those social issues as we are today, but that's how it was handled. It was sort of handled within the family.

The chaplain often got called out, when we had the duty, to go down into what were the slums of Newport, Rhode Island. We had an in-house rule in those days that when you were called to a domestic situation, you took another chaplain with you. Many times the DesLant duty chaplain called the base chaplain to go with him. I remember Chaplain Bill Hollis and I going down to stand between a sailor and his wife.* Both had knives, claiming they were going to cut each other up.

---

* Lieutenant William F. Hollis, Jr., CHC, USN.

Q: How did that resolve itself?

Admiral Stevenson: It finally resolved itself when security was invited in, and the sailor went off to cool his heels in the brig for the night. I suppose, in some respects, it's kind of like police work today. I mean, what do you do the next day? Well, today's world in the Navy, there would be more follow-up than there was in those days. In those days the question was simply what the command was going to do with him. Would they keep him on the base, restrict him for ten days, or respond to the wife's request on the third day that she wanted him to come back?

We dealt with many kinds of things: sailors' families with no money for groceries, some sticky legal problems, divorce situations sailors were involved with. Sailors getting married and the girl's parents flying in in a rage--fairly wealthy family, and their daughter had run off and married this sailor.

Q: Heaven forbid!

Admiral Stevenson: We wound up talking to them and introducing them to their new son-in-law. I remember one occasion in particular in which they were in a state of shock. The sailor *was* a college graduate. He did have very solid career plans; he was a very solid young man. But the parents were alarmed when they heard the daughter had married "a sailor!" I think that the daughter got by far the better of the deal, but the parents had the kind of money that they could fly into Newport, Rhode Island, and raise Cain with command. So you'd have the JAG officer involved.

Q: Well, the definite advantage you had from that tour in the destroyers is you knew what sailors were like by then. And you can't be too sanctimonious because you know what sorts of things they like to do and the culture in which they live.

Admiral Stevenson: Well, sailors are like guys I grew up with in Brooklyn. Sailors are like guys that I worked with in the railroad yards while I was in seminary. And, you know, you've got to end up a statement saying, "Sailors are very good people." For instance, I remember a very hard-working boatswain's mate in my destroyer squadron, who never went on liberty except in home port. I assume now that he was an alcoholic, because he would say, "If I go on liberty, I'm going to get drunk and get in trouble, and I promised the wife that I would not leave the ship." He went for years and years on that ship, and when we'd get to Newport, Rhode Island, he got off the ship and went home. Otherwise, he never stepped off that ship.

Q: Amazing self-discipline.

Admiral Stevenson: It really was. His name was Black; I remember him really well. I also remember that Newport, Rhode Island, in those days was a different town than it is now. Thames Street was loaded with bars.

Q: Much rougher.

Admiral Stevenson: Yes. I can remember my destroyers going into New York City for a weekend. Because of that, the chaplain and division officers were asked to speak to the sailors about the Murphy gimmick, or whatever it was called, where a girl approaches a sailor and says she's broke. Then the girl's boyfriend shows up and clobbers the sailor over the head, or threatens the sailor and takes his money. Well, the whole time we were in New York, it never happened. And, lo and behold, a couple weeks later, some of the sailors were in some small town in Rhode Island. Later, they came back to the ship claiming that what we had warned them about in New York had happened in this town.

    A prominent part of a sailor's life in those days was the YMCA in Newport.* It had lockers that sailors could rent at a reasonable fee for storing their civilian clothes. Because of the poor habitability aboard ship and the requirement that sailors were not to have

---

* YMCA--Young Men's Christian Association.

civilian gear in the ship, the YMCA became a very important part of the sailor's life. Today's sailor, I think, would find that somewhat different.[*]

Q: How much contact did you have with the civilian community in Newport?

Admiral Stevenson: In those two years, we had a fair amount of contact. Diane and I really got to appreciate the Newport community. We lived in Portsmouth, and we made friendships there that are still with us today. We lived in a very nice little community with five houses on the end of Glen Road. It was a great place to live. And, of course, we attended the jazz concerts in Peabody Park. We belonged to a wonderful book club. We were active on the base and in the civilian community with the Community Chest drive, etc. I attended the clergy fellowship.

Q: Were there other ways in which you grew during that period?

Admiral Stevenson: Yes, just observing how other chaplains operated; becoming more aware of what the requirements of command were; and becoming more and more comfortable with the Navy system, more and more involved in the social life of Navy things. One of the opportunities for maturation came because so many of those who attended the chapel were war college students. And, of course, conversations about what the war college students were studying broadened my view about things. Remember, those were the days when some folks used that dumb expression, "Better dead than red."[†]

President Eisenhower and then Kennedy stayed in Newport part of each summer in those days.[‡] Seeing the command get ready for the President to use command facilities during his visits was interesting. John Kennedy stayed at Hammersmith Farms, which was his mother-in-law's estate in Newport. He would come over on the presidential barge to the

---

[*] Since the early 1970s U.S. Navy enlisted personnel have been allowed to store civilian clothes on board ship to facilitate wearing them on liberty.
[†] "Red" referred to Communism, which was considered the incarnation of evil during the Cold War years.
[‡] Dwight D. Eisenhower served as President of the United States from 20 January 1953 to 20 January 1961. John F. Kennedy was President from 20 January 1960 until he was assassinated on 22 November 1963.

landing down at the officers' club and then walk up to the headquarters building, which had been turned over to the President and his staff during their stay. It was exciting to see the President from time to time walking up to headquarters.

I was very involved in the athletic program, so I played softball and some baseball while I was in that command. We became very comfortable with being in the Navy. In spite of the means by which I was augmented into the regular Navy, I realized how fortunate I was that the McQuaids and others had been active on my behalf.

Q: Well, from Newport you went to the aircraft carrier Saratoga.[*] How was being a chaplain in a big ship different from the destroyer squadron duty you'd had previously?

Admiral Stevenson: Well, it was a delight. I went to the Saratoga with some real concerns. It was not the usual thing for a lieutenant to go to aircraft carrier duty in those days. I'm speculating, but I have always thought that I got the carrier because Chaplain Floyd Dreith, who had been the officer in charge of the chaplain school when I first went to the naval station at Newport, was the Chief of Chaplains.[†] Jim Reaves, who was the detailer, had been up to the chaplain school quite often.[‡] I think chaplains like Ed Slattery, Tom Reilly and so forth had said, "Stevenson's a worker." So when they needed a Protestant in an aircraft carrier, I got the orders.

Before I went to the Saratoga, I talked with a Catholic chaplain, Father Frank McGann, who at that time was the force chaplain in DesLant.[§] He said that I was lucky because I was going to the USS Saratoga and because the skipper was one of the greatest naval officers I'd ever serve under. That was Captain Fred Moore, and what Father McGann said was true.[**] Fred Moore was one of the great naval officers.

---

[*] USS Saratoga (CVA-60) was commissioned 14 April 1956. She had a standard displacement of 56,000 tons, was 1,063 feet long, 130 feet in the beam, and had an extreme width of 252 feet. Her top speed was 34 knots. She was originally armed with four 5-inch guns and could accommodate approximately 70-90 aircraft.
[†] Rear Admiral Joseph Floyd Dreith, CHC, USN, served as the Navy's Chief of Chaplains from July 1963 to June 1965.
[‡] Commander James E. Reaves, CHC, USN.
[§] Captain Francis L. McGann, CHC, USN.
[**] Captain Frederick T. Moore, Jr., USN, commanded the USS Saratoga (CVA-60) from 3 November 1962 to 28 September 1963.

Q: In what ways?

Admiral Stevenson: He just exuded leadership. I mean, I think if he had decided to run Saratoga through an island or something like that, the whole crew and everybody would have been with him. He was that kind of dynamic individual. I can't name a lot of specifics, because he was not flashy. He was just a solid man of integrity. Six months later, we were in Istanbul when he was relieved, and I've never been to a party where the officers of a ship showed a greater respect for a CO. They really thought the world of him. He has a son who's a priest and a chaplain in the Navy today, Tom Moore.[*]

We all thought that Fred Moore would make flag without any question whatsoever, but a kidney operation knocked him out of selection for flag. It was said in those days that he was one of the few NROTC sure bets for flag.[†] He became chief of staff of ComCarDiv 6 after he left us and then to CNATRA.[‡]

Another great lesson learned: the guys who lead our Navy pay their dues. Here was Captain Moore, who had been deployed with Saratoga for six months; now he was becoming chief of staff of a cardiv that was going to be in the Med for yet another six months. We were going to be gone from our families seven months, but he was going to be gone from his family for 12 months. And prior to becoming the skipper of the Saratoga, he'd been the skipper of a deep-draft ship, and that was under way all the time.

Again, when you talk about luck or good fortune, we went to Mayport just when the new housing area was opening.[§] The Saratoga community was close knit. When we lost an aviator, we were in the Mediterranean, but the captain's wife was around the corner from my wife Diane. The captain's wife would pick up the chaplain's wife and the wife of the CO of the squadron, and they would get to that lost aviator's family promptly to provide comfort. The chaplain in Mayport or Jacksonville would know enough to call the wife of the chaplain when some word came in. Those were all part of a support system that was

---

[*] Commander Frederick Thomas Moore III, CHC, USN.
[†] NROTC--Naval Reserve Officers' Training Corps.
[‡] ComCarDiv 6--Commander Carrier Division Six. CNATRA--Chief of Naval Air Training.
[§] Mayport, Florida, which was the ship's home port, is adjacent to the Jacksonville Naval Air Station.

rather natural. The families had total involvement. I don't recall people thinking that that was a put-down or saying, "It's my husband's job. Why are you bothering me?" That was just considered part of the total community life and community obligation. It was a beautiful thing, just having the experience.

Q: It must have been a much harder thing getting to know the people in a carrier than in a destroyer because there were so many more of them.

Admiral Stevenson: So many more of them, and they're coming and going. But you have that great, glorious freedom of being able to <u>walk</u>. I mean, if you had spent a couple years in destroyers and you go to an aircraft carrier, you realize, "Hey, I can walk miles every day. I'm not confined to small spaces. I can really get out and walk around this ship and see people." Now, the senior chaplain, John Fay, preferred that chaplains stay in their offices.* He used to get a little annoyed with me once in a while, because I was out wandering around the ship. An aircraft carrier is a world with enough people that the chaplain really keeps hopping, just from Red Cross messages, emergencies, counseling situations, preparations for divine services, arrangements for different Bible study groups, etc. And if you're going to be at sea, you want to be hopping.

Q: Well, with all those things that you had to do, it probably took a real effort to get out and do your passageway ministry.

Admiral Stevenson: Yes, but you're there all around the clock, so it's not difficult to make the rounds.

Q: I can see the value of getting out, because a individual may not have the courage, or motivation, or whatever, to come in, but he's still got a problem that needs to be solved.

---

* Commander John P. Fay, CHC, USN.

Admiral Stevenson: You've got to be visible and available, visible and available. They need to see you as open and available. There's a tendency to be so busy that nobody wants to bother you because you're busy. But you've got to be available. There are a lot of places in the Navy where you can make yourself available as a chaplain. For instance, the dental waiting room is a great place. People who are waiting to see the dentist are very willing to talk; people who are in chow lines are willing. Any place where people are waiting for other services is an ideal place for a chaplain to circulate. I pulled a lot of liberty with the dentists in the Saratoga, so I would spend some time around the waiting room of the dentists. Again, like the barber shop, it's just a good place to pick up the realities or the myths that are making the rounds. Rumors are bad for morale.

Q: What role can a chaplain have a dealing with the duty rumors?

Admiral Stevenson: Well, I think the chaplain can squelch them. The chaplain is looked upon as a guy who knows the CO. The two guys that a sailor wants to check with are his division officer and the chaplain. That's one reason why it's important in our Navy for the chaplain to have rank. From time to time we run through this tendency where people talk about the fact that the Royal Navy chaplains do not wear rank, and that maybe our chaplains wearing rank is a put-off. I never found it that way in my experience.

In our Navy I think it's very important to realize that the chaplain has rank because we believe in separation of church and state. In the Royal Navy, the senior chaplain is always the Anglican, connected with the Queen's church. The rank that a British padre wears is the ecclesiastical rank. It has to be different in a world of separation of church and state.

Q: Did the CO and XO of that ship make a point of keeping you informed so you could squelch the rumors?

Admiral Stevenson: Lots of times. We had some very, very good skippers and XOs in Saratoga. I even had one XO throw me out of a department heads' meeting one day.

Q: What was the circumstance for that?

Admiral Stevenson: Julian lake, a very famous naval aviator was the XO, and I was too glib one day.* We were in the Norfolk Naval Shipyard. The one thing that the XO wanted to avoid during that yard period was giving coffee and other bribes to yard birds in order to get extra jobs done and so forth.† He was really down on that informal system of graft, as he called it.

Q: That's a Navy way of life, cumshaw.

Admiral Stevenson: Well, anyway, he felt that jobs ought to be done because they were the jobs to get done--never mind this coffee trade. He had strongly indicated to all his department heads that they were to keep their eyes open for that kind of stuff. Well, he called a department heads' meeting one day, and since the senior chaplain was not in the ship, I went to the meeting.

I'd been in Saratoga a long time by then and felt fairly comfortable, I guess, with the ship and staff. But, anyway, he started out the meeting by telling us that he had caught two sailors giving frozen turkeys to some yard birds for special jobs. He said he had caught them red-handed! It was kind of a tense situation, and he was certainly coming across in a very tense way about this to his department heads.

I guess I thought that I ought to ease the atmosphere, so I said, "XO, instead of catching them red-handed, you could have said you caught them cold-turkey." He was not in the mood to think that that was humorous, so he just dismissed me from the rest of the department heads' meeting. Me and my big mouth. But the telling of the story seemed to increase morale around the ship--at the chaplain's expense.

---

* Commander Julian S. Lake, USN, well known for his expertise in electronic warfare.
† "Yard birds" is a derisive nickname sailors use in describing the civilian workmen in a shipyard.

Q: Well, there was another tense situation you described yesterday when we weren't recording. That was about the visit by Herman Wouk that I would think is interesting for the record.

Admiral Stevenson: That happened prior to Julian Lake's tour. Saratoga was on a Caribbean cruise, and we went into St. Thomas. As soon as we dropped the hook, an honored guest came aboard, Herman Wouk, the author. We were advised to meet with Herman Wouk in the wardroom lounge prior to lunch. While we were meeting with him, the announcement came over the 1MC that liberty was being canceled because one of the statues from the quarterdeck, one of the brass fighting cocks, had been stolen.[*] All liberty was canceled until it was found.

It was kind of difficult carrying on a conversation with Herman Wouk and thinking of the strawberries episode in his novel The Caine Mutiny when we suddenly heard the XO's direct announcement that liberty was canceled because of a missing fighting cock.[†] And then a few minutes later, the announcement came over the 1MC that liberty could commence, because the dastardly culprit who had taken the fighting cock had thrown it out in the passageway somewhere. And to have those kind of things happen during a conversation with Herman Wouk is kind of a memorable occasion.

Q: Who was this other exec who was upset?

Admiral Stevenson: Mark Hill, and he was very upset.[‡]

Q: What else do you recall about the ship?

---

[*] 1MC--the general announcing system, with speakers located throughout the ship.
[†] Lieutenant Commander Philip F. Queeg, USN, was the fictitious commanding officer of the destroyer-minesweeper USS Caine in Wouk's classic naval novel of World War II, The Caine Mutiny, published by Doubleday & Company in 1951. In one episode, he went to unreasonable lengths to discover which crew member had stolen some frozen strawberries from the pantry of the officers' wardroom.
[‡] Commander Clarence A. Hill, USN, later a rear admiral.

Admiral Stevenson: Well, <u>Saratoga</u> was under way a good bit in those days. Once we got under way and got out of Mayport because a major hurricane was coming through. That's a great example, again, of Navy life. We went to the ship, and the ship went to sea. Wives and children stood the barricades for the hurricane. They organized themselves and took care of things. It was a devastating storm. Somebody had the idea in Mayport that one of the ways to protect the housing and the beaches was to put Demptsey dumpsters as a breakwater all along the beach there.* Fill them with sand and line the beach with Demptsey dumpsters. We found out about that when we came back.

But, again, note that difference in mentality. The responsibility of the naval personnel is the ship and the command. And one has to have a solid family that recognizes that, because in the civilian world it would be just the opposite: "Let's let all these employees go home to their families because there's a storm coming." The Navy has to be 180 degrees from that.

Q: In a large ship like that, you're likely to get more exotic religions, different from your standard three boxes you talked about. How did you accommodate some of the other religions?

Admiral Stevenson: Well, again, I don't think we did it as well in those days as they do it now. I think there's a much better recognition of meeting the needs of the individual today. We did some of that in those days, but I don't think we did it nearly as well. But we certainly did things like arranging for the Jewish personnel to celebrate Passover in the ship; arranged that the little chapel could be used by different Bible-study groups. I just think those were kind of standard operating procedures in those days.

Q: Did you have an active lay-leader program?

Admiral Stevenson: Well, we had a lay-leader program, but it was largely limited to small ships. The Catholic Church did not have lay eucharistic ministers in those days, so it was

---

* Dempster Dumpster is the trade name for large metal trash-collection boxes often used on naval bases.

basically the Catholic lay leader who led the Catholic services, using the rosary. So, no, we did not have an elaborate lay-leader situation. The lay-leader situation was more in the squadron of destroyers, where if the chaplain couldn't get to the ship, there would be a rosary service, or a Bible devotional by one of the lay leaders.

And those lay leaders were very faithful in their duties, but attendance was minimal at lay services.

Q: What do you recall about your interactions with individual crew members?

Admiral Stevenson: You're always amazed at the people who come up to you years later and say, "You know, you were a positive influence on me," etc. In most cases, I don't even remember talking to the man or woman.

I had the privilege when I was deputy chief and then Chief of Chaplains of traveling around the whole Navy. I was always surprised at the number of naval personnel who would come up and say, "I was in Saratoga with you. I remember this, or you were at such and such," and so forth. It's a delight to hear those kind of things, but you really don't keep book on that.

I've seen a lot of people in the Navy whose lives were turned around tremendously. I had a letter recently from a retired naval aviator who is now in seminary studying. I was really surprised at that. As a naval aviator he was a great guy, and very devout individual, and a fine family man and so forth. His wife of that time has since died, and he's come to the place now in his early 50s where he's decided that he wanted to go through seminary. But I also know that he was a disaster when he was a kid in Brooklyn. He's one of these guys whose dad, for the sake of the rest of the kids in the family, said, "Get out of here and join the Navy." And he did, served as an enlisted man and then became a naval aviator--you know, tremendous career and so forth. So everybody can tell a ton of stories about the Navy rescuing people who needed structure. The Navy and the Marine Corps were part of their formative years.

When I look back on it, I think I belonged to three different navies. The Navy prior to Vietnam, up through my tour in Saratoga, was a Navy very different from the Navy that came into being during the Vietnam era. The Navy that came out of the Vietnam era, starting in the mid-1970s to the Navy that I left in 1985, is a whole different Navy--a much more professional Navy. There is hardly any comparison in those three navies.

The Navy I joined had a very strong element of <u>Mister Roberts</u> about it.[*] Whether it was left over from World War II, or whether it was due to the large number of NROTC and OCS reserve officers who were getting out of the Navy, or what, it sort of had an element of <u>Mister Roberts</u> about it.[†]

The Vietnam era--I don't know what words would describe it--frustration, adolescent Navy trying to survive an identity crisis. Things had gone from the spit and polish of the professional touch to sloppy. Ships were dirty in comparison to the Navy of the '50s and the '60s. Ships looked seedy. Perhaps that was the cocoon period, and the butterfly came out after that. Now we have a Navy that's sharp and clean and targeted on getting specific things done.

Q: Well, we're right near the end of the tape, Admiral, any final thoughts for today?

Admiral Stevenson: No final thoughts for today. That's probably more than anybody needs.

Q: Thank you very much.

---

[*] <u>Mister Roberts</u> was a book of fictional stories written by Thomas Heggen on the basis of his World War II experiences as a Naval Reserve officer. Published in 1946, it depicted life on board an imaginary cargo ship in which the officers and crew flouted rules and regulations. It was later made into a successful stage play and movie, both starring Henry Fonda.
[†] OCS--Officer Candidate School.

Interview Number 3 with Rear Admiral Neil M. Stevenson, Chaplain Corps, U.S. Navy (Retired)

Place: Williamsburg Presbyterian Church, Williamsburg, Virginia

Date: Tuesday, 22 November 1988

Interviewer: Paul Stillwell

Q: Admiral, it's a real pleasure to see you again. This time we're on your home turf and ready to resume the narrative of your career. Last time we were discussing your service on board the aircraft carrier Saratoga.

Admiral Stevenson: I might mention to you in passing one of the lessons I learned about the chaplaincy. I was in USS Saratoga when John F. Kennedy was assassinated and was amazed at how several civilian Protestant churches asked me to be the speaker at memorial services they had for the President.[*] I learned subsequently that asking a Navy chaplain to lead the memorial service provided the civilian pastors with the safeguard they needed, or thought they needed, regarding a political figure. They were willing to have the memorial service, but I guess they didn't want to make any public statements on a congregational basis. So it was just one of those things you learn from experience.

Q: I remember that the Navy hymn was played during some of those ceremonies that I saw on TV, and not necessarily identified by the TV people but an appropriate backdrop for the funeral of a Navy man.

Admiral Stevenson: Yes, yes.

Q: Well, from the Saratoga you moved ashore to the naval air station at Glenview, Illinois. What was the nature of your duties there?

---

[*] This interview took place on the 25th anniversary of the assassination of President Kennedy, which was on 22 November 1963. At the time of the interview the news media made note of the anniversary.

Admiral Stevenson: Well, Glenview was one place in the world where we didn't want to go. I got some advice from Chaplain Joseph Dimino, now Bishop of the Military Ordinariate, who was my senior chaplain at that time in USS Saratoga.[*] He was one of the very, very talented chaplains, an ecumenical gentleman. Joe advised me that I ought to go by the Chief of Chaplains' office in Washington on my way to the Theological Institute in Princeton, New Jersey. Saratoga was in the Norfolk Naval Shipyard for an overhaul at that time.

So I drove up, and Chaplain Kelly was there at that particular time.[†] Having spent about a half hour in the Chief of Chaplains' office, I quickly determined that that was not a place to visit, and it would certainly be a place that one would avoid as far as duty was concerned.

Q: Why did you feel that?

Admiral Stevenson: I had called ahead and made an appointment to see Chaplain Carl Auel.[‡] I really didn't think I would be dragged in to see the Chief of Chaplains. I wasn't very comfortable with that. I didn't get any answers to my questions, except that Carl would try to let me know what they were slating me for. And, you know, the Chief of Chaplains' office is a very active place of business and not a sociable environment.

Anyhow, Carl asked me to call when I got back to the ship. When I called Carl, he told me that I was going to Naval Air Station Glenview, Illinois. Having served in an aircraft carrier, I had asked to go to an air station, but I must admit that I was thinking in terms of Naval Air Station Jacksonville or Naval Air Station Oceana, not little Naval Air Station Glenview, Illinois. I certainly was not thinking about going back to the Chicago area, having spent a year at Great Lakes previously. So that was pretty disappointing news.

---

[*] Lieutenant Commander Joseph T. Dimino, CHC, USN, at the time of his service in the Saratoga. He retired in 1977 as a captain and in the 1990s is Archbishop of the Archdiocese of the Military.
[†] Rear Admiral James W. Kelly, CHC, USN, was Director of the Chaplains Division from July 1963 to June 1965. He was subsequently Chief of Chaplains, 1965-70. His brief oral history is in the series conducted by the Navy's Chaplain Corps.
[‡] Lieutenant Commander Carl A. Auel, CHC, USN.

Q: Glenview primarily served the reserve community, didn't it?

Admiral Stevenson: Glenview was an air station unto itself in the reserve program. Then I discovered, when I got my orders, that I also had additional duty orders to CNARESTRA, Chief of Naval Air Reserve Training. I didn't know what that meant, but it was in the orders.

Q: Well, how did the actual tour of duty measure up to these expectations?

Admiral Stevenson: Like all tours of duty, it turned out to be tremendously good.

We hooked the two cars together, loaded in the dog and the three daughters, and left sunny Florida in December. I went through the mixed emotions of seeing the Saratoga pull out on deployment, leaving me on the pier. That's really mixed emotions. You wish you were with the ship; you feel kind of worthless watching her pull out without you after two years. At the same time, you're elated that you're going to be on shore duty and home every night.

I was relieved in USS Saratoga by a wonderful chaplain named Art Boyer.[*] We had a couple of parties for Art. Joe Dimino was still senior chaplain and had everything well organized, so the turnover was an easy operation.

For my last bit of horsing around, I left a case of Myers Catawba Juice with the assistant supply officer, Jack Leavitt.[†] I asked Jack to do me a favor--as Chaplain Stevenson's farewell gift to the wardroom--and break out the Catawba juice on the first night at sea. Jack reported to me that he did so, as I had requested, probably putting his own career in jeopardy. Of course, when the corks popped, Commander Julian Lake, the XO, according to Jack, went a little bit through the overhead. It took a while to get the XO to read the label that guaranteed that the Catawba was actually effervescent grape juice, instead of champagne. So I had my last fling at the XO.

---

[*] Commander Arthur C. Boyer, CHC, USN.
[†] Lieutenant Commander Jack B. Leavitt, SC, USN.

Q: One thing that these regular turnovers in the Navy guarantee is that you won't ever get to feel indispensable in any given command.

Admiral Stevenson: The arrival at Glenview was depressing. There wasn't any Navy lodge in those days.[*] We, like other Navy folk, were forced to find motel space somewhere near Glenview. Chicago prices were quite high in those days. It was also a bit of a letdown to discover that we were paying a rather large rent, compared with the people on either side of us. We learned that they worked for civilian companies. When their companies moved them from one place to another, they provided for their living expenses and that the civilian company bought their mortgages.

In addition, Christmas time is not the best time to report to a duty station. To this day I don't know why the chaplain at Glenview was so insistent that I get there before the Christmas season, because he stayed through the whole Christmas season, and Glenview didn't really need two Protestant chaplains at that time.

We bounced around. We met a supply officer who was traveling to bring his family, and he graciously offered the chaplain's family his quarters for two or three days. So we moved into Jim Holt's house, bought an artificial Christmas tree, and had our Christmas. Then, when the chaplain moved out in January, we moved into what they called substandard quarters. This was an apartment made out of part of the old dispensary building. I asked if I could paint the place, and the public works officer said if I was willing to do all the work, he'd let me have the paints, so we painted the place and fixed it all up. And that's kind of a happy memory. Diane insisted that the operating-room lights be removed from the dining-room ceiling. We got the kids settled in a very good school system and went from there.

The naval air station people worked from Wednesday through Sunday. The admiral's staff worked a normal week, so it was kind of a seven-day-a-week job for one chaplain, because you covered both the staff and the station. I was pleased that we lived right on the station. It was a wonderful place for good social life.

---

[*] The Navy lodges are essentially motel-like quarters for naval personnel in a transient status.

In that job I was introduced to staff work and being responsible to the admiral's staff for chaplains throughout the Naval Air Reserve Training Command. That included both active duty people at the air stations and inactive reservists in the program.

Q: Who was the admiral?

Admiral Stevenson: The admiral when I first got there was Admiral Koch.[*] His brother was also an admiral. He went from that command to ComCarDivSix. Then he was relieved by Admiral Fowler, who was one prince of a gentleman.[†]

Q: Why do you say that? What qualities did he have?

Admiral Stevenson: Well, he was a great morale builder. He was very interested in all parts of the command, including the religious program. He was as anxious to have good reserve chaplains as he was anxious to have good reserve aviators. So the Fowlers, including Mrs. Fowler, took a great interest in things that were going on. And I think I had only been there only about four or five months when Admiral Koch left, so I was part of the organization when Admiral Fowler reported.

Chaplain Don Jolly--another great chaplain and a great organizer--was a reservist who had the reserve desk in the Chief of Chaplains' staff.[‡] He was interested in the chaplains' program of the Naval Air Reserve getting some things accomplished. For me, it was an exciting time. I had the chapel program on the base, working with two inactive reserve chaplains who were Catholic priests: Chaplain Marty Witting, who later came on active duty, and Chaplain Tom Markos, who was a priest who taught at Notre Dame High School in Niles, Illinois.[§] I also had the assignment with the staff and supervision of active and inactive chaplains.

---

[*] Rear Admiral George P. Koch, USN, served as Chief of Naval Air Reserve Training from July 1963 to September 1965.
[†] Rear Admiral Richard L. Fowler, USN, served as Chief of Naval Air Reserve Training from September 1965 to January 1967.
[‡] Commander Donald W. Jolly, CHC, USNR.
[§] Lieutenant Martin J. Witting, CHC, USNR; Lieutenant Thomas Markos, CHC, USNR.

Q: What was your role in relation to these two priests?

Admiral Stevenson: I was the chaplain for the naval air station, and they did their reserve duty on weekends at the naval air station. I was the command chaplain, so I made sure everything was ready for Mass when they came. In the case of Father Witting, he was a teacher at Mormene Academy over in Aurora, Illinois. His abbot gave him permission to come on Saturday afternoon, so we would line up any counseling situation for him, as well as make sure the chapel was all set for Mass on Sunday mornings. After Marty went on active duty, I had to find other sources for saying Mass.

Nearby there was a Catholic seminary in Techny, right close to Glenview. And I was young and bold enough, and "Brooklynized" enough, that I went over to Techny and saw the provincial of the seminary, and said, "I need a priest to say Mass on Sunday mornings." (There was no 5:00 o'clock Mass on Saturday afternoons in those days.) So I struck an arrangement with the provincial of the seminary that they would supply a priest for us if we would supply a Navy car to pick him up, which we did. That meant that I had to call the duty office at 6:00 o'clock on Sunday morning and say, "You have remembered to send a car to pick up the priest," and so forth and so on.

Fortunately for me, the seminary provincial asked me, in turn, since the age of ecumenicity was dawning and Vatican Council II was the rage--this was around 1966--if I would come over to his seminary as a sort of the duty Protestant and teach a course. It was an Order of the Divine Word seminary. The initials of the order are SVD--"Smoke Ve Don't, Drink Ve Do." I taught a course on theology in modern literature, which I really enjoyed. We read and discussed Flannery O'Connor and Albert Camus and similar books--novels that were very popular in those days--and just tried to analyze theological themes within those kinds of novels. So for me it was a wonderful experience. I think the priests enjoyed coming over and saying Mass.

Q: Did these two reserve priests have their own parishes to tend to also, or what was their situation?

Admiral Stevenson: Marty Witting was a teacher at Mormene Academy, a military academy of the Benedictines. Among Marty's collateral duties at the academy, he was in charge of transportation, which meant he was charged to be responsible for all the buses and all those kinds of things. And that drove him up the wall and drove him into the Navy--or at least that's what we teased him about. Tom Markos was a teacher at Notre Dame high school and had a tremendous reputation in theater arts. I remember in those days, his high school kids put on the show Hello, Dolly. And I tell you, it had the quality of a Broadway production.

Marty Witting had the Mass at 6:30 in the morning. Tom Markos would come in and have Mass around 9:00 or something like that, and I had the Protestant service at 11:00. Normally, Marty Witting would show up and have dinner with us on Saturday night.

I was introduced to the requirements for "completed staff work" on the admiral's staff. I gained a close working and social relationship with chief of staff, the deputy, and the admiral. During that period of time, we put out a new instruction that spelled out how inactive reserve chaplains would be utilized in the Naval Air Reserve Training Command. So I wrote my first instruction and got it through command and signed. So all those kinds of things were really great learning experiences in a very nice, neat model world in which to learn those things.

Q: How were the reserve chaplains used?

Admiral Stevenson: The reserve chaplains were used at all the reserve air stations the same way we used Father Witting and Father Markos.

Q: How many chaplains altogether would you say were involved with CNARESTRA

Admiral Stevenson: Active duty-wise we had something like 10 or 11 chaplains, and reserve-wise we had something like 42 chaplains.

Q: How could a reserve chaplain fit this in, since both the reserve and his civilian job probably require being there Sunday morning?

Admiral Stevenson: We got the services of clergy who were teachers or clergy who worked in the field of counseling or social services. For instance, at Floyd Bennett Field in New York, you had an inactive reserve chaplain, the dynamic Rabbi Bill Kloner, who came in on Saturdays and Sundays to take care of Jewish personnel.[*] And he was assisted by the Jewish Welfare Board and Jewish Veterans of Foreign Wars and so forth and so on. They had a tremendous program at Floyd Bennett Field.

Q: How did you supervise?

Admiral Stevenson: In addition to writing the basic instruction, etc., I would visit these commands, inspect the chaplains' department, provide critiques, offer advice, and teach courses to reserve chaplains regarding what was current in the Chaplain Corps, pastoral counseling, etc. Supervision recognized both the chain of command and the chain of influence in those days. Calling cards helped in the latter area.

Q: In what ways?

Admiral Stevenson: Well, they were useful because when you went somewhere in the Navy, you knew that by custom you--you and your wife, if you were married--were required to call on the senior chaplain in the area, just as you made formal calls on the commanding officer. You called usually on a Sunday afternoon in your best bib and tuck, and paid your respects, had a glass of sherry, etc. They got to know who you were by name and by looks. And you left your calling cards according to the appropriate protocol.

Q: I guess what I mean is, in what ways was it useful to have made that contact?

---

[*] Lieutenant Commander William Kloner, CHC, USNR.

Admiral Stevenson: Well, it was useful because you then felt that you were known and you knew them. You had no hesitancy about then going about business with these folks. And then the seniors returned calls. A week or month or so later, they came by your home. By that time you certainly were more comfortable in going to the office, or being called into the office, and getting jobs done. It was just a nice manner for establishing a relationship. Sociologically it set the chain of command and, in the case of chaplains, the chain of influence.

Q: You said that you were able to get things done in this CNARESTRA organization. What accomplishments would you cite?

Admiral Stevenson: Oh, well, for one thing we became a more visible part of the organization through the writing of an instruction. This directive tied together all the chaplains' activities, and it set in the minds of commands throughout CNARESTRA what chaplains would do, including inactive reserve chaplains. It dealt with what contributions they could make to command and where they would be available, not only in conducting worship, but in offering services like educational programs and so forth and so on.

Q: It's hard to imagine that such a thing didn't exist before that, because the Navy lives by instructions.

Admiral Stevenson: True. There were areas in the Navy in which instructions regarding chaplains had been written--the good old 1730 series.[*] But a 1730 hadn't come about in CNARESTRA. The Navy did have the chaplains' manual, but that's another story for later on.

Q: And probably you codified things that were being done already in many cases.

---

[*] Instructions regarding chaplain matters were coded with the number 1730 in the Navy's correspondence system.

Admiral Stevenson: Sure. It was just a matter of getting the thing organized.

For example, when I first reported, the command received a death message. The next of kin lived in the northern suburbs of Chicago. As the chaplain, I was called out and told by the duty officer that the chaplain was totally in charge of CACO.[*] I informed the duty officer that I didn't think that was a very satisfactory way to handle CACO. And he said, "Well, that's the way we do it here."

So I went off in my own car and wandered around. It was wintertime. I remember it was bitter cold, and here I was, wandering around at night trying to find this address. I finally found it, and it was an apartment complex. I knocked on the door, and here was a woman and kids. My duty was to inform her that her son had been killed. The poor woman was so distraught she was convinced that her son in Vietnam was the one that I was talking to her about. But it was her other son, who was in a ship home-ported in Hawaii. He had been killed in a motorcycle accident. Anyway, it was a bad night!

That's how I found out that at Naval Air Station Glenview, the chaplain was charged with initiating and following through on the CACO responsibilities. I had never done the CACO thing before, so when I finished with that case, I can't tell you how many times I read the casualty assistance calls manual in those few days. Then I went to the XO and told him that the command's policy regarding CACO was incorrect and inappropriate. Commander Altmann was not pleased with me about that.[†]

Q: What was your objection to that being totally a chaplain's responsibility?

Admiral Stevenson: Well, two things. First of all, there existed in those days a chaplains' manual. The chaplains' manual stated that the chaplain would _not_ serve as the casualty assistance calls officer. The second thing was that CACO requires a division of labor. The chaplain should be involved in trying to provide some comfort and in actually performing or facilitating the religious rites that meet the needs of the next of kin. If the chaplain, or any other officer, is doing the whole thing, the family is not well served.

---

[*] CACO--casualty assistance calls officer.
[†] Commander Richard G. Altmann, USNR, a TAR officer.

Q: Why not? In what ways?

Admiral Stevenson: It takes a team to assist the family to deal with their legal benefits, to liaison with funeral people, to provide or facilitate the memorial service, etc.

Q: So you didn't object to being involved in the religious part.

Admiral Stevenson: I didn't object to that or to being part of a team that delivered the message. The Navy needs to send at least two people to deliver that sensitive a message. I did object to the family not being well served. You need more than one person and more than one visit. No one wants to be the angel of death, but you need experienced people to show the Navy's concern and compassion.

The XO, who later became a flag officer, was a hot jet jockey from Brooklyn. He thought his new chaplain was a pain in the neck. After all, the previous chaplain hadn't raised the question. Anyway, I waited a while, and I set up a briefing for the CO and the XO on the entire subject of what I thought the chaplain's duties were at a naval air station. I think they were kind of amused at that, to begin with.

Q: Why?

Admiral Stevenson: Because I don't think it happened very often, and I don't think they gave a damn, even though they were both good guys. Their attitude was essentially, "There's a chapel there, the chaplain's office is in the chapel. People who've got problems, go see him. Our mission is to fly airplanes."

Q: And everybody knows what the chaplain does.

Admiral Stevenson: Everybody knows--or thinks he knows--what the chaplain does anyhow. We're the real world, and the staffie is sort of a compensation.

Q: Did you win your point with the executive officer?

Admiral Stevenson: Well, I lucked out. I gave this little briefing about what I thought the chaplain's duties were and the contribution I thought he made. And I talked about what I hoped to accomplish on the CNARESTRA staff level. Evidently, it went over pretty well. Part of the total brief contained a recommendation on what the command's casualty assistance calls program ought to be. Nobody in command wants anybody, including the chaplain, to get up and say, "I think this part of the command is inadequate."

When I got finished, the CO was kind enough to ask me if I would brief the department heads at the weekly meeting. Once a month they'd have one department brief everybody else on what they were trying to accomplish in that year, etc. So I gave my briefing, and I included the casualty assistance business. The command medical officer, Glenn Lotz, said, "You know, you're right. It's a time of grief and crisis, and we ought to do better."[*]

The JAG spoke up and said, "The JAG knows more about the benefits, etc." So what came out of that was a little instruction, going back to directives again, in which we organized a quarterly training course. The chaplain, JAG, medical officer, and XO all took part in it. We trained officers on how to be CACOs and what should happen. We came up with a model that said a line officer CACO should be accompanied by the chaplain, night or day. If possible, medical should supply the driver. Having the driver be a corpsman proved helpful. I mean, you have people who faint; you have all kinds of things happen.

One of the big things was that the Navy provide the car, that we pull a car out of the transportation pool and go as a team, rather than having individuals use their own cars. It didn't take us very long to get the team together to go. Then, of course, things started heating up in Vietnam. We're talking 1965-66, etc. We dealt with more CACO calls from within and without the command than anyone ever wanted. Chicago had a lot of young men in the armed services--Marines and Navy. We were making more than our share of casualty assistance calls.

---

[*] Captain Glenn W. Lotz, MC, USNR.

Q: Could you guess how many during the course of a month, let's say?

Admiral Stevenson: Well, I'd say two or three a month--enough that you wished you were in Vietnam instead of in Chicago. I went with a Marine officer late one afternoon--about 6:00, 6:30--up to a suburb north of Glenview. It was really a scary situation. We were in a Marine Corps car. We parked the car, we went up, and we rang the bell. A man came to the door with a shotgun. He opened the door, looked at us, and he said, "Don't tell me my son is dead." Then he slammed the door. You know, you're in uniform; you've got the car; the whole neighborhood knows you're there. The Marine officer and I went back, and we sat in the car. We sat there, talking to each other, saying, "What are we going to do?" Neither one of us wanted to be chicken and go back and say we couldn't deliver the message. We didn't want to call the police or just phone the family. You're always trying to deliver the word before the news media does it.

Q: But you didn't want to get shot in the process.

Admiral Stevenson: No, we were well aware of that. We were in a little shock ourselves. We sat in the car. It seemed a long time, but it probably wasn't very long, maybe 15 minutes later the man's wife came out. She couldn't stand it; she wanted to know what had happened, and we told her.

Those casualty assistance calls were an absolute dread at that time and around that area.

Q: What kind of emotional burden did that put on you as a human being?

Admiral Stevenson: Oh, I don't know. I don't know. When you get the word you have to go, it's, "Oh, I don't want to. God, here we go again. I don't want to be the angel of death." Sometimes we'd have to drive for an hour or more to find the place. Then we had to make up our minds, "Are we going to wake them up after 10:00 o'clock at night? How are we going to handle that?" Sometimes the people had moved, and the emergency data form hadn't been updated, so we were involved with the police department, trying to find out where these people now lived.

Every one of them's kind of a bad memory, but, you know, you do as best you can. You may walk into a family that's religiously oriented. You find out very quickly that they are Catholic, and, yes, they would like the priest to come. So you call up an inactive reserve chaplain, and you say, "Please come by this Catholic family as soon as you can come by," or things like that.

I'll tell you about two instances that are well set in my mind. I had one family, elderly parents over towards Evanston. I delivered the message to them that their son had been injured in a helo crash. I did that on my own. I said that he was badly beat up, but he was alive. I went and saw this family a couple of times. They were Jewish. I'd tell them that he was coming along. He was in the Caribbean. I think they got him to Roosey Roads, where they mended his leg and then finally sent him to the Great Lakes Naval Hospital. He eventually returned to duty. Before the year was out, as I recall, I had to go back to that family and tell them he'd been killed. He was in a second crash and killed. I mean, that was really, really bad.

Then there was another case that was by far the worst one. I wish I could remember the names of people better from those years because they were so helpful. But we had an airplane that was configured for antisubmarine warfare. It was a twin-engine Grumman that they also used for COD flights in those days.[*] We had a Glenview reserve squadron of these planes go out on its two weeks of training. They left Glenview and went to the West Coast to do their training. On the way out, after stopping somewhere for refueling--I think Yuma--one of the planes took off and crashed, killing all five on board--pilots and crew. They called me down to operations around dinner time, and everybody was there: CO, XO, ops, etc. They said, "We've got five that are dead; we've got one chaplain. How are we going to handle this? You know, the damnable thing--it's going to be in the morning newspapers; we have to get the word out to these families."

---

[*] This was the Grumman-built S-2 Tracker, used for ASW; another version, the C-1 Trader, was used as a carrier on-board delivery (COD) aircraft.

God, that was a terrible night. We spent the entire night getting the word to the families. I can't remember the commander's name, but he was the maintenance officer. We got to the pilot and the copilot's families fairly readily. The XO volunteered to take one family all on his own. I remember we had covered a couple of families, and we ended up ringing a doorbell in South Chicago at something like 3:00 o'clock in the morning. The people didn't live there anymore. We had awakened a black family that had bought the house from a white family. The white family had moved out of the neighborhood. The black family didn't know where they had moved to. I still remember that they were very gracious after having us wake them up at 3:00 o'clock in the morning.

Our problem remained--how in the world were we going to find out where this family had moved to? We called the Chicago police. We called back to the base, and the base called what connections they had with the Chicago police. As I recall, it had to go pretty far up towards Mayor Daley's office to break out where this family now lived.[*]

Then we found out where the family was, and we decided that we would call them on the phone rather than just going at what was now 5:00 o'clock in the morning. We got as close to the house as we could, called them on the phone, woke them out of sleep, and told them we would be right there. They were still in their pajamas when we rang the bell. We went in, and that was terrible; the mother was hysterical.

We spent about an hour and a half with the family, and the dad said, "Who's going to tell his wife?" We didn't even know the guy was married. We found out where the wife was living with her parents up on the north side of Chicago. They wanted to tell her, so they got on the phone and called her and told her. Then we got in the car and drove up to there, and we spent some time with her. When we finally went back to the base, it was the next day.

Then we had to help make and coordinate funeral arrangements. Most of the funerals were in churches. I was contacting the priests and trying to discover what the families wanted the Navy to do. We would get pallbearers for that church, and then we'd go over to the next church. At some churches the priest would invite me to participate in

---

[*] Richard J. Daley served as mayor of Chicago from 1955 until his death in 1976.

reading scripture--early ecumenicity. Then we had one or two funeral services at the chapel in Glenview. It was kind of a long week by the time we did all that.

Q: Did you get some scar tissue after a while so that you could keep on doing this?

Admiral Stevenson: I don't know; I think it's like everything else. It is certainly easier to do as time goes on. And I don't think that's necessarily because of scar tissue. I think it's because you know what the requirement is, and you can meet the requirement. You begin to learn things that you never knew about grief; you begin to realize that grief has a great deal of anger associated with. And people are likely to take that anger out on whoever represents the organization in which their loved one was killed. That's okay. They should do that. You know, it's how they should react. Then you get to the numb stage with them. You have prescribed things that you have to do, and you're busy doing those things. You know, you're contacting other clergy, etc.

Funny thing happened at Glenview that's a little part of history, I guess. It illustrates the kind of legalisms that, thank God, don't exist anymore. It tells us what things were like. When I was at Glenview, the archdiocese of Chicago received a new cardinal who came from New Orleans.

Q: There was a Cardinal Cody about then.

Admiral Stevenson: Okay, thanks. When Cardinal Cody came, they were reorganizing a lot of things.* The Ecumenical Council's influence was having an effect. But in the meantime, one of the standing Catholic regulations was that a priest of the archdiocese of Chicago could not provide a committal at a gravesite that was not in a Catholic cemetery. Yet some service personnel who had been killed overseas were going to be buried in family plots that were not in Catholic cemeteries. The question was, how do we handle this situation where the priest can't give the committal, and yet the family has expectations that there will be something at the gravesite? Father Bill Walsh, whom I had known at

---

* John P. Cody became archbishop of Chicago in 1965.

Newport, was the senior chaplain at that time at Great Lakes. I probably told you what a blessing Father Bill Walsh was to me.[*]

Anyway, the word came in requesting that I officiate at some of these committals with the permission of the cardinal's office. The priest had the Mass; he had the whole funeral. As a Navy chaplain, I went to the funeral and then went to the cemetery following the funeral. When the priest gave me the high sign, I stepped forward and gave the committal. This was acceptable to the families or taken for granted. Then, oh, six months after I first started doing that, why, the rules of the diocese were changed. After that, priests went ahead and gave the committal. But that's just a little quirk out of history.

Q: You said before that systems rather than proximity were important in communications. What did you mean by that?

Admiral Stevenson: Well, I mean that in those years the Navy still had naval districts. We were geographically oriented. Being clergy we were geographically oriented anyway. Most clergy grow up and serve within a diocese, or within a presbytery, or a part of the country where they went to seminary. But with modern technology and communications systems the admiral can be in Glenview, and his command is all over the United States. That began, in my mind at least, to relate to getting things done systemically rather than just within geographical bounds.

CNARESTRA, in order to meet its mission, traversed all the CONUS districts.[†] Therefore, even in the line side of the Navy, there were both courtesies and concerns that took place as to who was operating in whose territory. It was an interesting thing to observe.

Q: In your efforts to standardize, through this instruction you mentioned, did you have to be concerned not to overturn local customs and mores?

---

[*] By this time, Chaplain Walsh had been promoted to captain.
[†] CONUS--Continental United States.

Admiral Stevenson: No, not when I was at Glenview. All our commands were within CONUS.

Q: You talked, also, on the line side about educating the CO and XO of the naval air station. Did you also have to do that on the staff side with the CNARESTRA people?

Admiral Stevenson: Yes, basically to give good rationale for 41XX billets.[*] When CNATRA would come and inspect CNARESTRA, I had to brief CNATRA on CNARESTRA's chaplains program and why CNARESTRA was running it. I had to explain any billets that were not filled, why they were not filled, what we were doing about it, etc.

A funny situation happened on one such brief. I really don't remember what command the visiting admiral was attached to, but we did have an inspection in which I had to give a briefing. Just before it was my turn to brief, I was told that the admiral was at that time the only Naval Academy graduate who was a Latter Day Saint. And I was told that he would likely ask me something about the Latter Day Saints. I was totally unaware, in those days, that there was some decision-making going on in Washington as to whether or not Latter Day Saints chaplain candidates could meet the academic requirements for naval duty. This involved the President, Mr. Marriott, who was later to be the endorsing agent for the Latter Day Saints--I think everybody knows who Mr. Marriott was.[†] When I finished my little briefing, the admiral said, "You don't have any Latter Day Saints."

I made a response typical of a briefing officer, I guess. I said, "Admiral, if there are Latter Day Saints chaplains who want to join the Naval Air Reserve program, we'll sign them up." Here I was, making this big statement, and, of course, in Washington, it was still a controversial situation.

Q: What were the misgivings?

---

[*] The officer designator for members of the Chaplain Corps is 4100 for those in the regular Navy and 4105 for those with Naval Reserve commissions. The use of 41XX is a generic way of indicating chaplain billets that can be filled by either a regular or reserve officer.
[†] J. Willard Marriott, chairman of Hot Shoppes and Marriott Motor Hotels, along with a number of other enterprises.

Admiral Stevenson: Nothing to do with faith groups. It had to do with the educational system. Do Latter Day Saints missionaries meet the academic requirements for the 90 hours of certified graduate work required of Chaplain Corps applicants. The Latter Day Saints did not have a postgraduate seminary program. I did not make the connection of my remark with what was happening in Washington until years later when I served with Chaplain Bob Radcliffe, who had been on the desk in Washington that dealt with that problem.[*] Bob Radcliffe informed me that it was a long, drawn-out negotiating situation because--and the Latter Day Saints agree with this as much as anybody today--the Navy Chaplain Corps, or any of the chaplains corps, should never compromise its requirements for the highest academic standards.

Q: How was it resolved in that case?

Admiral Stevenson: It was resolved, as it was with the Christian Scientists and others. Candidates are required to do postgraduate work within their faith group that is equivalent to 90 hours of postgraduate work in other faith groups.

Just to end up that sea story with some fun, when I was the Chief of Chaplains, I was invited to Salt Lake City for a briefing from the Latter Day Saints Church. They were having a meeting of all their chaplains, and so Air Force, Army, and Navy chaplains of the Latter Day Saints faith were there. I was given the opportunity to speak to them. The admiral, now long retired and working as an endorsing agent for the Latter Day Saints, was my escort that day. When I got on the podium, I had the good fortune of being able to say, "Admiral, in 1966, you asked me where the Latter Day Saint chaplains were, and I told you we'd recruit them. So now, here they are, all sitting out there."

Q: That same line officer was there?

---

[*] Captain Robert W. Radcliffe, CHC, USN.

Admiral Stevenson: Yes, he lives in Salt Lake City and, with his military background, he became active in the endorsing agency process for them.

Q: Well, it's good when something has a nice ending like that.

Admiral Stevenson: Nice little circle, closed the loop. Perfect.

Q: The Navy has a real fetish for these inspections, and you talked about being on the receiving end. What did you do when you went along as a member of the inspecting party with the admiral?

Admiral Stevenson: Each command was inspected once a year. First of all, the purpose was to meet the chaplains, active and reserve, and then to gain a view from those chaplains as to how the religious program at that command was meeting the needs. In those days it was a very simplistic format that I had in my mind, because we largely thought in those days as simply of Catholic, Protestant, and Jew. We had a checkoff list with questions like: "Do you hire an auxiliary priest? Is there a reservist in the area you use? How do you take care of Catholic needs? How do you take care of Jewish needs? Where are you in your own program? Is it an active chapel? Is there a Sunday School?" And so forth.

Q: Well, and you can, perhaps, become a clearing house. You can tell that guy in Olathe, Kansas, "Here's how the man in Los Alamitos or Dallas solved that problem."

Admiral Stevenson: You also dealt with the counseling business. In those days CNARESTRA was largely managed by TARs.[*] What are the particular problems that exist within the TAR organization? TARs knew all other TARs, and that had advantages and disadvantages.

---

[*] TAR--training and administration of reservists. Those individuals designated as TARs are reservists on active duty. Most of their duty involves the reserve program rather than the active-duty Navy.

Then there was the Navy Relief business, because we were all auxiliary Navy Relief providers: "How does your command feel about that, how do you deal with that?"

Then we looked into facilities. Was the chapel always going to be a Quonset hut, or were they going to relocate the chapel to the end of a barracks?* In most of the commands we were not talking about a chapel building that was strictly a chapel like the one at Glenview.

There were also a few chaplains who didn't fit that command very well, who thought that they were being sent out to left field. Most of them had very, very fine tours of duty. And some of the chaplains who really became top-notch chaplains through the years were the ones that I met in those commands.

Q: Any that you remember about?

Admiral Stevenson: Oh, yes. Chaplain Stan Beach, one of the first chaplains to be wounded in Vietnam had been up at Twin Cities.† He was relieved up there by Chaplain Don Krabbe, who's still on active duty and a very well-known chaplain.‡ Chaplain Clancy Lemasters was in Olathe.§ And reserve chaplains like Bill Kloner in New York. Actually, a really interesting and dedicated group of chaplains had gotten ordered into CNARESTRA at that particular time.

I also ran into the ROAD syndrome in a couple of places. These were "retired-on-active-duty" chaplains. A few were chaplains who were ordered into a command because they wanted to retire in that area. I had the frustration of going there and saying, "When I was here a year ago, this was an active program, and now it's just dead." One chaplain makes something out of it and does things for people, and another one goes and sits.

---

* A Quonset hut is a semi-cylindrical metal building that can be shipped to an advance base area and erected quickly. These huts were used widely in building Naval Reserve facilities in the years following World War II.
† Lieutenant Stanley J. Beach, CHC, USN.
‡ Lieutenant Donald L. Krabbe, CHC, USNR.
§ Lieutenant Commander Clarence E. Lemasters, CHC, USN.

Q: From what you say, these individuals probably had to be pretty resourceful, because they didn't have as many things to draw on as a person in an active station.

Admiral Stevenson: Yes, and they were on their own. They weren't around other chaplains.

Q: Was it a case where you had to relieve people that were too ill suited to the job?

Admiral Stevenson: No, I didn't have that kind of authority. But when I would be inspected by Chaplain Sneary, the CNATRA staff chaplain, he'd want to compare notes.[*] He expected me to motivate chaplains to provide good programs in line with the 1730 instruction.

If you want to look at my CNARESTRA plaque, it's hanging up in my garage, and it will give the names of all the air stations. All my memorabilia is hanging up in the garage.

Q: What was life like for your family living there?

Admiral Stevenson: Well, it was a great place. It just turned out to be a tremendous place. As I said, the school system was just outstanding in Glenview. The girls enjoyed living on the base.

There was one very traumatic situation there. Of course, I was on a trip when it happened. We lived across the street from a gigantic old wooden structure built during World War II. The one building housed administration, post office, movie theater, bowling alley, exchange, etc. Well, it caught fire one night and burned to the ground. The fire was so hot that they moved the families out of those substandard quarters where we lived for fear that they would catch on fire. Diane had to get up in the middle of the night, gather up the girls and the dog, grab the silverware and what have you, and clear the area. The heat was so intense that the firemen worried that our cars parked in front of the place would explode. I think that our oldest daughter is still somewhat shy of fire from that experience.

---

[*] Captain Earl D. Sneary, CHC, USN.

It was also a time in which two flag officers died in house fires. First, our Admiral Fowler died when his quarters went on fire at Naval Air Station Glenview.[*] And then Admiral Red Yeager died up at Ninth Naval District a couple of months later in a fire in his quarters.[†]

There was another one that was difficult. You talked about getting scars. I mean, I was called up late at night and told get over to the dispensary. Then I informed Mrs. Fowler, who was somewhat burned and who sensed that the admiral had been killed in the fire. Then I had to go and inform the two children still living at home, a daughter and a young boy. The daughter, I think, was in high school, and the young boy was still in grade school. Having to tell them that their daddy died in the fire was also part of the Glenview duty.

That was the first Arlington funeral I conducted.[‡] We flew the admiral to Washington in his own plane. We flew into Washington at night, and I had talked to Chaplain Don Jolly about these arrangements. He suggested I come by the Chief of Chaplains' office, and he would sit down with me and go through the Arlington procedures.

That's a tough one, when you are burying somebody who is a leader of the command. In <u>Saratoga</u> I had experienced the situation of losing a squadron commander during carquals.[§] Every funeral is a sensitive situation, but when it's the CO, it's particularly sensitive.

Q: What memories do you have of running the parish, or whatever it was called, attached to the chapel at naval air station itself?

Admiral Stevenson: Well, I got to preach every Sunday. We had our own little Sunday school. Children were always delighted to be at the chapel, because the chapel had a carousel altar. Between Catholic and Protestant services, the children liked to get up

---

[*] Admiral Fowler died on 19 January 1967.
[†] Rear Admiral Howard A. Yeager, USN, died at Great Lakes, Illinois, on 11 March 1967 while serving as Commandant of the Ninth Naval District.
[‡] The Arlington National Cemetery is near the Pentagon in Arlington, Virginia.
[§] Carquals--qualification landings and takeoffs on an aircraft carrier.

forward and ride on the carousel as it turned the altar from one setting to the next. That particular carousel had four sections: one Protestant, one Catholic, one Jewish, and one that was sort of generic. Someone had a big old radio on that fourth section. Perhaps it was prophetic of media ministry, or electronic ministry, or whatever.

We had a very congenial and close-knit group that worshipped in that chapel. Both Catholics and Protestants were very anxious to have coffee together before or after services. The "flying professor," a inactive reserve captain named Dick Schram, and his family lived in Glenview.[*] They came to that chapel. Dick put on a Piper Cub act for years and years at Blue Angels shows, and he was killed performing in one of those air shows.[†] He did, I think, a hammerhead stall and didn't come out of it. That was some years later, when I was in Vietnam.

The folks in the command that lived on the base came to chapel, kids came to Sunday School. So it was a rather satisfying time, and Diane and I enjoyed ourselves. The social life in both commands was delightful--lots of dances.

Q: Would it be fair to say that was the first job you had in the Navy that really had a large administrative overlay in addition to the ministerial duties?

Admiral Stevenson: It was, and it was enjoyable.

Q: So it was very much a growth experience in that regard.

Admiral Stevenson: Glenview was followed by being selected as an alternate for postgraduate school. I had the good fortune of being told I was going to Princeton and of being told I was going to study social theory instead of pastoral counseling.

Q: Why do you describe that as good fortune?

---

[*] Captain Richard A. Schram, USNR.
[†] Blue Angels is the name of the Navy's flight demonstration team, which has done close formation flying for air shows and other events since 1946.

Admiral Stevenson: Oh, well, in those days everybody wanted to study pastoral counseling. I think the clergy thought they could justify their existence through an emphasis on pastoral counseling. I don't think that's true, but I think that's how a lot of us felt about it. (I think the First Amendment stands without it.) Pastoral counseling had really come into vogue after World War II. I think clergy had always done their share of counseling, but it was becoming formalized.

I think my seminary class, the class of '55, was the first class to graduate with some specified hours in pastoral counseling. Clergy are like all other professions; there are trends, and the trend in those days was to learn as much about Jung and so forth as possible.[*] While I was at Glenview, I had taken some graduate hours over at Garrett Theological Seminary to try to hone my skills in pastoral counseling.

I had applied, like most chaplains, for postgraduate school. I was selected for the alternate list--just to let you know how lucky some people can be in life. And, lo and behold, the chaplain working the training desk in Washington, D.C., ended up with an extra billet or two. Thereby I got to go to graduate school as an alternate.

I was told not to sign up for anything until I met with Chaplain Harold Menges, who was on the Chief of Chaplains' staff.[†] Chaplain Menges was a rather forceful gentleman. He came out on a trip to Great Lakes, and Father Bill Walsh called me up and said, "Be up here at such-and-such a time. Chaplain Menges from the Chief's office wants to see you."

I went up and he said, "You received your letter that you were selected?"

I said, "Yes, sir."

He said, "We would like you to study under Dr. Sam Blizzard at Princeton. [Remember, seniors suggest and juniors recommend.] He's in the field of sociology of religion, social theory, and he lectures on clergy roles."

I said, "Well, I really would prefer to study pastoral counseling. I think it would be more beneficial to me," and so forth.

In a very nice way, Chaplain Menges said, "Stevenson, you're an alternate; alternates do what we tell them to do." So in August of 1967 I reported to Princeton to study social

---

[*] Carl Jung (1875-1961) was a Swiss psychologist and psychiatrist. He was the founder of analytic psychology.
[†] Captain Harold F. Menges, CHC, USN.

theory. I had the advantage of PG school and moving my family to Pennington, New Jersey, where there was another good school system, thank God. But that was a horrible move also. Heidi, who was seven years old, was sick with a temperature of 102, and here we were, driving in the car from Glenview to New Jersey. Those things happen to Navy families all the time. We got to Pennington, and there wasn't enough room in that little house for our belongings. We dedicated the little garage to a storeroom and left the car outside. You know, all that stuff that's just the norm.

Then I went and reported in, along with four other chaplains, as a student at Princeton Theological Seminary.

Q: What do you remember of the course of instruction?

Admiral Stevenson: Well, I'll tell you several things about that. First of all, Dr. Sam Blizzard, an interesting individual, was the academic dean as well as professor of social theory, or sociology of religion. His attitude towards chaplains was very helpful. He said, "Look, you're mature; you guys have been around; you've visited the world. You come to us, and at the same time you're going to be competing with people who've been full-time students all their lives." So he gave us some just good advice about, "Stay cool for a while." And he also said, "Let me help you pick out what courses you need and ought to take."

I made it very clear to him that I knew nothing about sociology, social theory.

Q: And didn't really want to learn.

Admiral Stevenson: No, no, I wasn't that dumb. No, orders are orders. Like any career Navy man, I knew when to turn to.

I did think that I really ought to stick to elementary stuff. He said, "I don't think you need that. I'll arrange for you to take this advanced course and audit some of the basic courses." So I'll never forget, I was placed in a seminar group of Ph.D or Th.D candidates.

The group met for two hours, and the discussion was about anomie.* I didn't know what it was. I would have given anything for a dictionary to find out what anomie was!

It was a very interesting environment to be thrown into, and have to get up to speed. I very quickly determined that this was the greatest experience of my life. It was the first time in my life I had ever gone to school since I was 11 years old without working--that is, without having to earn the money to pay the school bills, etc. You can imagine what it was like to go to Princeton. You got up in the morning, you got to the library at 8:00 o'clock, and around 6:00 o'clock at night you went home. You had some reading to do at home at night and stuff like that, but, golly, that was fabulous.

Q: Did you find out the rationale that Chaplain Menges had in wanting you to study this course instead of counseling?

Admiral Stevenson: No, I never found out. But I have always been grateful to Chaplain Menges that he had the foresight to put me in that place. That year of social theory made a real contribution to me for the rest of my career. I mean, it enhanced my understanding of clergy, why we clergy do things, how systems work, etc. Dr. Blizzard saw to it that I took a course in cultural anthropology under Dr. Hostettler of Temple University, the expert on the Amish societies. When you understand how cult groups formulate, it increases dramatically your dimensions of understanding of religion, religious groups, and religious people.

So, although a lot of the courses were not aimed at things that you might think were applicable, they became very applicable. I took a course under a radical liberation theologian, M. Richard Schall. Remember now, this was 1967. The Vietnam demonstrations were on the campuses. We Navy chaplains were sitting in class and studying strategies of social change--modified social change, radical social change, etc. It was an interesting year. And I studied under some very, very interesting people.

Q: Do you think this year helped you eventually to become Chief of Chaplains?

---

* Anomie is social instability resulting from a breakdown of standards and valuues.

Admiral Stevenson: Oh, I think very much so. I think the year made a tremendous contribution to my own understanding of how organizations work, how people's needs are met. It increased my appreciation of things ecumenical. It dramatically increased my view of what it really means to facilitate the religious needs of others. It introduced me to institutional ministry, in contrast to parish ministry. It opened my eyes to environmental awareness.

Added to my experiences at Glenview, it confirmed for me how many of our Navy chaplains were limited in their ministry to Navy folks because they were practicing only parish ministry. They had never looked beyond the model of ministry they had been given in the seminary.

All that started or was part of that Princeton year.

Q: It sounds as if it broadened you much more than the counseling would have.

Admiral Stevenson: Oh, yes. And probably gave me all the prejudices that social theorists have about counseling.

Q: Which are what?

Admiral Stevenson: That a large bit of counseling is meeting the needs of the counselor instead of the counselee.

Q: That's a cynical view.

Admiral Stevenson: It's a cynical view; it's a cynical view. [Laughter] But consider the numbers of people who are put through premarital counseling by clergy in order to meet the needs of the clergy. Actually, I feel we clergy ought to advertise and provide pastoral conversations, not pastoral counseling. Social theory gave me a lot of heretical ideas like that.

I mean, what a year to study social theory. Here we were studying anomie and Detroit was burning. Downtown Washington, D.C., was burning. Martin Luther King was assassinated.* I mean, that was one hell of a year.

Q: You had some real case studies there.

Admiral Stevenson: Yes, and you had people like Sam Blizzard, saying their schematics indicated that these 15-year cycles are applicable, and that you will probably have fundamentalistic religious tendencies and conservative government by the '80s.

Q: Pretty good prediction.

Admiral Stevenson: And you're sitting around in the '60s--well, they're looking at demographics; what is the mean age group going to be by this year. In those years the mean age of the population was in the 20s; now it's in the 30s. They knew it was going to be in the 30s. When I look back on it, I think they did a rather spectacular job of their predictions. It gives you some fears as to what's going to happen in the inner cities if we don't correct some of the problems by the latter part of the 1990s.

Q: Well, you mentioned these domestic problems that we were having. The country was also coming apart over Vietnam at that time. Was that addressed in these courses?

Admiral Stevenson: Oh, constantly, with a great deal of heat. As I said, Richard Schall was a liberation theologian, and Richard Schall was--it appeared to me, at least--to be extremely anti-American government.

Q: How did you weigh into these discussions, carrying the baggage of Navy chaplains?

---

* The assassination of Dr. Martin Luther King, Jr., on 4 April 1968 was followed by widespread looting and burning in cities such as Detroit and Washington that had large black populations.

Admiral Stevenson: Oh, we weighed, we weighed in. Particularly while we were there, some of us got orders to Vietnam, so we were in at a very realistic level.

Q: But what was your viewpoint, or your contribution to the discussion?

Admiral Stevenson: I won't speak for the other chaplains, but I still thought our people were making a sacrifice to give the Vietnamese people an opportunity for self-determination that certainly North Vietnam would never permit. There were a couple of guys in the seminary who had served in Vietnam and were out of the military. They spoke on several occasions about the fact that we as a nation were in the wrong place at the wrong time, doing the wrong thing. On the other hand, we had guys who were seminary students in order to avoid the draft. Don't debate with people who feel guilty! The vets were very rational and the "draft dodgers" very emotional.

Q: Did all this cause you to question your own views about the government's commitment?

Admiral Stevenson: Oh, yes. I had lots and lots of questions about our Vietnam policy. And I had the opportunity to read every textbook on Vietnam that every professor at the Woodrow Wilson School had placed on the reserve shelf for their courses.

Q: Well, the tendency now in retrospect is to view Vietnam as something we never should have gotten into because it turned out not to be a success.

Admiral Stevenson: Yes. The road to colonialism is paved with good intentions.

Q: But you don't know in advance what's going to work and what's not.

Admiral Stevenson: I think Sam Blizzard, who's been dead for some years, would be fascinated at our society's need to have a Vietnam memorial. I think when you lose, the need for some form of memorial increases dramatically. When you lose, you have to prove that people are not forgotten. The impact of the Vietnam memorial in my lifetime, as compared with any memorials for Korea or World War II, is just out of all proportion.

Maybe it's just like father, like son. My dad, a World War I veteran of the British Army, used to get so annoyed when I was a kid at seeing "veterans" selling pencils and playing on people's guilt. I would hope that the good I saw of our people in Vietnam is not totally lost because a bunch of veterans have a need to run around in ragged old fatigues. It's really kind of sad. It's really, really very sad.

Q: When you, as an individual or a nation, make a sacrifice, you want to believe that it was worth something, that you achieved something through that.

Admiral Stevenson: Well, I do think that there were positive things achieved. You know, I would sit back now like everybody else and say the overall policy of several administrations, starting with the colonial situation of the French and our support of them, led to an ultimate disaster for all involved. But it's a disaster of not one generation; it's a disaster of many, many generations. To use social-theory terms, Vietnam is probably a classic example of the law of unintended consequences.

Q: Certainly.

Well, in terms of intellectual stimulation, you would probably have to put that year at Princeton at the top in your entire life.

Admiral Stevenson: Yes, I would. Let me mention another contrast of that year. In the military you graduate in full-dress uniform, so there were the five of us in full-dress whites. Our baccalaureate speaker was William Sloane Coffin. He was the anti-war chaplain at Yale in those days. Dr. Blizzard looked at me and said, "Remember that William Sloane Coffin was in the OSS in World War II."[*]

---

[*] OSS--Office of Strategic Services, formed in World War II to collect and analyze foreign intelligence and to carry out special operations under the control of the Joint Chiefs of Staff.

Q: Were you a pioneer for the Navy in getting into sociology of religion?

Admiral Stevenson: I don't know. I know that if you spend time talking about a weltanschauung, your weltanschauung expands. I would interpret things afterwards differently than the way I did before I went to Princeton. And, of course, many of my peers down through the years have teased me because often I would end up quoting Dr. Blizzard. It got to the place where Joe Dimino and Jude Senieur and people I served with would tease me and say, "Oh, here comes another snowstorm."[*]

Q: How was Blizzard as a mentor?

Admiral Stevenson: Well, let me tell you a story about Blizzard. Sam Blizzard was selected to give lectures at the Chaplain Corps advanced course at the chaplain school in 1969. This was because of his notoriety for his work on clergy role models, etc. He totally bombed. It just didn't work.

Q: Why do you think that was?

Admiral Stevenson: Well, several reasons. And Sam Blizzard knew these reasons better than I did. Some years later he talked to me about it. First of all, most clergy of that time communicated with one another in psych language, not sociological language. He did not come and speak to them in terms of, "I'm okay, you're okay." It was the days of T-groups. It was the days of touchy-feely. That was not Sam's world. Sam Blizzard was the most articulate professor that I ever studied under. My own experience with him was that his way of teaching and his vocabulary was like learning a foreign language. And people who are good at foreign languages tell me that you study and study, and then suddenly you realize that you dreamt in that language. Well, for me the first few months at Princeton were days of study and study, but I had no idea where Dr. Blizzard was going.

---

[*] Commander Jude R. Senieur, CHC, USNR.

In Princeton they have the precept-group method, where you have a certain number of hours in class, but then you get together as precepts with the professor. Then one day it all seemed to sort of make sense to me. I was able to enter into the conversations and feel that I was beginning to learn some things.

Q: Did you go back to him and say, "What am I supposed to get out of this?"

Admiral Stevenson: I did a lot of that. I really did. And he would smile at you, and say, "You're fine. Just read it all over again!"

Q: Well, the Navy, in the person of Chaplain Menges, had set you on this course specifically. Did it then keep hands off for the nine months?

Admiral Stevenson: They did. They kept hands off, except for going to Philadelphia once to visit with Chaplain Hemphill, to be told that we were going to go to Vietnam.[*] He said that two of us were going to go to Vietnam and that we would be used in this special program called "personal response." And the more we knew about sociology and anthropology, the better off we'd be. Since that was what we were studying anyway, it was fine with us.

Q: What kind of a fitness report do you get for that kind of a year?

Admiral Stevenson: Well, since I was later on the training desk in the Chief of Chaplains' office, I think it's important to maintain the policy they had in those years. We received an observed--just strictly observed--fitness report, no grades.

Q: It indicated that you were doing what the Navy had ordered you to do.

---

[*] Captain Edward J. Hemphill, Jr., CHC, USN, who was on the Chaplain Corps Planning Group.

Admiral Stevenson: Yes. Well, our academic grades were sent to the Navy. The NROTC unit that we were attached to for pay purposes did not make any narrative report. And some years later there were some postgraduate students who did receive narrative reports. In most cases, having read some of them, they were not fitting, in my opinion. I mean, you don't want the chaplain to be judged by the CO of the NROTC unit. You order the chaplain there to hit the books and to absorb everything he can in nine months, not to be the school or NROTC chaplain.

Q: The professor of naval science is not really qualified to know how well you're doing what you're supposed to be doing.

Admiral Stevenson: Correct.

Q: Did you spend any time in the pulpit during that year?

Admiral Stevenson: Only at the local church that we went to. The minister got sick once or twice and asked me to fill in, and so I did.

Q: Well, anything else on that tour of duty to remember?

Admiral Stevenson: Yes. Writing has never been easy for me, and it was a good year of writing and rewriting and rewriting and rewriting.

Q: Well, we're close to our designated stopping time, so perhaps rather than get into Vietnam, we ought to leave that for another day.

Admiral Stevenson: Okay. That's a sad one.

Neil M. Stevenson #4 - 114

Interview Number 4 with Rear Admiral Neil M. Stevenson, Chaplain Corps, U.S. Navy (Retired)

Place: Immanuel Presbyterian Church, McLean, Virginia

Date: Monday, 17 April 1989

Interviewer: Paul Stillwell

Q: Admiral, what sort of preliminary preparations or briefing did you get before you headed over to Vietnam?

Admiral Stevenson: There was an organization within the Chaplain Corps in those days called the Chaplain Corps Planning Group. Some very well-educated and well-read chaplains were ordered to it when Chaplain Kelly was Chief of Chaplains.[*] He put some very sharp people in that group. Their offices were in the Washington Navy Yard in a building that had been a tower somehow associated with submarines.

Q: I'm not familiar with that.

Admiral Stevenson: Anyway, it used to be part of the intra-corps teasing: the planning group was highly elevated and lived in an ether far above the rest of the chaplains.

The good news about the Chaplains Corps Planning Group in those days was that they were innovative, extremely hard-working chaplains who tried to motivate current and futuristic ideas. Avant garde!

Q: Avant garde in what sense?

Admiral Stevenson: Well, in the sense that they would introduce the Chaplain Corps to using rock bands for worship, introduced the corps to new trends in liturgy and such things.

---

[*] Rear Admiral James W. Kelly, CHC, USN, served as the Navy's Chief of Chaplains from July 1965 to June 1970.

Q: So this was different from the stodgy old Navy that we all know and love.

Admiral Stevenson: Yes. Chaplain Mike MacInnes was senior.[*] Later it would be Chaplain Joe Tubbs.[†] Chaplain Eddie Hemphill was the number-two man in it; Chaplain Warren Newman was the junior man.[‡] All were very bright, well-learned men. Hemphill was also hyper and radically innovative.

The problem with the Chaplain Corps Planning Group was--from my position then and looking back at it now--was that it raised questions as to who was running the Chaplain Corps, the Chief of Chaplains' office or the planning group.

Anyway, like other chaplains, I had put Vietnam on my preference card. I certainly thought that anybody who was lucky enough to pull postgraduate work ought to pay his dues after graduation. I assumed that I would go from postgraduate work to Vietnam. I had never had any duty with the Marine Corps. I had had collateral duties with the Marine Corps at Glenview but never really served in the Marine Corps.

So I received a phone call in the wee hours of the morning while I was at Princeton. That was Chaplain Hemphill's style--impressing you that he was working long hours at the office. He said, "You know, your next tour of duty will probably be Vietnam."

I said, "Yes, sir, I assumed that."

He said, "Well, I'm going to tell the Chaplain Corps detailer and the Chief of Chaplains that you're going to be ordered to the Personal Response Program in Vietnam."

I don't remember if I was brave enough to say to him, "What is the Personal Response Program?" to tell you the truth. There were two billets--one with Marines, one with Navy. He told me I was going to be ordered to the Navy one in Saigon, although that was later changed to orders to the III MAF.[§]

I got another phone call one day asking me to come down to Philadelphia to meet with Chaplain Hemphill in between his dialogues with the faculty of the marriage counseling

---

[*] Captain Michael J. H. MacInnes, CHC, USNR.
[†] Captain Joseph J. Tubbs, CHC, USN.
[‡] Lieutenant Commander William Warren Newman, CHC, USN.
[§] III MAF--Third Marine Amphibious Force, based near Danang, South Vietnam.

course down there. It was one of the first times I had experienced the "Washington syndrome" where you go to Philadelphia to meet this guy from Washington. You sit for two hours because he's too busy to meet with you, and then he has only 20 minutes to tell you what you need to know.

Q: Did you get any pearls of wisdom in those 20 minutes?

Admiral Stevenson: No, except that I was reminded to study hard because I was going into this very special program. I recall he asked, "When do you graduate? What's the day and the hour that you graduate from Princeton?" And when he found that out, he said, "Then you've got to be in Washington that night, and we will begin briefings the next morning." So that was pretty impressive. I had never been involved in anything that seemed to have that kind of urgency or pseudo-emergency about it.

Q: Did you then find out during these briefings what the Personal Response Program was?

Admiral Stevenson: I found out what the Personal Response Program was from the viewpoint of those who were in Washington. And they had several terms for it. Chaplain McGonigal, who had been one of the original chaplains in this Personal Response Program, was back from Vietnam to brief us.* He later became a line officer.

Altogether, we were briefed for about a week. We were also taken around and introduced to a few people in Marine Corps headquarters and people on the Chief of Chaplains' staff. Some of them were so busy about their chores that they certainly weren't interested in giving us a lot of time, and I don't blame them for that. Others looked at us and asked the friendly question, "You guys volunteered for this?" Actually, I don't recall volunteering for it, except that I got a phone call. Eddie Hemphill said, "This is what you're going to," and I said, "Fine."

The presentations we received in Washington told us that the Personal Response Program was crucial to what Eddie Hemphill thought was the beginning of "peace-fare." I

---

* Lieutenant Commander Richard A. McGonigal, CHC, USN.

was the one who was dumb enough to ask, "What do you mean by 'peace-fare?'" Eddie explained that it's the opposite of warfare. I should have asked many more questions, but I didn't.

Churches in those days, Paul, were idealistic, because of Vatican II and because of what was happening within Protestant churches--partly because of Vietnam. Even my own church, the Presbyterian Church, was writing a new confession. The confession of 1967 reflects the ethos of the time, including reconciliation and the civil rights movement.

I discovered through that process that the confessions of the churches down through the centuries are beautiful little fingerprints of the environment and what's being emphasized at that particular time. The big thing in '68 was the "ministry of reconciliation:" how do you bring about peace and reconciliation between individuals, between communities, between races, and so forth? And here you are, you've had some education in social theory; you've gained some background in cultural anthropology; and you've had some time to read the reference shelf at Woodrow Wilson School of International Studies, the works of Bernard Fall, etc., so you're going to be an agent of "peace-fare."[*]

Personal response in Vietnam was briefed as an absolutely necessary tool to bring about a reconciliation between peoples. We were told that we had established this program to educate our personnel on the Vietnamese. From that concept it made sense.

Q: Did you accept this in the spirit in which it was offered, or did you have sort of a skeptical view?

Admiral Stevenson: No, I had a skeptical view, I guess, somewhat from the beginning, because I had just finished the year up at Princeton. I had been introduced to liberation theology for the first time in my life; I had been outside the Navy enclave for the first time in ten years. Seminary had drastically changed since my years in Pittsburgh. And the whole Vietnam-civil rights milieu had affected the campus, so I was questioning all kinds of things.

---

[*] Bernard Fall was a French-born Indochina scholar, author of Viet-Nam Witness: 1953-66 (New York: Frederick A. Praeger, 1966).

I can give you an idea of what it was like. A month before I came down to my briefings, I was washing the dishes after dinner, and the news said Martin Luther King had been assassinated. While I was getting my briefings on the Personal response from the Chaplain Corps Planning Group in the Navy yard, they had us stay in a real dump of a hotel right across from Union Station in Washington, D.C. I was getting my briefings when they brought Bobby Kennedy's body down on a train for the burial.[*] That was the atmosphere of the whole time, which I think had an impact on all of this. Anomie was pretty real.

I was a chaplain, but I was saying to myself, "This sounds more like a line job than it does a chaplain's job." Remember, we had just finished a period of time when the Chaplain Corps in the '50s and '60s had been up to its neck in character education and moral leadership. Then that was brought into question regarding its appropriateness to the chaplain's role. Now this personal response sounded like a wartime revision of moral leadership/character education in a form of "reconciliation ministry." Nevertheless, the Washington group felt that personal response had been well received by the Marine Corps and by the Navy, and that it was a crucial element of trying to bring about the reconciliation of our own personnel with the Vietnamese.

So they gave us all the briefings, and they told us about the work that Chaplain McGonigal had done with the CAP groups of the Marine Corps.[†] These were cadres of the Marines who went and lived in the villes to protect the villes. This was not too long after the Tet offensive and all the psychology of the Tet offensive's impact on our society.[‡]

Q: Did you establish some sort of game plan in your own mind after you heard all these briefings?

---

[*] Robert F. Kennedy, younger brother of John F. Kennedy, had been campaigning for the presidency in the spring of 1968. He died on 6 June after being assassinated in Los Angeles by Sirhan Sirhan. Kennedy was subsequently buried in the Arlington National Cemetery.
[†] CAP--combined action platoon.
[‡] On 31 January 1968 the North Vietnamese and Viet Cong launched a massive coordinated attack that came to be known as the Tet offensive because it occurred in conjunction with the lunar new year, a traditional Vietnamese holiday. Attacks were launched simultaneously against cities, towns, and military bases throughout Vietnam and resulted in many casualties. Although the American forces beat back the offensive, the news media at the time reported it as a North Vietnamese victory. Soon afterward, President Lyndon Johnson announced that he would not run for reelection and began scaling back the American commitment in Vietnam.

Admiral Stevenson: I really think I responded to the whole thing pretty much the way I had on the phone: "Aye, aye, sir. That's my assignment." I mean, the last thing in the world I was going to say to anybody is, "I'm not so sure I want to go to Vietnam." Instead, I was saying, "Yeah, it's time for me to pay my dues, and if this is the job you have ordered me to, these are the tools, and I'll turn to.

I remember going back up to Princeton after the briefings, and I was at dinner with a local Presbyterian minister and his family who had become friends while we were there. He was opposed to our Vietnam policy, and I was trying to explain to him the feeling I had at that time. I told him that, "If anybody can say 'Aye, aye, sir,' and get PR done, the Marines can. So maybe this reconciliation thing has its place. Let's see how it goes. If they think I can do it, then I'll have at it." I had been told through the years by people that I was a pretty good teacher, and this was an assignment of teaching. For the 13 months I was an instructor in personal response methodology. By the way, Marines were good at it, and many of the bravest young Marines died in an effort to be "agents of reconciliation."

So I took the family to my wife's home town, Tarkio, Missouri, because we were able to rent a house there on Main Street. I thought that it was good to have Diane and the girls near Diane's dad. I got the family settled in. That included doing all those things that you need to do at times like that: buy an air conditioner and get it put in the kids' bedroom, and paint rooms. Once they were settled, my father-in-law took me over to Omaha. I flew out to California with all my gear, went down to Camp Pendleton for, I don't know, three or four days of training that the Chaplain Corps provided to all chaplains on their way to Vietnam with Marine Corps units.

Q: What sort of training?

Admiral Stevenson: To listen to some sea stories about Vietnam from chaplains who had been there, things that they thought worked or didn't work. What the environment was like. Telling you to take your malaria pills, etc. We went out and climbed a minor mountain to prove we were in shape. Actually, I'd just as soon do anything in life except climb a mountain.

Q: Did you get some indoctrination in the Marine Corps ethic?

Admiral Stevenson: Yes, we sat through a bunch of briefings that Marines were going through in the areas of survival training, helicopter exiting, and things like that.

Q: Do you have any observations on the differences in working with Marines, as opposed to Navy men?

Admiral Stevenson: No, I think it's an adjustment to environment. I think when you're with the Marines, you've got to emulate Marines--start jogging, etc. I felt very strongly--still do--that if you're a chaplain with Marines, you have the privilege of wearing a Marine Corps uniform, etc. You play Marine. There's always a certain number of naval officers attached to Marines--doctors, and in those days lawyers as well, and chaplains--who always fight the program. They try to prove to everybody that they're Navy. All that does to a chaplain is diminish the opportunity for ministry. If you're going to be with Marines, play Marine; if you're going to be with Coast Guard, wear the uniform and go "Coastie."

Q: I would think that would hurt your credibility with the troops if you didn't do it their way.

Admiral Stevenson: True, but there are some people who have to be defensive. There are chaplains who say, "I joined the Navy to be in the Navy, and I'm unhappy that I'm with Marines." I was very happy to be with the Marines. They certainly treated me well, and I enjoyed duty with them. You know, I think the world of them.

Q: In what ways did they treat you well?

Admiral Stevenson: They never made me feel that I wasn't part of the outfit. They included me in their activities. I felt very much at home with the Marine Corps. I have a tendency to put things in religious categories, you know, the Marines are the charismatics--you know, they're the fundamentalists. From what I had heard in my briefings in Washington, one of the things personal response required was guts, and if anybody could pull it off, these Marines were the ones who would be brave enough, courageous enough to do it. Because it did mean, in many cases, asking the people to put their lives in jeopardy.

I was just talking to a college student the other day, because he had to write a paper on Vietnam. You would be surprised what a shocked look came over his face when I tried to describe Vietnam to him. He's 21 years old and he's a football player, nice big guy. I said, "Fine, let's just go back a few years and let's make believe it's you. You're 21 years of age; you're a big, hulking Marine. You've made sergeant, and you're in charge of a CAP outfit. You're told to go over and check out that ville, and see if there's any VC in that ville, or ascertain how much VC influence there is in that ville, or if there's a cadre of VC, or weapons there.[*]

"There are a couple of ways you can do that. You've got, say, 20 guys with you, most of whom are younger than you are. And, let's say, the average guy has been in Vietnam three months. You're loaded down with M-16s and hand grenades, and so what are you going to do?[†] Are you going to go over and have a conversation with the village elder, if you can find out who he is? You really don't speak Vietnamese, and he certainly doesn't speak English. How are you going to accomplish your mission?

"If you're somewhat chicken, you can almost find any excuse to stop at the edge of the village before you go stick your neck out, because you've seen what a dead Marine looks like by this time. So you can sit down with your weapon power and pulverize the place, and then go in and say, 'Are there any VC here?' Or you can put your ass in a sling and walk in, and see if they have been infiltrated or bothered by VC." The young student said that gave him something of a different view from what he'd gotten on television of what it was like.

---

[*] VC--Viet Cong, a derogatory term for Vietnamese Communists in South Vietnam.
[†] The M-16 became the standard U.S. infantry rifle in Vietnam in 1967. It had an effective range of just over 500 yards. It could be used either in a fully automatic mode or one shot at a time.

Well, personal response was a program that got young Marines together for inter-cultural training. The chaplain was handing out these materials of personal response and teaching the customs and traditions of the Vietnamese people, the history of the Vietnamese people, the kinds of things that make them angry, the kinds of things that turn them off. And they emphasized that they were over there to win friends.

To use a very realistic illustration that we used to use in class--you know, the laws of physics--every action has an equal and opposite reaction. I worked up a gimmick in class where I would step on some guy's toe and say, "You don't like me to step on your toe; in fact, probably if I weren't an officer, you would have shoved me a good distance across the room by now. Well, you know, that's what happens. Your action will probably bring about an equal reaction--for good or ill."

Q: How receptive were the Marines to your approach?

Admiral Stevenson: It varied. It varied with the amount of time they had been in the country; it varied with the amount of circumstances and situations that they had been in. It didn't take very long for the average Marine to distrust any Vietnamese. I mean, they were surrounded by guerrilla warfare basically, and you were asking these men to put their lives on the line, to be extremely slow with firepower in a totally threatening world.

There were a lot of things we worked up, Paul, that people said were helpful. We got involved with a poster series, trying to help Marines to understand that the Vietnamese themselves--I suppose under CIA sponsorship--had a thing called the revolutionary development cadre.* Vietnamese were brought in from the villes and trained at Vung Tau, a place down near Saigon. Young men and women, wearing "black pajamas" were trained to go back to their villes and instill in the population democratic ideas. Hopefully, this made them enthusiastic about the government of South Vietnam.

We got involved in putting out schematics, which I think helped a lot of our troops to recognize the fact that we came from a complex society, while the Vietnamese lived in a simple society. We were educating them to see the differences of priorities between a

---

* CIA--Central Intelligence Agency.

complex society and a simple society in order to give Marines an appreciation of why the Vietnamese were not enthusiastic about some of the things we did. I had a Marine Corps outfit that was really ticked off. And the general I worked for sent me out to talk to them, one of the multitude of incidents that I remember.

Q: What was the outcome of it?

Admiral Stevenson: Well, the outcome wasn't too good. What was happening was that our guys were building a road that we needed for LOCs, lines of communication. And, of course, it was going across rice paddies. Our guys were out there with a complex society mentality saying, "Hey, look, village elder, this is going to expedite you getting your crop to the market."

The village elder, however, was sitting out there and saying, "We've never taken a crop to the market. We eat our rice. We live here in the ville. We don't need your asphalt running over our rice." It was no different from World War II, when some of our own farmers were told that the government was taking over their farms to build a military base.

You know, while I was in Vietnam, our nation sent a man to walk on the moon.[*] I had with me a top sergeant, Gunny McEnroe, and an ARVN top sergeant was our interpreter, Gunny Wah.[†] They worked up a briefing to tell Vietnamese school kids about the moon shot. They tried it out on two elderly Vietnamese women who worked as building cleaners in the compound. The two women were brave enough to say things that normally Vietnamese wouldn't say. At the conclusion of this trial presentation, one of them said, "Why did you do that?" And the other one said, "I don't believe you." I mean, when you're in Vietnam and you look at that moon up there, the whole thing just was kind of ludicrous: "You've got a man walking on the moon, and we can't even walk outside the compound at night." It was really wild.

---

[*] Astronauts Neil A. Armstrong and Michael Collins made the first human walk on the moon on 20 July 1969. During the time they were on the moon, Edwin E. "Buzz" Aldrin, Jr., remained behind on board the Apollo 11 command module.
[†] ARVN--Army of the Republic of Vietnam, that is, South Vietnam.

Anyway, it was a matter of teaching courses, traveling around, and receiving from the legal officers reports of incidents in which the Vietnamese had been mistreated by rape, hooches burned down, etc. My personal experience was that the Marine Corps did not close its eyes to injustice. When Marines had committed immoral acts such as rape or something like that, the Marine Corps took it seriously, investigated, and court-martialed the accused. The CAP program was an attempt to really try to relate to the people of simple society. And yet the whole thing had all the marks of colonialism.

Q: Paternalism.

Admiral Stevenson: Yes, but not a paternalism that communicated itself favorably to the Vietnamese.

Q: So they resented it?

Admiral Stevenson: I think so.

Q: Did you have any successes in trying to bring this program into being?

Admiral Stevenson: Well, having read my end-of-tour report again recently, there were mechanical successes. Washington wanted this survey, and we got the survey run through. They wanted a Personal Response Program directive within the operational procedures of Third Marine Amphibious Force. We got some of those things done.

    I was in a Marine Corps command. I was working for the deputy chief of staff for plans, who was an Army officer, Brigadier General Warren Bennett.[*] So I was the only naval officer in a Marine Corps unit working for an Army general. And I was in a maverick program called personal response, which was looked upon largely by the Marines, in spite of how much we tried to identify with the Marine Corps, as a chaplains' goodwill program. As I wrote in my end of tour report, if the personal response concept really has any validity,

---

[*] Brigadier General Warren K. Bennett, USA.

it is really in the area of sociological warfare--as a counterpart to, or as a companion piece to psychological warfare. It is something that the line ought to be proficient with. I think that in any combat situation in the Third World, as a line program, it would have its place. But as a Chaplain Corps program, I don't think it would ever have legitimacy among the line. I don't think chaplains should be involved, for the good of the nation or the good of the church.

Q: Was that a frustration for you?

Admiral Stevenson: A great frustration. God, that was a constant frustration as was the whole war. I mean, I recently heard a North Vietnamese general interviewed on TV. He was asked by the American commentator, "What was the great difference between the Americans and the North Vietnamese?" His response was that we were there for a year, and that his troops knew they were there forever. And that's true. And he said something to the effect that if you're only there for a year, you're only there for six months, because when you get through that first six months, you really start counting down the second six months. Then your relief comes in and makes the same mistakes you made during your first six months.

Kind of a strange situation. While on duty in Vietnam, I was ordered to Saigon once a month, where I briefed people in the AID program and people in this RD, revolutionary development cadre program.[*] These were agriculturists and others who were coming into the country to assist the Vietnamese.

Q: It sounds as if your initial skepticism was borne out by the facts when you got there.

Admiral Stevenson: A very, very frustrating, uncomfortable year. My end-of-tour report probably still says it all. I hope we did some good. I still think about the young Marines in personal response. Some of them didn't come back, because they had the courage to try to make positive relationships with people in simple society, on a village level, creating an

---

[*] AID--Agency for International Development.

atmosphere of trust. And so those were the ones who put themselves the most in harm's way because of the love of fellow human beings. Peace makers lose their lives.

Q: Do you have any specific cases you can describe of those successes?

Admiral Stevenson: No, because the CAP program during that year dwindled, I think, in the number of Marines who were used in the CAP program. The colonels who were in charge of that program would have a better assessment of that than I would.

Q: Did you have a professional life as a chaplain apart from the program itself?

Admiral Stevenson: Yes, thanks to the two senior chaplains in Third Marine Amphibious Force, first, Ralph Below, who was there when I first reported in, and Bob Radcliffe, who was there my last seven or eight months.[*] Both top-notch chaplains in our corps.

They would invite me to preach at the III MAF chapel from time to time--my home when I was there.

Q: Was this up at Danang?

Admiral Stevenson: Along the Danang River. III MAF was next to the ARVN ammo dump that blew up in '68!

I was traveling in country a good deal. But as I think of it, let me tell you one incident in the whole personal response thing. Before I left Washington, I was handed a letter to the commanding general of Third Marine Amphibious Force from the Chief of Chaplains. This was a letter prepared by the Chaplain Corps Planning Group, indicating to the CG of III MAF that I was the one chosen to relieve Chaplain Otto Schneider, who was in the Personal Response Program, who was rotating out.[†] And my assigned duties would be as follows, etc., etc.

---

[*] Captain Ralph W. Below, CHC, USN.
[†] Commander Otto Schneider, CHC, USN. CG--commanding general.

Q: Who was the commanding general of III MAF then?

Admiral Stevenson: It was General Cushman, who went from there to CIA.[*]

I had never had a letter to carry like that before in my career, and I felt it was kind of strange but I carried it. I thought it was part of the routine. I had to stop in Hawaii to be briefed by the Fleet Marine Force chaplain, Chaplain Vinny Lonergan.[†] I don't know whether Vinny knew it or not, but he had a big influence on my life. I looked upon Vinny as one of the really solid chaplains in the Chaplain Corps.

I don't think Chaplain Lonergan was enthusiastic about the Personal Response Program, but he was in a position at FMFPac where he knew this was what the chief's office in Washington wanted done, etc.[‡] Anyway, I happened to mention this letter, or he knew about the letter--I don't know which it was--when I got to his office, and one of the dramatic memories I have of my life in the Chaplain Corps, is Chaplain Lonergan said, "Could I see that letter?" I handed it to him while sitting in his office. He read it, and he ripped it up. I was sitting there watching him rip up this letter and saying to myself, "Now, wait a minute." You know, the senior chaplain in Washington prepared that letter, and they handed me that letter and told me that I was charged with taking it to the CG of III MAF. Now I had handed it over to Vinny Lonergan to read, and here he ripped it up. You know, now what's my next act?

Q: Was this letter just essentially an explanation of the program?

Admiral Stevenson: Well, from the point of view of Chaplain Lonergan, the Chief of Chaplains and the Chaplain Corps never tells a commanding officer, not to mention a commanding general, how he's going to use the chaplain who's been ordered to him. It is not the way to start your relationship with a command. I think Vinny was absolutely right.

---

[*] Lieutenant General Robert E. Cushman, USMC, later Commandant of the Marine Corps, 1972-75.
[†] Captain Vincent J. Lonergan, CHC, USN.
[‡] FMFPac--Fleet Marine Force Pacific Fleet.

I think he did me a great favor in ripping up the letter. It was an act that represented the difference of the mind between those in Washington those in the field with Marines.

While I was in Hawaii, the chaplain I was relieving, Otto Schneider, was in Hawaii, and he gave me some additional, practical briefings as a fellow Brooklynite, a fellow Dodger fan. Otto Schneider was on his way out of Vietnam, and I was on my way into Vietnam. Otto was on his way to teach personal response to Marines at Camp Pendleton, staying within the program. I was on my way to Vietnam to teach personal response to Marines and others.

In Vietnam I had to defend personal response with many chaplains who felt that we were not doing Marines any favors. They were over there to fight a war and from their perspective, in combat. Their view was, "Why don't we just have all-out warfare and get this thing over with? And why does 'Washington' tie our hands behind our backs?" And so forth and so on.

You know, so many experiences, Paul--I remember we were having some inter-cultural troubles up at Okinawa. One of the Marine Corps generals from Okinawa was down in the compound, and a couple of III MAF generals and colonels thought that it would be good to sit down and discuss the problems at dinner, so they invited me. They had a separate O-6 mess at III MAF, which was the talk of a lot of junior officers, who did not believe that in the Marine Corps you had a separate mess for O-6s and above.[*]

But they had a separate mess, and I was invited this one night to talk to this general. There were racial problems with the troops, conflicts with the citizens of Okinawa, and a question of whether or not some form of personal response would be good in Okinawa. From a personal response approach, the beginning of the play <u>Teahouse of the August Moon</u> is a great example. And I can remember using that, and that ticked off the general right from the beginning. So I was a dead duck before we even got through the main course of the dinner.

You might remember the beginning of the play. The lead Okinawan character comes out and sits in the middle of the stage and says something to the effect that citizens

---

[*] O-6 is the pay grade for a captain in the Navy or Coast Guard and for a colonel in the Army, Marine Corps, or Air Force.

of Okinawa are the luckiest people in the world, that in thousands of years, they've never had to travel in order to gain culture--that the Chinese invaded and gave them Chinese culture, and the Japanese invaded and gave them Japanese culture, and now the Americans have invaded and given them American culture. You know, actions and reactions. It sets the tone that the Okinawans eventually win because they adapt.

Anyway, as I talked, this general bristled and informed me that Okinawa was a prize of war, a conquered territory. And I never will forget the look on his face when I kind of bristled back: "You know, General, none of your Marines were even born when we took Okinawa." We were talking about a whole new generation, who really didn't think in terms of World War II, and yet our leadership were all people like myself who had grown up in World War II, or were largely thinking in terms of who conquered what.

Q: It sounds as though you became something of a missionary in this program.

Admiral Stevenson: Yes, and at the same time I felt all the time that one of the great handicaps of the program was that it was considered a Chaplain Corps program. If the program has any validity--if the program were starting up today, Paul, I would have to say the same thing. The program has validity, but it will never be understood. It will never be the tool of valid manipulation that it ought to be unless it is a line program. If the Chaplain Corps is involved, it will always have the atmosphere of a "do-gooder" about it. Anyway, my social theory background helped me to appreciate the Vietnamese who referred to the United States is the "land of the big exchange," while our own troops talked about going back to "the world."

It was not easy for our troops to relate to simple society, although it was interesting to me that when I would talk to Marines who had grown up in the ghetto and who had experienced village life, that many of them were enthusiastic about village life. In the village life, everybody takes care of everybody. I mean, if you're born in a Vietnamese ville with no mama and no papa, you live a rather normal life. The people in the ville raise you. If you're born retarded or handicapped, you live in the ville and the people in the ville take care of you. I mean, you're not as institutionalized as in complex society. You'd find an occasional Marine who'd say, "Hey, let's trade in complex society for simple society. This is great."

I tried to do a little study one time on songs. And it didn't get anywhere, but, if you take the songs of previous wars, like "Over There," I doubt that they would have the constant negative impact that contemporary 1960s songs had on those of our troops.* And our troops sang those songs everywhere they went. They identify with those songs--"I'm going to get out of this place if it's the last thing I ever do," "The green, green grass of home." By the time I was ordered out in 1969, Marines had flowers in their helmets--the flower children. Marines were carrying cameras. Paul, you ever been in combat where everybody has a camera?

Q: No.

Admiral Stevenson: Everybody had an M-16 and a 35-millimeter camera. You're a warrior and you're a tourist. I don't think a real, in-depth study of that whole Vietnam thing has been done. I happened to be at some meetings in Danang when the word came in that Nixon was elected.† The ARVN generals were the ones that were the happiest at these meetings and toasting the celebration of Nixon's election, and so forth and so on.

Another observation I made in 13 months--I never met anybody in a leadership position in the ARVN who had not come originally from North Vietnam.

Q: How do you explain that?

Admiral Stevenson: I felt that this was a civil war, and that this civil war was between North Vietnamese. The real battle was between North Vietnamese families--those who had

---

* "Over There," written by George M. Cohan, was a stirring, patriotic song about American forces sent "over there" to France in World War I.
† Richard M. Nixon was elected President of the United States in November 1968. He took office on 20 January 1969.

stayed in North Vietnam and those who went south. I never heard any negative comments anywhere in South Vietnam, including ARVN officers, about Ho Chi Minh.[*]

Quagmire was not a bad illustration of where we were at and what we were up against. And I think, probably, the most impressive thing I ever read about it was Barbara Tuchman's book about the great follies of international relationships. "Folly" is in the title.[†] I can't think of it right now, but she talks about the way in which Great Britain handled the American Revolution as a total folly, and the way in which we handled Vietnam as a total folly. And if I read her correctly, one of her priorities is that each nation must act in accordance with its own self-interest. Vietnam was not in our self-interest, and yet we poured our blood and our treasure into it. I came away with the highest respect for the troops and for the law of unintended consequences.

Q: What qualities did you respect them for?

Admiral Stevenson: I respected their courage; I respected the fact that, although there was little enthusiasm to be there, they did the job, and at the same time had an enormous willingness to give of their own money and of their own--God knows--little spare time they had, to fix up villes, to build chapels. For every jackass who would knock down a Vietnamese shrine, there'd be 100 guys willing to rebuild it.

Q: Were the Vietnamese people as skeptical about the Personal Response Program as they were about the man on the moon?

Admiral Stevenson: I don't know. I could read the Vietnamese people a lot better in Princeton than I could in Vietnam. You know, I could get them in categories when I was in Princeton. The Vietnamese people are a beautiful people. I really thought a great deal of all the Vietnamese people I dealt with.

---

[*] Ho Chi Minh, a Vietnamese revolutionary leader, served as President of North Vietnam from 1954 until his death in 1969.
[†] Barbara W. Tuchman, The March of Folly: from Troy to Vietnam (New York: Knopf, 1984).

There was a young officer--I think he was with CIA--I speculate. At least he could get me, when I needed to travel, on Air America. Anyway, I went with him one time to look over these CHIC areas.

Q: What's CHIC?

Admiral Stevenson: CHICs: combined holding/interrogation compounds or centers. As the personal response type, I was asked to give my two cents to the planning for a CHIC. My great contribution to it was that when they made a CHIC compound, that they should have it where there was flowing water, a river or something like that, because the Vietnamese who were in the CHIC would be better served if there was water immediately available to them and so forth.

Now, the CHIC thing, from my experience, was absolutely typical of Vietnam. There was going to be heavy combat in an area. Our leaders knew that. And, thank God, our leaders were concerned enough about the hearts and minds of the people that they wanted to get as many innocent people out of that area as possible. So under threat to their own lives, our guys loaded helicopters and went into an area, went into the villes, and rounded up mostly women and children--the men weren't around by this time--and we hauled them to safer ground in the helicopters. Of course, they didn't want to leave the ville, and they didn't want to leave their rice paddies, and they don't want to leave their hooches: "Where are we being taken?" ARVN officers came with our troops, and the ARVNs were yelling in Vietnamese, "Get in these helicopters for our own good."

"But, surely," the people thought, "leaving my village is not for my own good, and will I ever see my relatives gain, and what will happen to my ancestors?"

Anyway, they did get in all these noisy helicopters, with dust, flies, and everything, and they got hauled out of there to a CHIC area. It was a big, gigantic compound with hooches in it, surrounded by barbed wire.

Q: So they were treated essentially as prisoners?

Admiral Stevenson: Yes, hopefully to stop them from being slaughtered.

Q: Protective custody.

Admiral Stevenson: Protective custody. So how are you going to treat them while they're in the compound? What kind of food are you going to have there for them? Are you going to have running water for them? Are you going to try to indoctrinate or interrogate them why they're there?

Then, when the battle was over with, you tried to get them back to where they were from. But did you have a negative or positive impact on them?

Q: Did you have a Navy chain of command in this billet?

Admiral Stevenson: No. No, my chain of command was through the deputy chief of plans to the CG. Our CG was relieved halfway through my tour by General Nickerson.* And . . . [Laughter]

Q: Why do you laugh?

Admiral Stevenson: I didn't get to talk to General Nickerson very much. I just was remembering a funny story about when he first came to the III MAF compound. He made a tour of the compound, and he came to the chapel. Chaplain Radcliffe was escorting him around the chapel. It was just kind of an old Butler building. General Nickerson stopped in the chapel and pointed to the American flag, and said, "That's not the American flag. The American flag is red, white, and blue, and that flag is red, white, and blue, and gold." It had fringe around the edges, so the gold fringe was removed from the American flag. Fight a war and take the gold fringe off the flag. That's Nam!

Q: It that a church flag specialty?

---

* Lieutenant General Herman Nickerson, Jr., USMC.

Admiral Stevenson: I don't know. You see American flags with fringe on them, and one of General Nickerson's things was that there's no gold on the American flag.

Q: What was your day-to-day existence like in that job?

Admiral Stevenson: Well, I had a gunny with me, a great Marine named Gunny McEnroe. Six days a week we would teach the courses to Marines. We traveled all over I Corps and around.* I had a Jeep that Chaplain Otto Schneider had acquired. Let Otto tell the story about his acquiring this personal response Jeep. It had a sign on it, "III MAF Personal Response Jeep." I also flew and heloed all over.

Most places we went I did the driving, and Gunny McEnroe rode shotgun. Noncombatants don't carry guns! We used to run into this controversy every once in a while, you know, as to whether a chaplain should carry a gun or not, and so forth and so on.

Q: What was your position?

Admiral Stevenson: Well, I didn't join the outfit to shoot guns. If I read the Geneva Conventions correctly, I don't see how it would help a chaplain very much to have a weapon. I am opposed to chaplains carrying weapons.

Q: Were you concerned about your personal safety?

Admiral Stevenson: Yes, but funny at it seems, I'd have to say that the year in Vietnam, in that sense, was one of the calmest I ever had. I mean, when I slept in Vietnam, I slept very well. We got rocketed when I was in Saigon and rocketed in Danang, and shot at a couple

---

* South Vietnam was divided into four corps tactical zones. The northernmost was I Corps (pronounced eye). It ran from the demilitarized zone on the north, past Danang, and down to Quang Ngai Province at its southern limit. Included in it were Hue, Khe Sanh, Quang Tri, and Chulai. Because of their initial landing at Danang in 1965, the U.S. Marines operated largely in I Corps throughout the war.

of times. The closest I came to being hit was when we had a rocket hit the pavement outside our room at the BOQ there at III MAF. Luckily they had put a delayed fuze on it, so it made a beautiful hole in the asphalt. It threw asphalt and sand all through the BOQ. But it would have been a whole different story if it had been a impact explosion.

We had guys who used to collect shrapnel and stuff, but I was not into shrapnel collecting. I saw my share of black bags and sure wondered if the price was worth it. I didn't see as many as other chaplains did.

Q: Now that you've had more time to reflect on it, what are your thoughts about that price?

Admiral Stevenson: Oh, the price was a devastating price, not only because of the price in Vietnam, but the price we paid here in the United States. Vietnam was not in our self-interest. I'd say the whole thing was the greatest example of the law of unintended consequences that ever happened to the United States of America. We got in, and we couldn't figure how the hell to get out. Each President's ego or pride, or something, became totally tied up in how do you get out of this thing without being a quitter?

Q: Well, especially Johnson.[*]

Admiral Stevenson: Yes, and I voted for him.

Q: Did you counsel the young Marines on their mortality and what they were facing out there?

Admiral Stevenson: No, I counseled them on personal response and what was required if they were going to relate to people in simple society. The danger of not following the principles of personal response is that your time in Vietnam will be to no avail, because there won't be any relationships of worth between United States and the Vietnamese.

---

[*] Lyndon B. Johnson served as President of the United States from 22 November 1963 to 20 January 1969.

Q: Did you have interactions with the line Marines in which you tried to get them to think more like a chaplain and vice versa?

Admiral Stevenson: Constantly, and, in fact, one of the greatest Marines I ever knew in my life later became a chaplain, Bill Gibson.* He tells me that one of my lectures influenced him, and it was his second tour in Vietnam, and he already had a Purple Heart.

History is interesting. The ministry of reconciliation really had to take place in our own people--not between the Vietnamese and the troops. One of my daughters recently saw a movie about Vietnam, and she was telling us at lunch how horrible Vietnam was. I said, "Well, you know, a lot of noble things happened in Vietnam."

She said, "Oh, Dad, how can you make a statement like that?"

I said, "Well, because it did. I saw our Marines take care of people; I saw our Marines put their own lives in jeopardy; I saw some of our Marines give up their own lives to try to relate to people. What you saw in a movie was a negative aspect that the majority of Marines were desperately working against." I guess she was talking about the burning of a ville and so forth and so on.

It was funny to me to hear this from my daughter who was seven years old or something like that when I was there. But she said, "Well, Dad, what do you know about it?"

Q: She has the celluloid truth.

Admiral Stevenson: Her mom said, "Well, your dad was there for a year." That was kind of the end of the conversation. "Well, Dad, what do you know about it?"

So it's better that the historians try to piece that whole thing together. I think Barbara Tuchman did a pretty good job.

---

* This was Chaplain William H. Gibson, who in the 1990s is Dr. Gibson of the philosphy department at the Air Force Academy.

Q: Do you have some sort of emotional reaction about your own time there, your contribution, your value?

Admiral Stevenson: I don't know, Paul; it was a very sad part of my life, very frustrating. I can remember Chaplain Kelly was the Chief of Chaplains, and he came to Vietnam for Christmas. Billy Graham also came, and I did a little escorting, for a half a day.[*]

When the Chief of Chaplains came over, I had to give him a briefing on personal response. Part of my briefing was to tell the Chief of Chaplains that I did not think it ought to be a Chaplain Corps program. I remember Chaplain Kelly got up and walked out. That's enough of that.

Chaplain Kelly visited Vietnam every Christmas. He'd have a luncheon for religious news services on his return and tell them what he saw: how many chapels had been built; how many orphanages the Marines and Navy people were helping with. And they were. And then he came over to 'Nam, and this guy he had ordered in there as personal response with Marines was saying that chaplains should be doing chaplains' work and not this stuff.

It was a state of shock months later when I got orders to the Chief of Chaplains' staff. In fact, I was told I was to see Chaplain Lonergan when I was on R&R in Hawaii with my wife.[†] I gave up some of the precious four days to go up to Vinny Lonergan's office, where I was informed that I would be ordered to Quantico, to Marine Corps Educational Development, where I was to continue teaching personal response. For the one and only time in my career, Paul, I said to Chaplain Lonergan, "I don't care where the Chief of Chaplains orders me, but I just can't. I'm a chaplain, and I'm not going to continue teaching this thing."

After the time in Hawaii, I went back to Vietnam and kept working away at it, because it was my job to teach. I think I did a pretty good job of teaching and getting around.

---

[*] Billy Graham is an American evangelist, well-known for his television ministry and revival tours.
[†] R&R--rest and recreation.

Q: So you gave it a good-faith effort, even though you thought it was a misguided program.

Admiral Stevenson: I really tried to say it all in the end-of-tour report. I tried to be honest with my relief. My relief was an extremely talented and brilliant chaplain, Skip Vogel.[*] And Skip Vogel found it the same way.

Chaplain Below, who had been the senior chaplain at III MAF, was ordered to the Chief of Chaplains' staff, to the training desk and, lo and behold, I got my orders to go into Washington and work for Ralph Below on the training desk.

Q: What's your Billy Graham story?

Admiral Stevenson: Well, Chaplain Radcliffe assigned me to escort Billy Graham when he came to Danang. The troops recognized him, and he was great with the troops! It was Christmas morning. We started out by having breakfast with General Cushmam at his quarters: Billy Graham, General Cushman, the Chief of Chaplains, and Neil Stevenson. The breakfast conversation led us to realize that General Cushman was born on the 24th of December, Chaplain Kelly was born on the 25th of December, and Neil Stevenson was born on the 26th of December. I recall putting my foot in my mouth by saying that you have to hope people born around Christmas don't have messianic complexes.

Billy Graham was a very pleasant gentleman. What interested me from a clergy point of view was the fact that in his appearance he was similar to the Hollywood people who had come through to visit the troops.

Q: Did Graham seem sincere, or was this more a political-type visit?

Admiral Stevenson: No, I think the man was extremely sincere. I mean, from the world of entertainment, the troops wanted to see Bob Hope, and from the world of religion, they wanted to see Billy Graham.[†]

---

[*] Lieutenant Commander Leroy E. Vogel, CHC, USN.

Of course, Cardinal Cooke came every Christmas, too, and I had the privilege of traveling with him for about a day.* What do you say about Cardinal Cooke? He was very sincere, very devout, very interested in all the troops--not just the Catholics but in all the troops. And he was a man who certainly didn't have to put himself in harm's way by any means. Yet he would leave New York right after midnight Mass and come right over there to travel around and visit his priests who were in combat areas and say Mass for the troops. He was the military ordinariate at that time. Very impressive, very impressive man.

Q: Was Admiral Zumwalt's influence felt at all as the in-country commander?

Admiral Stevenson: Well, my counterpart in Saigon worked for Zumwalt, and from what feedback I received, Zumwalt was very much into personal response.† The personal response office in Saigon grew substantially in funding, and it was seen as one of the tools in the process of turning over LSTs and similar gear to the Vietnamese Navy.‡ One of the officers on his staff over there in Vietnam was Captain Rauch.§

Q: That was his cultural relations staff officer.

Admiral Stevenson: Yes, and they looked upon personal response as a vital tool.

Q: I talked to Rauch, and it's interesting, he was strictly mister nuclear propulsion and systems analysis before that, but he really got wholeheartedly into the human relations program.

---

† For many years comedian Bob Hope took music-and-comedy shows to American servicemen overseas.
* Terence J. Cooke became archbishop of New York in March 1968, following the death of Cardinal Francis J. Spellman. Archbishop Cooke was appointed a cardinal in 1969 and served in that capacity until his death in 1983.
† Vice Admiral Elmo R. Zumwalt, Jr., USN, served as Commander Naval Forces Vietnam/Chief of Naval Advisory Group Vietnam from 30 September 1968 to 14 May 1970.
‡ LSTs--tank landing ships.
§ Captain Charles F. Rauch, Jr., USN. His recollections of service on Admiral Zumwalt's staff are in the Naval Institute's oral history collection.

Admiral Stevenson: I remember visiting his office in Saigon, and his walls were filled with a PERT chart.* He was going to handle intercultural and human relations in a PERT fashion. And, of course, from my studies in the human-relations field, it's nice to have a PERT for building a ship, but human beings don't get modified by using a PERT. But for planning it'd be better to have one than not have one.

I did have dinner that night at Admiral Zumwalt's table. I don't recall any dinner conversation that was going to solve the problems that confronted us.

You know, I might mention that one of the things we dealt with in Personal Response that needed to be dealt with was culture shock. For the Marines to come into I Corps was always a culture shock. For me to make my monthly trip to Saigon was always culture shock.† It was on visits to Saigon that I got the sense of colonialism.

Q: How do you mean that?

Admiral Stevenson: Well, I suppose one of the things was that I'd go down there in fatigues. I'd get a hop out of Danang, go down to Saigon, and work my way into Saigon for these meetings at our naval headquarters there. I gave these briefings to CORDS, AID, and others.‡ I couldn't get into the officers' club, because I was in fatigues, so I couldn't get any lunch. Correspondents were sitting in the hotels that the Americans had taken over. You know, the whole Graham Greene thing came back. I can't think of Graham Greene's novel on Vietnam right at the moment, but the novel had reality in Saigon. Graham Greene really knew Vietnam.

I'd been up in I Corps with the Marines. Then I would go down there to Saigon, and they were going out to a cocktail party. At the party were American businessmen and their wives, and they had their kids with them. They had an American school set up. They conversed like colonialists. A lot of ironies, a lot of ironies.

---

* PERT--Program Evaluation Review Technique, a system of milestones for tracking the progress of a program against its schedule.
† The headquarters for Commander U.S. Naval Forces Vietnam was in Saigon.
‡ CORDS--Civil Operations and Revolutionary Development Support.

Q: Did you get the idea that Saigon was kind of like a fairyland?

Admiral Stevenson: Yes, and back at Danang airport, you'd go by a plane that was loading up black bags. Then you went past the Air Force chapel there at Danang, and it was an air-conditioned A-frame chapel with offices. Guys weren't even wearing fatigues. You know, you open the refrigerator and get out a couple Cokes. Here you were in little America. To go back to your own billet, you went through three or four Vietnamese villes.

Q: Where you could get shot.

Admiral Stevenson: Well, it wasn't just a matter of getting shot; it was a matter of the combination of the poverty of the ville and the village elder was trying to keep the nature of the ville intact. It was a simple society surrounded by these gigantic American facilities. Just seemed like a lot of inconsistencies.

Q: Well, one point that we haven't made explicitly and probably should is that with Zumwalt, you did have a line officer running the program instead of a chaplain type.

Admiral Stevenson: No, the Personal Response Program in Saigon was run by a chaplain, but it became more integrated by Captain Rauch and Zumwalt into their total program than it did with Marines. And, you know, and in some ways I guess it probably had more accommodation to the kinds of things they were trying to do with assets, because they were talking about turning over assets to the Vietnamese: "We're going to turn this ship over to the Vietnamese, so for the first nine months of its operation, half the crew is going to be American, and the other half is going to be Vietnamese

I guess that there was more of a pragmatic application of personal response principles in the kind of a setting that Admiral Zumwalt and Rauch saw and utilized. More so, maybe, than this business of living in the villes, which the CAP program had, because in the villes, we weren't turning over any assets. We weren't giving them any rifles; we weren't giving them any tanks.

Q: So it was more of a short-term objective.

Admiral Stevenson: I suppose. I suppose the goal of the Navy, personal response-wise and intercultural-wise, was the early trend of that silly expression, "the Vietnamization of the Vietnam War." In other words, the Navy was actually in the position in 1968-69 that we were now going to turn these assets over to the Vietnamese so the Vietnamese could totally take over the burden of the war. It was a very nice, idealistic goal. So who ended up with all the assets?

Q: North Vietnamese.

Admiral Stevenson: North Vietnamese, I guess. Helicopters and everything else. History says some of them were more like colonials than we were. Ironic.

Q: I get this interesting mental picture when you describe the PERT chart, its objective: "We're going to win 3.2% of the hearts and minds this week," or whatever.

Admiral Stevenson: That's a little harsh, but in order to get this ship from 10% Vietnamese crew to 100% Vietnamese crew within this period of time, we're going to have these many personal response lectures; we're going to have these many language training sessions. At this period of time we begin to change the signs in the ships to multi-language signs.

Q: Makes a lot of sense.

Admiral Stevenson: Yes, to a Western mind.

Q: Right.

Admiral Stevenson: But, at any rate, the Vietnamese lady still sits there for the briefing on the moon and asks, "Why did you do that?"

Q: Well, if you can agree on the objective, that is, the turnover, the more common ground you can establish, the better you can do it.

Admiral Stevenson: Sure.

Q: Any more to say on the religious aspects of your job?

Admiral Stevenson: No. I baptized men in Vietnam. I met and associated with a lot of Catholic priests, Catholic nuns--Vietnamese Catholic priests, Vietnamese Catholic nuns. I remember we chaplains were all impressed with the Buddhist leader in the Danang area--Tek Nebu. I always wondered what happened to Tek Nebu, because he was very much opposed to the North Vietnamese and the threat of Communism to Buddhism.

I was always interested years later, Paul, in the undercurrent that always went on with Vietnamese leaders concerning Cambodia. I got the feeling that no matter who won this thing, the loser was really going to be Cambodia. No matter which of the Vietnamese sides won, they were going to take their assets and move on Cambodia. It was a feeling I had, and there was no way to express it to anybody.

Q: Well, it has certainly proved to be true.

Admiral Stevenson: Yes, but I mean it's--whether you were able to communicate your feelings and your predictions, your thoughts when you were there, that's what was important, not the Monday morning quarterback business.

Q: Did you have any interaction with the news media people when you were in that job?

Admiral Stevenson: I avoided them like the plague, as you would read in my end-of-tour report. One of the things--and it may have had a negative impact on my doing my job--was that the Chaplain Corps did not need any publicity about the fact that chaplains were in the personal-response business. I really felt that that would have a very negative effect on the Chaplain Corps.

I was influenced by a situation that I had observed at Princeton before I went to Vietnam. When I went to Princeton, there were at least five Princeton students who were interested in joining the Chaplain Corps. Four of the five lost total interest in the Chaplain Corps when they read in The New York Times about the interview of the Chief of Chaplains who returned from Vietnam and expressed his hawkish views.

And I said to myself, the last thing in the world the Chief of Chaplains needs is this kind of publicity. The Chaplain Corps doesn't need it. So that probably influenced me. I didn't think it would do the Marines any good; I didn't think it would do the Chaplain Corps any good.

Q: Did it require much effort to avoid them?

Admiral Stevenson: I can tell you a sea story that I'm not so sure I want to tell. I have to think twice about it.

Q: I always enjoy that kind.

Admiral Stevenson: I know you do.

When I completed my tour and reported to Chaplain Kelly's staff, they'd occasionally ask me to give a briefing on personal response, and I'd give this negative view. Chaplain Kelly, God bless him, would really get ticked off at me. Several times he told me he was firing me. He had a way of doing it; he'd say, "Now, if I understand correctly, you're renting your house, right?"

And I'd say, "Yes, sir, I'm renting it."

And he'd say, "Well, that's good. Don't buy a house because you may not be here long." Lots of things like that on Chaplain Kelly.

In fact, Chaplain Kelly's such a good man and a man of such good heart that when I became Chief of Chaplains, he came to Washington to serve on a reserve board. He walked into my office, and he said, "All right, Stevenson, I've never the heard the whole briefing on personal response. I want to hear it now." So we had our own sense of humor over that over the years, but I'm sure I was a great irritation to Chaplain Kelly.

Q: Well, it says something about him that he was willing to put up with you.

Admiral Stevenson: Oh, sure. Well, let me tell you how he put up with me. Anyway, he had a chaplain on his staff whose expertise was in public relations, Wendell Begg.[*] Wendell Begg is a Woody Hayes in chaplain's clothing.[†] Good ball player.

Anyway, Wendell Begg set up the Chief of Chaplains' press conferences. Chinfo required that there be a rehearsal, and Wendell Begg had to find people to come in and play the role of reporters.[‡] He asked me if I would do it this one particular time, and I said, "Sure."

So they had this dress rehearsal over at the Marriott the day before the luncheon and press conference. Chaplain Kelly walked in, pointed at me, and said, "I'm not taking any questions from Chaplain Stevenson, and he's dismissed." And I was sent back to the office.

Q: Did you have to actively avoid the reporters in Vietnam?

Admiral Stevenson: No, not really, just avoided them.

Q: Any more to say to wrap up Vietnam?

---

[*] Commander Wendell R. Begg, CHC, USN.
[†] Woody Hayes, a fiery, outspoken individual, was for many years the head football coach at Ohio State University.
[‡] Chinfo--the standard abbreviation for the Navy's Chief of Information, who heads the Office of Information.

Admiral Stevenson: China Beach was a beautiful place. And I thought the chaplains were fabulous. I mean, what I saw chaplains do over there, I thought the chaplains did a damn good job, great job. Eli Takesian, Carl Auel, Jake Laboon--those guys were really with the troops.*

Q: Any specifics that you could cite about their achievements?

Admiral Stevenson: They knew how to be chaplains. They gave of themselves. And a lot of them did not favor the Vietnam War. Those were the guys I admired the most. Eli Takesian--a guy who was not in favor of our Vietnam policy--did two tours, putting his life on the line right with the troops the whole time, the Hue conflict and Tet. But the troops were there; their needs came first; who else is going to give them communion; who else is going to baptize them; who else is going to say prayers with them when they die?

I mean, those guys to me are a bunch of heroes. I observed a lot of positive things. I guess in wartime there's a lot of positive things to be seen; you know, people put their lives on the line for their buddies. The young men we had over there drafted into the Marine Corps, a lot of them, they really knocked themselves out for the Vietnamese people. Seabees working like hell 12 hours a day and then going over with the bulldozer to help a Vietnamese school for four or five hours at night with the lights on the bulldozers and things like that.

Q: What was your own view on our policy in Vietnam?

Admiral Stevenson: When I went over to Vietnam, I had spent my time in debates--not formal debates but conversations--at Princeton defending our government, defending our policies. And my basic rationale, Paul, was, "We elected these guys, and they are not

---

* Lieutenant Commander Eli Takesian, CHC, USN. Commander John F. Laboon, Jr., CHC, USN, had graduated from the Naval Academy in the class of 1944 and served as a line officer before becoming a chaplain. The guided missile destroyer Laboon (DDG-58) is named in his honor.

dummies. They know more about it than I do, so I think they must be making the best decisions they can make."

Q: Did your view change over the course of the year in Vietnam?

Admiral Stevenson: Oh, yes. I became one of those who said, "What does the President know? He only knows what he's briefed. Who's briefing him? If he came over here, what would he see, through whose eyes?"

There was a change for me. I began to realize that decision-makers are largely victims of what information they have. It's a lesson that never left me. I've made bad decisions when I've been in positions of leadership. And I've tried to remind people who are around me that I'm like everybody else. (I assume that our senior decision-makers have the same problem.) You must make a decision in a certain amount of time, based on the information you have. When I got to be Chief of Chaplains and Deputy Chief of Chaplains, I used to tell the staff, "I'm in a position of making decisions, and I'm trying to make decisions on the best information I have. That's based on what you guys give me. I'm as dependent on you as you're dependent on me, and that chaplain in the field is dependent on us."

Q: Well, you finished up your assignment in Vietnam and came back to the States. What sort of job did you get into after you had been banished to this nether world from the Quantico assignment you turned down?

Admiral Stevenson: Well, I reported to the training division, J-14, on the Chief of Chaplains' staff. I thought the billet description was strange. It had been written prior to Chaplain Ralph Below going to Washington. I knew and trusted Ralph Below, so I figured when I got to Washington, Ralph would know what this was all about. The job description had to do with the development of an increased "spirituality" for chaplains. Well, it's not easy to define "spirituality." Besides that, the faith group that provides the chaplain deals with the chaplain's spirituality. The Chaplain Corps should enhance the chaplain's ability to do his or her job through continuing education, but spirituality is something else. In Greek and Hebrew, "spirit" can also mean "wind." I think the Chaplain Corps was demonstrating the fact that it hadn't made a clear division of labor between church responsibilities and Chaplain Corps responsibilities.

Another illustration of this was that Chaplain Kelly wanted any chaplains' annual professional development training courses to be in the area of evangelism. Well, of course, evangelism, which might well emphasize proselytizing, is not overly applicable to the military environment.

Q: Was there a perception by some group in the Chaplain Corps that there was a shortage of spirituality?

Admiral Stevenson: I think it was several things: a reaction to the swing toward using the behavioral sciences in the practice of ministry; uncritical thinking that the Chaplain Corps was a mini-church unto itself; and thinking about the parish instead of institutional ministry.

Q: How did you go about attacking the job once you were in it?

Admiral Stevenson: Well, I reported in, and Chaplain Vinny Lonergan had become the executive director of the chaplains division. (That billet eventually became officially the deputy's billet in 1980.) I greatly admired Chaplain Lonergan. Chaplain Ralph Below had taken over the training desk. Chaplain Jude Senieur, a brilliant Capuchin priest, and I worked for Ralph.

Anyway, Ralph agreed that the job description was unworkable in a Chaplain Corps of a pluralistic Navy. So with Vinny and Ralph we began to revise the training division, asking these questions: "What kind of training should chaplains have? How do chaplains get training?"

Q: I wonder, Admiral, how specific you got in these training programs. Did you get to the point of saying where individuals would go for training, or did you deal more in terms of groups?

Admiral Stevenson: It was a matter of trying to get the right people to the right course, and to be as fair as possible in distribution. There was a phobia in San Diego that because of their distance from Washington, that the San Diego guys wouldn't get as many opportunities as those in Norfolk. We had to deal with the reality of very false perceptions. I served for the first time on a selection board. I served on the PG selection board.

Q: Was there a perception among these individual chaplains that you were influencing their future careers by what schools they got to go to, or didn't get to go to?

Admiral Stevenson: Yes. Usually, if selected, they would have a preference, and we would try to work that out.

Because of this "spirituality," they sent me to a variety of things TAD, to look in on this church conference and that conference.* I went to many things that the Chief of Chaplains thought might be applicable to the Chaplain Corps, and then I would come back. Chaplain Kelly would say, "Well, you know, I have it on good authority from a wonderful preacher friend on the 'Lutheran Hour,' Oswald Hoffman, that this is a good thing.

Well, I'd go, and it would be a good thing. But I'd have to say to the Chief of Chaplains, "But it's only a good thing for the fundamentalists, or it's only a good thing for people of this ilk. The Chaplain Corps has got to be aware of pluralism." A lot of my Princeton stuff was feeding in on me at that time. You know, if you have the training courses based on Christo-centric materials, what do you do with your Jewish chaplain?

Q: But that's the Navy way--standardization.

---

* TAD--temporary additional duty.

Admiral Stevenson: But religion doesn't get standardized. You got to start with the religion of the sailor, not religion of the chaplain.

Anyway, Ralph Below was very supportive and backed me. In 1969 I was at one of these conferences, and I came up with the idea, "You know what happens in the Chaplain Corps is that some people get intense training, but there's no training across the board. There's no training that every chaplain shares. Why couldn't we send out, like once a quarter, training materials that all chaplains would receive?"

So I came back from that trip all excited and enthusiastic about this thing. And Ralph, being Ralph, said, "Why don't you work that up?" Then a friend showed me a cassette tape that he had received that had academic material. That was then a new thing. So I said to myself, "That's what we could do. Instead of chaplains going somewhere to hear a lecture, we can tape a lecture and send it out to all the chaplains, and everybody in the Chaplain Corps will get to hear the same lecture."

I was selling this concept to Ralph Below, and Jude Senieur was getting interested in it, because Jude was fabulous at working out the mechanics of stuff. So we decided that we should try a trial run. To make a long story short, I found out that Hans Kuhn, German Catholic theologian, was going to be at Princeton. And I found out that Langdon Gilkey was going to be at Pittsburgh Theological Seminary for a lecture. These were top theologians.

We wrote to Hans Kuhn and Langdon Gilkey, and we made appointments. Jude, being Catholic, went and got an interview with Hans Kuhn, and I, being Protestant, went to Pittsburgh and got an interview with Langdon Gilkey, which he gave me at 6:00 o'clock in the morning. Basically, we were asking questions about what was over the horizon in theology, what would happen with the ecumenical movement, etc.

Honest to God, Hans Kuhn and Langdon Gilkey were just as gracious as could be. Jude and I got back to Washington and duplicated a couple of tapes, and put a packet of materials together of articles from journals. We'd received permission to reprint the ones that were copyrighted. After we had done this, we said, "Now, see, once a quarter we can compile this material, tape, and all and send out a packet to update every chaplain on professional subjects. Wherever he is, the chaplain can listen to Langdon Gilkey and Hans

Kuhn, as well as read the enclosures. If he doesn't like it, he can throw it overboard; if he likes it, he can save it. It'll help his homilies." Gee, we really thought we had invented the wheel.

But now to do this you had to have money, and to get money you had to get the Chief of Chaplains to concur. I made the presentation, and Chaplain Kelly was not impressed. But Jude said, "Chaplain Kelly, take this tape home tonight."

Chaplain Kelly came in the next day. He still wasn't impressed. He said something very humorous. He said, "You know, the one guy even has a German accent." We thought we'd pulled the coup of a lifetime, one of the great Catholic theologians of our age, and we were getting a down because he had a German accent.

The next day Jude came in with a big smile on his face, and he said, "The professional training packet will be a go."

I said, "The chief's already turned it down." So Jude gave me a note that said, "KYMS." That stands for, "Keep your mouth shut." So I went with him when he briefed Chaplain Kelly. Jude said, "Chief, I was thinking about the professional training packet. It's really a good idea." He said, "But there's a major thing about it that we left out that we should have thought about and we want to apologize. We just weren't thinking."

The chief asked him what it was, and he said, "Well, the most important part of any packet would be a message from the Chief of Chaplains. Every chaplain in the Chaplain Corps, no matter where he is, would have his ministry positively affected by a message from the Chief of Chaplains." And we walked out of there with the chief's blessing.

We got our first packet out by staying till midnight, walking around tables with a box. You know, filling the box. We had had a printer make a stick-on label that said "Chaplain Corps Professional Packet," and so forth. We pasted this on top of the thing. We did the whole operation personally and by hand.

It had mixed reviews from the chaplains. We found out that when chaplains get a packet, they are more likely to say, "Why send me this article?" instead of saying what we thought they would say: "This is of no interest to me; I'll throw it in the circular file." Then if they found an article of interest to them, they would enjoy it and retain it. We got as many negative responses as we got positive responses.

While on that trip to Pittsburgh to interview Langdon Gilkey, I met a man named Frank Bates, who was setting up a professional tape cassette, clergy education outfit called Thesis Tapes. We arranged a contract with Thesis. But Thesis Tapes was too Protestant minded, so Jude and I had to tell Thesis Tapes every once in a while, "Hey, you've got to go interview this Catholic; you've got to go interview this Jewish rabbi. We've got to have a more pluralistic approach." In fact, I wish the Chaplain Corps were back into it today, but the Reagan administration knocked out the business of buying cassette tapes and other audio-visuals.* Irony--the Hollywood stars administration devalued audio-visuals.

The Chaplain Corps Planning Group had developed what the Chaplain Corps calls the advanced course for senior chaplains at the Chaplains School in Newport, Rhode Island. With the coming of a new Chief of Chaplains, Frank Garrett, it was time to get the advanced course under the training department.† That's a long story full of personality frictions, etc., but we in J-14 had the privilege of making the advanced course secure.

Q: What do you mean by secure? Was there a problem with it?

Admiral Stevenson: It had started out as an innovative idea: "Don't we need to expand the chaplain school to update chaplains in mid-career? Don't we need something besides the basic course the chaplains get as indoctrination when they come into the Navy? Don't we need to train chaplains to make the transition from chaplain to supervisor?" But in those days it had been a 22-week experimental course, and was ready to be changed into a nine-month course with better funding lines, etc. CNET was coming into existence.‡ It was a bit of a three-ring circus, which is always kind of fun to work in, if you come up with solutions.

Chaplain Below got orders to the naval air station at Brunswick, Maine. Much to my amazement and my delight, Chaplain Garrett was kind enough to let me relieve Ralph

---

* Ronald W. Reagan served as President of the United States from 20 January 1981 to 20 January 1989. His term in office ended a few months before this interview.
† Rear Admiral Francis L. Garrett, CHC, USN, served as the Navy's Chief of Chaplains from July 1970 to June 1975. His oral history is in the series conducted by the Navy's Chaplain Corps.
‡ Previously, the Bureau of Naval Personnel had administered education and training. In the early 1970s the Navy established a separate command, Chief of Naval Education and Training (CNET).

Below as head of the training branch. Jude Senieur and I worked together in the training branch from '69 to July of '72. It was a great experience working with Jude. The usual frustrations and things, but working with Jude, getting things done, planning training, preparing BuPers instructions, putting out the professional packet, etc.*

Q: Did the receptivity for that packet go up after a period of time?

Admiral Stevenson: Yes. When we started out with the cassettes, we received a half a dozen letters from chaplains who said things like, "I held the cassette to my ear for two days and never heard anything because I don't have a cassette player." You always get that kind of stuff from certain types of people. But I think most chaplains just appreciated the fact that the chaplain we were targeting with information was sitting in a destroyer on deployment. You can't take books with you, and 99% of your conversations deal with other people's professions. You get very little catalyst regarding your own profession. Chaplain Garrett made good use of the tapes to get the word out to the Chaplain Corps too.

And then we had kind of worn out our welcome, as you do sometimes in Washington. We had done about what we were going to get done, so it was time to move on. Chaplain Senieur was delighted. He got a set of orders to Miramar in San Diego, where he was longing to go and get back into the work of a chapel. The word I received was that there was going to be a six-month delay between his orders and my orders for the sake of continuity. But when Chaplain Hilferty reported in July, I think it was, he said, well, no, the word he had was that we were both leaving, and so it turned out we were both leaving.†

I was bold enough to go to Chaplain Garrett and say, "Well, you know, if I'm leaving, I would like to go to the advanced course. Most of my peers have already been through the advanced course, and I haven't." I think Chaplain Garrett and the detailers didn't feel that anybody from the staff should or needed to go through the advanced course, for a variety of reasons. But, thanks to Chaplain Garrett, I did get those orders.

---

* BuPers--Bureau of Naval Personnel.
† Commander Thomas J. Hilferty, CHC, USN.

Q: How did you go about promoting the money for these various programs?

Admiral Stevenson: Oh, I'm glad you mentioned that, because that was another very important part of my education. And I did have one other story I was going to tell you about.

When Chaplain Hutcheson had the training desk, he came up with the idea that a couple of chaplains ought to experience Navy Postgraduate School, Monterey, California.* Two chaplains had gone to the PG program at Monterey, one in fiscal management and the other in personnel management: Chaplain Jim Ammons and Chaplain Gene O'Brien.† They reported to the staff just about the time Chaplain Kelly retired. Chaplain Ammons walked into the office and informed us that the Chaplain Corps lived under paternalism. BuPers had a certain amount of money, and they provided some money to the Chief of Chaplains, and the Chief of Chaplains said thank you. The Chief of Chaplains' main concern was travel money: "How am I going to see my chaplains? I need travel money."

Jim Ammons, who was a brilliant guy, came in and said to the Chief of Chaplains, "PPBS."‡ And all the chaplains said, "No speaka the language. We don't know what you're talking about."

Chaplain Jim Ammons had very specific goals and ideas to turn the Chief of Chaplains' office away from paternalism into a legitimate place in the world of the Navy's planning, programming, and budgeting system. And, by golly, he did it. We listened to him and said, "Hey, this guy knows what he's talking about." And Jim would show us how to submit a budget, etc. He knew how to carry it up to higher authority on the basis of planned program budgeting. And that was a great education for me. It was also my introduction to the difference between personnel and manpower. It was when I joined the

---

* Captain Richard G. Hutcheson, Jr., CHC, USN. The oral history of Hutcheson, who retired as a rear admiral, is in the series conducted by the Navy's Chaplain Corps.
† Lieutenant Commander James E. Ammons, Jr., CHC, USN. Lieutenant Commander Eugene C. O'Brien, CHC, USN.
‡ PPBS--Planing, Programming and Budgeting System, which was started in January 1961 by Secretary of Defense Robert S. McNamara. For details, see Gordon G. Riggle, "Looking to the Long Run," U.S. Naval Institute Proceedings, September 1980, pages 60-65.

club of "young Turks" saying things like, "We ought to be part of the POM process. We ought to have a submission. We ought to inventory billets, etc."[*]

Q: What effect did that have on the Chaplain Corps's relationship with BuPers?

Admiral Stevenson: That empire was closing down a little bit in those days. We used to work directly with the people in Pers C, who were in charge of education and training. And the Navy was changing its system around to develop an education and training system--CNET in Pensacola--that was somewhat like the Air Force setup. We were beginning to realize that our paternalism, which came from the people upstairs in Pers C, wasn't going to continue. Paternalism, you can't justify anything. So Jim Ammons and I had to go down to Pensacola every once in a while and brief down there to get money, etc.

Q: So it was a real education process.

Admiral Stevenson: Yes. It was a big education process--like Princeton, like studying under Sam Blizzard, like listening to Jim Ammons. All of that gives you the experience on which you build your decision-making process when you get future breaks to come back in the office. And when you're a verbal young Turk, you know, and you say, "Well, what the Chaplain Corps ought to be doing is such-and-such and such-and-such." You know, there are people who overhear you. Then, years later, people like John O'Connor call you up, and they call your bluff. And they say, "Okay, Stevenson, you always used to say this ought to happen. Now I'm going to bring you into Washington, and you can make it happen."[†]

I was going to tell you about one incident in those days. You know, we had a chaplain who gained an awful lot of publicity, that I'm sure he didn't want, over a court-martial in Florida.

Q: Chaplain Jensen.

---

[*] POM--program objectives memorandum, an element of the budgeting process.
[†] Rear Admiral John J. O'Connor, CHC, USN, served as the Navy's Chief of Chaplains from July 1975 to June 1979.

Admiral Stevenson: Chaplain Jensen.* When the Jensen court-martial was over with, it was important that he get a set of orders out of the command. Chaplain Garrett was our Chief of Chaplains, and to show how things worked in those days, Chaplain Garrett called me in. I think Ralph Below had just left, and I'd just taken over the training branch. Chaplain Garrett said, "I think it's very important that Chaplain Jensen get out of that area, and he wants to go to graduate school. So arrange for him to go to PG school."

The PG slots had all been taken and assigned, and I explained all that to Chaplain Garrett. Chaplain Garrett looked at me very graciously with his blue eyes and said, "I have given you an assignment, and I expect it to be carried out." So I went up to Pers C and talked with our friends there. They sympathized and came up with an additional PG billet from out of the thin air, in terms of paternalism. I then phoned Princeton Theological Seminary, and I spoke to the president, Dr. McCord. I explained who I was and that I had graduated in '68, etc. I said to Dr. McCord that he may have read in the papers about this situation. And I stated that the Chief of Chaplains wanted this chaplain, who was freed of all charges, to be able to have the break of a year of graduate work. We would prefer for the sake of the man and his family and the Chaplain Corps, that there be no publicity. Would Princeton accept him?

Dr. McCord said, "Chaplain Stevenson, if the Navy wishes to send Chaplain Jensen to Princeton Theological Seminary, we will be happy to receive him. We know from our other chaplains that we won't have any academic problems about it." I went back that afternoon to Chaplain Garrett. I had the money and had the billet and told the detailer to go ahead and order him to Princeton.

Q: I would guess that there were both some pluses and minuses on each side of the ledger--on the paternalism side and on the PPBS side. Could you discuss those, please?

---

* Commander Andrew F. Jensen, Jr., CHC, USN, was accused of adultery while serving at Jacksonville Naval Air Station in the early 1970s. He was court-martialed and acquitted, then reassigned. He told his story in the book The Trial of Chaplain Jensen (New York: Arbor House, 1974), reviewed in U.S. Naval Institute Proceedings, December 1974, pages 95-96.

Admiral Stevenson: Well, what eventually became my motto was that paternalism is a good thing as long as you've done your homework. I mean, to use the old school analogy, to get a grade from your teacher because the teacher likes you, is, in and of itself, illegitimate. But if you really have studied and learned, and you can justify in the tests your competence, and in addition to that, your prof likes you, it's to your advantage. Right?

Another principle was established in those days, which, I think, continues--and it was established because of the guys who were young Turks, including Jim Ammons and others, was, "We are not going to lie. We are not going to ask for $10,000 because we need $5,000." I mean, there is that game, and there's a great temptation to get into that game. But in the long run, I think the game backfires on a lot of people. What we thought we had to do was establish the kind of integrity that says, you know, they're still chaplains, and they're not going to take clerical advantage, because in the naval service, there ought not be a 10% clergy discount.

Do your work and know the system, not because it's the Navy system, but because you are Navy; it's your system. There was a mentality in those days that the chaplains ought to be different from the system because the clergy are different, or some such thing. Just a bunch of nonsense. I mean, if you're part of the system, you've got to work the system. If there is some paternalism, fine, but it shouldn't be illegitimate paternalism.

Q: Do you think that the Chaplain Corps has been better served by making the change?

Admiral Stevenson: Oh, yes. I don't think there's any question about it. And I think the thing that's important is it's not the Chaplain Corps that's better served. I think it's the troops that are better served. I think the Chaplain Corps is in a better position by following the Navy system and knowing how to work the Navy system. It's in a better position to really relate to the rest of the Navy and relate to the personnel of the Navy. Oh, I don't think there's any comparison.

Q: Because the first P in all that is planning, did that bring the planning and training shops closer together?

Admiral Stevenson: Yes, and the planning shop eventually disappeared because, you see, now you're saying you've got to bring planning in the door of the chief's office. You can't have it on the other end of town--over at the Washington Navy Yard. You've got to bring planning and programming and budgeting right into the chief's shop. You can't have a separate entity doing that. And maybe that was part of the evolutionary plan that was in the minds of Joe Tubbs, Eddie Hemphill, and Joe Dimino to begin with. But that's how it eventually evolved because Chaplain John O'Connor came in, who was well versed in PPBS. When he came as Chief of Chaplains, he wanted that at his fingertips, in his office.

Q: Did the increase in the chief's role in the administrative side diminish him in the leadership or spiritual side in any sense?

Admiral Stevenson: Not in my opinion.

Q: Well, I would just think from the span of attention point of view, you've got to allocate your time differently.

Admiral Stevenson: Yes, but one of my pet peeves was that up until that time the emphasis of the Chief of Chaplains all had to do with detailing. Detailing had almost gotten to the point of gossip. The whole Chaplain Corps kind of went around asking, "Who's getting ordered where?" as though that were the central job of the Chief of Chaplains. And that's only one part of the Chief of Chaplains' responsibility.

In terms of planning, the issue of where the Chaplain Corps has to go in order to meet the needs of the next generation of sailors and Marines is always different than it was for the last generation of sea service personnel. You know, you've heard me saying I was in three different navies in 30 years. I really was, as far as I'm concerned. And if the Chief of Chaplains can't justify his budget in the Washington level, how can the local chaplain justify his budget in the command? Those things just had to become a natural part of the whole process: How many billets does the Chaplain Corps need? How do you justify those billets? That's all part of the system. You can be paternalized to a few billets forever.

If you don't have your justification, the manpower types will wipe you out overnight. I mean to an aviator, the most juicy billet to delete is the chaplain's billet, right? Because all he wants is aviators until the crash and funeral. So in order for the Chaplain Corps to stay alive, you've got to have honest data on how many billets you need, and you've got to have honest data on what kind of money it takes to provide the kinds of programs that affect the lives of personnel and their dependents in different kinds of environments--sea environment, overseas environment, CONUS environment, recruit training environment, etc. And you can't make believe that that's not all a part of doing exactly what chaplains are all about. It has a direct impact on ministry or not ministry. "Spirituality" won't do it!

Q: Well, how much role does the chief have then as a leader, a spiritual leader, in the sense that, say, a pope does?

Admiral Stevenson: Well, I think the Chief of Chaplains can set a tone in the practice of his or her own faith. He's not a pope. In fact, the chaplains he influences are under command authority. One of our Chiefs of Chaplains one time, when I was a rookie, made the statement that when he became Chief of Chaplains he wanted to be a pastor to pastors. That's a nice sentiment, but it's very illegitimate.

I can be Chief of Chaplains to a rabbi and to a Catholic priest, and to a Methodist, and to a Lutheran, but I can never be a bishop. I think the Chief of Chaplains makes a tremendous mistake when he allows people to think of the Chief of Chaplains in ecclesiastical terms. In fact, any chaplain in any supervisory role must supervise and not be a pastor to pastors. If he does, he compromises his primary job.

Q: Well, there's a little psychological twist to it, though, in that you've got a hierarchical structure in the rank system as the church does.

Admiral Stevenson: Yes, but not for life. Not for life, and not over ecclesiastical things. Don't ever mix Navy with your denominational or anyone's faith polity.

The Chief of Chaplains' desire is to have the right chaplain in the right billet--a chaplain who recognizes the environment of that command and provides the kind of ministry that meets the needs of service personnel in that environment. The institutional ministry is great in and of itself. It is not parish ministry. The biggest mistake a chaplain can make is to go through his career with the mentality that he is just a parish minister in uniform. Because Navy chaplains are not. Their job is in institutional ministry to a pluralistic, not a parochial environment.

In August of 1972, I went to the advanced course in Newport, Rhode Island, and that was a great nine months of settling down after working the kind of hours you work in Washington. At Newport I was going to school, having time for library reading, writing some papers, basically on my own interest of things regarding impact of myth on ministry, and listening to a lot of good lectures, and going through a lot of exercises and psycho-dynamic stuff, fellowship with other guys in the class, particularly with a chaplain we had from the Royal Australian Navy, named Wally Long. Dealing with a lot of the behavioral stuff: some of it was good; some of it was junk. Deciding what really applied to the Chaplain Corps and what didn't.

The senior two chaplains at the advanced course in those days were Chaplain Joe Tubbs and Chaplain Joe Dimino, whom I've already mentioned. Both of them had been down at the planning group in Washington, and I served with Joe in the USS _Saratoga_. It was a great nine months.

Q: When you were still back in Washington, did the winding down of the Navy's involvement in Vietnam have an impact on your planning and programming?

Admiral Stevenson: Well, in those days the dominant section of the office was the detailing section. The Chief of Chaplains' office has now moved toward the balance of manpower having as much dominance as personnel, which was very important. I can get into that a little later with Chaplain O'Connor.

Neil M. Stevenson #4 - 161

The Chaplain Corps had billets in those days that were unfunded, billets in excess.

Q: How did that happen?

Admiral Stevenson: <u>Bad paternalism</u>. History may show that the entire Navy was poorly managed from a manpower perspective in those years.

And, again, we suffered a Chaplain Corps myth. Chaplains talked as if billets were associated by faith group--Catholics, Protestants, and Jews. But all these billets are neutral and not identified by faith code or anything like that, <u>and ought not be</u>.

Q: Any other thoughts on the school period? Did it fulfill the expectations you had when you asked for it?

Admiral Stevenson: I'd have to say I not only learned a lot in the advanced course, but I would say two things happened for me personally. I think some of my Vietnam stuff got resolved.

Q: What do you mean by that?

Admiral Stevenson: Oh, I got away totally from anybody even talking about personal response. That subject used to come up every once in a while in Washington. It didn't come up at the advanced course. This was now 1973 when we were graduating and beginning to move.

I sometimes think I caused a problem for Chaplain Garrett. At Princeton I had studied under Sam Blizzard a great deal about collegiality. And collegiality is a good management tool for an organization like the Chaplain Corps, in contrast to other professional role models. Unfortunately, I did not define it in the restrictive terms it needs to be defined in the model that we had worked at Princeton.

Collegiality became a very popular term within the Chaplain Corps. But the sad thing about it was that collegiality had the connotation of "we're all together here and hugging, and we're all nice guys," and so forth. People interpreted collegiality as if it did not have an authority system connected with it, or an accountability connected with it. And, of course, true collegiality is very authoritarian. I mean, the college professor works for the department head, and the department head works for the academic dean, etc. So there is a structure. It became kind of the thought of many chaplains that collegiality meant that the Chaplain Corps did not have an authoritarian structure in it. This mixed signal made for much frustration.

Q: Anything more about the school?

Admiral Stevenson: No, I'm glad the school still exists, and I hope the chaplains that are there today get as much professionalism out of it as I felt I got out of it.

Q: Thank you for another good session, Admiral.

Admiral Stevenson: Okay.

Neil M. Stevenson #5 - 163

Interview Number 5 with Rear Admiral Neil M. Stevenson, Chaplain Corps, U.S. Navy (Retired)

Place: Emmanuel Presbyterian Church, McLean, Virginia

Date: Tuesday, 18 September 1989

Interviewer: Paul Stillwell

Q: When we met the last time, Admiral, you talked about entering the chaplains' advanced course in Newport. Your next assignment was down in Orlando, Florida. What was your role there?

Admiral Stevenson: I was very fortunate there. At first I was told that I was going to receive orders and be the senior chaplain at Quonset Point.[*] We liked New England, so we were pretty excited about that. In fact, we went over one Sunday to Quonset Point to chapel services. The chaplain there at that time was Chaplain R. Q. Jones.[†] They showed us where the quarters were, so we were all set for that.

A few weeks later I got a call from Washington that said that Chaplain Garrett had decided that I should go down to Naval Training Center Orlando, Florida, and relieve Chaplain Rodger Hill, who had decided he was going to retire.[‡] That was also very exciting news.

Incidentally, I had been selected for captain while I was in the advanced course, and that's a cute story. The day that I was selected for captain just happened to be the day on which they had planned a golfing activity for the afternoon for everybody in advanced course, including the faculty. So I called Diane and told her that I was bringing Wally Long, an Australian chaplain, and Frank Urbano, a Catholic chaplain, home for lunch, so I could tell Diane that I had made four stripes.[§] We raced around, and I bought Diane a

---

[*] Quonset Point, Rhode Island, was the site of a naval air station near Newport. The air station closed in the early 1970s.
[†] Captain Robert Q. Jones, CHC, USN.
[‡] Captain Rodger F. Hill, CHC, USN.
[§] Commander Francis J. Urbano, CHC, USN.

dozen roses, etc. When we were having lunch, Frank said to Diane, "Did you buy him his eagles?"

Diane said, "What eagles?"

Frank said, "He's supposed to wear eagles now."

She looked at me, and she said, "Don't you still wear those little bars?" Somehow, she'd lost the sequence of the oak leaves in there. Our family loved the Navy life but was not altogether that conscious of the symbols of rank.

Q: In contrast to some Navy families.

Admiral Stevenson: Well, we were a very Navy family, but it was just not one of those things that Diane kept very close track of.

Anyhow, we were delighted I had made captain, and we felt for the first time in our lives that we might buy a house. We went down to Orlando, where we found a big house, and we bought it. And that was a mistake. It was a wonderful house, and we got it at a good price. The only problem was when I got ordered out of there three years later, we could hardly sell the thing; we lost money on it. But I think a lot of Navy families have experienced that kind of thing.

I was delighted to be the senior chaplain of a chaplains department. It was that old story: "Now I've had these years of experience, and I've had this training at the advanced course, and I think I know what I want to do." This will probably seem silly to a lot of people, but somewhere along the line--and I don't remember when, Paul--I had started a thing I called an "if book." I don't know if I still have it around the house or not. Anyway, it was one of those old Navy green journals. And I actually used to write in that things that if I became the senior chaplain at a naval air station, these are things I would like to do. If I became the senior chaplain in an NTC, these are the kinds of things I'd like to do.* So I had my if book, and it went all through my career with me. I had it in Hawaii and used to write, "If I get ordered to Washington, these are the things I want to try to do," and so forth. So I always had some kind of a game plan out there.

---
* NTC--naval training center.

As I probably told you, the advanced course, I thought, was fabulous, great experience. And so now I was going to Orlando. And during the first three months I was there, Rodger Hill would be the senior chaplain, which was great. Rodger was a chaplain with a great background and reputation, one of the kindest gentlemen we ever had in the Chaplain Corps. He'd been a naval aviator in World War II, and in 1973 he had decided it was time for him to retire. So I went down, and I had two or two and a half months in which to observe everything in the chaplains department and be involved in things.

Q: Were the things in your if book radical departures, in any sense, from the way it had been done?

Admiral Stevenson: Well, I think it shook up some chaplains and line officers.

Q: What were some of the things on that agenda?

Admiral Stevenson: Well, they would go from things like using the system of developing a planning book within the chaplains department, so that everybody in the chaplains department was aware of what everybody else was doing, and who had specific responsibilities for what programs. Giving those programs dollar values so that we could request appropriate budget from command--that kind of thing.

One of the first meetings I went to kind of set the tone. It's kind of a silly story, but it will be all right. Rodger loved the sense of informality, kind of, "Get around the coffee pot, guys." So one of the first days I was there they had a staff meeting around the coffee pot. And there was a great emphasis--an incorrect emphasis, I think--that the spirit of "collegiality" was a spirit of non-accountability. In other words, that we all like each other so much, and our relationships--what the behavioral science called "maintenance"--were so high on our agenda that tasking diminished.

Q: Was there a sense of military hierarchy in all this?

Admiral Stevenson: No, there was a sense of not having a military hierarchy. And that's why I say it's a misinterpretation of collegiality, because collegiality has its authoritative system, that is, the department head may not be any better scientist than the other scientists in the science department, but he is responsible for scheduling and he is responsible to the academic dean. Collegiality has clear lines of authority. And I think the emphasis on maintenance had diminished the recognition that there does have to be authority. We are accountable--the senior chaplain is accountable to the executive officer, etc.

Q: How large a group was this?

Admiral Stevenson: About 13 chaplains. I think they had billets for nine, and they had four chaplains in excess.

Q: Were there things that were not getting done that should have?

Admiral Stevenson: Well, I'll give you a typical example. As we met, Rodger said, "Well now, I still have three worship services for next Sunday that I don't have anyone assigned to. Now, who would like to take one of those services?" [Laughter] Nobody volunteered to take those services. I must admit that I was not impressed with the fact that this sort of family gathering was not providing any volunteers to do the family chores. So--again, this is really part of a sense of humor--it ended up that when the meeting was over with and we were on the way back up to the office, Rodger said, in typical Rodger fashion, "Well, which one would you like of those three?"

I said, "I'll take any of them."

He said, "Well, I'll take this one and that one, and you take the other one." So I ended up with one of them, and Rodger--typical Rodger fashion--ended up with two, which meant he probably had three that day. But Rodger was the great example of the Christian heart that said, "Nobody else will do it; I'll do it."

Q: I suspect it was a handicap for you, having to try to impose a sense of discipline after that kind of regime.

Admiral Stevenson: But I had been to the advanced course, and I had my own ways about me. And I had been there long enough now that I recognized the variety of chaplains that made up the chaplains department. It's one thing to think about being a supervisory chaplain, and then it's another thing to be a supervisory chaplain. And there are basically two types of supervisory chaplains. There's what I call the autovon supervisory chaplain; that's the guy who sits miles and miles away from everybody, and he communicates with them mostly by autovon.* That's relatively easy in some ways compared with the supervisory chaplain who has to live with the team.

When you're a supervisory chaplain, you're basically the playing manager. There's a couple of disasters there. One is that you can end up in the Chaplain Corps with senior chaplains who stop playing ball. They just want to be the manager in the dugout. I don't see how you do that as a professional person. If you're not in the ball game, I don't give you much credit. So you've got to be a playing manager, which means that when you make an error, you're still the manager. And if you make a good play, you're still the manager. But you've got to be on the playing field.

I'm sure that my approach was an annoyance, and I'm sure there were plenty of chaplains willing to say, "Oh, Lord, here he comes with his advanced course stuff and brand-new stripes, and he'll drive us up the wall." But my intent was also to rectify a situation in which the command was not formally aware of the contribution that the chaplains department was capable of making to the overall command.

Q: Why was that?

Admiral Stevenson: Because over the years senior chaplains, I think, had a habit of more or less just indicating that the chaplains department was made up of good chaplains, and they

---

* Autovon (automatic voice network) is a term for telephone communication within the Department of Defense.

were doing their thing, but it wasn't a coordinated effort. There were no measuring tools as to performance. It was hard to quantify what any particular chaplain did or did not do. And there was sort of a relationship between command and senior chaplain that said, "Well, chaplain, you run your chaplains. I'm a nice guy, and I'll leave you alone."

Q: Benign neglect.

Admiral Stevenson: Yes, but even a paternalistic command found it difficult to understand that a chaplains department would ask for a specific slice of budget. In my day, rarely did the senior chaplain brief command on what the chaplains intended to do and seek command approval on whether or not they had made appropriate goals for the chaplains' performance. Now we were in a new environment, thanks to Joe Dimino, Joe Tubbs, Eddie Hemphill, and a bunch of people who had started this advanced course. Then I ended up in Orlando and said, "Hey, here's my opportunity to put this kind of program into motion."

Q: What were the functions that had to be carried out by this group of 13?

Admiral Stevenson: That was also a delight, because Orlando was the closest thing to a religious three-ring circus that you could ever have. Orlando was a relatively new base with old and new facilities, so lots of opportunity. We had chaplains involved in four basic areas: (1) chaplains in the recruit training command; (2) chaplains in the schools command, which before I left there involved also the nuclear school, although those were two separate commands; (3) chaplains at the center, which was the AdCom environment; (4) chaplains at the McCoy housing area. We took over the old Air Force chapel to set up a dependent-oriented chapel program with Sunday schools and CCD, etc.[*]

Q: Were there things that you needed from command that you felt you weren't getting?

Admiral Stevenson: Oh, a whole shopping list.

---

[*] AdCom--administratige command; CCD--Confraternity of Christian Doctrine.

Q: Such as?

Admiral Stevenson: Well, let me tell you how we got there first. It'd be easier to identify the things that way.

Another piece of good fortune was that in those days NTC Orlando was different from the other NTCs in the fact that in Great Lakes and San Diego the chaplains were under the administrative command. In Orlando there was no administrative command at that time. So the chaplains were directly under Naval Training Center. That was an advantage. I know they changed it over the years, because they want all the naval training centers to all look alike and so the chaplains are under the AdCom down at Orlando now.[*] But under the leadership of Captain Gillooly, who was the NTC commander and had his hands on for that operation, I thought it was a good way to run it.[†]

Q: So this meant you had one less layer to go through?

Admiral Stevenson: Absolutely. So I was directly under NTC, as were my chaplains, although we had them divided up into the four areas.

Okay, well, the easy way to get to this was the first thing that had to be done, which was to try to get the chaplains department together so that everybody in the department would recognize what our overall programs ought to be. By the way, every supervisory chaplain has to realize that he's the coach of a high school football team. He is not the coach of a college football team.

Q: How do you make that distinction?

Admiral Stevenson: It's a big distinction. In college ball, you have been out working scholarships, and you've been out trying to recruit specific ball players for specific positions

---

[*] In the mid-1990s, several years after this interview, the recruit training centers at San Diego and Orlando were closed, and all recruit training concentrated at Great Lakes, Illinois.
[†] Captain John F. Gillooly, USN.

and so on. But if you're a high school coach, you inherit the kids that are in the high school. Everybody knows the 11 positions in football, and those 11 positions have to be filled by the kids you've got. So you put into playing halfback and quarterback the guys that you think will best do those jobs. And the guy or the gal may not be a natural halfback, or a natural quarterback, or a natural tackle, but that's the one that you have to use. You just can't sit around saying, "Well, Washington didn't give me the tackle I needed."

Q: Did you meet some resentment?

Admiral Stevenson: Oh, sure. You meet resentment--and for a whole variety of reasons. First of all, this is new; second of all, I'm not so sure a Presbyterian can really coach a Catholic, or vice versa. Or, "You mean to tell me I've been passed over twice, and you were selected because you're now going to tell me how to play this position?" All those dynamics, all those human dimensions are all part of this thing. And in a degree they are the frustrations of it, which some people walk away from.

On the other side of the coin, I mean, that's what it's all about. For me that's the excitement. Okay, now let's see if this team can win games.

Q: What sort of psychological gimmicks did you use to make a team?

Admiral Stevenson: Well, I don't know that I was that attuned, myself, to playing psychological games. I would say my approach was basically skull sessions and education and saying, "This is what we want to derive." But at the same time I tried to maintain some sense of maintenance.

I'm laughing because I think you ought to interview the chaplains who were there in the department. They might tell you that from time to time Stevenson was certainly the son of a bricklayer when it came to getting some things done.

Thanks to the advanced course, to Princeton, and to being around Washington, the way in which I tried to do it was that I asked command to give me some time to get the chaplains all together, kind of pull them off the line for a couple of days. I gave the chaplains the task of coming together and putting together a workbook, a planning book, as we called it, that would identify for command everything that the chaplains did or ought to be doing. By working together to build the planning book, we started building some true collegiality within the chaplains department. We started identifying those things that needed to be done no matter who was in the job. What are we going to call these things? How are we going to program them? What kind of budget do we need in order to do these things?

Q: Well, there was one of your gimmicks right there--letting them participate in the laying-out of tasks.

Admiral Stevenson: It was a form of participatory management, but I think they also knew that Neil already had in his head a direction that he wanted to go. It's like getting together with the coach, but the coach has already decided that you're going to use the T formation.

But they came around. They already had a lot of things in place that they were doing, but they had not been necessarily identified by name or defined programmatically within a planning book. The things that were in the planning book would give you an idea of what we had to put together. We created a mission for the chaplains department that indicated we were part of a training command. We needed a table of contents for the planning book, which came down from what our mission was. And we had an agreement among the chaplains as to what our mission was. I think there were 27-some programs.

The first program was, of course, divine services and all the implications of that. How much funding do you need for musicians, particularly in recruit training command where you have these contemporary worship services? How many program dollars do you need for guitars, and so forth, for 18 year olds, who come to recruit training and all want to play the guitar in the contemporary worship service? (They were already doing contemporary worship when I got there.) So all the programs in each of the areas: Sunday school, CCD for down at McCoy, music program down at McCoy--how much do you need for money for schools command sailors to go on a retreat some weekend to get a break from the schools command environment and go with some chaplains out to the beach on weekend retreat? All those kinds of things came out of it.

We separated the <u>programs</u> from the <u>duties</u>. Programs were things you needed money for; duties were assignments that we had to stand--chaplains were going to stand the duty. The understanding that I had with my chaplains was that the chaplains rotated in standing the duty. As the senior chaplain, I was on call at all times, particularly when any of the commands could not find the duty chaplain.

Q: When you took over this football team, did you find, perhaps, that your best quarterback had been in a tackle slot and that you needed to make some switches?

Admiral Stevenson: Yes, but there were some that it was obvious you just weren't going to be able to switch, because they were locked in. They were programmed where they were, and you weren't going to be able to switch them.

Q: Well, you had a situation there that doesn't exist in a lot of commands. You've got recruits who are obviously new; they're away from home; they probably need more hand-holding than most sailors. Did you have a special contingent for dealing with that problem?

Admiral Stevenson: We did, and they were very good. We also learned a lesson that all senior chaplains need to deal with. Shipboard duty is essential. The chaplains may have had sea duty with Seabees, or they may have had sea duty with Marines, but if they have not had duty in a ship command, they really cannot be as effective in the recruit training environment as they ought. The Navy is trying to prepare this recruit to really respond to seagoing life.

Q: Was BuPers aware of this useful attribute in recruit-training chaplains?

Admiral Stevenson: They were, but you still ended up with chaplains reporting in who had come there and had not had shipboard experience, and that was a tough thing to get around. I had at one time three or four such chaplains. I actually called a friend of mine who was a commodore of a destroyer squadron up in Mayport, Florida. I asked him to arrange a tour of his ships for these chaplains. I hauled them all the way up to Mayport and had them go through ships from bilges to signal bridges, to living quarters, to try to impress upon them what sea duty was. I think it helped, but it was not the solution. The solution is you've got to live under a command at sea in order to know what the recruit training command is trying to do.

Q: You have to balance the needs of the individual with the needs of the ship and the service.

Admiral Stevenson: Right. And that's what recruit training is all about.

And so here you have the chaplain in a position where he can easily misunderstand the homesickness of a recruit, or the immaturity of a recruit, the academic deficiencies of a recruit who's got to go through remedial studies, whether he wants to go through remedial studies or not in order to meet the requirements of sea duty. If that chaplain is overly sympathetic to the recruit, then the chaplain conveys to the recruit the feeling that he is really being mistreated by his company commander.

Well, the Navy's not interested in anybody being mistreated by their company commander, but it takes a chaplain with some experience to know the difference between a recruit who's overreacting to his environment and one who is going through the culture shock that's basically required in order to make a sailor out of him. If you go through any Navy training without some culture shock, then probably the training didn't take.

Q: Or else you went through it in an earlier stage before you got there.

Admiral Stevenson: Yes. But that culture shock is an element that's required. You've got to have a chaplain who's been through some culture shock himself. I guess, also, Paul, in a larger sense it is very difficult for the Congress and others to appreciate that recruit training for Navy is so different than recruit training for Air Force and Army. The Army and the Air

Force are training people to live on land, while the Navy in a land situation is trying to train people to accept the sea environment. And that's difficult to do.

It might be better if the Navy had an element of recruit training that was actually in some old carrier. But, you know, the shock of suddenly realizing, "Hey, there's no land around. I cannot go to a shopping center. There's no gedunk available."* I don't know that we can ever really do that recruit training in terra firma.

Q: To go back to an earlier question, did you perceive some things that needed to be done that weren't being done?

Admiral Stevenson: Yes.

Q: What were those?

Admiral Stevenson: Well, for instance, to establish our divine service schedule on a quarterly basis. You can't come around on Wednesday afternoon and say, "Okay, who's going to take what service on Sunday?" We needed to firm ourselves up in all those kinds of things. From that time forth we did all our planning on a quarterly basis.

Some chaplains complained, "Well, this is impossible because maybe 13 weeks from now I want to go on leave."

My response to that was, "Fine. We have no objection to anybody ever putting in for leave, but we have our design, and if you put in for leave or if you get sick, then we'll make our contingency, and somebody else will take that divine service. But as of now you are assigned these divine services throughout these 13 weeks." So there'd be no question about anything.

Another thing that we needed was a specific time in recruit training in which a majority of chaplains would be available to recruits. So we paralleled the time of sick call with chaplains' call. In other words, instead of recruits asking company commanders at 3:00 o'clock in the afternoon, "Can I go see the chaplain?" or something like that, why not

---

* Gedunk is a Navy slang term for candy, ice cream, and sodas--snack-type food.

help the company commander and help ourselves and help the recruit by saying, "Fine, from 7:30 to 8:30 in the morning there is chaplains' call, and there will be enough chaplains there to see the numbers of recruits who show up in the chapel to get that taken care of." Recruits come to the chaplain--as the chaplains have to be reminded themselves--with non-religious problems.

You know, one of the nice things about being a chaplain, Paul, although it's one of the things that the coach has to constantly remind the team of, is that there isn't anybody who comes to the chaplain whom the chaplain can't help. I always remember a recruit who came to see me one morning at chaplains' call, and the kid had blisters on his feet. Now, why did he come to see the chaplain? Well, he came to see the chaplain because, first of all, he was scared of the company commander. He was afraid that if the company commander found out he had blisters on his feet, the company commander would call him a tenderfoot, which is what he was. He had the wrong size boots. He didn't want to go to medical, because he'd heard about other people who went to medical, and medical set them back. So instead of getting out of recruit training in nine weeks, the guy would be around for 12 weeks. He's looking forward to going home in uniform, showing off to his girlfriend that he's out of recruit training. So what's his alternative? He's anxious, so he comes and sees the chaplain. The chaplain's something of a father figure or a mother figure. And the chaplain convinces him, "Okay, you need to get to medical."

That is a training point for chaplains. We would be constantly fighting the chaplain who said to the recruit, "No use of you seeing me, go to medical." Well, that doesn't help the recruit, and that doesn't help the chaplain too much, because we haven't made an <u>authorized referral within the system</u>. So one of the things that we were constantly trying to emphasize with the chaplains was, "Let's use the Navy system; let's have an authorized referral system; let's get either the chaplain or the chaplain's clerk to make an appointment in medical for this recruit; let's provide this recruit with a chit, a copy to medical, a copy to the company commander, and a copy that is maintained in the chaplain's office that says that in the chaplain's opinion this recruit does need to go to medical. An appointment has to be made for him at such and such a time. A copy of that memo also went to the executive officer of recruit training command. That way the XO of the recruit training command knew that the chaplain was making a valuable contribution to the whole business of recruit training. By the way, "copy to" is a great tool in any organization.

Q: Well, another situation that undoubtedly came up: you've got the guy who's looking forward to going home in uniform and seeing his girlfriend, but before he can do that, he gets the "Dear John" letter. How do you deal with that?

Admiral Stevenson: Well, sympathetically, hopefully. You get that; you also got the person who came in and said, "I haven't gotten a 'Dear John' letter. I've gotten a letter that tells me that my fiancée is pregnant, so we want to get married as soon as I get out of recruit training," or, "Can I go home right now and let us get married?" And, in some cases, "There are requirements for premarital religious counseling that I have to have in order to get married in the church at home. Can I get those while I'm in recruit training?" Chaplains can provide or facilitate such arrangements.

But homesickness is the toughest one, probably, to deal with, because it is a sickness, and it is debilitating.

Q: What are the remedies?

Admiral Stevenson: Well, I think the remedy is to motivate the person to get outside himself. You might use the expectations that the parents have; this is an opportunity to be proving oneself. You have to remember that recruit training in those days was probably made up of more young men and women who were not high school graduates than today's Navy. Today's Navy is different. I was in Orlando at the time in which the government was debating the giving up of the draft.[*] So we still had that kind of recruit.

But I would say it's basic motivational skills. Trying to get the individual to gain some self-awareness, and to realize how important it was for the individual at that time to succeed. Of course, the majority of the ones who came to you with homesickness were

---

[*] In 1972 the Defense Department announced it would end draft calls in mid-1973. Secretary of Defense Melvin Laird announced on 27 January 1973 that the use of the military draft had ended as of then, several months prior to plan.

people who already had a record of flunking high school. And you try to motivate them to realize, "Hey, you've already started a tendency to fail. You've got to stop it somewhere, and this is the place to stop it. Otherwise, you're going to really have just a habit of failing."

Q: One advantage you've got is that there are probably very few totally new problems. You get an experience base in what works in various situations.

Admiral Stevenson: And that's where you're fighting the boredom of counseling. You've got to fight to make sure that the recruit who comes in is seen as a person whose name you want to learn--not a number. And you want to avoid the cheap shots that a sleepy chaplain early in the morning might be tempted to fall and say, you know, "You're the sixth guy who's come in with this ridiculous story, and you're all a bunch of crooks."

One of the things that comes back to mind, Paul, with the--I hadn't thought about it in a long time--is that we had a couple of chaplains who were sharp enough to say, "Let's group some of these people. Let's group the six who showed up with homesickness this morning; let's put them in a group, and let's get the chaplain to play them one against the other. And let them start motivating each other, and let them recognize in some other recruit the very thing that they're expressing."

Someone might say, "My recruiter twisted my arm unfairly, or I wouldn't be here." Finally, one of the other ones speaks up and says, "Oh, that's baloney. I was going to use that line, and, you know, he really didn't. I wanted to get out of high school, and I twisted my parents' arm to sign the papers, and here I am."

Q: I interviewed a recruiter a while back, and I quoted to him the classic line, "My recruiter lied to me."

He said, "Maybe so, maybe not, because recruits have a tendency to hear what they want to hear and not necessarily what the recruiter said."[*]

---

[*] This is in the Naval Institute oral history of Rear Admiral Jackson K. Parker, USN (Ret.), who was a recruiter during his enlisted service, prior to being commissioned.

Admiral Stevenson: Well, the advertising of anything--you know, you choose your vacation based on the advertisement, and then when you get there it's not quite that way. I wouldn't put it past the recruiter to say, "Well, you know, I can get you to Orlando, and that's where Disney World is." The fact that the recruit only gets one day of liberty to go to Orlando to go to Disney World is another story from what he may have had in mind.

Q: Well, I guess a Navy chaplain in that situation needs to have a healthy blend of both sympathy and cynicism.

Admiral Stevenson: I guess. And not to allow his own personality to dominate the whole situation but to try to have some genuine sympathy for what it's like to be 17 or 18 years old, first time away from home, first time you're thrown into a structured environment.

Q: How big a part did religion per se play in that command?

Admiral Stevenson: Well, in Recruit Training Command in Orlando, it has, fortunately, had a major part. I guess Fred Brink was the first senior chaplain down there.* Eddie Hemphill was the third to be the senior chaplain down there. And I think it was probably during Eddie Hemphill's time that they started the contemporary worship service.

One of the things we needed to do also was identify different kinds of worship services, so that the recruit, in an age of non-compulsory chapel attendance, would want to seek out worship on Sundays, and receive from that worship those things which met the needs of the recruits. There's only one kind of Mass, but we advertised two kinds of Mass. Okay? We advertised contemporary Mass, and we advertised traditional Mass. All these titles came out of putting the planning book together in order to describe for command and to advertise to recruits what we were doing.

On the Protestant side of the house, we had liturgical Protestant services, which would catch the eye of an Episcopalian or Lutheran, who wanted to go to a sacramentally oriented worship service. We had contemporary worship service, which was what caught

---

* Captain Frederick F. Brink, CHC, USN.

the eye of the majority of the recruits. The majority of them came to the contemporary Mass and contemporary Protestant services.

Q: How would you explain that?

Admiral Stevenson: How to explain that? That was the opportunity for two chaplains to take a worship service and make it contemporary in the eyes of the chaplains. In other words, instead of giving a sermon, let's get the recruit drama team to write a play about the Scripture and to act out in simple dialogue that portion of Scripture. Then, instead of having organ music for the hymns, have more contemporary hymns or songs. And have a rock band, sort of, with an organ in the middle of it, and guitars and drums, occasionally a saxophone player or trumpet or something. Take all these talented kids who come through, try to get them involved in this program, and let them, with costumes and bands and music, put together a worship service based on a Scriptural theme, more in the mode of what they were about from 1973 to 1975.

In the main, it worked very well, and it worked well for a lot of reasons. One major factor was that the Navy had brought female recruit training down to Orlando. So we did have women recruits as well as men recruits. And that worked rather well.

We also had to maintain certain rigidity, though. We had some chaplains who said, "Well, you know, the recruit training has come together. We need to combine them in worship." And we had to learn that you cannot really allow 18-year-old recruits not to be sectioned off in the chapel for contemporary worship. We had a couple of chaplains who had to learn that passing the peace in normal worship services, and allowing the passing of the peace in 18 year olds who have been in a very structured environment for a whole week, doesn't always work, because there are those who will take advantage of the situation.[*]

You know, all those kinds of lessons. We had some extremely talented chaplains there who were great with working with drama and color, and audio-visuals. All those things that we thought would not only attract recruits' attention, but also would lower the tension level, we were all in favor of.

---

[*] "Passing the peace" involves greeting fellow worshipers, including handshakes and, sometimes, hugs.

Q: Recruit training is necessarily very rigid and ritualistic, so I can see the appeal of a church service that was not also very rigid and ritualistic.

Admiral Stevenson: We also had gospel services for the more evangelical Protestants--more of the hymn-singing, revival-type of environment.

We tried to offer titles for worship that recruits would feel comfortable. And once a month we established a program in the recruit chapel so that the recruits could be introduced to a cultural program. We hired the Rollins College drama group to put on the play Godspell one Sunday afternoon, and it was interesting. We discovered that the majority of the recruits had never seen a Broadway-type production.

And we also had a disaster one Sunday afternoon. We had the chaplains taking turns in being responsible for these afternoon programs. And Chaplain Pohlman, who was the first female chaplain, had come from a highly educated and cultural background.[*] She had, of course, never had any sea duty or shipboard duty. And she felt, for instance, that the recruits would be bettered by having an afternoon program of Bach. So she had the Orlando Bach Chorale, which she and her husband belonged to, come out and perform for the recruits on a Sunday afternoon.

Interesting phenomenon, Paul--first of all, these things were announced in all chapel services and so forth, so recruits were aware that on that one Sunday afternoon the opportunity existed for them. In this case the majority of the recruits didn't hear the words "Bach concert," but had thought they heard the words "rock concert." The chapel was packed, and the chapel held between 800 and 1,000 recruits, and the concert began. I was there, because I was very worried about what the reaction would be. About a dozen or more recruits got up and walked out during the first number. The senior usher came to me and said something like, "Don't worry, sir, we'll stop them from leaving."

I said, "No, no, no! Let the ones who want to leave, leave." You know, I was a little worried about crowd control. Interesting thing, at the end of the first number, the

---

[*] Lieutenant Florence Dianna Pohlman, CHC, USNR, was the first woman to be commissioned as a chaplain in any of the U.S. armed services. A portrait of her appeared on the cover of the October 1974 issue of U.S. Naval Institute Proceedings.

recruits handled it pretty well themselves, because they greeted it by clapping like this [slow clap-clap].

Q: Very unenthusiastic.

Admiral Stevenson: Very unenthusiastic. Now, the conductor was a wise man. He got the message, and he immediately turned around to the microphone and said, "I realize that most of you don't know about Johann Sebastian Bach." So he said, "Let me tell you a couple things about Johann Sebastian Bach." And he told them a little history, and so forth, which was very good--how this man was a genius in music, and so on and so forth. And he said, "Now, what we're going to do, just so you can appreciate what Bach did, we're going to sing one more number and that's all we're going to sing." And turned around and led the group in one number, and the recruits sat there and listened to it. And then they gave him a legitimate applause.

If that man had not been attuned to his audience, it really could have been a disaster. But, again, see, Chaplain Pohlman was trying to take the environment she had come from--college, seminary, Bach--she was a musician who said, "Hey, these recruits are 17-and 18-year-old kids. They haven't been invited into that world. And they need to." You just can't get there from here.

Q: Well, I can see your role as a psychologist in this. You could have told her it wouldn't work, but it wouldn't have had the impact as letting her see it didn't work.

Admiral Stevenson: Well, I think I could have told Dianna it wasn't going to work, and it wouldn't have made much difference. She'd do it, anyhow. But, anyway.

Q: What else do you recall about her?

Admiral Stevenson: Well, Dianna was an extremely attractive young lady and well educated. So the Chaplain Corps recruited well in selecting her to be the first female chaplain. She graduated from Princeton Theological Seminary. Chaplain Garrett felt that the best place for her to begin her ministry was in a recruit training environment, so she received orders to Orlando.

She went to chaplain school, and the basic course was under the leadership of Chaplain Chuck Greenwood, whose record in the Chaplain Corps was absolutely outstanding: former aviator, Naval Academy graduate.[*] Chuck and I were old friends from my first tour of duty, and his first tour of duty as a chaplain. I got to talk to Chuck several times about Chaplain Pohlman, and he was worried. Some of Chuck's concerns were that she had been in and out of class quite a bit, because she had had publicity, notoriety, about her being the first chaplain. She'd been on TV quiz shows, etc. He felt that she had not gotten as much out of the basic course as maybe she should have.

Second thing was that he was somewhat concerned--because Chuck was very sensitive to the women's liberation movement--that she was not as well versed in that as she might have been. But by the time she got to Orlando, she felt that she was highly versed. And, lo and behold, right after she had graduated and become ordained in the church and commissioned in the United States Navy, she met a Presbyterian pastor, and they fell in love. Right after chaplain school she got married, and her husband was a minister whose experience was parish experience, not institutional experience. So I think she really thought largely in terms--and I'm sure it was reinforced at home with her husband--of parish ministry within a Presbyterian church, rather than the Navy world of getting recruits ready for sea. Dianna had a tough time and in some cases, the chaplains had a tough time with Dianna. She decided after three years in Orlando that the Navy way was not her way.

Q: Well, coach, how did you go about playing this new team member while she was there?

Admiral Stevenson: Well, we tried to have a lot of skull sessions; they didn't all take.

Q: Did things improve as you went along?

---

[*] Captain Charles L. Greenwood, CHC, USN. Greenwood was in the Naval Academy's class of 1950. He retired as a captain in 1982 after serving as the senior chaplain of the Naval Academy, 1979-82.

Admiral Stevenson: I think things improved somewhat, but I think Dianna was very uncomfortable with being a Navy chaplain. I think she really wanted a civilian parish situation. She and her husband, both being Presbyterian clergy, sought a parish together where they could minister as husband and wife.

There are some people who are made to do institutional ministry. There are other people who should only be in parish ministry, and then there are some people, who, perhaps, can do both environments. Just as there are some people who probably do well in missionary work, and others who do not do well.

Q: Would you explain that by saying that some people are better suited than others as chaplains?

Admiral Stevenson: Well, I think almost all chaplains come out of seminary trained for parish duty. And when they come into the Navy, they're coming into an institutional environment. I don't think that we were always as attuned as we ought to be, that there is an environmental impact that needs to be dealt with. And it needs to be dealt with openly and honestly. Some people need to say, "This is for me," or "This is not for me."

Let me step out of the ministry for a minute. You know, everybody thinks it's very legitimate for a medical doctor to come into the Navy. And during the first tour of duty in the Navy, this physician has to work at sort of a force field analysis of pros and cons as to whether or not he is comfortable practicing medicine in the Navy. The doctor may say to himself, "I like the idea of standing the duty with other physicians. I like the collegiality of other physicians," so forth and so on. "And I don't want to go out and practice and fight the insurance bills, and so forth and so on, so institutional medicine satisfies me and I enjoy doing it."

Another physician could say, "I don't like the pharmacy limiting the drugs that I'm going to prescribe. I don't like having a senior medical officer over me," etc., etc. "I'm going out into private practice. I can make more money there anyway," and so forth. Well, they make an honest, clear decision. Now, put a chaplain in that same situation. A chaplain should be making those same kinds of decisions. I was trained for parish ministry. I really like the support of people in my own parish. I'm such a Presbyterian that I really don't want to have Baptists and Lutherans and everybody else in the chapel that I have to be aware of. If I'm a Presbyterian pastor, hardly anybody's ever come to see me except a Presbyterian, or somebody who has been in a Presbyterian church. So I don't feel that I can meet the needs of a Muslim, or a Jewish person, etc., etc.

But, you see, if I'm a Navy chaplain, I'm doing institutional ministry, and in institutional ministry I have equal requirements, not only to provide for the people of my own faith, but to meet the needs of persons of other faiths. If I'm not comfortable doing that, then I'm a disaster in institutional ministry. If I don't recognize the fact that a chapel is a chapel, not a church, I'll be a disaster.

Let me give you the standard illustration. If a couple comes to be married in the chapel, and they do not meet the requirements of my faith group to be married, I can't tell them that they can't be married in the chapel. In institutional ministry, it's my job to direct them to where their needs will be met, where they could find the person to officiate at their wedding, and to see that their wedding is properly scheduled at the chapel.

If you cannot adjust your profession, or enhance your professional outlook to meet that kind of challenge, you shouldn't be in institutional ministry.

Q: When you were senior chaplain, did Chaplain Pohlman and perhaps some of the others come to you and say, "But, Captain, with due respect, the world has changed since you became a naval chaplain."?

Admiral Stevenson: Oh, yes. Lots of dialogue.

Q: Did you make adjustments?

Admiral Stevenson: Oh, I think I made some adjustments, but I doubt that many people in the chaplains department thought that old Stevenson made too many adjustments.

Q: What ones do you remember making?

Admiral Stevenson: Well, I made some adjustments in my own background in contemporary worship. Contemporary worship was not the most comfortable thing for me. I worked in it; I enjoyed the work I had in it. I learned a lot from it. But we did have a few chaplains who asked not to get involved in contemporary worship.

I have a funny story about that. I had a chaplain who was of an evangelical background, and he was very uncomfortable in contemporary worship services. He came to me and said he wanted out of contemporary worship services. I asked why, and he said because the music was non-theological. I said okay. A couple weeks later he went on leave, and he wanted to know who was going to take over the gospel services. And I said, "I will."

He said, "Well, I don't think that you know how to lead those services."

I said, "I think I'm adaptable." And I said, "I can do that. What is involved?"

And he said, "Well, you know, it's a free spirit type of worship service. You have to ask people to pray; you don't do all the praying. They pray. The choir sings." He said, "We have a special song book."

I said, "I know. We've ordered the song book."

He said, "They call out the numbers that they want to sing."

And I said, "I know. Have a sing-along, things like that."

He said, "Yeah."

So I said, "I've handled this before. I think I can do it." It wasn't until I was involved in the worship service that it really struck me how humorous the circumstances were. Here I was, standing in front of a group of recruits, and singing, "Climb, Climb Up Sunshine Mountain. The Heavenly Breezes Blow." Well, Paul, that's about as non-theological music as exists.

Q: When Admiral Zumwalt was the CNO, he had set the Navy on its ear.[*] Were there impacts from that at the Orlando level?

Admiral Stevenson: I think perhaps Captain Gillooly was there as the commander of Naval Training Command because of that. Orlando was one of the places where we were experimenting with the training. For instance, in schools command there was a great deal of self-paced learning. There was the coming together of both male and female recruit training in the one environment. Recruit training for women had come down from Bainbridge, Maryland, to be part of one RTC. I think our contemporary worship services in recruit training were part of the accommodation of that era.

There was a classic thing that happened when Captain Bill Fisher was the commanding officer of recruit training--an outstanding commanding officer.[†] He realized that different terms had been used in the training of male and female recruits. For years company commanders who led male recruits "pushed" the recruits. It was a common expression. Female company commanders said that they "carried" their recruits. I really thought that was a fabulous designation between the way in which male and female recruits were handled. It expressed the roles that their company commanders adopted. Bill Fisher got the company commanders all together and said, "From now on company commanders must lead." He changed not just the words but the approach.

Q: Did the racial awareness training get involved in your area at all?

Admiral Stevenson: The racial issue was very high priority in those days. It was a very sensitive subject--very hard to change some of those racial tendencies. Sailors who had joined our Navy in the Philippines were being given an opportunity to get into all the ratings of the Navy, not just stewards. Things had to be changed, because we were moving from the time of the draft to the time of volunteer services.

---

[*] Admiral Elmo R. Zumwalt, Jr., USN, served as Chief of Naval Operations from 1 July 1970 to 29 June 1974. He introduced a great many social changes to the Navy during his tenure.
[†] Captain William G. Fisher, Jr., USN.

Q: Some of the people who had been in the Navy for a while resisted this training. Was that as much a problem for the new recruits who hadn't been through the previous setup?

Admiral Stevenson: No. It was not, but it was a problem for getting the right people to teach them.

Q: Was that part of your responsibility?

Admiral Stevenson: No, I would not say that. I had a minor part of it. But, you know, when you talk about these kinds of sensitivities, let me give you an illustration of sensitivity. I reported in and was told a chaplain in the chaplains department had volunteered to be in charge of the annual prayer breakfast. It was held at the hospital mess, and 100 to 150 people attended this prayer breakfast, including Captain Gillooly and other commanding officers. I went and sat next to the chaplain in my department who had made the arrangements. The speaker, who was invited by the chaplain for the command, came from a very evangelical, Christian background. He led us in a half-hour revival. I was embarrassed. But I had been in the Navy long enough that I knew what to do. I went immediately from breakfast to the commanding officer's office. I thought it'd be best for me to get there before he called for me. I went in, and Captain Gillooly said, "Well, Neil, I'm embarrassed."

I said, "Yes, sir, I'm embarrassed too. It won't happen again."

I was somewhat surprised to find out from my chaplains that this format was sort of a standard operating procedure for a prayer breakfast. It's amazing how insensitive one can be to a pluralistic environment. For the annual prayer breakfast the next year, we invited a rabbi to speak to us. The rabbi spoke about his own escape as a child from Nazi Germany. It was much more appropriate for a pluralistic setting, but even then, some of the "real Christians" complained.

It's interesting how religious people are insensitive to other people's religions. Again, part of institutional ministry is part of the Navy's becoming aware of the pluralism.

How much of the WASP Navy had a negative effect on Rickover?[*] How did that play out in Rickover's career and impact? How much of an impact did the WASP Navy assumption that the Navy was an Anglo-Saxon Protestant organization have on the chapel situation at the Naval Academy? I understand there wasn't even a Catholic chaplain assigned until the 1940s.[†] Or where there was never a senior chaplain who was a Catholic until John O'Connor in the 1970s. So it's not just a matter of our society and our Navy and Marine Corps recognizing needed changes over the years in the racial things, but also of chaplains understanding their requirements to be sensitive to the religious needs of all.

I don't have the facts, but I think Chaplain Merle Young's tour as senior chaplain at the Naval Academy was shortened in the '50s because he did not want midshipmen to be forced to use the Episcopal prayer book.[‡] You know, was it an Episcopal chapel or a Navy chapel?

Let me tell you one other story about contemporary worship. We had a call one day from a retired chaplain who was in his 70s. I forget his name, but he called, and he said he and his wife had heard about contemporary worship services at Orlando, and would it be permissible for them to attend the service? I said, "Of course," and I escorted them to the service. I also alerted the two chaplains who were in charge of the part of the Protestant contemporary service for that day that these guests would be there. When the service was all over with, the chaplains, feeling that they were very much with it were somewhat taken back when the long-retired chaplain's wife--a beautiful, white-haired, old lady--said, "Oh, I enjoyed the worship service. It reminded me so much of what we did in Chautauqua when I was a child."[§] What comes around goes around.

---

[*] Admiral Hyman G. Rickover, USN (Ret.), ran the Navy's nuclear-power program for many years. He came from a Jewish background. WASP--White Anglo-Saxon Protestant.
[†] Commander Henry J. Rotrige, CHC, USN, was the Naval Academy's first Catholic chaplain, serving there from 1947 to 1951. The oral history of Rotridge, who retired as a rear admiral, is in the series conducted by the Navy's Chaplain Corps.
[‡] Commander Merle N. Young, CHC, USN, served at the Naval Academy from 1950 to 1953.
[§] Tent Chautauqua refers to traveling groups that operated in the United States from 1903 to 1930. They went from town to town, giving a program of lectures, concerts, and recitals in a large tent. Their popularity declined with the development of radio and movies.

Q: Well, you mentioned earlier there was not too much consciousness of religious concerns and the chapel program on the part of the line command. How did change that?

Admiral Stevenson: I had to insist that we would brief command on the religious program, like other departments were expected to brief on their programs. As I said, we had put this planning book together, and the planning book became a constant companion to every chaplain. The planning book allowed you to explain any program the chaplains' department had: the outline of every program; which chaplain had the conn; what the title of the program was; what the description of the program was; what the funding of the program was; what the publicity requirements of the program were; what the requirements of the program were, etc., etc. That enabled us to give command copies of our planning book. It enabled command to make decisions regarding our budget: do we keep this program, or do we delete it? If we keep it, it costs so much; if you wanted to modify it, it would cost so much less. What do you want us to do? How do you want us to do it?

In that planning we also had report cards. Near the end of the fiscal year, every chaplain filled out an evaluation for the whole chaplains department. You had to grade every program we had: A, B, C. A meant it's a good program, keep it going; B meant I don't know enough about this program, or I haven't heard enough about it so I can't make a judgment; C meant as far as I'm concerned, dump it. Now, the chaplain who had the conn on a program that got a C was often shocked. It was because either he hadn't shared it enough with the other chaplains in the department, or it really was a bomb and ought to be scratched.

Then we'd go back to command at budget time with the reworked planning book and explain to command: "We're recommending that we drop this program because it hasn't worked. It's been a failure. Nobody has signed up for it; nobody has a need for it. Whereas, on the other hand, we have increased attendance at this program, evidently we need some extra funding for it."

It was a delight to me that the comptrollers liked what we were doing, and the comptrollers recommended to other departments from time to time that they do similar things. The comptroller and the commanding officer and the executive officer had a real feel for, "What are you doing, and when do you do it, and why do you do it?" And then they got in the ball game telling us "We don't want you to do that," or, "yes, we want you to do it," or "why don't you put more emphasis on this?" The chaplains increased their sense of professionalism, recognizing the fact that it was the command's religious program, not just the chaplains'. My job as the senior chaplain or as a chaplain is, as a professional, to recommend to command what kind of religious program fits this environment. Then it's their job to determine whether or not it's worthy of funding. Then it's my job to execute it in the way in which they want it executed. That's institutional ministry. That is not parish ministry.

Q: Were there any items on your Orlando list of projects that we haven't talked about yet?

Admiral Stevenson: Chaplains down in the McCoy chapel handled that family program very well. They did not get as great a music program out of it as I hoped. One of those things on my list was to have dynamic music programs because that's a drawing card for the chapel. We never got that in the McCoy area. In fact, at some expense we moved a big, powerful Hammond organ down to McCoy, because it wasn't heavily utilized in the recruit chapel.

Q: Going back to the idea of the football coach, did you, after you'd been there a while, have a chance to recruit some of your own players?

Admiral Stevenson: I had a chance to recruit some chaplains, thanks to the detailer up in Washington. I also had the opportunity to refuse some. One day a detailer called me and said that he was going to give me a couple of additional chaplains beyond the billet allowance. I told him I didn't want them.

What you need on a ball team is a team of nine guys who know how to play ball. Don't give me chaplains that other chaplains need to take care of. You remember there was a softball team with four men, the King and his Court. They beat teams with nine players. That's professionalism!

Q: Eddie Feigner was the pitcher. They played in Annapolis in the summer, I know.

Admiral Stevenson: That's my ideal chaplains' department.

Q: There's a pitcher, catcher, first baseman, and one other fielder.

Admiral Stevenson: Just give me players who really know how to play this game and who want to play this game. A large number of chaplains will not do as much as the small group who really knows how to play the game. Well, of course, what I was saying to the detailers is impossible. The detailers can't give you a ready-made team, but that's what it ought to be.

In the game of ministry, you all know your positions; if you've got to cover somebody else's position, you can cover somebody else's position. And, you know, you don't run around saying, you know, "But I'm just a shortstop. I don't do anything else."

I was talking to the detailer, Tom Hilferty, who was one of the best chaplains I think we've ever had, one of the wisest we've ever had on the Chief of Chaplains' staff. He was saying, "We'll give you these chaplains."

"I don't want them." The last thing a senior chaplain wants to do is babysit mediocre chaplains.

One of the problems with senior chaplains is that a lot of senior chaplains want to act as though they are now in a pastoral capacity to their chaplains. They want to play bishop. That's not the Navy. The senior chaplain is a department head and responsible to the command for the department. You cannot have a counseling or pastoral relationship with another chaplain. You can try to coach them and motivate them, but you cannot become a pastoral counselor because you cannot maintain confidentiality for the people in your department. You've got to start off your relationship with them by reminding them-- and being honest with them up front--that, "I'm not here to be your pastoral counselor."

Q: Where do they go for that?

Admiral Stevenson: Everybody should have a pastor. And if the pastors don't know who their pastors are, then they aren't too swift.

In the Roman Catholic Church, your bishop is your pastor. And in the Protestant tradition, you select your pastor, just as the people in the church select their pastor. If you need marriage counseling, you should not get it from your senior chaplain any more than the senior chaplain should get it from a junior chaplain in his own department.

If a chaplain who is supposed to be celibate is running around with some lady and contemplating marriage with her, a senior chaplain cannot handle that situation as confidential. That's a situation that has a direct effect on that man's calling and, therefore, his endorsement, and therefore, on his commission.

Q: Because you have to deal with that fellow as the reporting senior in the Navy chain.

Admiral Stevenson: That's exactly right, which eliminates the confidentiality. You can't have the Chief of Chaplains or anybody else hand-grenaded and then turn around and say, "Oh, well, I knew that all the time because I heard it in the counseling situation."

So I think from up front you've got to make it clear to your chaplains, "I'm the department head. I want us to have a professional relationship, I want us to have a friendly relationship, but I cannot and will not be your pastor. I'm a supervisor of chaplains, not a pastor to pastors." By the way, 29-plus years of experience taught me that the senior chaplains who most often degrade ministry to people, hurt the Chaplain Corps, degrade the Navy, and the faith groups are the ones who play the pastor-to-pastor game for the sake of their own egos.

Neil M. Stevenson #6 - 193

Interview Number 6 with Rear Admiral Neil M. Stevenson, Chaplain Corps, U.S. Navy (Retired)

Place: Williamsburg Presbyterian Church, Williamsburg, Virginia

Date: Thursday, 16 November 1989

Interviewer: Paul Stillwell

Q: The last time, Admiral, we talked about your time down at Orlando. We're ready to move you back to Washington to the office of the Chief of Chaplains. What sorts of duties did you have in that role?

Admiral Stevenson: Well, I was on the staff of Chaplain John O'Connor, and the director of the Chaplains Division in those days was Chaplain Jerry Sargent.* Maybe it would be good to give a little background about how I got to Washington on that tour. John O'Connor was selected for rear admiral and went in as Chief of Chaplains.† John is the kind of individual who has always gotten things done, and so he came into Washington like a storm.

I was very happy to still be in Orlando, but I knew I was coming up for orders. It was the first time we had bought a house, so it was the first time that I realized that I was going to come up for orders when it was the worst possible time to sell a house. Having bought it on the high, I was going to have to sell on the low. I talked to the detailer about going out to the Third Marine Division for a year, an unaccompanied tour in those days, leaving the family in the house in Orlando.

Q: The Third Marine Division being in Okinawa.

Admiral Stevenson: Yes. The Chief of Chaplains made a visit to Orlando at a time when I was in the Midwest getting my daughter Holly in college. Shortly after that, he called me up and asked me if I would be willing to come to the staff in Washington. I had never

---

* Captain Gerald H. Sargent, CHC, USN.
† His tenure as chief was from July 1975 to June 1979.

gotten a call from anybody before asking me if I wanted to do anything. [Chuckles] And not having served directly with John O'Connor, but having known John over the years, I wasn't so sure that I was the guy that he wanted on his staff.

Q: Why did you feel that way?

Admiral Stevenson: Oh, because John and I had had several debates in which we were on opposite ends of the spectrum. I think we were somewhat opposite on the Vietnam War, and we had been opposite on other things down through the years when we had met at lunches and things.

Q: Could it be that that's why he wanted you?

Admiral Stevenson: It could have been. But he had written a book on Vietnam which I felt was very much to the disadvantage of the Chaplain Corps and so forth.[*]

Q: In what ways?

Admiral Stevenson: Well, his view at that time was a strong justification for the war in Vietnam, and I found it very hard to justify the war in Vietnam. Nevertheless, I was called up to Washington, as I recall, on two separate occasions to work with the planning group, which was located over in the Navy yard. John came into town and said, "We've got to do something about the Chaplain Corps and the POM. We've got to get the Chaplain Corps to be a part of the Navy system."

We worked a week on justifications and researching the interpretations of the First Amendment in regards to not depriving people of their right to religion and how it applied to the Navy Chaplain Corps and sea duty and things of that nature.

Q: What had been the status of the Chaplain Corps before it got into the POM situation?

---

[*] John J. O'Connor, A Chaplain Looks at Vietnam (Cleveland: World Publishing Company, 1968).

Admiral Stevenson: Well, as I mentioned before, Paul, those of us who were the so-called "young Turks" were very frustrated with the position of the Chaplain Corps. The atmosphere regarding the Chaplain Corps was largely paternalistic. You know, the Chief of Chaplains was in the Bureau of Naval Personnel, which said, "Just don't worry. The Chief of Naval Personnel will take care of you guys." The Chief of Chaplains' staff was dominated, as I've also said before, by the detailing desk, and the detailing desk handled both personnel and manpower. You had the same individual charged with, as it were, manipulating billets and PCS orders.[*] John O'Connor had a much larger vision, as he's always had, of the Chaplain Corps's position and of the place of religion in Navy life. And he was not hesitant to express those views.

At that same time, you may recall they were doing away with the naval districts at this time. For the older generation of chaplains, this was a great crisis because the hierarchy of the Chaplain Corps was largely based on district chaplains.

Q: Were they, in effect, bishops for their districts?

Admiral Stevenson: Sort of, yes. I think that's a good illustration. That was kind of the mentality. And, of course, one of the great disasters for the Chaplain Corps at any time is for a corps that is made up of clergy to gain the mentality that the Chaplain Corps is organized in similar fashion to the polity of any particular church, whether it be Presbyterian or Episcopal or Congregational or what.

Anyway, I went up there to talk these things over with the planning group and others under the sponsorship of John O'Connor. We were discussing things like, "Well, if the district chaplains are going to be done away with, if the bishops are going to be removed, you know, what do we need to have now as an organization in the Chaplain Corps? How do we establish the domain?" [Chuckles]

---

[*] PCS--permanent change of station.

It just so happened that week that Jerry Sargent, who was the division director, was wrestling with this problem. I got to thinking about it, and I asked the question, "Well, what is the Navy system?"

And the response was, "Well, the Navy has gone over into this crazy claimancy thing," which I think even to a lot of line officers at that time looked a little strange.

From the kind of training I'd had under Sam Blizzard and others at Princeton, I started just harping about the fact that, "We need to imitate, in our small organization, what the primary organization is doing. You've got to relate through claimancy chaplains. You've got to develop the claimant chaplain as the kingpin, rather than the district chaplain, because that's the funding line.

Q: Could you explain a bit what you mean by the claimant?

Admiral Stevenson: The claimants are those major commander-in-chief commands which have authority over an entire system of the Navy, like Pacific Fleet, Atlantic Fleet, Commander in Chief U.S. Naval Forces Europe, the Chief of Naval Education and Training, etc. The Navy was realizing that it could not be bound by the geographic rigidity that the districts had put it in. In a new world of communications, you were moving into the systemic world. I think the Navy at that time was recognizing the move from an industrial society into a service-oriented society, moving from printing presses into computers. Well, the Navy had reached that kind of technology, and the organization of the Navy was a handicap to its technology. And the claimancy system was a way of moving into a more realistic world.

Q: What sort of alternative internal structure did you come up with to deal with this new system?

Admiral Stevenson: Well, I don't recall it being that difficult. And at the time I'm talking about, you know, it was a conversational thing, and Jerry Sargent was the one who said, "I think maybe Neil's on to something here. Let's look at this."

On a human level, you're dealing with some of the personality clashes, because higher authority has redrawn the map and you are now saying, "Wait a minute. This chaplain down at Pensacola, who just happens to be at Pensacola, who was not ordered to Pensacola to be a claimant chaplain, but he happens to be the senior guy in Pensacola, and as of next Thursday, is going to be attached to the Chief of Naval Education and Training. He is now a kingpin. He is now the guy who is going to be the closest to the billet-and money czar. If the chaplains are going to have any budget and have training programs and so forth, he's got to act."

The claimant's chaplain has to be recognized as "the chaplain who belongs to the claimant," therefore the one who has to be the Chief of Chaplains' man on the scene.

Q: So it was being divided up along the lines of these major commanders, rather than geographically.

Admiral Stevenson: Right. And, of course, this process had started back when I was in the bureau previous to that, for instance, CNET coming into being. So what we're talking about is the Chaplain Corps, like, I suppose, all other small communities, deciding under the new game plan, "How do we now play the game and how do we get things done?"

Well, what had happened was that between '72 and '76 the Navy evolved in this fashion, and the Chaplain Corps in '76 with John O'Connor and Jerry Sargent was saying, "Well, wait a minute. We haven't made the adjustments. We're still thinking in terms of districts. We've got to do something right away."

And, as it turned out, by the time I had gotten back to Orlando, that off-the-top-of-the-head thought of mine probably caught Jerry's attention and John O'Connor's attention, and they said, "Well, maybe we can use Neil up here."

I got some phone calls from John O'Connor saying he would like me to come to the staff, but he didn't want to order me to his staff unless I wanted to come, and that was very much John's way. Of course, I suppose I should have said, "Yes, of course." But I'm a little stubborn, so I had to make statements to John O'Connor like, "Whenever I get a set of orders, I follow the set of orders." [Laughter] In other words, "If you want me up there, you order me up there, but I'm not about to volunteer to come back into that whole thing."

Q: So he ordered you there.

Admiral Stevenson: So he ordered me there, and I went up. [Laughter] Just for the sake of Navy families, I repeat the fact that the selling of the house was a horror, and we lost money. And, thanks be to God, my wife insisted that we were going to go as a family, whether we had to leave the house vacant or what we did.

We rented a house in McLean, Virginia, so we could get our youngest daughter into the same high school her sisters had been in--all those kind of Navy things that you try to do. I went to work on the Chief of Chaplains' staff on the sixth of August 1976, and the family didn't come up until September.

The reason I mention the sixth of August is to give you an idea what a productive year it was, Paul. One of the few pieces of memorabilia that I have kept over the years is this plaque that I received from John O'Connor--who greatly disliked mistakes--when I left the office. They made a mistake, and I kept it simply because of the mistake. According to this plaque, I joined the staff on the fifth of August 1977, and I left the staff on the first of August 1977. That may be somewhat symbolic of that year.

Anyway, I reported in. It was that feeling of, "I'm back." I wasn't too happy about it. I was also somewhat frightened, because it was only when I reported in and talked to Jerry at length and then the Chief of Chaplains at length that I felt that their expectations about what I could contribute to the staff were beyond my capability. They seemed to identify an awful lot of worms. John had come in and stirred things up, which is exactly what needed to be done, but I mean, the loose ends were just going in 50 directions. And those first couple of weeks just seemed absolutely horrible. We were just working all day and into the night, just trying to get a handle on how big a mess we had.

Q: Well, what examples do you recall?

Admiral Stevenson: Well, first of all, let me say this. The good part about joining the staff, for me, was that people I admired were on the staff: Joe Dimino, whom I had served with in USS Saratoga; Tom Hilferty, who had relieved me on the training desk years before, was now the detailer.* And Joe Dimino is one of the finest administrators I have ever been around in my life. Tom Hilferty knew the Bureau of Naval Personnel better than any chaplain. Tom was the first detailer of the Chaplain Corps who would admit, and knew, that personnel should be separated from manpower. The tendency of most people--if you're the king of both those empires, you try to hold onto it. But Tom's recognition was, "No, these things are separated in the Bureau and they need to be separated in the Chief of Chaplains' office."

They talked to me about being in charge of planning, budgeting, and administration. It was kind of an overwhelming load to look at.

Q: Why do you think that Chaplain O'Connor's expectations outweighed what you could bring to the job?

Admiral Stevenson: Well, I think one of the strengths of Chaplain O'Connor was that he was willing to see in other people the talent and abilities that he has, you know. He's a character larger than life.

Q: So perhaps he can get more out of you than you think you can deliver?

Admiral Stevenson: And he will. [Laughter] Some days he will have you the happiest guy in the world, and some days he will have you the angriest guy in the world, but the production will tell.

Q: Well, I wonder if you have a list of these loose ends that we could go through one by one and discuss.

---

* Both of these officers were by now captains.

Admiral Stevenson: No, I don't have a list, but let me give you an idea of the environment. First of all, we changed the fiscal year in the Navy that year.* I arrived for what was known as the T quarter, the temporary quarter.

Q: July to September.

Admiral Stevenson: I arrived in August. And one of the problems was that if we didn't expend what money we had, we would lose it. But no decisions had been made, no contracts had been written. [Laughter]

Q: It sort of put some time pressure on you.

Admiral Stevenson: Yes, and so I can recall a couple of long weekends I was glad the family wasn't there yet. Joe Dimino and Tom Hilferty and I sat there and tried to work through what we should be expending money on.

When you come into a period like that, you end up with people coming in with all kinds of strange requests. People were convinced that this was a great opportunity for seed money. And I hate seed money. I had big arguments with Chaplain O'Connor over seed money, because he liked the thought of sprinkling seed money and things happening out in the Chaplain Corps. And my view from previous days was that an awful lot of seed gets bought, but I've never seen a crop, because you really can't put the kind of accountability on that money that ought to be put with it, particularly when chaplains are getting orders and the next chaplains can't pick up the ball on that particular "hobby" that the outgoing chaplain got seed money for. Pretty wasteful.

Anyway, we got the budget done, but it was a challenge. The shop that I inherited had three chaplains. One left before I got there, and another one left, I think, the next day. And the third one, who was the finance chaplain, was an outstanding finance man, but he had already put in for leave and his leave had been approved. [Laughter]

---

* Up to 1976, the U.S. Government's fiscal year ran from 1 July to 30 June of the following calendar year. In 1976 the government switched to a fiscal year beginning 1 October and running through 30 September.

Q: You probably didn't pick up too much finance from Sam Blizzard. So how did you adjust to this kind of environment?

Admiral Stevenson: I picked up finances in three ways: first of all, Jim Ammons when he was on the Chief of Chaplains' staff in the early '70s, was a very good tutor; I had been through the advanced course; and, number three, I had had the chaplains department down at Orlando and had submitted the budget and worked with the comptroller down there. So anyway, we went at it, and with the help of everybody on the staff, those kinds of things were resolved.

Another admin nightmare was a complex system in those days of yeomen who were given a designation that they would be eligible to work in chaplains' offices. We had to establish a system for recording who they were, and then a negotiation to try to give them a little training. It was a very poor compromise in comparison to the religious program specialist rating that came into being during that year that I was there, under the leadership of John O'Connor.

Q: Was he the one who got that changed?

Admiral Stevenson: John O'Connor was the one who got the RP rating into existence, along with Chaplain Steve Jones, who came in and did the mechanics over and over again in that process.*

Q: Would it be fair to say that Chaplain O'Connor's approach to BuPers and the rest of the Navy was to start demanding things, rather than just depend on this paternalism?

Admiral Stevenson: Well, yes and no. With the caveat--you've got to remember that everybody knew that Admiral Watkins, who was CNP, was a very close friend.† There was

---

* Commander Stephen N. Jones, CHC, USN.
† Vice Admiral James D. Watkins, USN, served as Chief of Naval Personnel from 10 April 1975 to 21 July 1978.

a great mutual admiration between Chaplain O'Connor and Admiral James Watkins.

Q: So the environment was helpful.

Admiral Stevenson: Right. I guess I was the one that developed this expression, which is one I've used with chaplains ever since, "paternalism with homework." In other words, you're not going to get more than anybody else, but if you do have a daddy and you do do your homework like everybody else, or better than anybody else, you're going to get a hearing. And if you've got a hearing, at least you're working the system. You're not going up there looking for a handout; you have to prove that you can do it.

And so in that year, as I said, John O'Connor stirred things up. All kinds of things were going in all kinds of directions. One of the things he had done was he recognized, along with Admiral Watkins, that the Chaplain Corps, like the rest of the Navy, needed to put on a full press regarding minority recruiting.

Chaplain O'Connor brought a black chaplain, Gil Gilbert, into the staff.[*] In the personnel section there was Chaplain Dave White, whom I had the privilege, when I was on the training desk, to select to be the first chaplain to go to Postgraduate School in Monterey.[†] Dave White, who's now the Deputy Chief of Chaplains, is one of the solid citizens, one of those guys who really got things done. When you go back to those years, the guy who put the Chaplain Corps minority recruiting really under way in a sound, good, bureaucratic fashion, etc., was Dave White. And the chaplain who was there as a minority to work the problem was Chaplain Gilbert. So all these things were going on. It was a very exciting staff to be a part of.

Q: Did you come to a point where you overcame your reluctance and got caught up in the excitement of it?

---

[*] Lieutenant Leroy Gilbert, CHC, USNR.
[†] Commander David E. White, CHC, USN. As a rear admiral, White subsequently served as Chief of Chaplains from August 1991 to August 1994.

Admiral Stevenson: Actually, it was just hard work. I mean, it looks a lot better now than it did on a day-to-day basis then. I remember one night my oldest daughter indicated that the subject of POM would not be discussed at the dinner table. Evidently through the years I had said there were some things that should not be discussed at the dinner table, so she decided that one of the things that would not be discussed was the POM. I think I was all POMmed out that year.

John O'Connor had said to me that he wanted the Chaplain Corps within the POM within my tour of duty there in three years. It was looked upon as a three-year tour of duty. You know, Paul, it was a time of a lot of ups and downs. One of the things that Chaplain O'Connor insisted on was that in order to be part of the system, every element of the staff needed to be involved in the committee meetings and all the things that were going on within the Bureau of Naval Personnel. So you're talking about a lot of man-hours, as I told you. I'd go to meetings, and Admiral Smedberg and Admiral Metcalf were there, and they were also stirring things up in those years.[*]

Q: What sorts of things?

Admiral Stevenson: Well, now you're really stretching my memory. We even had a three-day weekend in which the entire leadership of BuPers was hauled down to Yorktown, and we worked on this overall--I'm trying to think of the name of it now--this overall personnel plan for the Navy.

Q: How would you, in general, characterize the relationship between the Chaplain Corps and BuPers at your level?

---

[*] Rear Admiral William R. Smedberg IV, USN, Assistant Chief of Naval Personnel (Peronnel Planning/Programs); Rear Admiral Joseph Metcalf III, USN, Assistant Chief of Naval Personnel for Financial Management and Management Information.

Admiral Stevenson: Well, I have never had a time in the Bureau of Naval Personnel in which I didn't feel that there was not a high degree of harmony between the Chief of Chaplains' staff and the elements of the bureau that they worked with. I think because we set the stage, that we wanted to do work the same way that they wanted to do work. In talking about cooperation and harmony, that meant for chaplains that we had to go to elements of the Bureau of Naval Personnel and say to them, "How do you do this thing? We didn't learn this in seminary. You know, how do we do these the Navy way?" (By the way, years later some of our chaplains, like Mel Ferguson and Bill Gibson, taught their counterparts how to do some things.)[*]

I can remember one night when I had a whole list of sheets to fill out mechanically for our submission to POM '79. I had loused up about a half of them. When I took these in the next day, they were looked over and they called me up. And a couple of lieutenants sat with me and said, "No, this is not how you do it. This is how you do it."

So in those years, throughout the bureau, I don't think the Chaplain Corps got any advantages over any other community in the bureau, but I think the atmosphere in the bureau was that there are people there, both GSs and active duty, and their attitude was, "We'll help!"[†] Everybody was so busy that sometimes tempers got a little short. But I think the atmosphere was, "If you guys need to know how to do this, we'll teach you how to do it." And it was our job to get it done.

Q: You talked about the switch-over from the naval-district system to the claimant system. Did you have a problem that maybe one claimant wouldn't be as enthusiastic for the chaplain role in his command as others would?

Admiral Stevenson: Well, you had chaplains who went to a billet with the mentality that they were going to emulate their predecessors, put out a newsletter and to be, as you said earlier, sort of the bishop. Now, all of a sudden, somebody was saying to them, "Hey,

---

[*] Lieutenant Commander Melvin R. Ferguson, CHC, USN; Lieutenant Commander William H. Gibson, CHC, USN.
[†] GS refers to civil service employees.

throw that stuff all out of your head. Where are you on manpower? What billets do you have? What budget?" etc.

You'd get a phone call, and the chaplain would say, "Well, I went over and I talked to these people, and they said, 'Chaplain, don't worry about it.'"

And we would say, from Washington, "Well, you damn well better worry about it, because that's not acceptable to us."

But you've got to remember that the chaplain is under the local command, not under the Chief of Chaplains. The Chief of Chaplains--again, like a high-school football coach--inherits the team. John O'Connor was able to change some people around, but you're under financial restraints in detailing too. You just can't come in and say, "Well, no, I don't want that guy there. I'm going to move him and put someone else in." It doesn't work that way.

So we had to go out, in some cases, and try to give briefings to claimants and educate claimant chaplains. The first claimant chaplains conference was in 1976, and they've had one every year ever since. I went up for a couple of hours to the one they had last April. And, you know, the chaplains all look so professional and they're all so familiar with the lingo and all this stuff now, that I sit there and smile, because, believe me, those first couple of major claimant meetings were absolute disasters. You know, you're talking about senior chaplains who were going back to school and learning a whole new system, and some of them are saying, "I'm too old. I'm not interested in that. My command tells me we'll be taken care of, so I'm not going to worry about it."

Q: So it was an education process.

Admiral Stevenson: It was an educational process. And we, as a staff, when we put together the first major claimant staff chaplains conference, we would sit there and say, "What are we going to have as an agenda? What are we going to look upon as a successful conference? For instance, can we get these chaplains convinced that personnel is one domain and manpower is a separate domain, and that the word "manpower" means billets, and that billets is a funding question? It really comes down to how many dollars a billet costs and how many billets can you buy for how much money? Most chaplains were not aware of the relationship to the cost of a billet.

Q: What were the consequences of separating manpower and personnel?

Admiral Stevenson: First of all, you began to play honestly with the Bureau of Naval Personnel, and that is "No billet, no body." In the Chaplain Corps, the whole emphasis had been on bodies, who was going to get what job. We had chaplains where we didn't have billets, because nobody had ever bought the billets. And the claimant thought, "Well, I don't have to pay for this. This is the Chief of Chaplains' domain, and he's going to keep sending some chaplain here, because he's not going to leave this space empty." And we found out that if you're going to play the system, you've got to play it honestly. If you don't have a billet, you don't have a body.

Q: Did that cause any unhappiness?

Admiral Stevenson: Oh, sure! That caused a lot of unhappiness. Threatened a lot of people.

Q: Well, it probably forced you to do a better job of justification too.

Admiral Stevenson: Absolutely. And two programs of justification come to mind: DOPMA and SHORSTAMPS.[*] Chaplain O'Connor called me in one day and handed me paperwork the size of the New York phone book. And he said, "I want you to be our expert on this. This is called DOPMA." [Laughter]

---

[*] The Defense Officer Personnel Management Act (DOPMA) was sent to Congress in 1973 and finally passed in 1981. For its provisions see Brayton Harris, "At Long Last: DOPMA . . . How Long Will It Last?" U.S. Naval Institute Proceedings, September 1981, pages 129-131. SHORSTAMPS--Shore Requirements, Standards, and Manpower Planning System.

I went back to Chaplain White, and I said, "Dave, what in the world is this DOPMA business?" Dave gave me some strokes on DOPMA, and I started to try to understand DOPMA.

At the same time, in a little office in BuPers, a couple of naval officers were trying to put together with some civilian consultants a Navy justification of billets that the Air Force used, called SHORSTAMPS. Chaplain Hilferty introduced me to these gentlemen. I wish I could recall their names, because they deserve credit. I went up, and they talked to me about SHORSTAMPS. I was in a position where I was trying to justify getting the chaplains' 4100 billets as a legitimate part of the POM, and they were trying to get somebody to be willing to be operated on.[*] They were looking for candidates willing to put their communities into the SHORSTAMPS formula. This was part of being young and bold, so I said, "What's wrong with us? Why don't you experiment with us?"

They said, "Well, that's not a bad idea, because the Air Force chaplaincy has their equivalent to SHORSTAMPS." I think it was an Air Force general named Snavely who originated this personnel concept, and his daughter was a consultant to the Navy.[†] The Air Force was using it effectively with the Congress in justifying the billets. The Navy wanted to work the system in the shore establishment and called it SHORSTAMPS.

Our job was to try to work the SHORSTAMPS business, and we took it very seriously. It's like experimental surgery. When they open you up, you may be found to be worse off than they thought. So there were a lot of communities that were not willing to be opened up and looked at by other people. We had to have the gut-level feeling that, "First of all, we can't be any worse off than we are, and number two, let's look at ourselves. Let's sit down and write justifications under the SHORSTAMPS formula for billets."

Well, this had the funny side to it. It turned out that, of course, the SHORSTAMPS formula had been reduced to a mathematical formula, equation. [Laughter] I am not a mathematician. We discussed this, and Tom Hilferty said, "Well, you know, Dave White is

---

[*] In this case, the number 4100 refers not to a quantity of billets but to the officer designator for individuals in the Chaplain Corps.
[†] Major General William W. Snavely, USAF.

our bright boy in math and chemistry." So, lo and behold, who could work the SHORSTAMPS formula but Dave White?

They used to turn the heat off in BuPers on the weekends. But in order to get into the SHORSTAMPS, we had to have something in by Tuesday. So Dave White and Tom Hilferty and Neil Stevenson sat in overcoats in the Bureau of Naval Personnel all day one Saturday and then all of Sunday afternoon. Dave White worked his little calculator, and we put this packet together. That actually worked out to become the homework side of the paternalism of getting the Chaplain Corps into the POM.

Chaplain O'Connor was disappointed that it showed an increase of only 124 billets over a five-year period of time, but I was delighted. I still look back on it and say it was a legitimate justification and a sound approach of about a 25-billet yearly increase in the Chaplain Corps, over a five-year period starting with POM '79.

Q: Was it a case of trying to legitimize the status quo, or to just start with a clean sheet of paper?

Admiral Stevenson: No, we started with a clean sheet of paper.

Q: What was your formula? How did you go about this justification? Did you start with the major commands and work down?

Admiral Stevenson: You started with the population and the responsibilities for active-duty naval personnel and other requirements in that area. Home-ported ships were part of the equation. Boy, you're really pushing the memory here. You've got a percentage of the personnel of home-ported ships, you've got a full percentage of active-duty personnel. You didn't get any credit for dependents, but we had areas where there was heavy impact, particularly in overseas billets. I think in overseas billets you got a certain percentage. I didn't keep any of that kind of stuff, but that was the kind of formula it was.

Q: Was it a major change from what had been?

Admiral Stevenson: It was a major change in two respects. For the first time you were justifying the billet structure in an area, rather than just saying, "Well, I've been around the Navy for 30 years, and I know how many chaplains we ought to have there." So you actually were coming up with a justifiable formula. That related to other communities in the Navy. Second, we also proved that we could modify SHORSTAMPS in relations to ships, home-ported ships, which was not in the formula that the Air Force had used.

Q: I guess my question was, did this cause a significant realignment in where the billets were?

Admiral Stevenson: Yes, and it projected over five years. And I'm smiling because I'm remembering what those of us who got carried away with the fact that it should be a quantified system, called all previous systems the "whim-shit" method. You know, "How many billets--how many chaplains should you have here?"

"Well, you know, I think . . ." With this SHORSTAMPS program we did not have a proof positive, but we had at least a recognized, organized system that was applicable.

Q: Well, those gut feelings of past experiences were not completely invalid.

Admiral Stevenson: No, no, no, no. But in a sense the Chaplain Corps was joining the Navy.

Q: You talked about this in terms of shore billets. What about the shipboard billets?

Admiral Stevenson: The shipboard billets part of that package did not come into being during my tour. Those decisions were more subjective, because the debates got into things like the size of the ship. You had a Navy in which your newer ships, because of technology, had smaller crews, but you still have, under the First Amendment, the need to provide an opportunity for the expression of their religious faith to the men and women serving in those ships.

The old formulas had applied in World War II time and had remained in the Navy through those years: 3,000 men in an aircraft carrier, 1,200 in a battleship, so many in a cruiser. All those things were dropping out of the system. Not only the Chaplain Corps, but the whole of BuPers was beginning to deal with different kinds of configurations of personnel to ships. Now, how do you work your chaplains' billets for that? But that was really worked after I had been ordered out to the fleet job.

Q: Was there more emphasis on circuit-rider chaplains after that?

Admiral Stevenson: Yes, and then the complications of where you were going to put RPs when the RP rating came into being.* By that time I was out in Pacific Fleet, and I was fighting, in the beginning, to keep RPs out of the squadrons and to limit the beginning RP billets to major combatants. From a fleet point of view, it's easier to justify RPs in an aircraft carrier and see the value and the contribution the rating makes than to try to do it in a squadron environment. Where does he fit into the mess decks, and where does he fit into mess cooking, every time you change this enlisted guy from ship to ship? Do you keep him on the same ship in the squadron as the chaplain?

My gut feeling from the very beginning, from PacFlt, was, "Lord, keep them out of the squadrons, because we need the rating operating well before we get involved with all these subjective judgments that are going to be made by XOs." You know, I've got an enlisted guy for two weeks, Paul. Do I put him in a gun crew or not? I mean, the Navy just wasn't programmed for an enlisted type who changes ships every couple of weeks. They can handle a chaplain, because you've got to put up with him. [Laughter] But the RP rating was a different story.

Q: Well, talking about this mess-deck issue, when it came up and Chaplain O'Connor was fighting for a specific rating, was there any concern about how he would be perceived in

---

* RP--religious program specialist.

shipboard crews, that this would be, say, kind of a "wimpy" rating compared to gunner's mates or BTs?

Admiral Stevenson: I'm certain it was, but the emphasis at that time was just to get the darn rating. And so the year that I was there, the chaplains who specifically worked on that, Geoff Gaughan and Steve Jones, were working on the mechanics with other people in the Bureau of Naval Personnel, who were telling them how to prepare the mechanics for the hearings.[*]

For years and years the rumor was that the Chaplain Corps had tried to get a rating, and it had always been turned down. I remember when Ross Trower came to the staff in 1971 and asked to look in the file and see what all had been done about it.[†] It turned out to be a matter of only a couple of letters. [Laughter] From those letters the myth developed in the Chaplain Corps that the corps had actually done something to establish a chaplain's assistant rating, like the Army and Air Force had always had. Nothing was really done until John O'Connor.

By the way, I always through it interesting that the RP rating and O'Connor have the same birthday, January 15, which they share with Martin Luther King, Jr. Chaplain O'Connor knew the Navy system, and he was like a bulldog. He wouldn't let go. They would say something to him like, "Well, if you'll submit a letter."

He'd say, "No, no. Letters come up and get turned down all the time. I want in on the meeting. I want my chair around the conference table."

Q: What were the arguments he used to make it work and get the billet established?

Admiral Stevenson: I left in August of '77, and the billet was officially established on the 15th of January, 1978. Part of the justification was that the Army and the Air Force had such a specialty. Part of the justification was the uniqueness of the Navy. And so, you know, in my Sam Blizzard-trained mind, it is not by accident, by any means, that the three

---

[*] Commander Geoffrey E. Gaughan, CHC, USN.
[†] Captain Ross H. Trower, CHC, USN.

similar ratings for enlisted personnel in the three separate services have different titles. In the Army, for 200 years the chaplain's assistant is called the chaplain's assistant. When you go back and look in the history, the chaplain's assistant was in charge of the chaplain's horse and the chaplain's mule. The chaplain's mule carried the chaplain's tent, which had the chaplain's flag. The assistant put up the tent in which they had the chaplain's office, etc. He also fed the mule and this kind of stuff. And if you were around an Army chaplain's assistant today, it has a lot to do with the Jeep, you know.

In the Air Force, the title is chapel manager. Now, the Air Force lives in the suburbs. They're suburbanites, and they always have a chapel. Even in Danang, you know, it was a big A-frame, air-conditioned and with a coffee mess. [Chuckles] These chapel managers are a group of professional enlisted personnel who manage the religious education programs and everything else in the chapel.

The Navy is a whole different world. First, you've got a percentage of these chaplains who are with the Marine Corps and likely to get shot at. The RPs are definitely combatants, you know. You're not talking about wimps; you're talking about combatants. You're talking about a whole variety of sea duty. Now you have, in 1978, the coming of this new rating for the Navy in a time in which the term "systems" is a prominent term. So you end up with the religious program. This is an enlisted rating for programming religion within the variety of environments in which Navy chaplains serve.

We knew from the very beginning--and we accepted wholeheartedly--the statement from the Secretary of the Navy at that time, Claytor, that he would favor the rating, but that the rating would never serve where there was not a chaplain.[*] I admired Claytor's remark, "The difference in sea duty and the responsibilities of sea duty between peacetime and wartime is very little."[†] It's a great statement that he always made. Very effective and a very truthful statement. In comparing sea duty in peacetime and wartime, the margin of difference is small.

---

[*] W. Graham Claytor, Jr., served as Secretary of the Navy from 1977 to 1979.
[†] He knew from personal experience. As a Naval Reserve lieutenant commander, Claytor was commanding officer of the USS Cecil J. Doyle (DE-368) in early August 1945 when she rescued survivors from the heavy cruiser Indianapolis (CA-35), which a Japanese submarine had torpedoed and sunk a few days earlier.

Q: Why did he argue that there should not be an RP without a chaplain?

Admiral Stevenson: Well, you can expect a professional ordained officer to be responsible for facilitation of religion to other groups. You can demand that maturity of professionalism. In an enlisted rating, you may have the danger of religious fanaticism or single-mindedness. You need to have the chaplain to be accountable to command for what happens in the command's religious program.

I would never want an RP who was highly motivated towards his own religious faith, beyond reasonableness. So many of the most successful RPs have been religious, but understand their rating as one like all other ratings that provide service to all service personnel and their dependents.

Q: Was there a concern that an unaccompanied RP might be viewed as a surrogate chaplain and wouldn't be equipped for that role?

Admiral Stevenson: Absolutely. I think that will always be something that's of concern. That's one of the concerns in squadrons where a chaplain may be separated from the RP.

Q: During your time in the front office, did, heaven forbid, any religious issues come up?

Admiral Stevenson: Oh, yes. Let me mention one more thing about that SHORSTAMPS business, though, before I forget. The SHORSTAMPS was the beginning of justification for RP billets, because its Air Force counterpart model had incorporated the chapel managers in the formula. You had a time there with Chaplain O'Connor in which a lot of things were coming together. Besides that, John O'Connor was stirring up the pot, and John O'Connor was, as I say, a very strong individual. John never had any doubts about the course he was on. I never knew that he had any doubts, although we had a lot of wide-open and free debates about things.

When you talk about religious issues, I'm trying to think back. You mean in the broad context of what was happening in the nation or some such thing?

Q: Right. We've been talking about planning and programming-type issues here.

Admiral Stevenson: But that's what I call the world of the snipes. One of the misconceptions of some chaplains, I think, including--well, not just chaplains, but line officers--the Chief of Chaplains' staff is a place for snipes.* The job of the Chief of Chaplains' staff is to keep the ship and the engines going.

The Chief of Chaplains is not a bishop, the Chief of Chaplains is not a pope, the Chief of Chaplains is not the head of a religious organization. When I was later Chief of Chaplains, I know some line officers were very disappointed that I did not come out as a spokesman regarding certain moral issues, such as abortion. But the moral issue from the perspective of what faith group? Faith groups differ on moral positions.

You're not talking about the Chief of Chaplains being the head of a faith group. The Chief of Chaplains is in charge of the provision of chaplain services to all the fleet, so that the religious practice of individual sailors may be accommodated. The individual chaplain does that by either providing that service because these people are of the same faith group as the chaplain, or the chaplain facilitates that service by ensuring that those personnel have access to chaplains or religious leaders of their faith.

Q: So what you're saying is that the front office doesn't get into the substance of what these individual chaplains do.

Admiral Stevenson: Yes and no! The Chief of Chaplains acts to provide the training chaplains need to carry out their special missions. That is substance, but the chief cannot dictate certain moral policy.

The front office also is in a position of relating to, as John O'Connor would call them, the senior decision-makers of the Navy, with a moral impact. The moral impact of

---

* "Snipe" is Navy slang for someone in a ship's engineering department.

that day would be that John O'Connor's voice parroted or emulated or motivated, maybe--I don't know--the voice of the Chief of Naval Personnel regarding the Navy and minorities, and the involvement in the Navy with minorities and what needed to be done within the Navy not just to recruit minorities, but to have open sessions throughout the whole Navy on race relations, and seminars and all these kinds of things. John O'Connor was there.

That year we also dealt within the Chaplain Corps concerning the subject of alcoholism. We dealt openly with the concern of chaplains with alcoholic problems. Again, there were a lot of things going on. But you're right, most of us in Washington were working the mechanical and the budget problems to get the money to see that these programs existed. What we were doing was urging this new breed called the claimant chaplain to do these things within the claimancy: "Are you pushing your claimancy to deal with the minority issues that exist within that claimancy?" And where is the chaplain in the racial strife that was going on in some ships in those days?

Q: Who managed the training pipeline to make sure that sufficient people were coming along to fit these billets that you were justifying?

Admiral Stevenson: Well, one of the great helps was that the advanced course of the chaplain school had come into being. So the opportunity existed now to reprogram the curriculum at the advanced course at the chaplain school so that chaplains at the commander level were being instructed to serve the Navy of that day.

The officer in charge of the chaplain school in those days, Ross Trower, was also a man who understood the Navy system and how chaplains ought to be trained to relate within the Navy system. Ross would not use the same language that I use. In fact, sometimes Ross would frown a little bit, because I took the language from my Sam Blizzard training and stuck it into the Navy things. To this day I still talk about the chaplaincy as institutional ministry, not parish ministry. Ross would cringe at that a little bit.

I also would freely use the term "the command religious program." It's not the "chaplain's religious program." It's "what does the command want?" It's only when the command is confronted with the fact that it's their program that they have to decide how they're going to fund it. Part of a good command religious program is that it has funding, and it has the proper number of billets. The bottom line is economics. If you're going to pay for a religious program, you're going to pay for the billets. If you're going to pay for the RP billets, then you've got the potential, if you get the right chaplain and you get him properly motivated, to get the religious program that Navy people deserve.

Q: Was there measurable progress in that area?

Admiral Stevenson: I think there was. In fact, one of my major burdens when I was Chief of Chaplains started in those days. If you will let me just tie this together and jump ahead a little bit. I was in the office when Dave White and Gil Gilbert were working the minority situation. The Chaplain Corps felt strongly that the Navy needed to improve the entire atmosphere of minority recruiting and minority relations and so forth.

The Chaplain Corps needed to take a leadership role itself. That was not easily done, because, like in all other fields, the minorities had been environmentally deprived of education in some areas. The minority had been "ghetto-ized." And when you are "ghetto-ized," it is harder for you to relate to the larger society that is reflected in the Navy.

Even Jewish chaplains had this problem, because the Navy Chaplain Corps "ghetto-ized" them and, at the same time, they chose to "ghetto-ize" themselves. So there were only certain billets in which Jewish chaplains ever served. I mean, the Jewish chaplain knew he was going to be in about three places if he stayed for a whole career. But when you change over to a systemic view of the world, you're saying, "Wait a minute. These things don't fit and aren't fair." Every billet is a chaplain's billet.

Well, when we started with the minority business, there was great concern in the detailing world about where to order a minority chaplain. Are we going to put him where the most minorities are? Are we going to put him in Marine units that are heavily populated with black troops? And so forth. This kind of discussion was going on. The same thing with the female chaplains.

So I saw this thing in the beginning, and I also saw that you really have to make compromises to sort of make up for the ills of society when you recruit minorities. I suppose I ought to put that in other ways. In other words, when you decide that a percentage of a class at Harvard is going to be minorities, then you've got to provide for those minorities some kind of tutorial service to make them competitive.

Now, when I became Chief of Chaplains--and even before that when I was the deputy--one of the things that bothered me greatly was that there was still a mentality that you had to make exceptions for minorities. Okay? Now, again going back to the training that I think I had at Princeton, as well as my own experience, there comes a point at which within an institution you are handicapping minority people by maintaining the support systems that they have in exception to others.

Q: What sorts of exceptions did they get?

Admiral Stevenson: When I was Chief of Chaplains, Paul, I think we had gotten to the place where we had somewhere between 13% and 16% minorities in the Chaplain Corps, which was great. I'm very proud of that, because I know the work that went into recruiting chaplains to get us to that point. The Chaplain Corps far exceeded the percentage of minorities of the rest of the Navy.

But when you get above 10% minorities, then it seems to me that you are jeopardizing the careers of some of your minority chaplains, whether they be black or Oriental or female or American Indian or Jewish, although the Jewish would not want to be associated with the word "minority." You get to the place where the detailer is saying, "I can't order this minority chaplain to a proper billet, because I must send him or her to a billet circled for a minority." After a while, what you're doing is you're building a ghetto rather than tearing it down. You are negatively affecting a person's career--the law of unintended consequences.

Q: Why did certain billets get circled as minority billets?

Admiral Stevenson: Sometimes because "there would be seniors around" who could provide paternalism for them or because of the population of that minority in the unit, or it was a part of the United States that restricted their living in the area.

Q: Did you develop a system to get the minority chaplain developed into an all-purpose chaplain?

Admiral Stevenson: Yes, and I think the minority chaplains did it themselves by adapting, but I think we had to do it. So that's when I had to make some decisions that I lost a little sleep over. I had to make some decisions to do away with what minorities had begun to accept as normal support systems, but if continued I knew it would be counter-productive to their careers.

For instance, John O'Connor started a program by which once a year all black chaplains came to Washington and had individual meetings with the Chief of Chaplains and called on the Secretary of the Navy and the Chief of Naval Operations. But there comes a time, in my opinion, when that's to the disadvantage of the minority chaplains.

When you pull them all out of the normal requirements of duty, when you make an exception of them, when you have a lieutenant chaplain of a minority who is serving with three other lieutenants, and the three other lieutenants are beginning to say, "Hey, what's the scoop? This guy goes to Washington for special feeding once a year, and I don't." And yet in the real world of doing ministry within that command, you've got to produce, and your evaluation system is based on your producing, not on your minority status. How do you prepare that chaplain for the real world when he's going to become a supervisor of chaplains--all chaplains as chaplains?

They also had a separate meeting for the female chaplains, so that they could get together and be a support to each other. Again, in my opinion, they were relating to each other, and in the early years they needed that support. But they were not relating to command or the wider ministry. They were relating largely to, "What are our problems as a minority?" more than relating to, "What are the problems of the troops who are minorities?

What are they facing?" After too much individual attention, it seemed to me we were handicapping minority chaplains more than helping them.

So I urged Ross Trower as Chief of Chaplains, and then made the decision myself as Chief of Chaplains, to treat chaplains as chaplains. In my opinion, when you get over 10% minorities, as unpopular as it is to the minority chaplain, who has become accustomed to special status, you've got to say, "A chaplain is a chaplain, and we are going to start ordering people as chaplains."

When I was Chief of Chaplains, I decided that we had to put Jewish chaplains on sea duty for that very purpose. For instance, how could you ever have a Jewish chaplain become the detailer of the Chaplain Corps if he has never been eligible or served sea duty in his career? What you've done is you've truncated his career. I think it's very, very important from now on every chaplain be a chaplain. A chaplain of the Jewish faith can provide and facilitate religion in an aircraft carrier just as well as any Presbyterian or Catholic chaplain. At least, he should be put to that test as well as anyone else.

Q: Did you get any resistance or unpleasant feedback when you made this decision that a chaplain is a chaplain?

Admiral Stevenson: Yeah, because I think that people who have gotten used to a support system are hurt when that support system is pulled away. And I talked to some chaplains. I had a bunch of illustrations that I used to throw out, and I'll tell you a sea story on that.

One of my illustrations used to be that there's a big difference between a pioneer and a settler. Somewhere along the line, you have to make the decision of what you're going to do as a settler. You go through a romantic period in which everybody wants to claim that they are a pioneer, and in a sense they are a pioneer. What we forget is there were pioneers who broke out into the frontier and then said, "Hey, this is not for me," and went back. We always think of the pioneer as the one who was successful. You know, some pioneers just got shot and never made it back. So sometimes when somebody is a pioneer in a field, they don't last in that field and that's their sacrifice. That's their cross, if you want to call it that.

But there are also pioneers who have to realize the time has now come to be a settler, and that's what I was trying to say in the Chaplain Corps. You've had these pioneers, but somebody's got to blow the whistle and say, "Stop your pioneering. It's time to plant the crop and stick around and do the job that the other settlers are all doing. You're here to stay. The only thing that will be threatening from now on out is a lack of performance. You know, you're no longer a tutorial student. You are now a full-fledged student, and you're out there competing with the rest of the people."

We are colorblind. And some of them would say to me, "You may think we're colorblind, but this outfit is not. We're not convinced that it's colorblind." And my heart would bleed for them, because, yeah, they came from the inner city, they came from ghettos, and naturally they would be more conscious of the distance they had come and the prejudices that they were up against. But I still think it was the time to call down the barrier and say, "Hey, you know, for the sake of really being incorporated into the whole system, there's got to be a time in which you are not recognized in detailing and in other ways and in special training as a minority."

Q: Were you able to sell this idea?

Admiral Stevenson: I think I sold it to quite a few of them, and I hope that it's working--for their sakes. I don't know how long a paternalistic system is to their advantage.

Let me give you a sea story that brought that into focus for me. When I was in the training desk--and I may have already told you this story--I was in the training desk years ago with Jude Senieur in the early '70s, and we went up to the chaplain school to speak to the advanced course. And one of the students in the advanced course was one of the first black chaplains in the United States Navy, a man whom I had the privilege of serving with several times, was Carroll Chambliss.[*] Carroll Chambliss was a member of the class, and I was told by the detailer that we were allowed to share with some of the students at the advanced course where they were going for duty. So Jude and I shared with Carroll

---

[*] In the early 1970s Chambliss was a commander.

Chambliss that he was going to Camp Lejeune, because the general at Camp Lejeune wanted a black chaplain. This would have been '72, I guess.

We went home to have dinner with Carroll and Chris Chambliss that night at their house and watch a ball game or something, and through the whole ball game, Carroll and Chris talked about the fact that they really didn't like the idea of being ordered to Camp Lejeune as a black chaplain.[*]

I went back to Washington, and I went in to see the division director in those days, who was Vinny Lonergan, one of my favorites of all time. And I said, "Chaplain Lonergan, I think Chaplain Chambliss is very disappointed in his orders, and he doesn't like the idea that he is ordered as a black chaplain."

And Vinny Lonergan said, "You're right. He's a chaplain. He ought to be ordered as a chaplain."

From that, Carroll Chambliss got orders to the USS Franklin D. Roosevelt.[†] And home-ported where? Mayport, Florida. "You mean to say we're going to have two chaplains and one of them is going to be black?"

"Yeah."

"You're not worried about this black chaplain being in Mayport, Florida?"

"No. The time has come." So that was the early expression of the idea, as far as I was concerned.

Q: How well did that one work out in practice?

Admiral Stevenson: I think it worked out very well. Carroll certainly had a successful career; he made captain. He himself was claimant chaplain on one or two occasions. So I think that move at that time was the right move. And that event of 1972 was certainly in my mind in 1978, 1979.

---

[*] Their son Chris was a major league baseball player in the 1970s and 1980s for the Cleveland Indians, New York Yankees, and Atlanta Braves.
[†] USS Franklin D. Roosevelt (CVA-42) was an aircraft carrier.

Q: What can you say about Chaplain O'Connor's working style, his personality?

Admiral Stevenson: [Chuckles] John O'Connor will stand up and make a speech about how he's not a workaholic if somebody accuses him of being a workaholic, but he is. If he's not a workaholic, then he is the most dedicated individual I've ever been around. [Laughter] There's no way any of us could keep the hours that he kept. He was always the first one there in the morning, the last one to leave at night. And he always claimed that he was not doing that to put any pressure on any of the rest of us, but when the senior guy comes in at 5:00 in the morning and goes home at 9:00 o'clock at night, it does put pressure on the rest of us.

Q: You felt that pressure, I take it?

Admiral Stevenson: Oh, yeah, I felt the pressure. Sure.

Q: Well, he didn't have a wife and daughters to interrogate him about the POM.

Admiral Stevenson: No, but that's not necessarily the working style of all celibates, whether they be Catholic, Protestant, or Jewish. John O'Connor had a history in his whole life of being that kind of student and that kind of person, and a very gifted person. One of the great gifts that John O'Connor has had in his lifetime is his ability to write.

Q: What can you say about his intellectual gifts?

Admiral Stevenson: Well, I think they're proven in his ability to get his Ph.D. from Georgetown. He's a fast read; he's an easy person to brief in some ways. He's an easy person to brief if you are briefing factual-type things. If you're briefing him on personnel moves and things, it gets a little more difficult, because he had a tendency not to appear to be proactive in his decision-making, but rather he wanted to have you come up with what he had already thought.

So occasionally, we used to play a game. When Tom Hilferty was the detailer, we would know that Chaplain O'Connor wanted a certain chaplain in a specific place, but Chaplain O'Connor would not say, "I want this guy in this place." Occasionally, we'd have a detailing meeting, and Tom would say, "I'm going to say Norfolk. Neil, you say Charleston. Joe, you say Newport." We'd go in, and Chaplain O'Connor would say, "What are we going to do about So-and-so?" And we would each play our role, and then if one of us was lucky enough to hit the thing, then Chaplain O'Connor would say something like, "Well, that's a possibility." We used to get a little frustrated and say, "Geez, why doesn't he just say such and such?"

Q: What was the point of a game like that?

Admiral Stevenson: Oh, I don't know. The point of a game like that was maybe to give him time to reassess his own thinking about it, to get you involved today where he's already been yesterday. I don't know. Maybe it's just one of those quirks we all have. I mean, I'm sure the guys quite often went back into the cubicles after talking with me and said, "What's Stevenson all hot about that for?" you know, trying to figure out. Considering his abilities, I think John O'Connor was a patient man, but if you were not conscious--and we were not always conscious--of all his gifts and abilities, he came across to us certainly as a very impatient man.

Q: Can you give an example that would illustrate that dichotomy?

Admiral Stevenson: He insisted one time that I give a briefing on the POM process, because he was testing to see whether I really understood the POM process. I had borrowed slides from over in the Pentagon in order to do this thing, and got the slides screwed up in the presentation. He just hauled out of there. For a few minutes there, I was definitely wasting his time, because he already had the POM process in his mind.

Q: So it was for your benefit, not his.

Admiral Stevenson: I suspect it was for my benefit. But a daily dose of that is sometimes a hard thing to deal with. We used to tease in the office that if he got a good night's sleep, he would feel guilty about it and he'd give us all a hard time all day long. [Laughter] Whereas if he only got three or four hours' sleep, he was in a good mood and we were going strong.

I remember one silly thing. He wrote an esoteric letter to all the Catholic priests as priests, and then a similar letter to all the rabbis as rabbis, and to the Protestants as Protestants. Since I was, as they used to occasionally say, the token Protestant on the staff, he asked me one night to look it over, this letter he had written to all the Protestants. It was a good letter. It was a very flowery type of thing. He also liked long letters, and I liked short letters, and that used to lead to controversy.

I think one letter I rewrote seven, eight times--getting it larger and larger and larger. Bottom line was that he didn't like the letter because the letter said no to the request, and I had written my kind of letter, which was a letter that said, "No!" I needed to write his kind of letter, which said, "We have considered what you have proposed. It certainly has great merit. We admire the fact that your brain thinks these things up, but no." [Laughter] So he was far more gracious than I in those kinds of replies, but the answer was the same--"No!"

But in this particular letter to Protestants, he had written that the Protestant chaplain's wife--I think the expression he used--is the chaplain's daily bread and so forth. I went in the next day at a staff meeting, and I critiqued the letter. He was very unhappy with my critique, because I said, "This is a bunch of romantic nonsense, a woman-on-the-pedestal type of thing. You must have seen some old movie in which the minister's wife was a saint. They are wives and they are not unlike other wives. The husband's ordination does not come with marriage for them," and so forth.

I came from a school where one's profession is to be divided from one's family. One's family is not expected to fall into a bunch of categories just because you happen to marry somebody of that profession. I still think that's very, very important. But John did not feel that way about it. He felt that this expression needed to be in there, and he was very unhappy with me. So he challenged me by saying, "When you met Diane, did you not think of her in terms of what a wonderful minister's wife she would be?" I indicated to him that when I first met Diane, when we were both in college together, my reaction was, "Wow!" and had nothing whatsoever to do with the ministry! [Laughter] And I was dismissed from his office in no uncertain terms.

One of the ways John's sense of humor was expressed, I think, would be to put people down. I remember when I asked to be considered for the Pacific Fleet billet, he finally made the decision that I could go to PacFlt, then he would introduce me for the next month or so that I was there as "the traitor on the staff," who was trying to escape the heat of things. I was darn glad to get out of there, to tell you the truth, and get out to PacFlt.

Q: Was he an arbitrary man in decision-making, or was he willing to listen to other viewpoints?

Admiral Stevenson: No, I think he was listening to other viewpoints, but I think you'd have to appreciate again John's abilities and say that there were few issues that he probably had not made up his mind about ahead of time.

We had one thing come in--talking here about a man who's working around the clock, a man who's ahead of the rest of us. But I remember one time a chaplain sent in a letter complaining that the people in my end of the shop had not given support to this chaplain in this aircraft carrier like we should have, and so forth. I was gone on TAD to something at the time, and when I came back, I found out that the chaplains in my shop had been hauled into the chief's office and roundly thrashed with this letter.[*] It was one of the angriest times of my life. I did take the time to put the facts together, because it was a bad call by this chaplain in the carrier, whose name escapes me.

Q: What was the issue?

Admiral Stevenson: This chaplain claimed that he had not received some kind of support that he felt was his due. You know, there are people, in my opinion, who have to prove

---

[*] TAD--temporary additional duty.

their ignorance, and in my opinion, this chaplain proved his ignorance. I was not going to let anybody off the hook on it. I went in with my briefing sheets, and I think to my satisfaction, at least, and also to Chaplain O'Connor's satisfaction, confronted the fact that I didn't think my guys were being treated fairly. I said I thought that this chaplain on the ship was a horse's--and why, A, B, C, D. I think that caught the chief up a little bit. Then our problem was that he was so kind to us for the rest of the week, we got to the place where we were sitting back there saying, "Gosh, if he'd only get off this being-nice-to-us business, we'd get back to doing business on the norm and get some things done around here."

We talked a little earlier, just you and I, about the reaction of people to Admiral King.[*] Maybe this will seem to everybody in the world an unfair statement, but in some sense I suppose there were some similarities maybe. Chaplain O'Connor was ahead of us. He had thought these things out. He had lived in this world, and he knew he had a certain number of years available. As I learned later on, you've got a certain amount of time to get done what you want done. He was the guy who was turning the Chaplain Corps upside down at a time it needed to be turned upside down. He had only four years to do it, and he wanted all these things done. I guess he had more people ordered in and out on that staff. I don't know what the record is of the numbers of people who served the Chief of Chaplains' staff, but I would daresay John O'Connor had the record.

Q: From what you describe, it sounds as if he came in with a long agenda that he had developed over the years leading up to that.

Admiral Stevenson: He is a natural politician. That is not a put-down. He would do things in a more political way than any of the rest of us would ever think of doing, and he got them done.

Q: How do you mean that?

---

[*] Admiral Ernest J. King, USN, served as Chief of Naval Operations from 26 March 1942 to 15 December 1945 and as Commander in Chief U.S. Fleet from 20 December 1941 to 2 September 1945; he was promoted to the rank of fleet admiral in December 1944. He was widely regarded as an extemely capable, no-nonsense officer.

Admiral Stevenson: Oh, like going out to the Chaplain Corps, as he did one time, requesting everybody to send the Chief of Chaplains letters as to who the detailer ought to be. Come on, the Chief of Chaplains is the detailer. There's a guy on the staff who's called the detailer, but the Chief of Chaplains signs the paperwork, like the CO of a ship. So asking chaplains who they would like to have as detailer is not necessarily the way to go about it. Plus the fact that the vast majority of chaplains wouldn't know what the detailer's job demanded. I mean, the detailer's job is looked upon as a surrogate bishop to most chaplains, but if you've served in the Bureau of Naval Personnel, the detailer's job is to justify money for detailing chaplains like other communities are justifying money. You know, again, you're in the realm of economics and accounting as much as you are this business of deciding who's going to go where. That's the easy part.

Q: But he was trying to create the impression, apparently, that he cared for their opinions.

Admiral Stevenson: Yes.

Q: What other things did he do to upset the Chaplain Corps besides the minorities and moving on to the POM system?

Admiral Stevenson: Well, I think the alcohol seminar that year was a breakthrough, dealing with actual problems in the corps itself.

Q: Please tell me more.

Admiral Stevenson: I think John O'Connor probably related more on a one-to-one with line admirals than Chiefs of Chaplains had, willing to challenge their thinking at staff meetings, willing to go to all the meetings, certainly willing to posture himself as an equal, rather than a "staffie." So I think all those things were of benefit. When John traveled, I think people were aware of the fact that John had access to people in the Washington area and that he was willing to speak up when he thought something was wrong somewhere or needed to be done better, so forth and so on.

[Chuckles] For some reason, I remember some of the more humorous things that happened. He was on a trip, and his division director, Jerry Sargent, had suffered a heart attack and was on the binnacle list. So, lo and behold, Neil Stevenson was the senior guy in the office. A phone call came in, and the Chief of Chaplains' secretary said that a CEC admiral, whose name I forget, was calling and needed to talk to the chief.[*]

Another one of the things that John O'Connor brought to light was the fact that the Navy had just not built any chapels. "It is 1977 and chapels are still in Quonset huts or the like all over the world. Other buildings are getting built. Where is the Chaplain Corps share of construction dollars?" And he had provoked that. So the phone call came in. Again, the background studies had all been done. The admiral said to me on the phone, "Can you get ahold of Chaplain O'Connor within the next 15 minutes?"

I said, "No, I can't."

He said, "But I need an answer within 15 minutes, because I've got to go back into this committee hearing, and I either have to present the fact that we're going to build a new chapel in Naples, Italy, or Pearl Harbor. What do you want?"

I don't remember whether I said, "I'll call you back in five minutes," or whether I just gave him an answer there. [Chuckles] But I said to myself, "Well, I'm here and there has to be an answer. I can't contact the chief, so I'll write a memo to the chief." And I said Pearl Harbor.

The admiral said, "Fine. It's going to be Pearl Harbor." Pearl Harbor was the one that was approved within that POM.

Q: Why did you decide Pearl Harbor?

Admiral Stevenson: Because it was American territory. And when the chief came back, he wasn't particularly happy with my choice. He had visited both areas, and he felt that it was more important to have one in Naples. [Laughter] So he let me know that I had guessed

---

[*] CEC--the Navy's Civil Engineer Corps.

wrong. His decision would have been based on having visited the areas. My decision was based on the fact that Pearl Harbor was American territory. And who knows? Maybe we won't be in Italy two years from now. So let's go for Pearl. I had been to the Quonset hut in Pearl Harbor.

All those kinds of things. As I say, I was there for one year and things were happening. It was a good time. I left there with a very secure feeling that I could do a job as a fleet chaplain because of where I had been and what I had learned.

Q: You had gone in initially with some trepidation about being able to live up to expectations. Do you feel, in retrospect, that you did live up to those expectations?

Admiral Stevenson: Oh, I hope I did. A good deal of this business of the POM, etc., was to be done over a three-year tour of duty. It happened in one year. Again, it happened because Admiral Watkins was there. It happened because John O'Connor was there. I was down working with the mechanics. But it happened.

One day one of the lieutenant commanders, the wonderful snipes in the Bureau of Naval Personnel, called, and he said, "Chaplain Stevenson, the '79 POM went through. You got a buy for 124 billets." I had the thrill of going into the Chief of Chaplains, along with Chaplain Dimino and Chaplain Boreczky.[*] And I said, "I'm able to report to you that the Chaplain Corps is in the POM for a 124-billet buy for five years." And I don't think he believed me.

He said, "You're sure? What's your source for this?" and so forth and so on. And I'm sure that later on he checked. [Laughter] He checked to see if I was having a mirage or something like that. But that was a very thrilling time in my career. You know, you think back to all these bull sessions with Jim Ammons and all these guys back in the early '70s, and then in 1977, the thing came down the pike and it was there. The Chaplain Corps was in the system.

Then they were debating at that time ad infinitum the fact that Chaplain Moore was coming in from PacFlt, because one of the other things that went on in those days was to

---
[*] Captain John V. Boreczky, CHC, USN.

fight for legislation to change the office of the Chief of Chaplains and the structure of the Chief of Chaplains.[*]

Q: Change it in what way?

Admiral Stevenson: Well, the Navy had the only Chief of Chaplains who was directly under the Chief of Naval Personnel. In the Army and the Air Force, the Chief of Chaplains was under the Chief of Staff of the Army, Chief of Staff of the Air Force. The endorsing agents looked upon that as a sign that the Navy didn't take religion as seriously as the Air Force and the Army had. So legislation was proposed, and the legislation did go through. There was a great debate in those days and arguments whether the Chief of Chaplains ought to be under the Secretary of the Navy or under the Chief of Naval Personnel or under the Chief of Naval Operations.

I was one of the voices, just within the staff, who constantly cried out that the Chief of Chaplains should <u>never</u> be directly under the Secretary of the Navy. I think that's very inappropriate. I think the Chief of Chaplains and the Chaplain Corps belong to the blue suits, not the politicians.

Anyway, there were a lot of debates, and a lot of that was debated within the DOPMA issues. Then DOPMA fell apart that year and sort of disappeared. That which was high on the list when I first came to the office just sort of disappeared, and nobody knew what to do with it. Then that came down from the Hill, from Senator Nunn, when I came in as deputy in 1980.[†] DOPMA came crashing down on everybody. That's another story.

But the legislation that John O'Connor started did eventually get approved. It got approved as part of, believe it or not, of all things, the National Emergency Act, as I recall, in 1979-1980. So that I became the first legitimate Deputy Chief of Chaplains in the Chaplain Corps.

---

[*] Rear Admiral Withers M. Moore, CHC, USN, was the command chaplain for the Pacific Fleet. His oral history is in the series conducted by the Navy's Chaplain Corps.
[†] Sam Nunn (Democrat-Georgia) was chairman of the Senate Armed Services Committee.

Q: What had been the setup before that?

Admiral Stevenson: The Chief of Chaplains was directly under the Chief of Naval Personnel, and a Chaplain Corps captain served as the executive director of the Chaplains Division. The second flag of the Chaplain Corps had always served somewhere else--CinCUSNavEur, PacFlt, etc. I personally felt that that was not the way it ought to be, that it ought to be a system by which the deputy comes in, runs that office while the chief does the chief's things, and then the deputy fleets up to chief, and that you get the kind of rotation that the JAG and other corps have.*

Q: You brought up the alcoholism problem. Was that viewed as a religious issue, leadership, medical?

Admiral Stevenson: That was a two-pronged thing, I think. It was that alcoholism is a problem in the Navy, as it is everywhere in the world, that chaplains ought to be educated as to what alcoholism really is, what recovery treatment really demands, and so forth. The by-product is that, like all communities in the Navy, you've got to confront those who suffer from the disease within your own community. Doctors have to recognize alcoholics in their profession; chaplains have to recognize people with alcohol problems within their profession. So the training program that year provoked that kind of response.

Q: Was a specific remedy established then?

Admiral Stevenson: No. No specific remedy, other than the remedies all other people who are afflicted with that disease face. The Navy was developing a fairer policy regarding alcoholics in those days, and chaplains who suffered from the disease would be subject to the system. Chaplains would not be an exception to the rule. If a chaplain had an alcohol

---

* JAG--Judge Advocate General, the Navy's top legal officer.

problem, he ought to face it, or senior chaplains needed to have a confrontation and say, "This is your work record, and is alcoholism one of the root causes here?"

Q: What had been the approach before then with alcoholic chaplains?

Admiral Stevenson: Oh, sometimes it was ignored, like the rest of the Navy. We tried to ignore things, or else we would try to work around the individual. You know, all the standard things that were done for others who had alcohol problems. Or in severe cases, we just discharged the individual. But if some chaplain was a regular naval officer, everybody would be trying to work around his problems: "He's only got another two years to go until he retires, so let's do what we can." But now the Chaplains Corps had to change with the rest of the Navy; alcoholism was confronted head on.

By the way, the training required a mandatory attendance for all chaplains at that seminar, and I'm one of the few chaplains who did not attend the alcohol seminar that year. The Chief of Chaplains said it was mandatory attendance, and when it came my time to attend one of the seminars, he told me there wasn't time for me to take off from his staff. [Laughter]

Q: One of the observations, it seems to me, about this tour of duty is that it did a lot to build the foundation for you being the chief later.

Admiral Stevenson: I think it built on the graduate work, it built on the advanced course, it built on the previous experience on the Chief of Chaplains' staff. Yes, I have always said that I'm one of the fortunate ones. I had the good fortune of these kinds of experiences, although I was not always happy at the time that I had them. Life is training.

Q: And you realized that more in retrospect.

Admiral Stevenson: Yes, more in retrospect, it looks like they all fell together. And I'm not being a Presbyterian predestinarian, either.

Q: Is there anything else that you want to put on the record from that tour of duty?

Admiral Stevenson: I was happy it was over. They had a party for several of us who were leaving the staff. At that time, Dave White was leaving the staff, and I was leaving. I remember that Diane and I were asked to say a few words, and Diane and I decided ahead of time that we would say, "Free at last! Free at last! Thank God Almighty, I'm free at last!" [Laughter] And "Aloha." So after one year in Washington, we had a set of orders.

Just to let you know how I got there--one morning, very bold, I went in around 7:00 o'clock. The chief was in the office alone. I interrupted him, and I said that I wanted to privately ask for consideration to be the fleet chaplain in the Pacific. He said, "Get out of here." So I figured that was the end of the subject. Then other people like Chaplain Dimino kept bringing it up. "Why don't you send Stevenson out to the fleet?"

It was a month or six weeks later that Diane was stopping by with Heather. They were out shopping for Heather's wedding dress. It was a very rare occasion for them to come by the office to go to lunch with me. While we were standing in the cafeteria line, Chaplain Boreczky came up to my wife, not to me, and said to Diane, "Well, you should start buying some clothes to go to Hawaii, because the chief decided this morning."

Q: What sorts of duties did you encounter once you got out to Hawaii?

Admiral Stevenson: Well, another learning experience. We reported in to CinCPacFlt and LogPac.* Actually, the orders in those days were to be chaplain at LogPac and yet additional duty orders to CinCPacFlt.

Q: Why was it done that way?

Admiral Stevenson: I think it was done that way so that the headquarters billets would be minimized because of congressional interest always in the numbers of headquarters billets.

---

* CinCPacFlt--Commander in Chief Pacific Fleet; LogPac--Logistics Command, Pacific Fleet.

Q: But your real job was for the fleet commander in chief?

Admiral Stevenson: No. Both were real jobs.

Q: I see.

Admiral Stevenson: Because PacFlt was unique in the fact that it had a LogPac, and LogPac had direct control of all the bases that rimmed the Pacific. In my LogPac hat, I was force chaplain, as it were, for the naval stations at Subic Bay, Yokosuka, San Diego, Long Beach, Pearl Harbor, Diego Garcia, etc.

Then with my fleet hat, I was fleet chaplain to the forces of the fleet, such as SurfPac, NavAirPac, LogPac, etc.[*] Organizationally, it was a good arrangement.

Q: What were the responsibilities in connection with LogPac as far as dealing with these various bases you've enumerated?

Admiral Stevenson: The bases existed to support the fleet. One of the major priorities, as I saw it, was to see that chaplain-wise, the bases supported the fleet. There was a tendency then, as I suppose there is a tendency now, that when a chaplain goes to work and reports to Naval Station Yokosuka, Japan, the chaplain thinks of himself as the pastor of the First Church of Yokosuka, Japan. And that the church is made up of this Sunday school and this CCD and this chapel and people who live there on the base and who come from off base to be part of the religious program.

God knows that's probably plenty of work, but the other reason that the chaplain is there is so that when ships come to Yokosuka, the chaplains in Yokosuka extend themselves into religious support for those ships. With the minimized number of Catholic priests in shipboard duty and, in those days, no rabbis on shipboard duty, when ships get

---

[*] SurfPac--Naval Surface Force, Pacific Fleet; AirPac--Naval Air Force, Pacific Fleet.

into a place like Yokosuka, Japan, it's essential that the chaplains be proactive in providing services for the ships. So that's one of the things that I went to PacFlt to emphasize.

Q: You do, indeed, have to be proactive, because most sailors on Sunday morning on board a ship are not eager to get up and go to church.

Admiral Stevenson: Unless they've changed drastically over the years--the sailors who will go to worship in their own ship will not be likely to walk across a brow to another ship to go to worship. So it's important for chaplains to hold a multitude of services. In your fleet job, you're trying to train chaplains to have the eyes to see and to meet those needs, to make themselves, in that good old expression, <u>visible and available</u>. To ensure that the naval station chaplains have the provisions that any seagoing chaplains might need in the way of wafers and grape juice and so forth.

Then part of the task was to travel around and to motivate chaplains to recognize the ministry that was around them. Visiting a naval air station and finding out, for instance, that the chaplains had a nice program at the chapel, but are they visiting the hangars? That kind of thing. At the same time, I was also the chaplain for the chapel at Makalapa.[*]

As fleet chaplain, you are also reporting to your seniors what the tone of religion is throughout the fleet and the force. You are also indicating to command where you feel that there are human-relation problems that need to be addressed. And there's another chore. When I was in Washington, I was disappointed that the fleet and force chaplains were not as active as I thought they ought to be in identifying for the Chief of Chaplains the type of chaplains needed in particular billets. I did not call the detailer and twist arms for certain personalities, but I certainly felt that my job was to inform the Chief of Chaplains' office as to the kind of personnel we should have.

When I ran into the situation where I thought that we had not done justly by a command, where I told them, "I'm not blaming the guys in Washington, because this is information that's hidden from Washington, but you've ordered a chaplain into an overseas

---

[*] Makalapa, near Pearl Harbor, is the site of the headquarters compound for Commander in Chief Pacific Fleet.

billet. His wife has a problem [maybe it's an alcohol problem, maybe it's a timidity problem] and here you've got her overseas." Or, "You've got a chaplain who's the only chaplain in an area of the Philippines, and his religion will not allow him to give communion to anybody but the people of his own denomination." Why do we do that?

Q: How responsive was Washington?

Admiral Stevenson: I think as responsive as they could be. John Boreczky was detailer in those days, and John would take stuff like that on board and deal with it.

I would also tell you that I made some great mistakes in that system. I'll tell you about one of the worst mistakes, because it might help somebody else some day. I had a report on a chaplain who was considered to be having personality problems, that he was holing himself up in his stateroom on the ship, he was not being seen by crew or wardroom, that the executive officer considered him uncooperative or perhaps in need of a mental evaluation. I received these reports from several sources, including chaplains outside the ship. I did not meet the chaplain, nor did I have the opportunity to visit the ship. The ship was visiting Subic Bay. So I contacted the senior chaplain at that base, and I said, "Get to the root of this thing. We need to know what's going on."

He came back and said, well, he felt the man was under a lot of pressure and so forth and so on. A long story short, the man was ordered to medical and back to a hospital in the States. I was very frustrated about the whole situation. He was given a mental evaluation, and they said he was okay. They sent him back down to the home port of the ship while the ship was still deployed. Then, about a month or two months later, I was talking to the senior chaplain of the force in San Diego, and he told me, "The man is okay. Just leave him alone."

Then this force chaplain said to me that ever since this man's first cancer surgery, they felt he had a problem. I will never forget saying, "What cancer? Where are all the facts?" I couldn't believe over the months that no one had informed me that the chaplain had had major cancer surgery.

That is a sad story, and I mention that sad story because I became a great advocate from then on of being very quick to inform anyone around me that people make decisions based on the information they have, and therefore I want all the information I can get. I suppose after that, some chaplains probably felt that I was probing more than I needed to probe from time to time, but I had learned the hard way.

Q: What was the ultimate outcome in his case?

Admiral Stevenson: Well, it so happened that the man ended up with a second operation. He was discharged from the service for a period of time and then brought back on active duty. But from a fleet chaplain's perspective, I don't know whether some of the chaplains involved thought that they were protecting some kind of confidentiality or whether they were playing pastor to pastor, rather than playing just plain senior to junior. They should have been forwarding facts for the decision-making process. You have to make decisions, and you make the decisions based on the knowledge you have.

Q: In that fleet chaplains are spread fairly thin in ships, did you find a high degree of dedication to cover as much as they could?

Admiral Stevenson: Not as much as I wanted. It was a constant battle of pushing chaplains. I would imagine to this day it's a subject that needs to be pushed. As human beings, I guess it is. We get very much at home with our immediate environment and need to be motivated to get into other environments. I think chaplains do an exceptionally good job in the helo-hopping, getting to other ships and so forth, but the business of availability and visibility when the ships are at the pier and you're the chaplain assigned to the station, you've got to fight laziness to get yourself out of that office. Because they announce the chaplain is aboard doesn't mean everybody's going to come pouring out on deck and say, "Hallelujah!" Because they've all got work to do and so forth. But the fact that they know that you make the regular rounds is essential.

In that same line, Paul, another battle you fight is the sailor who goes to the hospital. You have to constantly remind a chaplain that if that sailor is from his ship or squadron, he should go see that sailor. The chaplain, with some degree of legitimacy, can say, "Wait a minute. The chaplains assigned to the hospital should go see him."

"Yes, they should see him also, but you need to go see him if he is from your command."

It's the same fight you have when you say to a chaplain on shore duty, "Mrs. So-and-so has had a baby in a civilian hospital. Her husband is assigned to USS Gumstump. Make the hospital call."

"Well, wait a minute now. You know, Gumstump is not part of my . . ."

"Doesn't make any difference. You go see her and you send a chaplain's message out to that ship and say the chaplain has seen Mrs. So-and-so and that the baby is doing well, and send a copy to the XO of your own command, etc."

But you have to deal with all those kinds of things that are outside the immediate domain of your set of orders, and force and fleet chaplains have to motivate their chaplains to do those kinds of things, and to use "copy to" to see that they are reported.

Q: Let's say that a certain ship is in port, and the base chaplain is motivated to go to that ship. He is interrupting work, so how welcome is he made by the command?

Admiral Stevenson: There isn't any such thing as a ship where you weren't invited to have a cup of coffee. Again, availability and visibility may be nothing more than getting an appointment with the XO. Don't just drop in on an XO.

And, again, rank has its privileges, so the guy that you may have to motivate as fleet or force chaplain to do this is the senior chaplain at Naval Station Guam, okay? And the senior chaplain goes down to that ship and has an appointment to see the XO, and he may be senior to the XO. And the XO says, "Come on in the wardroom and have a cup of coffee."

And the chaplain says, "You're going to be in port for ten days, and I've got a rabbi, I've got a Catholic priest, and I've got myself. If you want divine services, fine. If some of your people need to talk to somebody, fine. If you'd like me to walk around the decks and just say hello, fine. But we want you to know if we can help you, we can help you.

He may say, "Gee, I think we're in pretty good shape, Chaplain, and the guys can go to the chapel if they want to go to the chapel." Fine.

Q: At least he's taken that first step.

Admiral Stevenson: You've got to take the initiative. The only time the initiative is going to be reversed is when you have an XO or a CO that's Catholic, and they come in and call you up and say, "We want a priest for Mass," which is great. Doesn't necessarily say anything about what's going to happen to the guys or the gals in that ship who do not happen to be Catholic. I learned early on in destroyers that when I got into any port with my ships in the Mediterranean or anywhere else we were, the expectation was that as the chaplain, I was going to go out and find a Catholic priest and get him to that ship.

As I told you, I had an "if book" that I had compiled in case I became a senior chaplain somewhere, and I used it at Orlando. Then I had also said to myself, "If I go out to PacFlt, I want to do this." Well, in this case my agenda included making sure that the LogPac and the PacFlt billets were in good shape, because I was going to take my manpower knowledge with me. So I went over and talked to the manpower people in the fleet shop, and, lo and behold, by the time I got to LogPac, they were working SHORSTAMPS for LogPac.

I was interested in the budgets for the command religious program everywhere I went. I know that some chaplains got the word around that, "The bigger your budget is, the better Stevenson will like you, so you've got to have a big budget when Neil comes by." But I would be hoping that what I was saying was, "I don't care if your budget is ten bucks, if that covers what you need to cover to meet the needs of these troops. I mean, if all you need is rosary beads, at least you've got the ten bucks to buy the rosary beads."

Q: How do you think you got that reputation?

Admiral Stevenson: Because I was of the vintage that raised questions about a budget. Again, John O'Connor's breaking the tradition of the paternalism. We were trying to break paternalism in places like Orlando, where I had worked the command religious program budget. So I was anxious to see people using those same kind of tools, not to see how big a budget somebody had, but to see that the chaplains were in the system, that the chaplains recognized the fact that they were doing institutional ministry, that they were not dependent on buying the equipment that the chapel needed out of the so-called chapel fund in those days. The title in itself caused all kinds of confusion in budget matters. One of my joys of going back to Washington as deputy and chief was to get chapel funds renamed as religious offering funds.

Q: Where did that come from? Was that made up of donations from the congregation?

Admiral Stevenson: Donations by those who attended chapel. It had been called for years the chapel fund, and it got everybody confused each year when Navy did its accounting on non-appropriated funds. The chapel fund was a non-appropriated fund which people associated with the chapel and thought that it was being used for the upkeep of the chapel. It wasn't, because the upkeep of the chapel is appropriated money.

Q: What was done with this chapel fund?

Admiral Stevenson: Well, what should have been done was that it should have been expended within the will of the donors. That is to Catholic, Jewish, or Protestant charities. For instance, while I was stationed at PacFlt, we had the boat people problem, and we took up collections in the chapel to assist the boat people.* Charitable giving, rather than support of the local chapel program, which should be the command's appropriated fund.

---

* Boat people were refugees who set out from Vietnam in small, often unseaworthy boats in an attempt to escape to a better life elsewhere.

Q: I think of all the times I ever attended Navy church services, only once was it explained what happened to the collection.

Admiral Stevenson: Well, that's a sad statement. Religious offering funds should not be making up any difference of a lack of appropriated funds.

Q: Had various chaplains used that as a crutch?

Admiral Stevenson: Oh, sure. See, you don't even have to write up a budget if you're going to use that. You don't have to confront command with a program. You don't have to do any PPBS. You can send the funds to the seminary at home, as some guys did, and look good.

Q: You mentioned in passing the Makalapa chapel. What was the story with that?

Admiral Stevenson: Oh, the Makalapa chapel. Well, the Makalapa chapel was a great place. The Makalapa chapel was the building that had been used as Admiral Nimitz's mess in World War II, and sometime after that became the Makalapa chapel.[*] It was one of the famous buildings in Makalapa, held together by the termites. In my day, along with Father John Glynn, who was relieved by Chaplain Al Sullivan, we used to tease that you really couldn't leave anything in the sacristy, because when you came back, it was polluted with termite manure.[†] That was the famous Makalapa chapel, pews in an elongated Quonset hut-type structure with no air-conditioning.

Q: How much time did you spend in Hawaii and how much out on the road?

---

[*] Fleet Admiral Chester W. Nimitz, USN, Commander in Chief Pacific Fleet and Pacific Ocean Areas, 1941-45.
[†] Captain John J. Glynn, CHC, USN; Captain Alen P. Sullivan, CHC, USN.

Admiral Stevenson: I probably spent half of my time in Hawaii, the rest on the road, Paul. When I wasn't going to be at the Makalapa chapel, I had to get somebody to hold services for me, which was okay. The naval officers quartered in Makalapa were the ones who largely attended, although Catholic Mass had a larger attendance than just people who lived in the Makalapa area, which is kind of flag row.

Anyway, you recall that I said that this quick decision had been made in the phone conversation to build a chapel in Pearl Harbor. [Chuckles] And the Navy built a beautiful chapel in Pearl Harbor. Even though I was the force chaplain for LogPac, it didn't exactly get built the way I had hoped it would be built, because it got built stuffed with pews, and if anybody's interested, to this day I still don't think that that chapel needs pews. In fact, I think most chapels are handicapped by pews, because the chapel ought to be flexible enough that it looks good when you have 25 people and it looks good when you have 250 people. You do that more with chairs and cushions than you do with pews, which are fixed entities. But, anyway, it's got pews. It shows you the lack of power that a fleet and force chaplain has with his opinion. [Laughter]

Q: I imagine there was a sense of satisfaction as you saw this new chapel going up.

Admiral Stevenson: Yes, that was kind of fun. The chaplains over on the base and the CO of the base at that time, who became a very close friend of mine, Shep Shapero, was a great CO, Jewish, to have when that chapel was built.[*] He knew how to celebrate the coming of a new era. The chapel was built so that it is right smack down with the ships.

Well, the Makalapa chapel was supported, as everything in Makalapa was supported--special services-wise and so forth--by Naval Station Pearl Harbor. There wasn't any money around to refurbish the Makalapa Chapel that was falling around our ears. So when the new chapel came into being, I felt very strongly that people who lived in Makalapa, which is a mile and a half away from the new chapel, ought to be part of the larger chapel community. My recommendation was that the Makalapa chapel be closed. That recommendation went through. There were some people who were unhappy about it.

---

[*] Captain Allen L. Shapero, USN.

I was amused at the senior officers who lived in Makalapa, who, to the best of my knowledge, never attended chapel, but were upset that the chaplain was closing the chapel. Anyway, it was closed, and it was made into a photo lab or some such things.

Q: So the termites could pollute the photos.

Admiral Stevenson: Well, no, I think there was some money to renovate the building from the photo people that was not available on the chapel basis. But, anyway, long story short, just so that you can have a sense of humor about this thing, shortly after I went to Washington as Deputy Chief of Chaplains, the Vice Chief of Naval Operations was ordered out as CinCPacFlt. And when Admiral Watkins, devout man that he is, got to Hawaii and found out that there was no longer a Makalapa chapel, he was one very unhappy man.[*] [Laughter] My rationale for closing the chapel, I'm sure, never made any sense to Admiral Watkins. In fact, he told me it never made any sense to him. He wanted his own chapel, and one was provided, but that's a long story.

Q: What are your recollections of Admiral Hayward as the fleet commander in chief?[†]

Admiral Stevenson: Very, very pleasant. I had never been around a man who had a more natural ability to exude leadership than Admiral Hayward.

Q: What examples do you recall?

Admiral Stevenson: Well, he's a good-looking, charming gentleman who has that kind of magnetism that makes people like him. He makes himself open to people and available to people. He and his wife Peggy entertained and included everyone. He was always in the pew on Sunday morning, so he was a man who was practicing his own religious belief.

---

[*] Admiral James D. Watkins, USN, served as Commander in Chief Pacific Fleet, 31 July 1981 to 28 May 1982.
[†] Admiral Thomas B. Hayward, USN, served as Commander in Chief Pacific Fleet, 12 August 1976 to 9 May 1978.

I remember when he was selected for Chief of Naval Operations, it was written up in Time magazine that he was the only admiral in the United States Navy at that time who would receive a unanimous vote from every other admiral in the United States Navy that he should be the Chief of Naval Operations. I think that was true. I mean, it was true. Before I ever met Admiral Hayward, that's what I had heard about Admiral Hayward, and when I met him and worked for him, I was just thrilled to work for him.

His deputy was a big Irishman from Boston, Admiral Tom Bigley, and Tom Bigley did me an enormous favor.* When I reported in as fleet chaplain, he immediately asked me to come and see him, told me that he was interested in what I was doing and interested in what was happening within the fleet, that it was my task to get an appointment from his EA, for me to be in to see him once every two or three weeks.† If I had no agenda, that was fine, but I was still supposed to be there. If I was there for ten minutes, fine. If I was there for half an hour, fine. But he wanted me on his calendar once every two or three weeks to bring him up to date with what was happening with religion in the fleet. And you can't ask for anything better.

That opened doors for me, allowed me to share with him exactly how I saw things. Of course, he knew the Navy, he knew what was going on. He could also steer me, that maybe I ought to visit such and such a place, because he would have received word--before I would through a chaplain's circle, he would have received word through a command circle that maybe the fleet chaplain ought to drop in on this place and see if he couldn't solve some problems.

Q: What sorts of things were you able to accomplish through that access?

Admiral Stevenson: Well, a silly illustration comes to mind, but there was a chaplain in the fleet, in one of the LogPac commands, who, when I had visited the place, there seemed to be a good relationship between command and the chaplains department. The word had come in that the chaplains department was not doing the job very well, that maybe I ought

---
* Vice Admiral Thomas J. Bigley, USN.
† EA--executive assistant.

to stop in. A couple of months later, I made a point of getting to this place, and it will sound silly to a lot of people, but what had really happened was that the senior chaplain, although he'd been in the Navy 20 years, had never really gotten out of a parish mentality.

To make a long story short, what I found was that the command had kind of an awards ceremony type of thing. Because of weather conditions, it was decided that the best place to use was the religious education building on the base, which was perfectly fine. For the numbers of spectators, they needed many additional chairs. All of this had been discussed at department-head meetings.

Lo and behold, when it came near the event, the chaplain asked the public works officer on a Sunday morning when he was coming out of church to see that the chairs were there for the ceremony and taken down after the ceremony. But the senior chaplain had blown his stack when he found out that the cost for putting up and taking down the chairs had come out of the chaplains department budget. The senior chaplain blew his stack by claiming that the public works officer was cheating him, and making statements that the command didn't support religion. [Laughter] Of course, if he had been attuned to institutional ministry, when they were discussing setting, he would have asked, "Where's the funding coming from?" Like any other department head would, "Is this money coming out of contingency? Where's it coming out of?"

When I talked to the public works officer, it was interesting, because he was a faithful member of this chaplain's flock. His view was, "I hate to tell you this, but all clergy are lazy. So when the chaplain said he needed the chairs, I went and did the paperwork for him. I filled out the requisition, I sent it in. I did all his work for him, and then all he does is criticize me."

It's just a great example in my memory of a chaplain who had been in the Navy for 20 years without ever being aware of the fact that he was in the system and that he ought to work the system like everybody else. Instead, what you had was all kinds of bad relationships. The senior chaplain was ignorant of the way in which he should have handled a very common funding requisition type situation.

Q: Chaplains get involved in a number of other collateral duties besides just religious things. Did you supervise any of these things: Navy Relief, dependent programs, or whatever?

Admiral Stevenson: Well, each command would have a different approach to it. In some cases I would have to remind the command, as it specifies in regulations, that the chaplain should not be synonymous with Navy Relief. I think most commands appreciated that, but occasionally we ran into the situation where the commanding officer thought that the chaplain ought to be Mr. Navy Relief.

That's a problem, because Navy Relief, like all charitable organizations, has specific regulations regarding how and who they can give funds to. It's really not good for the overall cause of religion or of counseling for the chaplain to be the one who refuses to give an individual the money that he needs at that time. So you lose out on the counseling relationship, and you may lose out on the family relationship, and you may even lose out on the religious relationship. That the chaplain is a supportive part of the whole Navy Relief picture, fine. But the chaplain should never be the one who handles the funds for Navy Relief. Every once in a while you have to either be in the job of reminding a CO or an XO that a chaplain should be as active as all get-out, but he is not the one who writes the check or makes the decision as to who gets a check.

Ministry is always filled with a certain amount of collateral duties. Some of them are more appropriate to the chaplain's role than others are. You also have to remind commands that the endorsing agents who represent the faith groups are going to be somewhat judgmental concerning the collateral duties. For instance, a Southern Baptist chaplain who is on the officers' club board might not be looked upon as an appropriate collateral duty, and you might have to educate command to the sensitivity of that in regards to a specific chaplain.

Most naval hospitals, I assume, now have ethics boards--a very, very sensitive issue, because you have to remind the endorsing agent of a specific chaplain that the chaplain's job on the ethics board is to speak in behalf of the patient's religious convictions, not the chaplain's convictions. <u>Sometimes you have to remind the chaplain of that</u>. You may have an extreme case where the patient was a Jehovah's Witness, and the hospital feels that he had to have a blood transfusion, but the man's religion says he shouldn't have a blood transfusion. The chaplain needs to represent the patient, not the chaplain's ethics or moral theology at the meeting of the ethics board.

Q: Even if it's going to do harm to the patient.

Admiral Stevenson: That's why the chaplain should only be a member of an ethics board. There are medical types, I would assume, who are speaking for other parts of the ethical situation. Just as the chaplain might be a part of the decision process concerning the sincerity of a conscientious objector, but that should only be one piece of a conscientious objector appeal. You know, pluralistic society, and you're representing--under the employ of an institution--that pluralism.

Q: Is the Chaplain Corps small enough that you could essentially know most, or all, of the chaplains in the Pacific Fleet?

Admiral Stevenson: I recall in those days we had in PacFlt 270-some chaplains or something like that. In your visitations, you can get a very good handle on them, particularly the ones who are deployed and the ones who are assigned overseas. Because when you meet with them, they're not absorbed, as it were, into the normal civilian society of a place like San Diego or San Francisco. You meet with them out on those ships, you meet with them in an overseas isolated circumstance. You get to know people pretty fast. That's by far the better part of being a fleet/force chaplain.

I still say the best job in the whole Chaplain Corps is PacFlt. It's a much better job than deputy or Chief of Chaplains or any of those jobs. [Laughter]

Q: Why do you say that?

Admiral Stevenson: You're involved hand to hand in ministry. You are under direct authority to supervise and train chaplains. Everywhere you go there's an opportunity for training, observation, passing on ideas. "Hey, this is what the guys in Subic are doing. Why don't you try it in Guam?" At the same time, you get this tremendous education of the pros and cons of every duty station. I used to enjoy going around and finding out that the chaplains in Yokosuka were envious of the guys in Subic. The chaplains in Subic, of course, were envious of the ones who were in Yokosuka. They think the grass is always greener, and you get to say that, "It ain't necessarily so."

The Hong Kong chaplain's work was having a very direct effect in reducing drug usage and in actually cutting down on the loss of lives. We had Chaplain Dick Day in Hong Kong, and he set up a program so that one of the wives of a chaplain or an American citizen in Hong Kong would go out to a ship before liberty commenced, and give a briefing over the 1MC about the drug problem in Hong Kong.* We had had a couple of deaths in Hong Kong the years before, and Dick Day was working to combat the situation.

Dick Day had set up a system so that he knew the service resources in Hong Kong, and he was there to emphasize to local police, ambulance drivers, and so forth: "If you get a sailor in distress, you take them to the British Military Hospital. You don't take them to the Chinese hospital. You give me a call, you get me involved." I don't know if you've ever been to Fenwick Pier, but the chaplain's operation in Fenwick Pier when the fleet is in, I think is a pretty vital operation.

One thing that should be remembered, Paul, is that every so often the chaplains want the fleet or force chaplain or the Chief of Chaplains to come and tell them what's going on in the fleet, or what's going on in Washington, what's going on in the Chaplain Corps. That's fine, and anybody in those jobs should be capable of doing that. I discovered that the shock for many of them was when I said, "I really didn't come here to tell you about Washington or the fleet; I came here to find out what you're doing." I think I had kind of a reputation as being a little hard-nosed, because what I was saying was, "They didn't pay my way out here for me to tell you about the fleet as much as they paid me to come out here

---

* Commander Richard T. Day, CHC, USN.

and find out what you're doing. If you're doing something worthwhile, we'll pass it on to other people."

One of the things I developed when I went out there, tying some of these things together--speaking of memorabilia--was having experienced the chaplains' planning book and how it fit into my Orlando experience. I decided when I got to be fleet chaplain that I would develop a loose-leaf notebook to put in the hands of every chaplain in the fleet so that the chaplain would have his own command religious program book. Again, I was pushing the phrase "command religious program." I sent it out, and I listed in it all of the advantages for each chaplain to organize his own planning book. That was a means I had of trying to see if anybody was using it. If they were using it, how were they using it, and was it being as effective as it ought to be, and as applicable to every command in PacFlt as I had found it to be in my chaplains' department in Orlando.

Q: One question that has occurred to me as we talk is whether chaplains are rank-conscious to the degree that line officers are.

Admiral Stevenson: Well, I think that depends on who the chaplain is. I think one of the great privileges of being a chaplain is that you are the only officer who, by Navy regulations, is allowed to be called "Chaplain," no matter what your rank. When you're wearing a uniform, it's quite obvious what your rank is, so what's the big deal? The big deal is that you should be called "Chaplain" and referred to as "Chaplain." You approach things as a chaplain and you do that without an apology. What the line officer who is in command is looking for is not a competitor or an advocate who thinks just the way he does. When he wants a chaplain's opinion, my assumption is he wants a chaplain's opinion coming from the frame of references that a chaplain has.

At the same time, I don't think the chaplain should be the one who advertises himself as an expert in single fields, because I think a chaplain should always be a generalist. So I'm somewhat suspect of the chaplain who touts himself to be an expert in moral theology or an expert in counseling or an expert in this and that. To have, as the Navy calls it, a subspecialty in those fields, and to be able to give advice like other staff officers from the perspective of your education in those areas, that's fine. But the weight of the decision-making is still on command.

Within the Chaplain Corps I was always turned off by junior chaplains who referred to me by rank, I guess in two ways. I didn't know what they were saying. Number one, did they think I was rank-conscious? Is that why they called me by rank? Or number two, were they so ignorant of the regulations of the Navy that they didn't know any better? Either way, I wouldn't be impressed by it if somebody called me by rank.

At the same time, I never referred to any of my seniors by rank. The chaplains I worked for through the years, I always referred to as Chaplain Sneary and Chaplain O'Connor and so forth. In friendship, certainly I served with Father Bill Walsh and Father Tom Reilly. I think that's another subject that comes up among chaplains, as to whether they carry their civilian title into the military. Again, I think that's okay among those who are members of their faith. By all means, a Jewish sailor is going to call the rabbi "rabbi" before he calls him "chaplain." That's great.

The other side of the coin, though, is that the chaplain wants to be visible as the chaplain of the ship or the chaplain of the command, no matter what his religious affiliation is. As I probably told you, if I put up a sign that said "Presbyterian chaplain," then I've already indicated to everybody except Presbyterians that I'm not interested in seeing them, or I'm turning them away. So you know, as I've probably recommended before in this text, I think every chaplain's door ought to just say "Chaplain." That's an open invitation for anybody to come in. The chaplain can provide and meet the individual's need by religious practice or by facilitating for that person by making the proper referral to another chaplain or another resource.

Q: Did you have any input into the fitness reports of these chaplains you went to, or did that come through their own commands?

Admiral Stevenson: No, that came through their own commands, but I was not averse to educating command that, "Chaplains' fitness reports are written with very high-water marks, so if you think your chaplain is a top-notch chaplain and you want him to compete, you're going to have to write in these ways."

From time to time I would alert some commanding officers that they had hurt their chaplain in the grading or mostly in the narratives. You know, to write a narrative and say, "This is the best Presbyterian chaplain in the whole world," is to say to somebody who's on the chaplain selection board, "Well, he may be the best Presbyterian chaplain in the world, but is he the best chaplain in the Navy?" [Chuckles] That's what they're dealing with. So many times if you want to kill a guy in a chaplain's fitness report, you just write how wonderful he is to the people of his own faith group, and you leave out the fact that he has an ecumenical spirit and that he goes out of his way to take care of the needs of those who are not of his faith. You're killing him right there in the eyes of the kind of chaplains who ought to be on a selection board.

Q: Did you put out any formal communications to line officers on this?

Admiral Stevenson: I think maybe once in a while we wrote kind of a standard letter along those lines.

The other thing is that the Chaplain Corps is not a Sunday school. It ought to be a competitive world. There are also myths out there--terrible, terrible myths--that are a great disservice to the Chaplain Corps in the Navy. For instance, one myth is that people are selected for rank on the basis of some kind of a denominational faith-group rotation. "We selected a Lutheran, so this time we're selecting a Presbyterian." Or "We selected a Catholic, so this time we're going to select a Jew," or something. I mean, it was ridiculous. The only way they will ever have a good chaplaincy is by the best of the ability of people who serve on boards selecting the individuals they think are best qualified to do the jobs.

The other problem with fitness reports is a mentality among senior chaplains when they write a fitness report to be signed by a CO. They write what the junior chaplain has done, ad infinitum, but never say anything about his potential. So if you write on a lieutenant commander, you've proven that he's a good lieutenant commander. [Chuckles]

But you'd better get something in there about the chaplain's ability to serve higher purpose and wider needs.

There's also the frustration of chaplains who reflect the Peter Principle. They have reached beyond the height of their competence. So you may have a chaplain who has been promoted and now he's a force chaplain, but he doesn't know anything about training chaplains. He sees all chaplains doing what he did, rather than motivating them to be better chaplains.

Q: Do the selection boards make any attempt at all to balance the selections by denomination?

Admiral Stevenson: I don't know how many selection boards I served on over the years, but it was probably 20 to 30. I don't recall ever being on a board that made a decision in regards to a faith group.

Q: That's a very specific answer.

Admiral Stevenson: Yes. Let me just add a little story. I can also tell you from my experience in Washington, because occasionally I've heard the myth that Chief of Chaplains knows pretty much what a selection board is going to do. Speaking for myself and having observed the four Chiefs of Chaplains that I worked for, I have never been around any other Chief of Chaplains who did not express the same view that I felt when I was Chief of Chaplains. When they hand you that sheet of paper and you look at it, you say, "Oh, yeah, sure. I mean, I'm pleased as punch that the following were selected. I am totally mystified that the board would select these guys." Then you look at the selection list, there's always one chaplain that causes you to say to yourself, "My God, what will I ever do with him? He's now a commander or he's now a captain. I haven't got the faintest notion in the world where to use him."

Q: What are your recollections of Admiral Davis, who relieved Admiral Hayward as CinCPacFlt?

Admiral Stevenson: Oh, that was a great surprise to everybody when Admiral Hayward came back. He was in Washington when word came out that he was selected for Chief of Naval Operations. Headquarters command just went wild with joy, and everybody went to the airport when Admiral Hayward came back to Hawaii with 100 leis and so forth and so on, to celebrate. And who got off the airplane with him but Admiral Red Dog Davis.[*] So then the word spread that probably Admiral Davis was going to be the new CinCPacFlt.

I did not have as close a relationship with Admiral Davis as I had with Admiral Hayward, but I enjoyed him. I enjoyed his sense of humor. When I was selected for flag, I was frocked in his office, in the old Nimitz office, a place of nostalgia for any naval officer.[†] Of course, Admiral Red Dog Davis took that beautiful new cover that my wife had bought, dropped it on the deck, put his foot on it, and said, "We don't need any flag officers around here with these fancy-looking hats." [Laughter] So I enjoyed him, and he had the interest of the troops well at heart, but I didn't have the opportunity to formally brief him and so forth as much as I had with Admiral Hayward.

Of course, by that time, Admiral Carlisle Trost was Deputy CinCPacFlt.[‡] He wowed us all with his brilliance, his affability. He's another salt-of-the-earth kind of guy who seriously practices his religious faith. We always used to get a kick out of Admiral Trost, because when he came to chapel, he would always be the last to leave. He would be standing around at the coffee, talking to some sailor or somebody afterwards.

He is the epitome of a professional, but certainly more demanding on himself than he ever would be on anybody else. But the thing that really got us at PacFlt--it was the talk of the whole fleet when he first came out there--was his brilliance. We marveled at the way in

---
[*] Admiral Donald C. Davis, USN, served as Commander in Chief Pacific Fleet, 9 May 1978 to 31 July 1981.
[†] "Frocking" a naval officer refers to the practice of allowing him to wear the uniform and assume the title for which he was recently selected. The officer does not receive the pay for the higher rank until a vacany appears on the lineal list so he can be officially promoted.
[‡] Vice Admiral Carlisle A. H. Trost, USN. Later, as a four-star admiral, he served as Chief of Naval Operations from 1986 to 1990.

which he could handle stacks and stacks of paperwork with dispatch. You would wonder if he really had read and absorbed it all. You'd find out not only that, but he could quote it, and that he had also found the two "T's" that weren't crossed and one "I" that wasn't dotted. The man takes his gifts for granted.

I was telling somebody the other day--this is a silly thing, but one time my daughter and the other high-school kids had established a picnic-softball family gathering down in the crater on some Sunday afternoons. So we started just a community potluck affair with the families there. It was daughters and dads against mothers and sons in softball. At one of the first games, Admiral Trost got a hit, but he tripped halfway to first base and took a bad fall, scraped up his arms and knees and everything. Captain Dewey Feuerhelm, the intelligence officer, was coaching first base.[*] Dewey looked over and said, "Gee, Admiral, you started your slide a little early." [Laughter] I've always thought that was one of the great illustrations of tact.

We got to know the Trost family, and then they left for duty in Seventh Fleet. Admiral Briggs, who was my boss in LogPac, became Deputy PacFlt, another brilliant naval officer.[†]

Q: Did those two keep going with the same policy that Admiral Bigley had of calling you in regularly?

Admiral Stevenson: No. I saw Admiral Trost on a regular basis, but not on the basis that I made an appointment every two weeks as I had with Admiral Bigley. Admiral Trost's approach was more, "If you have a problem and you need me, I'm here. Or if there is a problem and I need to know about it, then I'm here."

Q: So you didn't lack for opportunities.

---

[*] Captain Duane L. Feuerhelm, USN.
[†] Vice Admiral Edward S. Briggs, USN.

Admiral Stevenson: There were times that he would be going home from work, and I'd already gotten to the tennis courts, so he would see that his chaplain had already left the office and was on the tennis court. [Laughter] So he was aware of where I was and what was going on.

Q: Was Admiral Hayward a workaholic to the extent that Chaplain O'Connor was?

Admiral Stevenson: No. All naval officers are workaholics. I mean, anybody who stays in the Navy has a degree of being a workaholic. I mean, shipboard life is a natural for a workaholic. People who stay in the Navy, I assume, are workaholics. I guess that's why in Washington, D.C., when you call around, the Army and Air Force guys have legitimately gone home, and the Navy guys are still sitting in all those little cubicles. Have you ever noticed, in making the rounds in Washington, D.C., how the Navy comes ashore?

Q: No.

Admiral Stevenson: Well, if you looked through the eyes of a Sam Blizzard, you would be inclined to say, "Isn't it interesting that the Navy brings the ship to the shore?" PacFlt headquarters looks like somebody grounded a ship. It's got all those decks around it. The Navy comes ashore and they decide you can work in the same kind of spaces that are berthing spaces at sea.

    The endorsing agents would go visit the Army Chief of Chaplains' office in the Pentagon--impressive. They'd go over to Bolling Air Force Base, and the Air Force Chief of Chaplains has half of a building, with a giant mahogany desk and so forth and so on. And then they come over to the Navy Annex and be in a state of shock.[*] They'd think we'd taken a vow of poverty. But that's the Navy ashore. The Navy can squeeze into a building 100 people. Where else but in the Bureau of Naval Personnel would you have 100 to 150 people for each head?

---

[*] The Arlington Annex, adjacent to the Arlington National Cemetery, is near the Pentagon in northern Virginia. The annex has for years housed the Bureau of Naval Personnel and Headquarters Marine Corps.

Q: I remember one line admiral commenting on the Washington mentality. He said, "We worked half-days when we were there, 7:00 till 7:00."

Admiral Stevenson: PacFlt once had--I don't know if they still have it--a very unique tradition. Wednesday afternoons was a rope yarn for PacFlt.* Senior decision-makers usually were up on the golf course. Of course, they all worked on Saturdays. But Wednesday afternoon was a special time. For me it was a special time, too, because it was a great time to start working on a homily for Sunday. Most of my days in PacFlt I was home from the office around 1700 in the afternoon. I'd get out on the tennis courts and be playing while all the brass were on their way home to their quarters.

Q: You had something else in your notes you wanted to mention.

Admiral Stevenson: I wanted to mention that we got involved in a lot of counseling problems. One of the most heart-breaking counseling situations I was introduced to in Hawaii involved people cohabiting sans marriage. A lot of reasons for that: Hawaii is a very romantic place; sailors not having money, and so the advantage of four or five or six sailors going together and getting an apartment. The higher visibility and career potential for female sailors. But the saddest part of all the excesses that took place in cohabiting outside of marriage was when one member of the relationship decided to break up the relationship.

Having dealt over the years with people who got divorced or who had marital problems, I was absolutely shocked at the higher degree of dysfunction in breaking up a living-together relationship. I became aware of the fact that when a marriage breaks up, there are things to negotiate. There are other people in the target area--"Your mother, your father, or kids." But in the majority of these situations where they had just lived together,

---

* In the years before World War II, the Navy typically worked half a day on Saturday. To compensate, a free weekday afternoon, usually a Wednesday, was known as rope-yarn Sunday. The term comes from the old Navy, when sailors were given time off from their duties to make and mend uniforms.

people suffered from a very high degree of just straight rejection. "Why are you walking out on me?"

"Well, I don't like you anymore." Period. It was almost as if they were saying, "All I do is I take my stereo and leave. You are nothing more to me than this stereo. You're a thing. I choose to leave this stereo here, or I choose to take the stereo with me."

Q: I take it you wound up talking to the rejected partners.

Admiral Stevenson: Yes. They're the ones in crisis who then say, "Well, who am I going to talk to? I can talk to my friends, but after a while, my friends kind of laugh at me. I can talk to my command, but in a sense, I'm putting myself on report. So who am I going to talk to? I can't talk to my parents because they're back in the mainland U.S.A. I'm going to talk to the chaplain. And when I talk to the chaplain, what am I going to tell him? I'm going to tell him that I'm depressed. I'm depressed because I've just plain been rejected."

Q: Did you wind up with more men or more women in this rejected category?

Admiral Stevenson: I would say it was more women.

I recall a restaurant in Hawaii that was open 24 hours, and abused spouses were spending the night in the restaurant. It was a place you could stay when you couldn't go home. Where else were you going to go?

So along with all the paradise of Hawaii and all the joy of being involved with dynamic people like Admiral Hayward and Admiral Trost, you know, I also had my task as a chaplain. That included experiences such as the bride whose wedding was being ruined because the groom was drunk.

What I'm really trying to indicate is that I hope people realize that the fleet chaplain's office deals with a lot of regular chaplain activities. It's not just a matter of rank. It's rank used in service of people. Just like you go to the good lawyer, you go to the chaplain in the Navy that's made rank in hopes that he is willing to use that rank in your behalf.

Q: Did you find any particular techniques or words of comfort that were helpful in these rejection situations from the couples breaking up?

Admiral Stevenson: No, I had no secret formulas.

Q: Probably just being a sympathetic ear was helpful.

Admiral Stevenson: I think so. I hope so. No pat formulas. Part of it, too, was that the person rejected is usually in a financial state where they have to move back in the barracks. And when they've been out of the barracks for six months to a year, they don't want to go back into that environment.

Q: I think an advantage for having that facet to the job, though, is it keeps you current on the types of things that are happening.

Admiral Stevenson: Yes, that was one of the advantages of having an office in the midst of the headquarters with people of all ranks and rates.

Q: What was Hawaii like as a place to raise a family?

Admiral Stevenson: Great place to live. Our youngest daughter was a senior in high school there, and she had some wonderful friends. But she and other girls raced home after school to get to the bathroom, because the bathrooms were controlled by a tough crowd. There was always the rumor and reality of "Kill Howlie Day."

Q: I'm not familiar with that.

Admiral Stevenson: Well, we had some problems out there at Barbers Point and other places from time to time in the local school system.[*] The locals would gang up and beat up

---

[*] Barbers Point Naval Air Station, to the west of Pearl Harbor on the island of Oahu.

a couple of Howlies. I mean, It could be a fistfight over a football game, but people could read into it a "Kill Howlie" or get even with a local situation.

Q: Anything else to say about that tour of duty?

Admiral Stevenson: Let me mention one or two other things. In that tour of duty I was also dealing with people who didn't make selection. For anybody in the Navy, that's a heart-breaking experience. Sometimes you get so caught up with pass-overs in your own community that, as a chaplain, you forget that it's not just the chaplains who didn't get selected for promotion. Other officers get bad news, too, and the chaplain should know them. So you rejoice with those who rejoice, and you <u>weep with those who weep</u>.

I'm trying to think how much I should say about my own circumstance out there. When it came time for the word to come out on flag selection, I didn't necessarily think that I would be the one selected. People had been kind enough to tell me that they were sure that I would be in the running and so forth, but I felt I had had a great career. I had felt earlier on that if I made lieutenant commander and completed 20 years, it would be the happiest thing in the world. [Laughter]

So, anyway, a little sea story about being selected for flag that's humorous and true. I got a phone call about 4:00 o'clock in the morning out there, which would have been 10:00 o'clock in Washington from Chaplain Withers Moore. He told me that I had been selected for flag. The phone call had awakened Diane. So she was so excited, she decided she needed to tell somebody. So she called her dad in Missouri, where it was 9:00 o'clock or something, and told him about it. I listened on the other phone. She said that Neil had been selected for flag, and her dad said, "Does that make you happy?"

And she said, "Yes."

And he said, "Well, it's snowing here."

Later that day, she called to tell her aunt, who was in a nursing home in Kansas City. Just to put in perspective the civilian view of the United States Navy, Aunt Georgie said to Diane that she thought that was nice, as long as Diane was happy about it, but Aunt Georgie thought "commander" sounded better.

Q: Anything else?

Admiral Stevenson: I'm trying to think of the issues concerning Diego Garcia and all that while we were out there.[*]

Q: Did you have to provide a contingent for Diego Garcia as it built up?

Admiral Stevenson: We had one chaplain there with the Seabees, and then as it changed its command structure, they debated as to whether it should be under PacFlt or AirPac and then under LogPac. We were involved in the buildup. I was one of the privileged people to get out there to visit the scene when they decided before you left Clark Air Force Base as to whether they had a bunk for you or not.[†] So we saw Diego build up. Of course, years later when I was going out from the chief's office for the Christmas trips, I could see how Diego had really grown.

We really had a lot of good chaplains out in PacFlt, and it probably was my most enjoyable tour of duty.

Q: Thank you very much. I look forward to our next session when we'll get you back to Washington.

---

[*] Diego Garcia is an atoll about 1,000 miles south of India; it was formerly British territory. In the 1970s the U.S. Navy made a significant investment in facilities there to support ships operating in the Indian Ocean. See Kirby Harrison, "Diego Garcia: the Seabees at Work," U.S. Naval Institute Proceedings, August 1979, pages 53-61.

[†] Clark Air Force Base was about 50 miles north of Manila, on the island of Luzon in the Philippines. It was closed as part of the U.S. military withdrawal from the nation in the early 1990s.

Neil M. Stevenson #7 - 261

Interview Number 7 with Rear Admiral Neil M. Stevenson, Chaplain Corps, U.S. Navy (Retired)

Place: Williamsburg Presbyterian Church, Williamsburg, Virginia

Date: Thursday, 1 March 1990

Interviewer: Paul Stillwell

Q: Good morning, Chaplain. I hope we can wrap up your career today and get this project ready to make it available for historians.

You talked last time about your time out in Hawaii with the Pacific Fleet chaplain's job. How did that lead to your being the deputy in Washington?

Admiral Stevenson: For the sake of people who are selected and non-selected, let me start out by telling you that I was surprised and delighted that I was selected. I received, as I think all people who are selected receive, some wonderful congratulatory phone calls and messages. But I don't know that anybody always tells the other side of the coin, so I thought it might be interesting.

There was a senior admiral in Hawaii who was somewhat upset by the news. He had a close friend in the Chaplain Corps whom he had assumed, as I suppose others had, would have been the one selected. He felt he had the need to tell me that he was disappointed that I was selected. That's kind of an awkward situation. It happened a couple of times. There were a couple of chaplains as well who let me know in no uncertain terms that they were disappointed that I was selected, and I can appreciate that.

Q: How did you respond to something like that?

Admiral Stevenson: Well, that's what I thought might be interesting to you. In the admiral's case, he told me this at a social gathering, in a private kind of a corner. I just simply said to him, "You know, I'm sorry. I can appreciate your being angry and disappointed that your friend was not the one selected. But you ought to realize I wasn't on the board. The board selected me, so like anybody else in the Navy, the only thing I can do now is do as good a job as I can do." You know, it's really on the same level as somebody saying, "I was disappointed that you got orders to such-and-such instead of somebody else." You can't turn down the orders. What you can do is just do the best you can. I just thought it may be interesting to some people to know that you do get negative feedback as well as congratulations. [Chuckles]

Q: Did he expect you to fall on your sword? [Laughter]

Admiral Stevenson: I don't know what he expected me to do. But I think he felt better after he told me that he was disappointed.

Q: Do you want to put a name with this person that expressed disappointment?

Admiral Stevenson: No. [Laughter] You must respect your seniors.

Q: Well, to move you to Washington, could you, perhaps, address the split in duties between the Chief of Chaplains and the deputy which you then became? Who handled what?

Admiral Stevenson: Once again, I was a fortunate guy because I'd had previous experience. Chaplain O'Connor, when he was Chief of Chaplains, saw the necessity of getting many things in the Chaplain Corps tied in a truer fashion to government and Navy. He had commenced a change in legislation regarding the office of the Chief of Chaplains, which had been approved.

I always thought it humorous that that piece of legislation was approved with the signing of the National Emergency Act. In other words, Chaplain O'Connor set the legislation in motion, and it got approved as a piece of the National Emergency Act in 1980. I was selected for flag in 1980, and, therefore, not only did I go to Washington with some background in what previous division directors had done in the "deputy slot," but I went to Washington happy that I was the first official, legal Deputy Chief of Chaplains.

Q: What was the status of the deputy before that?

Admiral Stevenson: Before that, an officer, usually a senior captain, was ordered into the Chief of Chaplains' office as the executive director of the Chaplains Division, rather than being "a deputy." Those who know the technical differences can appreciate the fact that the deputy certainly has more authority to act than the executive director does.

Q: So the new arrangement was statutory rather than ex officio.

Admiral Stevenson: That's correct. And I would continue to hope that the two flag officers of the Chaplain Corps serve in the Chief of Chaplains' office in Washington. I also believe that if the chief is on the road, the deputy ought to be there, and vice versa. I really believe in somebody keeping the store. Things happen very quickly in Washington, and there are many times that you need the flag of your community to be involved. By the way, any duty that is productive in Washington may be expected to be both frustrating and tedious.

Q: Are you saying that the two of you were essentially interchangeable?

Admiral Stevenson: Yes. There's no doubt the chief is the chief, but in many respects, to get the job done, the deputy's got to be--well, let's say the chief's got to be comfortable enough with the deputy that he's given the deputy a signal to make decisions if need be. And the deputy's got to know that he is the deputy, and stay not only in close contact with the chief, but also have a sense of how the chief would want things done.

Q: Well, it's interesting, though, that the chief doesn't pick the deputy. The selection system picks the deputy, so there could be a potential for friction there.

Admiral Stevenson: There could be. But at that time the chief was on the board that was selecting the deputy. The system has changed. I still think the community should dominate the selection process, not the line. The line depends too much on the math.

Q: In your case, apparently, it was a very harmonious relationship with the Chief of Chaplains.

Admiral Stevenson: Yes. I was very fortunate. I had known Ross Trower for years, and I think I knew Ross Trower real well and I think he knew me very well.* I think we also knew that we were opposites.

Q: In what ways?

Admiral Stevenson: Oh, the guys on the staff used to tease. Chaplain Trower had a habit when he wanted to think about something he'd say, "Whoa, whoa, whoa, whoa," you know. It was a habit of his over the years. Ross is far more cautious than I am. Ross is far more exacting than I am. Much better writer than I am. There's nearly ten years' difference in our age.† He came into the Chaplain Corps right near the end of World War II, and I came on active duty in 1957. So you have those experiences that Chaplain Trower had that I did not have, and so forth. When he was an O-6 in the Chief of Chaplains' staff, I was one of the "young Turks," and yet Ross was always a good listener. So, yes, we had much in common. We were both churchmen.

And we both liked to go with our wives to dances. We both have big families with a lot of joy in our lives. I knew Ross's children, and he knows all my children. We had an ability to disagree with each other, and I also knew who the chief was. [Laughter] The guys in the office used to tease and say that, "Go in and see the chief, and the chief would say, 'Whoa, whoa, whoa.' Then you go in and see the deputy and the deputy would say,

---

* Rear Admiral Ross H. Trower, CHC, USN, served as the Navy's Chief of Chaplains from June 1979 to August 1983. His oral history is in the series conducted by the Navy's Chaplain Corps.
† Trower was born 2-22-22; Stevenson was born 12-26-30.

'Go, go, go.'" There are many times I wish I were more like Ross, and I hope there were times he wished he were more like I was. But, anyway, it was pretty harmonious.

Q: Did you find cases in which you had to prod him when you thought he was too cautious?

Admiral Stevenson: I think a better way to put it and a more honest way to put it was that if you're going to go to Chaplain Trower with a proposal, you go enough in advance to give him time to really think about it. He wouldn't want anything at the last minute. I knew Ross well enough to get ideas planted in advance so that he really had time to think them out and question them.

Q: So that way you could counteract that sense of caution by putting in a percolation period.

Admiral Stevenson: Sure. And even when we would play tennis from time to time, that's another place where we would be teased. The guys would say, "The chief responds, and the deputy reacts." And that's the way we played tennis. Ross can hit that ball, just keep that ball in play. I would get tired and go up there and kill that sucker. [Laughter]

Q: Are there any specific cases that you might cite as an example of how these two approaches worked on a problem?

Admiral Stevenson: Well, I'll give you one example that comes to mind. Bob Ecker was the EA at the time I got to Washington, which was in July 1980.* Chaplain Ecker and I talked about the fact that we thought that the chief, like Chaplain O'Connor, should travel to be with the troops in difficult environments. The Chief of Chaplains or the deputy should be visible, setting a model for ministry for junior chaplains and showing the importance of sea duty.

---

* Captain Robert J. Ecker, CHC, USN. EA--executive assistant.

The IO was sort of the gravity point of the Navy in those days.* So shortly after I arrived in Washington, we began talking to the chief, saying that the Chief of Chaplains ought to have the visibility of visiting the task force in the Indian Ocean during the Christmas season.

Q: Had that not been done before, sending the chief out for these visits?

Admiral Stevenson: Kelly had visited troops in Vietnam. O'Connor went to Antarctica, etc., but Ross hadn't. So I thought it was important to do that. The chief went in Christmas of '80, and then I went the next two years, because Ross broke his ankle in November of '82. So I went out two years in a row, and then when I was chief.

I think those kinds of things are important because it's not only for the feedback we received, it's not only something of value to the sailors, but the Chief of Chaplains or the Deputy Chief of Chaplains must get away from the Washington desk and came out and did ministry for Hanukkah and for Christmas. We made the rounds of the ships. It was a case of saying to the Navy community, "What I'm doing is no different from what all chaplains do. Chaplains, like other sea service personnel, are deployed, serving their nation."

Q: And you doubtless found that people would tell you things on those visits that they would never communicate in any other way.

Admiral Stevenson: Very true, and one of the sad experiences to me was the reaction when I came back from my first trip. I looked upon the Chief of Chaplains and the Deputy Chief of Chaplains as being in the business of religion. But when I came back and spoke to people in Washington, some of them were disappointed, because it was almost as though they wanted me to talk to them about operational things, of which I don't think I have to be knowledgeable. I could give a sense of what I found in the way of morale. I could tell them what the religious tone was and what the attendance was at religious functions. See,

---

* IO--Indian Ocean. In the wake of untoward developments in Iran and Afghanistan in the late 1970s, President Jimmy Carter directed the establishment of a strong naval presence, usually at least one carrier battle group, in the region.

that's my world. I think some flag officers in Washington--and some told me--were somewhat disappointed that I did not come back with the kinds of data they thought I would come back with.

Q: What did they expect?

Admiral Stevenson: Well, I think they expected more of what they received from line officers, who look at things through line eyes, as they ought to. Maybe I didn't spend enough time finding out before I left what they wanted me to look for. Maybe that would have been a better idea, in retrospect. On the other hand, it might have been a handicap, too, because the last thing in the world a chaplain who is a jaygee needs, never mind a chaplain who's a flag officer, is this sense of being a junior IG, or a spy.[*]

Q: And you didn't really have the background to do that sort of evaluation either.

Admiral Stevenson: No. We brought greetings from CNO and so forth and so on, which I think is what we ought to be doing. I mean, we're sort of a traveling Christmas card. And in the smallest ship in the fleet in the Indian Ocean, I think it's great for a flag-rank chaplain to come aboard by helo and get up on the 1MC and tell them that CNO sends special greetings to these guys--which is true--and SecNav, and so forth and so on. Then you get about the business of saying, "And I'm here to hold Christmas services."

Q: What specific experiences do you especially remember from those trips?

Admiral Stevenson: Well, there's one in particular that's humorous. When I was going out on my first trip, there was some function of the Navy officers' wives club at the Navy yard. My wife was the president of NOW (Naval Officers Wives). Admiral Arleigh Burke and his wife were at one of these functions a day or two before I left for the Indian Ocean.[†]

---

[*] IG--inspector general.
[†] Admiral Arleigh A. Burke, USN (Ret.), had served as Chief of Naval Operations from 17 August 1955 to 1 August 1961. His oral history is in the Naval Institute collection.

Admiral Burke asked me where I was going, and I told him I was leaving for the Indian Ocean. He said, "Well, if you get any spare time, you tell the sailors that Arleigh Burke sends Christmas greetings." I carried those warm greetings to the sailors in the Indian Ocean.

Arleigh Burke was hospitalized over that Christmas in Bethesda.[*] He told me later that a call of Christmas greetings had come for him from one of the ships in the IO. It was named for a personal friend of his, perhaps Oldendorf. The admiral said, "Now, if you want to have an experience, you're coming out of this anesthetic at the hospital, and so forth and they tell you that this friend is trying to call you. You wonder if you are here or approaching the world to come!" Not exactly the return we wished for extending his personal greetings to the deployed ships.

Q: As you carried his greetings to the fleet, did you find that his name was still recognized?

Admiral Stevenson: Yes, in the officer community, not necessarily among the young sailors.

Q: Did you make a deliberate attempt to downplay your rank during these visits?

Admiral Stevenson: No, I don't think there was any need to downplay the rank.

Q: Well, some people would be put off by dealing with a flag officer, certainly some junior enlisted people.

Admiral Stevenson: Well, you know, a worship service is a worship service. [Chuckle] If you have a problem, and part of that problem's back in the States, and here's a guy with some rank who's going back to the States who might be able to do you some good with a phone call, and so forth and so on, I think sailors know the system, and they want to use the system. One of the reasons our chaplains have rank is that we do have separation of church

---

[*] National Naval Medical Center, Bethesda, Maryland.

and state. The thing that the chaplain oftimes does in ministry, legitimately, is he allows other personnel to use his rank. In other words, how else do you get that thought or that concern into the meeting at that level if that chaplain's not made aware?

One issue that comes to mind was talking to some enlisted personnel in Bahrain about the problem they had when one of their wives got pregnant and the kind of medical care that wasn't available. How do we solve this thing? These women had to fly all the way to Frankfurt, Germany. I remember passing that word on in Washington.

To my knowledge, the chaplain is the only officer honored in by Navy regulations in being given the privilege of always being referred to as "Chaplain," no matter what his rank. Now, I've run into chaplains who forgot that. As I probably told you before, when I would run into a chaplain who called me "Admiral," I didn't think too much of that. I mean, my immediate reaction was not to be too impressed with that chaplain.

Q: What mechanism did you use to deal with these inputs? Did you have a flag lieutenant to take notes to call about Seaman Jones's allotment, or what?

Admiral Stevenson: No. I would write these things all down and carry them back with me. I did travel with another chaplain, a Catholic chaplain so that we would be a Protestant-Catholic team. They wrote things down, I wrote things down, we compared notes, we came back to Washington, we made phone calls. Sometimes we phoned mothers and sometimes wives. The Chief of Chaplains was also part of the staff of CNP, and so I had a place within the Bureau of Naval Personnel to express opinions and bring feedback. We always debriefed with Deputy CNP, CNP, and Vice CNO when we came back.

Q: How well could you assess a religious program during a hit-and-run visit when, presumably, people were putting their best feet forward?

Admiral Stevenson: Pretty well. [Chuckle] And, again, I would say that you take any part of the Navy--I would not think it would take very long for a JAG officer to size up a JAG office. I don't think it'd take medical long. Within your own profession, you can size things up very, very quickly. One of things, for instance, Paul, that I was always interested in was the call on the commanding officer, which is a mandatory courtesy. If you hear the commanding officer say--and I used to hear this every once in a while--"You must be pleased, because my people tell me that the people who go to the chapel are pleased with the chaplains in that chapel over there."

Well, that's a real indication that you'd better start asking the chaplains if they're spending all of their time in the chapel. Or if they think that chapel is a church. Or whether they're involved in the command religious program. Whether the needs of just people of the chaplain's own faith group are being met, or whether the needs of other people are being met. No, it doesn't take very long after those many years for your ears to perk up.

Q: Suppose the skipper says he's not too pleased with the chapel and the way it's going. Do you think that's a good sign?

Admiral Stevenson: I think if he says so, that interests, sure, and then you start talking to him about what you want to look at. And you get back with him, and you might find yourself, as I did in one or two occasions, saying, "Yeah, these are some of the things that I think are problems. Some of them are answered with money. You haven't given the command religious program enough money to get done the kind of things you're sitting here thinking about." Sometimes you'd have to say to a commanding officer, "You are only seeing religion through your eyes. You think the whole world is Presbyterian and that this chaplain ought to be a Presbyterian. That's not meeting the needs of the Navy."

Q: Where does that command chaplain's first loyalty lie--to his skipper, or to the Chief of Chaplains?

Admiral Stevenson: Oh, that's a good one. [Laughter] There's no question. When you talk about the skipper, you're talking about the chain of command. When you're talking about the Chief of Chaplains, you're talking about the chain of influence. The Chief of Chaplains wants to use the chain of influence to better religious programs throughout the whole Navy. So that may be in the form of giving advice, it may be in the form of changing chaplains at a particular duty station, etc., etc. The Chief of Chaplains is not in a position to command change. He's in a position of trying to persuade through influence the chaplains and the command that there's a better way of meeting the needs of people.

As a chaplain, you never have command. You are always part of the chain of command. But as a chaplain, your tool is influence. An effective chaplain of any rank has learned to use influence.

Q: In your visits to the individual commands, I wonder about the command chaplain who's trying on the one hand to please his boss who writes his fitness report, and, on the other hand, the emphasis that that skipper places may be different from what's coming from your office. How do you help him resolve that?

Admiral Stevenson: I suppose, Paul, just from years of experience knowing that you can't go in and override a situation. You don't go in making demands.

Q: Well, maybe you can use some of your influence on the skipper, also.

Admiral Stevenson: True. And you hope you did. Usually the goal was to have skippers see a larger picture concerning the place of religion and means of ministry.

Q: Well, one testimonial to the value of these trips is that they have since become institutionalized and are now done on an annual basis.

Admiral Stevenson: As I said, John O'Connor traveled a great deal. He even got to Antarctica. But I think the biggest impact was the number of sailors in places like Harold E. Holt in the North West Cape of Australia and the ships in the Indian Ocean, the isolated places where sailors would just simply say, "The flag officer coming from Washington made Christmas a little different. Made us remember that we're really not forgotten, we're part of the larger organization, and that people do have an interest that we're out here for the sake of the United States of America."

Q: And this Chief of Chaplains is also giving up his Christmas at home.

Admiral Stevenson: Sure. Because he knows that that's a norm for Navy families. It's the point in every chaplain's career at which the chaplain begins to be a Navy chaplain rather than a civilian pastor. It is the day he realizes that, yes, babies are born and husbands stay at sea. [Chuckles] What is the norm for the Navy is not norm for the civilian world, and vice versa, and so on.

Q: The Chaplain Resource Board was helpful in providing some suggestions for questions to explore during this interview for their benefit as well as whoever else might use these. One of them is to get your assessment of how the changes that you had put in in the Chaplains Division during your earlier tour there had come to fruition by the time you got back as deputy. Did it meet your expectations for those reorganizational changes?

Admiral Stevenson: I was pleased and ready to run with the organization as it was, and I was not interested in changing the organization of Chief of Chaplains' office. It was to my advantage to know that I was going back into an organization I was familiar with, that I thought was properly organized. And so there wasn't a question about spending time reorganizing this outfit, which is a total torture in Washington--this constant business of reorganizing.

I'd gone down the roster, and I went back to Washington pleased to go in as deputy to a Chief of Chaplains' office that had talented personnel in it. I had been unhappy when I was in the office on previous tours of duty with the mentality that sort of said that the Chief of Chaplains' office was a house of representatives--that we have people on the staff because they represent this element or that element and so forth.

Q: Are you talking about faith groups?

Admiral Stevenson: I'm talking about faith groups, I'm talking about racial groups, I'm talking about minorities. At one time, we even ordered people into the chief's office who'd been passed over so that the guys who had been passed over would not feel unhappy about being passed over. I don't think that's healthy for an organization. I think the healthy way to put together a Chief of Chaplains' staff is to order in the best "snipes" the United States Navy Chaplain Corps has. It's interesting to me, Paul, that the people who were very successful in the chapel and in shipboard duty were also, in my opinion, the ones who were successful in Washington.

Q: How do you account for that?

Admiral Stevenson: I think they just were people of ability. I don't want this to be as sarcastic as some people would read this to be, but, you know, reading, writing, and arithmetic go a long way.

Q: Had it been during the time that Chaplain O'Connor was the chief that the office changed from this house of representatives to a more talent-laden organization?

Admiral Stevenson: No. Chaplain O'Connor advocated the house of representatives approach. In fact, I used to be teased when I was back there that I was the token Protestant. [Laughter] Anyway, I think Chaplain Trower had already put together an outstanding staff. I think we kept outstanding people in the time that I was there. I was very proud of them all. We worked them all very hard.

I had had a part in forming the organization the way it was with the four shops. But this is another situation like the chicken or the egg. I could sit here and say to you that I had a lot to do with the development of the organization of the Chief of Chaplains Office in the days of Chaplain O'Connor. I would also have to say to you I suspect that Chaplain O'Connor knew exactly what he wanted, and what he was allowing me to do was to put it together the way he wanted it put together.

Q: Letting you think it was your idea.

Admiral Stevenson: Yes, and including the pieces from the Joe Diminos and the Tom Hilfertys and the Dave Whites, and so forth, who were there at the time. The most important single part of that was that the Chief of Chaplains' office separated personnel from manpower.

Q: I think you covered that pretty well the last time.

Admiral Stevenson: So I came back, and I was working for a Chief of Chaplains who said, "We know each other, and I want things done correctly. I want things done right. I want them done with integrity." And I agreed wholeheartedly. "When we put in a budget request, I want it to be an honest budget request. I don't want it to be inflated with the idea they're going to cut us back. We are the Chief of Chaplains' office."

I had my "if book," and I began--with the concurrence, of course, of Chaplain Trower--to start initiating some of these things. There were many times when he and I would talk about them, he would say, "Whoa, whoa, whoa, whoa." But we did move on some of those things. You want me to read off some of those things?

Q: Please.

Admiral Stevenson: One of the things I came in with was the concept that there should be a rotation of flag officers in the Chaplain Corps, whereby the deputy would fleet up as chief, and the chief got out of the way in a timely fashion.

Q: What had been the situation up till then?

Admiral Stevenson: It had been a mixed bag. Many Chiefs of Chaplains were selected for flag and came in immediately as chief, such as Chaplain O'Connor, such as Chaplain Garrett.

The O-7 flag officer had not been in the chief's office at the time of selection, so you had only one flag officer in the chief's office and the other one out in Hawaii or out in London or somewhere.

Now, thanks to O'Connor, the deputy is a regulation deputy. It seemed to me the sensible thing for the organization would be to have the stability that the deputy runs the office. He gets to know all the problem areas and then fleets up as chief. That way the average flag officer in the Chaplain Corps would serve something like five years. So you're deputy for half the time, you're chief for half the time, and you get out of the way.

Q: Was there a specific tenure up until then for the chief?

Admiral Stevenson: The tenure, legally, was four years for the Chief of Chaplains.

Q: How has it worked out in practice on the length of the tour?

Admiral Stevenson: I was there three years as Ross's deputy, and then I was there two years as Chief of Chaplains. Chaplain McNamara fleeted up to relieve me as chief. I think John McNamara was chief for three years, so John McNamara was a flag officer of the Chaplain Corps for five years.[*] I was a flag officer for the Chaplain Corps for five years.

You know, if you're going to get things done--if you have a wish list and there's certain things you want to get done, you can get them done in five years.

Q: How did it happen that your tour was two years instead of three?

Admiral Stevenson: Oh, many reasons. First of all, I'd been there five years. I had 29 years in the United States Navy. Maybe, I tell myself when I look at my paycheck now, I should have stayed for 30. But CNP and CNO did not want me to stay another whole year plus some months in order to satisfy my getting 30 years, and I take that as a legitimate concern

---

[*] Rear Admiral John R. McNamara, CHC, USN, served as the Navy's Chief of Chaplains from August 1985 to June 1988.

from their perspective. I know the Secretary of the Navy wasn't pleased with me, and the more I read of history the more that's okay with me.[*] I also suspect CNO thought he might become Chairman of the JCS, and he wanted to be sure John McNamara became Chief of Chaplains, etc. Lots of stuff.

And then, you're looking at other things. You're looking at the amount of travel you've done. When is it time to make a transition? I remember when the paperwork came down for planning the flag rotations of the community, it was marked secret. I looked at it, and I said, "Gee, I either put in now recommending a selection board, or I wait another whole year to recommend a selection board." What does that do to everyone's timing? What does that do to gentlemen's agreements to step down in timely fashion?"

And so I put in for the board, and I got a very nice courtesy phone call from CNP, Admiral Lawrence, which was good, but I know he was also reflecting the fact that CNO and SecNav wanted me to retire.[†]

When I got that envelope, I called Diane, and I said, "Guess what? I think I'm going to put in that it's time for this board to be held."

She said, "Fine, go with it."

I think if you're planning to continue your career, you're also thinking about the fact that you're going to be 55. If I am going to go to a parish, what does my dossier look like?

Q: What were some of the other items on your agenda when you came in?

Admiral Stevenson: I think that the Chief of Chaplains needs to have as his emphasis providing the best religious opportunities for Navy, Marine Corps, Coast Guard personnel and their dependents. I think other people may look to the Chief of Chaplains as the duty ethicist or the moral theologian in the castle. But the number-one job is to provide worship services to the people of the fleet.

Just briefly, Paul, every naval person has moral and ethical responsibilities, both personally and to the government of the United States. And I hope chaplains can be helpful

---

[*] John F. Lehman was a controversial Secretary of the Navy during his tenure from 1981 to 1987.
[†] Vice Admiral William P. Lawrence, USN, served as Chief of Naval Personnel from 28 September 1983 to 31 December 1985.

to them, but I don't look upon chaplains, per se, because of the variety of faith groups, as across-the-board ethicists or moralists. I think it's true that every commanding officer can look upon his chaplain as somebody who had a valid input, but not the automatic arbiter.

One of the battles I had when I was Chief of Chaplains is something I think we've talked about before. One medical officer thought that it would be good for each hospital to have an ethics board and that the chaplain should be the chairman of the ethics committee at each naval hospital. I thought that would be an absolute and utter disaster. I fought that, and JAG helped me. It was disapproved. The chaplain is the last person to be the chair of an ethics committee at a naval hospital.

Q: Why is that?

Admiral Stevenson: Well, you would assume that the chair signs the findings and perhaps makes a public statement of the findings of that ethics committee. The ethics committee's decision under command may be in opposition to the chaplain's faith group position. That would be untenable. For example, if you had an ethics committee in a hospital decide that an abortion was the correct procedure in a given situation, and the Catholic chaplain was the chairman of the committee, it would be untenable. So you're already handicapping the job of an ethics committee.

Q: But you weren't in any sense contradicting the idea of an ethics committee for the hospital?

Admiral Stevenson: Not in the least. I also felt that it was extremely important that the chaplain be a part of the committee. The problem is training the chaplain that the chaplain's contribution to the committee has to be divided between that which the chaplain understands as his faith group's ethic and the ethic of the patient. The chaplain's duty is to explain to the ethics committee <u>the ethic of the patient</u>.

For instance, if it's a Jehovah's Witness, it's not my task to go to the ethics committee and explain that Presbyterians believe in blood transfusions and that Jehovah's

Witnesses are ridiculous because they don't believe in blood transfusions. My job is to explain where the patient's coming from, which is something that takes training for chaplains, because we all start out in a parochial world. This is not to compromise the ethics of the chaplain or the chaplain's faith group. It's a recognition of the chaplain's responsibility to the pluralistic society.

Q: What happens if there's a medical issue in which the best medical interests of the patient are in contradiction to the preachings of his faith? Is it up to the medical community to try to overrule those in his behalf?

Admiral Stevenson: Well, as you well know, many of those issues have become court cases. The ultimate authority becomes the law of the land, not just medical ethics and not just religious ethics. When religion and medicine and science cannot agree, the arbiter becomes the government in our system.

That's what happens with Christian Scientists taking inoculations. That's one illustration. I don't think that the Chief of Chaplains or any chaplain should be considered automatically the IG for morality. The primary task of the chaplains is the provision of religion to meet the needs of individuals in a pluralistic nation. I think a lot of my predecessors would disagree with what I've just said. [Laughter] Now, when I would come back with ethical issues, those ethical issues did not become public. They were kept internal to the Navy, because that's, in my opinion, where the answers were.

Q: Do you have any examples?

Admiral Stevenson: Oh, I came back from a trip to the Mediterranean one time and raised with CNP the whole question of single parents in the Mediterranean area and our responsibility for day care. The numbers of single mothers or mothers standing duty was increasing. How do these young mothers meet their responsibilities as parents as well as standing the duty at night? Does the Navy not have a responsibility to provide 24-hour day-care facility? Those are real moral and ethical questions, and they demand funding for answers. And it was not just chaplains being aware of these things. Commands were dealing with this all the time, and old senior officers had not served in a Navy that demanded that kind of decisions.

Q: Was the issue of homosexuality in the Navy something that came up?

Admiral Stevenson: That question came up. The policy was very clear-cut in regards to all personnel, including chaplains.

Q: I see in the newspaper it was reaffirmed by the court again this week. The Supreme Court refused to hear a case.

Admiral Stevenson: I think that one of the things that nobody speaks about that's very important is not only the problems that are addressed in regards to homosexual activity within a military organization, but what impact it will have on recruiting if the policy is changed. Will parents allow their children to join an organization that openly condones homosexuals? The issue may be more pragmatic than idealists would recognize.*

Q: What other items did you have on your agenda as you came to the front office?

Admiral Stevenson: Well, I thought that the O-6s, the captains in the Chaplain Corps, needed to be more involved in a leadership role and needed to be somewhat separated from the rest of the chaplains. They needed to be made accountable for getting the job of religion done. So we invented this little thing called "O-6 Minutes." Minutes were sent out from the Chief of Chaplains' office directly to the O-6s, giving them the early word, alerting them to the chief's thinking and what was coming out. Hopefully, it was to get them more

---

* Subsequent to this interview, the policy was changed with the advent of the administration of President Bill Clinton in 1993. The new policy does not openly condone homosexuality in the services; it maintains the traditional prohibition. Its "Don't ask, don't tell" provision indicates that the armed services will react only in response to overt evidence of homosexual activity.

involved in a leadership role and to be more recognized for the kind of leadership they ought to supply.

Q: How well did it work?

Admiral Stevenson: Ah, sixes and sevens. Again, you know, you're trying to change and motivate people who have gotten awfully comfortable in their ways--trying to shake them up.

Q: How frequently did you send these out?

Admiral Stevenson: I think we sent them every other week. The frustrating part was that some of our O-6s used it in exactly the wrong way. You know, like it was a poker game: "I know this, and you don't know it." That was not the intent. The intent was for them to get the information out so they would look good among the juniors. It would enable them to be proactive in getting out the word and in getting action. In some cases I think it worked pretty well, and in other cases it was a nothing. The guy in your organization who takes information as power is a disaster. We had a few of those.

One of the major things I wanted to accomplish in Washington was to get across the concept that the chaplain exists to <u>provide</u> for his own and to facilitate religion for others. That the job of the chaplain is not just to do his own thing, but to meet the needs of others. That's a battle I fought as fleet chaplain. It's a battle that will always have to be fought, but I think it's part and parcel of the First Amendment, of the chaplain's ecclesiastical endorsement, and the chaplain's commission.

I was told when I went to Washington that the chaplains' manual was due to be revised. I looked upon the chaplains' manual as a disaster, and so one of the things I went to Washington with was a desire to eliminate the chaplains' manual. [Chuckle] A little bit of heresy to some. And I think the chief was a little concerned that my views along that line were a little radical.

Neil M. Stevenson #7 - 281

Q: He said, "Whoa, whoa, whoa"?

Admiral Stevenson: He said, "Whoa, whoa, whoa" a couple of times. We talked this thing over, and we went about it in a variety of ways. We had documents on documents of how the chaplains' manual should be changed. I had been in Washington when the former chaplains' manual was put together.

I think the first manual was published during World War II. It had come down through the years and been revised during Chaplain Garrett's era. But a manual is a how-to book. It belongs at the force level. I had seen enough things to say, "Look, we don't need a Boy Scout handbook." That's what the chaplains' manual had become. Society and the Navy had changed during the Vietnam era.

I wanted a SecNav policy regarding religion, something that was part and parcel of the whole Navy system. Over the years we were able to evolve a SecNav policy, SecNav instruction, and a companion OpNav instruction, which sets policy regarding religion and chaplains.

Q: Rather than just guidance?

Admiral Stevenson: Rather than just handbook guidance. The handbook guidance business is very important, but it ought to be at the force level, and the king of it ought to be the force chaplain. In other words, you know, what is operationally sound for a chaplain in SurfLant over against those things that are unique for chaplains who serve in AirLant. And there's a difference. There's much of chaplaincy that is the same, but there are also those things that are unique to the force that you're serving.

What's the difference operationally for chaplains with Navy and chaplains with Marine Corps? Well, the place that needs to be explained is at the force level. Fleet Marine Force should have a handbook. I got the CRB, the Chaplain Resource Board, to get with the force chaplains to develop force-level manuals. I told them, "We will expend the money to put together handbooks at that level, which should be maintained at that level, which should be funded at that level, and so forth, updated at that level." But at the Washington level, you should be dealing with SecNav policy. Thanks to Bill Gibson and Mel Ferguson, we were able to pull that off and develop the 1730 series of instructions.

Q: In what ways had the Vietnam War rendered the guidebook ineffective?

Admiral Stevenson: Well, the Vietnam War was also a watershed period. It was a watershed for the American people, along with the civil rights movement. We had moved from a WASP-oriented society to pluralism. You want some Navy examples of that?

Q: Sure.

Admiral Stevenson: Minority recruiting is a must. We no longer can be a lily-white Navy. Chaplain O'Connor was ordered to the Naval Academy, first senior chaplain at the Naval Academy to be a Catholic. Amazing. Go back and look at the Naval Academy in regards to worship. Absolutely amazing. Highly restricted to the Episcopal prayer book up through the '40s, I think even into the '50s. Well, that's not pluralism; that's not a recognition of provision and facilitation. Look at the history of compulsory chapel attendance at the Naval Academy.

If I'm correct, there was a period of time in which the Catholic services were only held in a side part of the Naval Academy chapel, rather than in the main part of the chapel. America became more of a secular society, and it also became a society in recognition of pluralism. We needed to make that kind of change in an honest respect for the First Amendment of the Constitution. To me it was very important to have that kind of SecNav policy and to make the Chaplain Corps, therefore, more viable to the age that it was serving the Navy.

Q: How did you go about seeing that these SecNav policies got implemented, that they weren't just words on paper?

Admiral Stevenson: Well, you bring up a favorite subject of mine. Having been in Washington, I was aware of the fact that a lot of chaplains and a lot of church groups don't recognize the difference between legislation and implementation. The way in which the Chaplain Corps tried to do implementation was through training. As Ross Trower would say, "The sidewalk has changed; have you changed?" [Chuckle]

To educate chaplains regarding the fact that there now is a SecNav policy that impacts on their command and the very work that they do, and it's not just a whim that the chaplain's ministry be open and inclusive, but that they have to actually watch out that they're not being exclusive. We were trying to train chaplains that it's very important that the sign on the door of the chaplain's office say "chaplain." Not Presbyterian chaplain, not Protestant chaplain, not Catholic chaplain, not Jewish chaplain, etc. But just--chaplain.

Q: One size fits all. [Laughter]

Admiral Stevenson: Well, one size does fit all, if the chaplain realizes that he can help all. The chaplain can provide for his own faith group and make referrals or facilitate for others. The word "chaplain" is a very open invitation in this society. You've got to train the chaplain that, "No matter who comes in the door, the chaplain can help him."

Let's say the person who comes in the door needs instructions from a Catholic chaplain in order to get married. Then I know I can make an honest-to-God referral to the Catholic chaplain. I can get you an appointment, I can get you a time, a date, I can be helpful to you. And I don't do it by just saying, "Go see the Catholic chaplain." I actually do an honest-to-God memorandum of referral with appropriate copy-to notations.

Now, in order to implement these kinds of things, chaplains have to be involved in establishing a level of trust. Chaplains are not into the business of proselytizing. Chaplains are into the business of trusting each other, knowing that those who come to the chaplain's office for assistance, will receive honest assistance to meet their need.

Q: Well, one thing that helped you was the changing of the times themselves. Such an approach wouldn't have been useful before John the XXIII was Pope, for example.*

Admiral Stevenson: That's very true.

Q: So what you were really trying to do, as much as set down a policy, was to sell a philosophy on how you would operate it. And we were talking during one of the breaks the idea of building a consensus on these changes rather than trying to ram them down people's throats by directive.

Admiral Stevenson: Right, and not threatening people, but explaining to them, again, that what you're trying to do is meet the needs of eligible people within the military services, within the sea services. It's a big job, and you've got to have some appreciation of where chaplains come from and that some chaplains have not moved beyond the limited seminary environment they were educated in. And a lot of chaplains have not left the parish environment from whence they came.

Sometimes I used to think the more parish experience a chaplain had, the less able he was to operate in the institutional environment. Some people would say the other way around. They'd say, "Oh, no. We want to make sure this guy's had at least five years in the parish before we bring him in the Navy." And many times I'd say, "Yeah." And all he's done for 20 years, 26 years, 30 years in the Navy is replay that parish experience as though everybody was a Presbyterian. That's very narrow, very sad. A chaplain must be provoked into a bigger world and appreciate that he is an employee of the U.S. Navy. If he wants just the parochial parish, he ought to go home and let the parish pay him.

Q: Indeed that chaplain does work for the Navy.

---

* John XXIII was Pope from 1958 to 1963. He had a more open, ecumenical spirit than his predecessors. Vatican Council II was convened during his tenure as Pope.

Admiral Stevenson: Yes, but if you'll deal with any clergy, you'll find out that many have difficulty recognizing the fact that they are employees and have specific responsibilities to an employer.

Q: Do they think of themselves as working directly for God?

Admiral Stevenson: Well, you know, they get out of the seminary and don't know whom they work for. I mean, if you work for a lot of committees, you don't work for anybody. You need to recognize the relationship to an employer. And if you have a problem with the Navy as your employer, then, in conscience, you need to pursue that. You don't hide it within yourself and get angry about it.

I was recently at a continuing education program for senior pastors down in Orlando, at the hotel I ran into an old executive officer of mine, who also was raised in Brooklyn, New York--Admiral Dick Altmann. It was a delight to see him again after all these years.

We went and had a drink together, and we were laughing about when I first went to the Naval Air Station Glenview. They had it that the chaplain did all the casualty assistance calls work and so forth. I went to him and said, "You know, this is against regulations, and it's against conscience, and this is not the way it's to be done." And I think something good came out of it. I could have sat at that duty station for two years and fumed and fussed and gotten angry. But, no, I had an employer, and I went to the employer and I said, "I don't think this is good for the business. I don't think you've got the right guy doing what he ought to be doing. I think you need to get the medical and the JAG and them all involved." It turned out to everybody's benefit, especially the next of kin we served. It certainly turned out to my benefit, and my employer did not knock me down for it.

Q: How successful were you in the minority recruiting campaign?

Admiral Stevenson: Well, the Chaplain Corps was very successful in minority recruiting. The Chaplain Corps had the highest percentage of minority recruiting in the Navy. And, as

I think I've explained, having been on all sides, that became something of the law of unintended consequences.

Q: What do you mean by that?

Admiral Stevenson: Well, we went from 1% or 2% minorities in the Chaplain Corps to somewhere between 13% and 16% of the Chaplain Corps being minorities, which I think is extremely good. That, of course, depends on what you consider minorities; sometimes they count women, sometimes they don't.

But in the development of that, when you start an equal opportunity program and a minority recruiting program, the problem is in the kinds of reinforcement that they need. So there were, correctly under Chaplain O'Connor's time, meetings for black chaplains and meetings for female chaplains. Once a year, as minority groups, they would get together and say, "Well, this is how I'm being treated." Or, "This is what I still see as the problem." And, of course, in the Navy you're recruiting them all pretty much at the same date of rank, so they're becoming competition for each other in the system.

There comes a point where somebody's got to make a decision, and I thought I was the one that ought to make the decision since I observed this problem of the law of unintended consequences. I decided that the isolation or separation from the norm that we were providing was hindering individuals from the minorities in becoming regular chaplains, because they are much more interested in being members of the minority club.

They looked forward to just getting together with other black chaplains more than they did to being involved with all chaplains. So I tried to initiate, with the help of minority leaders, the fact that we had come to the day where we were truncating the careers of minority chaplains and hindering them by separating them from having normal chaplains' responsibilities.

Q: I think the way you put it before was that you wanted to take away a crutch and let everybody stand on his own.

Admiral Stevenson: And compete on his own as best qualified. I think when you reach a certain degree of minorities, you've got to do that for their sake. That's a tough call.

Q: Was there resentment when you put that out?

Admiral Stevenson: Oh, I think so, sure. I mean, if you've got guys going to a club meeting once a year and then you close down the club, you're going to get some flak.

Q: Because that probably developed a camaraderie of its own.

Admiral Stevenson: Yes, because they always came to Washington and would call on CNO. There's a prestige in that, but there's also a problem in that. You go back and you say to the other guys who are working in the trenches, "I've been to the mountain, and you haven't." [Chuckle] You also get this mentality in commands that we just talked about in this business of pluralism. You get to the place where commands begin to have the mentality that the minority chaplains minister to minorities. You get the mentality that only a woman chaplain can minister to women. Well, that's not the Chaplain Corps. That's the opposite, in my opinion. Unfortunately, clergy are often most comfortable in their own ghetto, but that's parish ministry, not institutional.

Q: By the time that you had completed your tour as chief, was the situation as pluralistic as you had hoped?

Admiral Stevenson: No. It never will be, but I think it had certainly moved in that direction. It's a long voyage. You handle the rudder lightly, I was told, and over a long course, the course correction takes place. That's basically what it is. What I'm basically talking about is trying to have a course correction for the benefit of everybody. But I took some heat personally.

Q: Were you accused of being racist?

Admiral Stevenson: I didn't hear that term, but I did hear people say, "You really don't have an interest in our minority needs."

I was trying to say, "I think I have to make a decision. I think it's time that all chaplains are chaplains.

You know, I'm a manpower person. Billets are not color coded; billets are not faith group coded; billets are billets. It was the same thing in my mentality with the Jewish rabbis. A Jewish chaplain, in my opinion, has the right and obligation of sea duty. When the Chaplain Corps decided because of the low numbers of Jewish personnel in the Navy that Jewish chaplains would always pull shore duty, we were, in my opinion, mistreating the Jewish chaplain. The Chaplain Corps truncated the Jewish chaplains' opportunity to be a part of the Chaplain Corps at every level. How are you going to order a rabbi in to the Chief of Chaplains' staff if he's never had sea duty? I mean, is anybody going to respect his handling of the detailing or the training desk? You're going to put in charge of Chaplain Corps training a guy who's never been in ships? You know, that's ridiculous.

Q: Did you change that policy during your time?

Admiral Stevenson: Yes. And we got some flak on that one too. Some letters from the Jewish groups and some questions from the Jewish endorsing agent, Jewish Welfare Board. But what you're trying to explain professionally is you realize that the rabbi's ministry in the ship is as valid as my ministry in a ship. And they say, "What do you mean? There's only ten Jewish personnel on this aircraft carrier." And I'd say, "Okay. I understand that, but what I want the rabbi to understand, and what I want ship's company to understand is that the sign on the door says 'chaplain.'"

Q: Read my lips. A chaplain is a chaplain. [Chuckle]

Admiral Stevenson: And if you come see that chaplain, he can help you. He can help you. Now, he cannot provide Christian sacraments, but he can get you to a Catholic padre, he can get you to a Protestant padre, he can get you to Medical, he can get you to JAG, he can do all these things. The chaplain has to see this larger world as he gains responsibilities in the Chaplain Corps. He's not to become the victim of his own parochialism or the development of his own ghetto. And what I was saying to people, "Well, you can continue having a minority ghetto, you can continue having a Jewish ghetto, but the United States Navy, under the First Amendment, ought not have a Chaplain Corps made up of ghettos.

Q: Well, the chaplain in a ship or other command is going to develop a reputation that the sailors will know, yes, you can or, no, you can't get help from this man or woman.

Admiral Stevenson: Very quickly. And one of the excuses that the sailor can use is if the chaplain makes it very evident that the chaplain is not part of that sailor's experience, that because of race, color, creed, etc., that that chaplain is unavailable.

Q: Did you, through the mechanism of selection boards, have a way of not promoting the people who were too parochial?

Admiral Stevenson: Well, you would hope that was true, but selection boards depend on records and reputations. So if the fitness reports of all those up for selection all look alike, then boards start leaning on reputations. The selection system is not perfect, but you'd like to have it as pure as possible and deal with records. So if I would want to handicap a chaplain coming up for selection, I would start writing the narrative of his fitness report by saying, "This Presbyterian chaplain takes outstanding care of Presbyterians." I would look at it as a negative statement. Whereas, it should be positive if you write in the fitness report that this chaplain is of a ecumenical spirit and is open to people.

A chaplain can be a person opposed to alcohol. . . a teetotaler. But does he put a sign on his door that says, "Teetotaler Chaplain"? [Chuckles] And then other extreme, of course, is the guy who says, he has to go hang out in the bars and all that, which is nonsense. Again, the extremes are always a bunch of nonsense. It has do with openness.

During this five-year period, I thought that we needed to communicate to chaplains very clearly and distinctly the business of double jeopardy.

Q: We talked about that before the tape recorder started. If you could put that on the record, please, what you mean by double jeopardy.

Admiral Stevenson: I think that every time you take upon yourself a major obligation in life, you naturally add to your jeopardy in life. In the case of clergy, double jeopardy comes from being ordained and being commissioned. You have total obligations to your faith group, because you are ordained by that faith group. And you have total obligations to the United States Navy, because you have freely received a commission. You're the one who raised your hand. To dishonor either one's ordination or one's commission puts you in double jeopardy.

Q: How do you mean dishonor?

Admiral Stevenson: For instance, you could have a chaplain come to you who has a major problem. And sometimes even the chaplain's endorsing agent would say, "Now, you know that if a line officer did this same thing, that it would not be as much of a jeopardy to his career as a chaplain doing this thing."

And I'd say, "Sure, but the chaplain ought to know he willingly accepts double jeopardy. He did accept ordination, and he did accept a commission."

Q: So he needs to live by a higher standard?

Admiral Stevenson: Well, I guess I'm somewhat concerned about the word "a higher standard," but it's just the standards that he accepted for himself, and so it provides double jeopardy. And in my opinion, it ought to, because if you are not a good commissioned officer, the Navy needs to respond. And if you do not follow your ordination vows--you were commissioned on the basis that you were endorsed as an ordained clergy--well, then, you're letting your faith and people down.

I ran into a couple of ridiculous things with chaplains, but even more so with endorsing agents. We had spent so much time--I felt, legitimately--trying to get people on board with the concept. We were trying to explain to endorsing agents and chaplains, DOPMA, for instance, and how DOPMA impacted on the Chaplain Corps. [Laughter]

I got the feedback one time that they thought that we had written DOPMA. Part of DOPMA came up from the military bureaucracy, but then Senator Nunn said, "This is what we want."

Q: We were talking about this double jeopardy concept before the machine was on. You used as an example the chaplain who committed adultery would be held to have done worse than, say, a line officer who did so. Was there not that sort of double jeopardy before you came back to the front office?

Admiral Stevenson: Yes, but I had the impression as a young chaplain that it was often handled with a gentlemen's agreement.

Q: What do you mean by that?

Admiral Stevenson: I mean the chaplain confronted would just resign. But in an age of litigation, you got to the place where fewer chaplains would just resign out of a "sense of honor" or a sense of responsibility to one's endorsing agent. Today we are more apt to play what I would call legalistic games: "Well, I'm an employee and I have the rights of all other employees. And if other employees have committed adultery and they don't have to resign, then I won't resign."

Q: So did you sort of codify the expectation then so that it would be on the record what the consequences would be?

Admiral Stevenson: I tried to codify it in my own philosophy as I shared my philosophy with members of the Chaplain Corps.

Q: I wonder if that would stand up in a court of law?

Admiral Stevenson: Oh, I don't think so. What I was doing was writing what my expectations would be regarding a chaplain and a chaplain's behavior.

Q: This was not all that long after the notorious case of Captain Jensen, who was accused of adultery. Was there still a legacy of that as you came into the chief's Office?

Admiral Stevenson: No. I think that was gone. I was in the chief's office when that case was prominent. I really think that was gone by the time I became the deputy chief.

Q: Was that case an aberration, really? It's not too many instances where, I think, a chaplain would be falsely accused of adultery.

Admiral Stevenson: I really don't know how to respond to that, Paul. I really don't have a lot of knowledge of that other than newspaper stuff.

Q: Did you have the sense after you imparted this philosophy of a double standard that behavior was improving, or what?

Admiral Stevenson: No. However, I do think that my training under men that I admired, like Admiral Hayward, taught me that it is very good to put your expectations up front. You realize that some people are going to read into that that you are a hard-nosed SOB, but you are hopeful that others will say, "Well, look, this is the expectation, and I know where I stand with this guy." There were some tragedies while I was Chief of Chaplains, and like any human being, I would hope that my attempt to make my expectations clear did not add to anybody else's burden.

There were a few chaplains who exited the Navy because of homosexuality while I was Chief of Chaplains. There was a chaplain who committed suicide while I was Chief of Chaplains. These things that happen in life happen to individuals within the Chaplain Corps. I would trust that my emphasis on this business of the double jeopardy, or dual standard or whatever you want to call it, has just been a matter of reality. Now, if that added an overbearing burden on other people's lives, then I would regret that. But I thought it was very, very important from the very beginning to try to let chaplains know clearly how I saw things.

For instance, I also borrowed from a letter that he sent out to flag officers. I admired that letter. I thought it was really straight-shooting. Well, I took that letter and I adapted it to the O-6 community in the Chaplain Corps. In other words, I feel that the Chief of Chaplains' detailing policies for O-6 chaplains should imitate the CNO policies toward the detailing of flag officers. Captains have come a long way and had a lot of experience, so there is no excuse for an O-6 not to understand the United States Navy and the requirements of the United States Navy.

We are the fortunate ones. The line between those selected for O-6, O-7, O-8, and others is a very narrow line. But since we're the ones who got selected, since we're the ones who get the pay, then let it be clear that where we need to be is where the Navy thinks we need to be. We don't need somebody making O-6 and deciding, "Well, I've not only made O-6, I'm not only assured now of successful retirement pay, but I also choose to be in San Diego with my grandchildren for the rest of my career." That's not serving the United States Navy or its people.

Q: Could you talk briefly about what the detailing policies and practices were?

Admiral Stevenson: The majority of the chaplains, unless they've served in the office of the Chief of Chaplains, don't understand the burden of detailing. They don't understand that the entire detailing system of the Navy is under a budget, and that there are restrictions in regards to PRDs.* The detailer must get the right chaplain to the right job, having the money to get that move made. The Chief of Chaplains may know a chaplain who would be ideal for a specific billet, and you have frustration when you can't get that guy to that billet because he's already tied in to a projected rotation date.

One of the things I wanted to do and that Chaplain Trower allowed me to do when I first went back to the office was to prioritize O-6 billets. What are the most important, influential billets from the Chief of Chaplains' perspective.

Q: Approximately how many of them were there?

Admiral Stevenson: I think there were about 60, so where do you put your top O-6 people? And, again, it's accommodation. You've got to have top-notch people in the Chief of Chaplains' staff. You've got to have top-notch people at the chaplain school. You've got to have somebody at the Naval Academy--I used to call it Camelot--who knows what he's doing. You've got to have claimant chaplains who understand manpower.

So you go through those prioritized billets and then look at your stable--I hope nobody gets offended at all these little terms--and try to decide how you're going to get the best guy in the best slot. Sometimes, it's by exception. Because after you've done those things, then you say, "But, we don't have the money to move this guy." Or you may have an ideal chaplain and he almost breaks your heart because he says, "I don't want to go. I don't want to leave San Diego." Geez. No sense of the mission of training, motivating other chaplains, and fulfilling the religious needs of people.

You also run into the problem of detailing where you recognize the fact that the chaplain out there is still thinking in terms of his church rather than institutional ministry. You get the O-6 whom you want to be a claimant chaplain. You think he'll be able to do the job, and you find out that he's filling the role of a bishop. You don't want him to fulfill the role of a bishop. You want him to fulfill the role of a supervisory chaplain who's

---

* PRD--projected rotation date, the time at which an individual in a given billet is expected to move on to other duty or to retire.

working night and day at the force level, at the claimant level, to influence chaplains to meet the needs of sailors.

I initiated a letter that I sent to O-6s, particularly those who were newly selected for captain. I would have thought that the guy who has just been selected for O-6 is looking for the Chief of Chaplains to send him a set of orders. Say, I'm in an O-5 billet. I want to get my feet wet as an O-6. I want to go to a place that's a challenge. I want to establish my reputation and my record as a leader. So, okay, "I'm only halfway through my tour here in San Diego, but, by golly, the selection board has recognized me as a potential leader of the Chaplain Corps." And if the Chief of Chaplains says, 'We want you to go and become the senior chaplain of Third Marine Division, you're young, you're athletic, you've got a good mind,' my assumption would be, 'Yeah, let me have at it.'"

In some ways, it's disappointing, and my letter was in hopes of sharing with that individual specifically why I wanted him to go to that place. It was a system by which I shared personally with the O-6s that I was very much in the O-6 detailing act, although the detailer brought the recommendations to me. I wanted everyone to know that there was no use blaming the detailer. I signed the paperwork. I had to write, in many cases, to a flag officer, to a general officer and explain to him why I was ordering this person in and why I thought this person fit the particular command.

Q: So you had to be kind of a salesman on both sides in that role.

Admiral Stevenson: Yes. And in most cases it worked out very well, and in some cases it bombed dramatically. Sometimes, on rare occasion, you ran into a situation where a flag or a general officer said, "Well, I really want Chaplain So-and-so." I was in a position of saying to them either "Fine," or "Do you really know what you're asking for?" [Laughter] Because in some cases, they didn't, because things had changed since they served with that person; relationships had changed.

The detailer would handle the chaplains with problems. I was proud of the detailers we had when I was in Washington. I thought they handled things with a great deal of sensitivity. I don't think that priorities ought to be given to people with problems. I think the Chief of Chaplains can be too involved with the problem of a specific chaplain, and that sometimes those chaplains need to be treated like a medical officer with a problem, or a JAG officer with a problem, and not on the basis of pastoring that chaplain with a problem.

If you have a bad doctor, his reputation has a negative impact on his profession. If you have a bad chaplain, a chaplain with a problem, it impacts on his reputation, and it impacts on the contribution he can make to command.

Q: Is alcoholism a problem in the Chaplain Corps?

Admiral Stevenson: Oh, we had chaplains who were alcoholics. I don't think it was any more so than other communities. My policy regarding chaplains with alcohol problems or who suffered from alcohol disease was the same as the Navy's. One would encourage them to recognize their own problem and to get into rehab.

One of the things we set up in detailing was a selection process that went even beyond the Bureau of Naval Personnel's requirement. In most communities, selection for indefinite extension, that very first level of attrition, is strictly done by the community's detailer. Because of the uniqueness of the Chaplain Corps for faith group endorsements and the involvement of faith groups, we decided that we needed an indefinite extension board to go through all the records like a regular selection board and to determine who should receive an indefinite extension.

Same with making regular Navy--another selection board process rather than just a detailer for the Chief of Chaplains making the decision. I think that's good for the Chaplain Corps. I think it's good for individuals. Like all selection boards, they bring in results that are sometimes disappointing to the Chief of Chaplains. You look at it, and you say, "How could they select that guy and not that guy?" But those are the breaks, and you go along with those breaks.

Q: How good a relationship did you have with NMPC and the Chief of Naval Personnel in implementing what you wanted to do?*

Admiral Stevenson: As a member of his staff, I had an open audience with him. That was a very workable relationship. And when a chaplain got in trouble, it was the Chief of Chaplains, or the deputy if the chief was on the road, who would be called in to a private session to talk about the information that had come in on a specific chaplain. It was kept as confidential as possible. In fact, in cases where confidentiality broke, it was broken by the chaplain himself. He felt that he was being mistreated or put upon.

Q: It sounds like there were still some holdover of the old gentlemen's agreement business then. The person was allowed to go away quietly with no furor.

Admiral Stevenson: Oh, not if the circumstances warranted legal action. The chaplains did not receive--to my knowledge--a benefit over against other officers of the Navy. Where charges were brought, due process was carried out. There's no way in which anybody can influence the due process. I don't think there's ever been a deputy or a Chief of Chaplains who has not had a few sleepless nights, concerned both for the Chaplain Corps and for the individual who has committed an infraction, hoping that all the right decisions are made and that people make reasonable choices.

Q: Well, you're a caring person or you wouldn't be in that business to begin with.

Admiral Stevenson: You're also a person under authority. We had some major personnel problems regarding some chaplains, and we agonized with them and with their endorsing agents.

Q: What types of cases were these?

---

* NMPC--Naval Military Personnel Command, a title used for a time in the 1980s. Before and afterward, the organization has gone by the title Bureau of Naval Personnel.

Admiral Stevenson: Oh, a case of rape in one situation, a case of homosexuality.

Q: Does this create bad blood between the Chaplain Corps and a faith group if one of these cases comes up?

Admiral Stevenson: Sometimes the initial reaction of the faith group is to come to the Chief of Chaplains and say, "This has got to be a put-up case. I'm going to protect my chaplain to the hilt."

And you say to them, "Please do. I can only share with you what the law will allow me to share." The endorsing agent did not always comprehend the requirements of the military.

I remember one endorsing agent who came to me. The chaplain of his faith group did not have a discipline problem. It was a simple attrition situation. The chaplain had not been selected either for regular Navy or he had not been selected for indefinite extension. I'll give you two examples that readily come to mind.

In one case, the assumption of the endorsing agent was that this decision had been made because the individual represented a minority and that this was a case of the Navy being prejudicial to a minority. Well, the chaplain had a bad record. He was not sharp; he was not on the ball. He was in a league that was over his head in competition. And what it's like, Paul, it's like somebody coming and saying to the manager of a ball team, "You're prejudiced against this guy."

And you say, "No, he can't play the position, so we're sending him down to the minors." In that particular instance, that community felt that they needed to go outside their faith group to make a complaint about the Navy. And in that particular case, I received the toughest letter I have ever read in my life. It was an accusative letter from an agent of the NAACP.* My detailer came in and said, you know, "What are we going to do with this?"

I said, "What we're going to do is we're going to sit down and we're going to write a long, specific, explicit letter explaining the entire process, providing him with the statistics

---

* NAACP--National Association for the Advancement of Colored People.

of the numbers of people who were selected and the numbers of people who were not selected. The numbers who were selected who were minorities, the numbers who were selected who were non-minorities. Tell them the whole story, lay the whole thing out." I mean, it was a three-page letter. Never heard another word. Just had to lay it out candidly.

There was a separate situation in which the endorsing agent came and said, "You cannot attrite this man from the Navy because he is the only chaplain on active duty from our faith group." Now, see, at the surface level, where this guy was, that seemed to make sense. His mentality was that the Navy had a quota for each faith group. Now, how many hundreds of faith groups are there in the United States?

Q: I have no idea.

Admiral Stevenson: You could end up with one chaplain from each faith group in the United States. It had to be explained to him in detail, and he didn't understand it at first. But I met the guy a year later, and he said, "I know what you're talking about now." I had to explain that the selection board operates on the principle of best qualified, not on the basis of faith group. On best qualified. The Chaplain Corps does not have to be a religious house of representatives. Which would mean you could have an ineffective chaplain of this little faith group who would be guaranteed a 30-year career because there isn't anybody else that--I mean, that's ridiculous. The Navy has to run professionally on the best-qualified basis, and chaplains have to know that it's a competitive system. I'm not saying it's the fairest system in the world. I'm saying it's the fairest one that anybody could invent to meet the needs of sea service personnel.

That endorsing agent was really ticked off. Now, I'll give you the humorous line of it. As a wedge in his argument, the endorsing agent said to me, in the confines of my office, "You've got to keep this guy because I don't have any place for him." [Laughter]

I was sitting there saying, "Hey, if you don't have a place for him, he may be in the wrong profession."

But each one of those personnel decisions is a tough thing to deal with. We had good detailers while I was in Washington, and to the best of their ability, they got the right guy at the right place at the right time.

Q: On this matter of expectations, some people may have looked at you as hard-nosed. On the other hand, sometimes by setting those high expectations, you can inspire people to do more than they thought they could.

Admiral Stevenson: The most important thing is to have integrity. I tried to explain to people that what Neil Stevenson was trying to do was to reflect as honestly as possible the policies of the United States Navy.

You didn't go to the Naval Academy?

Q: No.

Admiral Stevenson: You know, in Christianity, St. Paul talks about the Jewish community, Israel, the faithful. Well, who are Christians? Christians, Paul says, are those who are adopted into Israel. So we come by adoption. Okay. Those of us who did not go to the Naval Academy must recognize that we came into the United States Navy by adoption. I'm being serious. I mean, the true children are the Naval Academy; the rest of us have the joy of adoption.

Now, the adopted need to understand that in the Naval Academy, everybody's numbered. From the day that that person goes to the Naval Academy, they recognize that they are in a competitive environment. Somebody's going to graduate number one, and somebody's going to graduate number 251, and that's a norm. And everybody who went through the Naval Academy lives with that norm.

Now, this chaplain comes in from a church in Fruit Jar Junction with an ecclesiastical mentality, from a polity with a bishop or a good-old-boy school. And then he comes into the Navy, and he's told by his endorsing agent, "It's the same as the church except you're in uniform." No way! Somebody's got to get to that guy for his own sake and say to him, "Do you know anything about the Naval Academy? Do you know anything about competition? Do you know anything about attrition? That's the real world. You don't live in ecclesiology land anymore. You live in the United States Navy." As far as I'm concerned, it's just a matter of being honest.

Endorsing agents play a very critical part in the world of separation of church and state. They endorse--in a sense, verify--for the Department of Defense that these clergy are of an ecumenical spirit.

One of the policies we had under Ross Trower, and certainly one that I tried to continue, was that we, in our annual briefings of endorsing agents, ought to be wide open and share with them the whole load. In some respects, that was very frustrating, because the questions they asked when you had your division leaders over there briefing them were often questions that indicated they didn't exactly understand the requirements of manpower and personnel and integrated planning, and so forth and so on. Nevertheless, we tried to share that with them and bring them on board.

It used to get frustrating, because sometimes we felt that the Army and the Air Force would just make some generalized statement like, "All is well," and that the endorsing agents left happier with the Army and the Air Force than they did with us. We sort of felt we bared our souls to them and didn't get that much back. They didn't always seem to understand the system and the laws. They were pretty parochial in their view.

Q: Well, it's interesting that maybe part of their purpose in sending an individual to the Navy was to be a representative of their faith group. And, yet, you're saying, "Well, we'd rather he be ecumenical."

Admiral Stevenson: Yes, and that's part of the uncoupling. I don't think that the majority of endorsing agents, including the ones that had been on active duty, understood the concept of institutional ministry, or didn't want to understand the implications of institutional ministry. And, of course, that's one of my hobby horses.

For instance, I'm not so sure that it always impacted as much on them as it would on me that you have provided this person with an endorsement so that he is qualified to work for an employer. The agreement is that if you pull the endorsement, the employer is going to fire this guy. But while he's employed by the Navy, it is the Navy that has the prerogatives of an employer. I'm not so sure that that is always quite clear. We tried to make it clear.

As I said before, they used to come around occasionally with the idea that we had invented DOPMA. I used to recommend they write to Senator Nunn. I was a fan of DOPMA, because I really think it straightened out an awful lot of inconsistencies. One of the inconsistencies at that time, by the way, was that by an anomaly in the previous code, O-6 chaplains were allowed to stay on active duty until they were 62 years of age rather than exiting the naval service at the end of 30 years of service. We recommended that chaplains be under the identical laws of all other naval officers. I would hope that would always be true. After DOPMA passed and some of the chaplains who had served more than 30 years and were not yet 62 years of age, were very unhappy that they had to get out of the Navy. They, too, thought that we had invented DOPMA. So much for endorsing agents.

By the way, do you do want me to mention some of our mistakes?

Q: Please do.

Admiral Stevenson: As I've told you in previous tapes, I worked the '79 POM--the first one to include the Chaplain Corps--under John O'Connor's leadership. John was unhappy with that POM, because it called for only 124 billets. When I came back to Washington in 1980, a lot of work had been done under John O'Connor to expand the POM buy for the out-years.* This was a true example of the law of unintended consequences. The Chaplain Corps by now in the POM had bought too many billets.

There was a lot of pressure. The expression that was being used was, "Use it or lose it." In reality, it meant that the Chaplain Corps had gained too many billets in too narrow a period of time. We had to recruit something like 100 chaplains within one year in

---

* "Out-years" refers to planning for years beyond the immediate fiscal year for which the budget is being developed.

order to meet the POM level, etc. We would have been better off to have immediately gone back and asked to extend the POM over and beyond the FYDP and acquired chaplains at a lower rate per year.

Chaplain Al Plishker headed up the recruiting process, including minority recruiting.* He did an outstanding job to meet the mark that was set, but that just created the hump. Through the work of Chaplain Bill Gibson and Mel Ferguson and others in the G-2 shop, we recognized that we had to deal with our own problem. We wanted a smooth attrition level. When I first went in there as deputy, we should have spotted that. Eventually, we got an integrated plan. That established an improved means of managing a small community.

At the same time, there was a lot of pressure on us--throughout the Chaplain Corps--that the Commandant of the Marine Corps wanted more and more chaplains. We were hearing that our reluctance to recruit to the highest was causing the Chaplain Corps not to get as large as it had potential. I think two things about that are important to keep in mind. One is that there probably wasn't any community in the Navy at that time that had as high a retention. Second, the Navy paid for the billets, not the Marine Corps, and you do have to maintain some sense of balance regarding Catholic chaplains in relationship to Protestants.

The highest retention rate in the Navy happens because chaplains get a taste of institutional ministry, and I think the impact of this is positive to those who are married. Their wives are positive about it. When you have a high retention, you've got to establish some system of attrition. [Chuckle] At least we felt over the years that one of the ways the Chaplain Corps had suffered was from too high a retention, really. Whereas, the rest of the Navy was thinking of its low retention among staff corps officers.

Q: How would you account for that high retention rate in the Chaplain Corps?

Admiral Stevenson: Oh, first of all, it is an exciting form of ministry, particularly for those who get caught up in the advantage of the ecumenical, institutional environment.

---

* Captain Richard Alan Plishker, CHC, USN.

Q: Is the security an asset?

Admiral Stevenson: Security and salary, I think, are major factors, particularly the retirement factor. There's no church that I know of that offers anything equal to it. And I think the camaraderie, both in the Chaplain Corps and with the whole sense of shipmate, is a major part.

Q: Did you, as chief or deputy, do anything to foster that camaraderie?

Admiral Stevenson: I hope so. It was fostered to me early on. Lots of good fellowship and get-togethers and serving together. And, you know, there's something, also, about serving in an ecumenical environment. You're sharing the same spaces, but there's a division of labor between Catholic, Protestant, and Jewish, and so forth, and that engenders a cooperative relationship. It's exciting to work in the same command and facility with men and women of other faiths.

Q: Interesting that you're trying to foster this camaraderie, but at the same, they're competing with each other for promotion and retention in the Navy.

Admiral Stevenson: So are the line officers.

Q: That's true.

The Catholic Church has had a drop-off in recruiting, if you will, for priests. What impact did you feel in the Navy from that?

Admiral Stevenson: Oh, that's a good point. Since World War II, the Catholic priests have represented approximately 25% of the active duty Chaplain Corps. That has been a pretty constant figure.

What has happened is, the recruiting of men to the priesthood in the United States is at a critical point. The average priest in the United States, when I was on active duty, was 54, 55 years of age. So how do you overcome that problem? It's a demographic problem. And our approach was that we did have a chaplain on the staff working specifically, almost entirely, in the area of recruiting Catholic padres.

Another point about the Chaplain Corps growth in numbers is that there's no sense of the Chaplain Corps growing when you can only recruit Protestants, and you can't keep a certain balance--say, 25%, or something like that--of Catholic padres.

Q: Did that number decline during your time?

Admiral Stevenson: No. We were able to stay a little ahead of the curve, thanks to the work of people like George Dobes and others who worked on Catholic recruiting.[*] By the way, many a bishop was surprised at how hard Protestant chaplains worked on recruiting Catholics.

Q: Could you tell us more, please, about some of the other staff members of the front office? You've talked about what an excellent team it was. What do you remember of them as individuals?

Admiral Stevenson: Well, as individuals they all had a willingness to work Washington hours, and they maintained a certain degree of tension between their shops, as I would hope they would. The G-1 was watching out for training assets, and the G-3 was making sure he didn't lose anything to his detailing and personnel and so forth. We benefited from the leadership of men like John Glynn, Walt Hiskett, Gene O'Brien, Al Koeneman, Murray Voth, Al Plishker, Tom Hiers, Vic Smith, Mel Ferguson, Bill Gibson, Joe O'Donnell, and John McNamara.[†] You know, these were all chaplains who had solid careers, solid records,

---

[*] Commander George A. Dobes, CHC, USN.
[†] Captain John J. Glynn, CHC, USN; Captain Walter A. Hiskett, CHC, USN; Captain Alvin B. Koeneman, CHC, USN, later Chief of Chaplains; Captain Murray H. Voth, CHC, USN; Commander Homer Thomas Hiers, Jr., CHC, USN; Lieutenant Commander Victor H. Smith, CHC, USN; Lieutenant Commander

in their own right. I don't think any of them were ever shy about letting us know where they stood on issues and what they thought should be prioritized. One of the things that you have to do is to let the staff run you.

Q: How do you mean that?

Admiral Stevenson: Well, you know, I think I've alluded to that maybe with myself and John O'Connor. That you've got to share with the staff what your priorities and what your goals are, and then you have to receive from them the advice on how you're going to get there. And you have to remember that they are interacting, if they're good staff officers, with their own counterparts outside the Chief of Chaplains' office. This is one of the big improvements that I saw in the Chief of Chaplains' staff over the years.

When I first went to the Chief of Chaplains' office, I got the feeling that we largely just talked to each other. By the time I left the Chief of Chaplains' office, I think that all the members of the staff were interacting with their counterparts throughout BuPers and throughout OpNav on an equal basis. That we had the kind of staff people who had learned their functions and tasks well enough that when they went to meetings in OpNav and BuPers, they were not looking for a 10% clergy discount, as I would put it, but to be a full part of the deliberations. That they learned to speak the language, that they learned the terminology. And that wasn't easy, you know.

There was a generation of chaplains before us who talked in providential and ecclesiastical terms, and then the Navy types would say, "Well, now, they just don't understand any of this manpower stuff, etc., so we have to solve the mysteries for them." Whereas, I saw a crew of chaplains like Bill Gibson, Mel Ferguson, Tom Hiers, Vic Smith, who really studied the issues and who took a leading edge in thinking and in proving that they could help other communities in managing assets. So they were, in some cases, provocative, but always productive. They led BuPers in small community integrated planning.

Melvin R. Ferguson, CHC, USN; Lieutenant Commander William H. Gibson, CHC, USN; Captain Joseph F. O'Donnell, CHC, USN; Captain John R. McNamara, CHC, USN.

Q: That must have created some surprise. [Laughter]

Admiral Stevenson: Oh, they were great. I really thought they were great. When I said, "Go," it established an atmosphere in which there was a design, but the contingency was dependent on the ball players. The staff pursued the game plan and were capable to meet the contingencies.

Q: Well, to stretch the sports analogy, you were the coach, but these guys still had to execute on your behalf.

Admiral Stevenson: Yes, and sometimes you don't come back and check everything with the coach. I mean, there's got to be that kind of relationship, and when you foul up, you both foul up. And you go from there. But we couldn't have had a finer staff, in my opinion.

Q: You've talked about the relationship when you were deputy and Chaplain Trower was the chief. What about when you were the chief and Chaplain McNamara was the deputy?*

Admiral Stevenson: Well, John was a great assist. John had been a the detailer on Chaplain Trower's staff. I had met John at chaplain functions over the years. I had always admired John, because John speaks his mind and is extremely articulate, and I recognized, also, that he was a great preacher.

He had handled the detailing job in a most admirable fashion. It was interesting that John had ordered himself to a parish more than a bureaucratic job. Now, I wish sometime later that he had had the experience of being a major claimant chaplain, going out to the fleet and wrestling with the manpower business, and so forth and so on. But I was delighted when he was selected and came in as deputy.

And, again, there was a balance there that was somewhat different from Chaplain Trower and myself, because I was prone to manpower thinking because my time under John

---

* Admiral Stevenson became the Chief of Chaplains in August 1983.

O'Connor had such a manpower emphasis to it. John McNamara brought in the personnel side of things, and he knew the people in NMPC.

One of the things we did before John McNamara came back as deputy was change the detailer's status. The Chaplain Corps detailer, unlike other detailers, had primary duty to the Chief of Chaplains' staff and ADDU to NMPC.[*] I arranged for the Chaplain Corps detailer to become primary duty to NMPC and ADDU to the Chief of Chaplains. They kept the location in the Chief of Chaplains' spaces, but I think that it's important that the Chaplain Corps detailer be basically accountable to NMPC--again, following the Navy norm.

Q: What sort of division of labor was there between the two of you when you were the chief?

Admiral Stevenson: Well, except on rare occasions, we maintained the rule that one of us would be in town at all times. When I did go to the Indian Ocean one Christmas, John asked if he could make the rounds of our Caribbean area, and he and the detailer went down and covered the Caribbean. I think John and I had a very smooth working relationship, very open, very candid.

Q: Any more examples on his personality, his capabilities?

Admiral Stevenson: One of the things that was somewhat different is you have the dynamic of the Protestant-Catholic thing, which is advantageous. I don't think the line fully appreciates that factor. John was extremely helpful in the Beirut crisis.[†] In August of 1983 he had come up to be deputy from being the senior chaplain at Camp Lejeune.[‡] So when the memorial service was planned for Camp Lejeune, since the Marines knew John as

---

[*] ADDU--additional duty.
[†] On 23 October 1983, a suicide terrorist drove a truck filled with the equivalent of 12,000 pounds of explosives into the Marine Corps barracks in Beirut, Lebanon. The resulting explosion killed 241 Americans and wounded 70.
[‡] Camp Lejeune is a major Marine Corps base in North Carolina.

intimately as they had, I received a call asking if I, as Chief of Chaplains, would object to John, my deputy, being the main speaker at the memorial service at Camp Lejeune.

I said, no, I didn't object at all. It made a lot of sense to me since he knew people intimately down there. That's one of those cases, I guess, where some protocol officer was concerned that the deputy was going to do the speaking, and the chief was going to give a prayer. It was a sad day in dismal weather. The rain soaked us clear through, and the whole memorial service I stood up there and could feel the rain running down my T-shirt.

A little aside to that that I will never forget was that Mrs. Reagan was sitting between the President and the Commandant of the Marine Corps.[*] Somebody had given her a wonderful see-through umbrella with a very high dome. Mrs. Reagan sat with the see-through umbrella over her head, and I could see the rain running down the sides of the umbrella and going directly into the collar of the President on one side and the collar of the Commandant of the Marine Corps on the other. I am happy to report to you that, to my knowledge, neither one of them flinched, although I think they both were getting a torrent of rain down their necks. [Laughter]

Another thing about it was that I was very pleased to turn over the corps, to be relieved by John McNamara for several reasons. One reason was that I was so delighted that we had been able to have Neil Stevenson fleet up and relieve Ross and then John McNamara fleet up and relieve Neil. And then as this happened, John was chief for three years and retired, and Al Koeneman, who was his deputy, fleeted up.[†] Just, experience-wise, it just all makes so much more sense to me than what we had in the past in the Chaplain Corps.

In the past, you know, I was in the office when Chaplain Kelly retired and Chaplain Garrett came in. Chaplain Garret came in from LantFlt. He hadn't been around the office, so the whole staff was saying, "Okay, new broom. Where do we go from here? What changes?" It's just not as smooth a transition, I would think, as it ought to be. This is a work place, this is a place where the engines are, you know, the ship is steaming. You don't get all new chief engineers when the new skipper comes aboard. You still maintain the

---

[*] General Paul X. Kelley, USMC, served as Commandant of the Marine Corps from July 1983 to July 1987.
[†] Rear Admiral Alvin B. Koeneman, CHC, USN, served as the Navy's Chief of Chaplains from June 1988 to August 1991.

same wardroom, on a rotation basis. People rotate in and rotate out, but the ship keeps on going. It seemed to me that made more sense than all of a sudden, one guy's gone and another guy comes in.

Q: The obligation, though, that that puts on the selection board is that whoever's picked for rear admiral, then three or four years down the road is going to be the chief.

Admiral Stevenson: Yes, well, that's not going to happen if CNP and CNO don't make the nomination, you know. And one of the things that the O-7 and the deputy needs to do is he needs to do some work on the E-ring.*

Q: So you're saying it's not automatic.

Admiral Stevenson: No, it's not automatic. It's a gentlemen's agreement. And whether it's still a gentlemen's agreement or not, I don't even know, as I speak now. I just think that if you can work that way, that's the way it ought to be. For the good of the Navy and the good of the Chaplain Corps, I think that's the way it ought to operate.

Q: Were there some things you were able to accomplish as chief that you couldn't when you were the deputy?

Admiral Stevenson: Well, we pushed ahead with the SecNav policy business. It was a major goal of mine.

Q: And you talked about getting away from the affirmative action on minorities.

---

* The Pentagon has lettered corridors, going from A at the innermost to E at the outermost. E-ring offices, which go around the perimeter of the building are considered the most prestigious.

Admiral Stevenson: Again, you know, the pendulum swings, so I just would emphasize that I'm talking about my time therein. The SecNav instruction was signed off 14 December 1983, and I became Chief of Chaplains the first of August 1983.

When I became the chief, I had laid out for myself some very specific goals, and I measured myself. You know, I still sit down on a Sunday afternoon and grade my homily before I put it in the file. So, as I used to tell people, I do do Monday morning quarterbacking about myself.

When I found out that I was going to be the Chief of Chaplains, I asked the reserve flag officer of the Chaplain Corps, Chaplain Floyd, to come on active duty for a few days.[*] And I asked Chaplain McNamara to come up from Lejeune. We went down for three days to Marine Base, Quantico, where we thrashed out an agenda and goals. My idea was that, from the reserve side of the house, from John's personnel background, so forth, it would be good for the three of us to decide what ought to happen in the next couple of years.

We concluded that the organizational goals of the next few years, commencing with fiscal year 1984, would be, as I wrote to the whole Chaplain Corps, a restatement of policy, that is, "To provide a clear, concise directive to increase the chaplain's awareness of the environment in which he or she serves and to make commands more conscious of their requirements of the chaplain's ministry." For me, that was accomplished in the establishment of the SecNav policy 1730.1, dated 14 December 1983. Chaplain Bill Gibson, who had been a Marine Corps line officer in Vietnam and gone to seminary and come back in as a chaplain, was the point man and did an outstanding job on that.

By the way, I did not have any paternalism attached to SecNav 1730.1. I didn't have that kind of relationship with the Secretary. It made it because it is proper and had top-notch staff work. We did have it go through with all the chops, including the JAG chop when I was away on a trip.[†] There was some language in it that had gotten by JAG, and then the Deputy JAG saw it again and realized that this particular language in relationship to

---

[*] Rear Admiral Emmett O. Floyd, CHC, USNR.
[†] Based on the original Hindi meaning of "stamp of approval," the Navy usage of "chop" in this sense is figurative rather than literal. Essentially, it means that a certain level in the hierarchy has signed off on a particular document.

the First Amendment was a major problem. I don't know if you want the whole story on this thing or not.

Q: Might as well.

Admiral Stevenson: Okay. There was an Army chaplain, rabbi-type, a reservist who was brought on active duty by the Army Chaplain Corps, because the Army Chaplain Corps, at that time, was working a major litigation. He was an Army chaplain and a civilian lawyer.

Q: That's quite a combination.

Admiral Stevenson: Yes. Rabbi, lawyer, Army chaplain. I'm trying to think of the gentleman's name. Very, very brilliant man, but had given us some legal language which was really not advantageous in the military environment. I could give you that language if you give me a minute to look it up. But it had been chopped. But then when JAG rediscovered it, JAG went over to CNO and CNO got all exercised that we hadn't done our job. And maybe we hadn't, but I felt that since JAG had already chopped it, that it was acceptable language. So I was kind of ticked off because I was out of town and by the time I got back to town, I really wasn't in the mood to go to CNO and say, you know, "I think JAG gave you the impression that this thing got through without JAG chopping it," and that it was strictly Chaplain Corps problem in language. But, anyway, I didn't do that.

Q: What was the outcome?

Admiral Stevenson: The outcome was that we made a change in the language of the instruction, which we should have. So the signing-off date was the 14th of December 1983, but the change in the language that was required was a good change. The original one, the difficult terminology as recommended by the Army chaplain-lawyer-type was "to observe the requirements of their religious beliefs and principles, except when precluded by a compelling military need."

Now, there are certain legal implications to the word "compelling military need," which would be to the disadvantage of a commanding officer. To the best of my memory, the word "compelling" puts the onus on command rather than on the individual. And we can all appreciate that it cannot be that way in a military setting. So the language was changed to read, much more simply and directly, "in keeping with sections umpty-ump of Article 0722 of Navy regulations and Title 10 of the United States Code, it is the Department of the Navy policy that commanders and commanding officers shall provide for the free exercise of religion by all personnel of their commands as specified in Enclosure 1." So, anyway, having achieved our goal for a policy from the highest level of the Navy, which I had been working on as deputy, and people on the staff, like Bill Gibson, had taken the point on, we were able to execute pretty fast after I became chief.

The second goal was a reemphasis of accountability. That is, to provide a structured method for communicating, identifying, measuring, reporting requirements and accomplishments through the chain of command. Chaplain Corps had done away with in the '60s the requirement for a quarterly report from chaplains. In those days, I favored doing that when I was on the staff. [Laughter]

Q: Favored doing away with it?

Admiral Stevenson: I favored doing away with it because it went nowhere. It was a piece of paper sent from chaplains to chaplains. Now, as Chief of Chaplains, I felt that we needed to do everything we could to reestablish lines of accountability and to make chaplains more accountable to the chain of command.

One of the ways you do that is by making chaplains make out a report that goes to command for endorsement and that is fed up through the force/fleet level for evaluation, knowing that, in proper staffing, it's going to go to the force and fleet chaplains. Not only to share ideas and concepts up through the line, but to set an environment of accountability and to remind chaplains that they are accountable to command. That you've got to fill out your quarterly report and have in mind that this CO wants to know if you're making a contribution to command. A contribution to all the people of the command, not just people of your own faith group. So, to me, that was important to reestablish that kind of accountability.

When we, the deputy or I, traveled, we had quite often been greeted with chaplains who've said, "Wonderful. You've come to see us. Please brief us on what's going on in Washington and what's going on in the Chaplain Corps." That's kind of an ego trip, so you like to get up and tell them what you're doing and how you're doing it, and so forth. Well, you can suddenly realize that you're leaving, and you've never sat down and said, "Now, wait a minute. Now you get up on your two feet and you tell me what's going on here." [Chuckles] Which is another form of accountability.

Third thing was a reassertion of practical factors, to provide impetus to the networking of professional expertise, and to encourage on-the-job training to the benefit of all clergy practicing this specialized field of ministry called chaplaincy. Nothing aggravated me, I guess, as much in my time as deputy and as chief as the fact that our training dollars would get away from practical factors, and yet, largely expended on what I looked upon as more theoretical aspects of our ministry.

Q: Such as what?

Admiral Stevenson: You've probably heard this before from other people, but it was a real--remember, I'd been in the training business thanks to Chaplain Garrett. I had been given the privilege of having the training desk in the chief's office, so I had dealt with setting up professional development training courses for chaplains, etc. I attended professional development training courses down through the years. Now, in the main, the Chaplain Corps, like other parts of the Navy--I mean, if Navy medical wants to bring somebody in for a training course, they go to medical schools and they get somebody. If the Chaplain Corps wants to do it, we go to the seminaries and we get somebody. You spend all your time trying to get these experts--and I'm not saying they're not experts in their field--but you try to get these civilians to understand the Navy. And those consultants do not appreciate the requirements of military life.

Q: Well, you're explaining to them what the Navy's about.

Admiral Stevenson: And I hope I have more patience now than I had then. Maybe I don't, but let me try to explain. And I'm sure other people in the Navy have felt the same way.

You get this civilian consultant and you're paying this civilian consultant wages, and at the same time you're chewing up all kinds of man-hours trying to explain the Navy to the guy. Two examples. When I was leaving the Navy, the professional development training course was being developed around the subject of ethics. I had one meeting at Georgetown University with the ethicists from the various universities and seminaries. Within an hour, they were ticked off at me, and I was ticked off at them. Some of them thought I was a pope, some of them thought I was a bishop, and almost immediately they started talking in terms, "Well, you will study the ethical issues and you will make a pronouncement." No! You have what, 50 different faith groups in the Chaplains Corps?

Q: They were looking at you as a stereotype.

Admiral Stevenson: Well, they were also looking at the Chief of Chaplains as the leader of a religious community. And the Chief of Chaplains, may God bless him, if he thinks of himself as a bishop, in my opinion, he's a fool. He's the senior chaplain in the United States Navy. And it's a secular, pluralistic world that is served, and he ought to be able to articulate the ethical, moral, theological views of his faith. But he cannot make them synonymous with the United States Navy.

Q: Well, taking a devil's advocate approach, shouldn't there be some ethical standards for chaplains in the U.S. Navy?

Admiral Stevenson: Oh, yes, there should be. And those ethical standards apply to chaplains as well as to all persons of the Navy, and they don't just apply to recruits. One of the things that used to always gripe me was the concern of senior officers that the recruits get character and moral training. We had many senior officers that needed as much moral and ethical training as recruits needed it. [Chuckle] It's at what level, at what need, and what is the question? And who has the expertise and who has to make the decision and who is the adviser on the decision? I can tell you some sea stories about myself and Admiral Watkins along that line in regards to terrorism and so forth.

But, anyway, another year we had counseling as the primary interest. And one of the things that bothered me, and I got quite agitated about it, was the fact that the counselors were standing up in front of Navy chaplains training Navy chaplains about counseling without any appreciation of the requirements of the sea service environment. They were talking about marriage counseling but don't know anything about talking to people who are required to be gone from home six months a year. Don't know anything about the fact that one does not receive leave because one's wife is giving birth to a child. They don't understand any of these things. And what they're doing is feeding chaplains misinformation because of their lack of knowledge of environment. It frustrated me, because I was sitting there saying "Now, these chaplains are going to leave with these concepts in their minds as the latest concepts from the expert. But it's going to be a disaster, because this chaplain's going to go back to his command, and he's going to espouse some of this stuff, and the XO and the CO are going to say, "Where has this guy been? He's lost the load."

I must confess that my frustration boiled over at one PDTC, and I unfortunately blew my stack.* Chaplain O'Connor used to do that from time to time, and as a member of his staff, I'd ask myself why he did it. Then I did it in Jacksonville at a dinner, and--even realizing it was a mistake--I could appreciate John's frustrations.

I discovered that the most successful way to do training was to do it in house. So we had one situation while I was chief. It was one of the cases where I went bulldog on the guys. CNET and others told me I couldn't do it. Others came to me and said, "Chaplains will not be accepted by other chaplains as experts." And yet, I was committed to having one professional training course that was totally designed by Navy chaplains for Navy chaplains, to deal right down the line with practical factors, particularly the chaplain as naval officer.

---

* PDTC--Professional Development Training Course.

Q: Was this the integrated training plan?

Admiral Stevenson: Yes.

Q: Could you explain that, please?

Admiral Stevenson: Briefly, to take all the elements of Chaplain Corps integrated plan for the out-years and relate it into the practical terms of what chaplains ought to be doing to understand it and its implications to the ministry in the command where they serve, under the policy of the Secretary of the Navy. How chaplains need to know the policy of the Secretary of the Navy and brief command on what command responsibility is for the command religious program. How it applies to all faith groups, the needs of the individual sailor and his dependents, not the needs of the chaplain, and so forth. How you go about setting up programs, getting funding at the local level to accomplish the provision and the facilitation of ministry in that command.

Q: Was this plan a course, or how did you implement it?

Admiral Stevenson: We wanted to train the most junior chaplains to understand the system and thereby enable them to do better ministry for service personnel and their dependents. I wanted the Chaplain Resource Board and CNET to provide the product, the tool, that would enable the chaplains who have had the course to implement the best professional ministry of provision and facilitation the Navy ever had.

Q: Was this tool a curriculum?

Admiral Stevenson: The tool was entitled correctly "The Chaplain as Staff Officer for Religious Ministries, Policies and Practices Workshop." So it covered the whole spectrum that all the good minds of the Chaplain Corps could put together.

One of the things that needed to be done, as I look back on the situation in Beirut, as I look back on other situations in my career, is have the chaplains work through every aspect of a mass casualty situation. You hold an operational exercise on a practical level and make it as real as possible: chaplains in teams, message traffic, an exercise commanding officer and executive officer and Chief of Chaplains. You spend an entire day putting them through the exercise of a mass casualty situation, forcing them to write the message traffic. You learn just where your mistakes are, and you share at the end of the day which team did it better. Is the Chief of Chaplains a major player in this thing? No. Do you have to remember to keep him informed because maybe somebody in Washington is asking him, "Are the chaplains going out with the casualty assistance calls officers?" Yes!

How do you get chaplains from other commands? Do you just call the chaplains on the phone and say, "Hey, guys. Be nice guys and come over here"? Or do you go through the chain of command? Do the chaplains know that you've got to be in the uniform of the day? That you're not helping anybody if you come racing over and you're in khakis, we can't use you to go out on a casualty assistance call. For crying out loud, get in the uniform of the day. So we emphasized all these things.

How do you approach families with tragic news? How do you train your chaplains ahead of time to know how to handle that situation? Do you just assume that he's clergy and, therefore, he knows how to do these things? How do you provide feedback? Do you keep a log? Do you make the log available to command, following the mass casualty so we can check on what we could have done better, or what feedback we got? Have chaplains been alerted to record where they were and who they saw, and so forth?

Q: These are the kinds of things that line officers do routinely.

Admiral Stevenson: Absolutely. These are the kind of things Navy does routinely. And, see, what happens is there's a tendency among chaplains to misuse the opportunity for professional development training--to go off for a week and play church. Which is counterproductive to understanding institutional and reinforcing institutional ministry. The Navy doesn't need a chaplain on Navy money to go off and play parish ministry for a week.

Chaplains enjoy all the stories of the civilian professor who's teaching homiletics. That's fine. Some people call that spirituality, which, again, is fine. But when I was on the training desk, my "if book" said I wanted this outfit to do things the Navy way. Not because I want chaplains to be line officers but because I want to ensure the kinds of professionalism that meet the needs of this environment and these people. That's why, no matter who is the Chief of Chaplains, my recommendation would be to aim at the practical, practical, practical, practical.

Q: Did you implement part of this integrated training plan through the chaplain school?

Admiral Stevenson: We hoped to. I requested that the chaplain school invite me--then you're dealing with commands and influence--to every basic course so that I had two hours to teach a little course on institutional ministry. To say to them, "Hey, you're no longer in the parish. It's institutional ministry, these are the differences." At least I had the feeling that I had told them what the difference was.

On the advanced course level we worked it right into the curriculum. The chaplains graduating into supervisory positions in the Chaplains Corps should be more aware of practical factors, doing things in accordance with the professionalism of the Navy.

Q: Was the chaplain school as a whole fulfilling your expectations for it?

Admiral Stevenson: Rather well. The chaplain school had evolved over the years, depending on the officer in charge, as well as influence from the Chief of Chaplains' office. Again, it's one of those things where there's influence from the Chief of Chaplains' office. Funding and immediate accountability is with the officer in charge of the chaplain school and CNET. But it had evolved well, in part because Chaplain Ross Trower was the officer in charge of the chaplain school when he was selected for flag.

Q: Was any part of the training there a sensitivity to minority groups, minority religions?

Admiral Stevenson: We sure hoped so. And, remember, in the basic course these guys were civilians two or three weeks before. You're having conversation with them at a cocktail party, at a lunch, or something, and they want you to know how they have improved, how they've come along. They're beginning to understand the system. And a chaplain says, "My roommate is a Catholic priest, and I'm really impressed. I'm really impressed. And he knows his Bible."

And you're tempted to say, "Oh, God, you idiot, how will we ever make you into a Navy chaplain?" But, instead, you've learned over the years to say to the guy, "Oh, that's interesting. Have you ever met a Catholic priest before?"

And the guy says, "No, I've never met one before. We had one in our town," or "I met one once." It's interesting. And you're talking about guys who've been to college. You're talking about guys who've been to seminary. You're talking about guys who've lived in a parochial world, and all of a sudden they're thrown into pluralism, endorsed by an endorsing agent who most likely says to them, even though he's been in the military himself, "Well, you just put on a uniform and you're just like a pastor." It's not so! It's just not so!

If I were around, Paul, I would be still probably hounding everybody that the most important thing you can do in the Chaplain Corps is practical factors. I don't think I'd ever get off the guys' backs on that. I think we should have done a lot more of that. I turned it around a little bit, maybe, but I think you can turn it around a whole lot.

Q: You mentioned, in passing, the Chaplain Resource Board. What is its role?

Admiral Stevenson: The Chaplain Resource Board is one of the great delights of all times. When I was in Washington in the '60s and early '70s, we had a Chaplain Corps Planning Group. The Chief of Chaplains doesn't have chain of command; he has chain of influence. And what had happened in those days was the Chief of Chaplains had allowed the planning group to have so much influence that chaplains in the field received a mixed signal: the Chief of Chaplains going to the right or the planning group going to the left.

When I arrived in Washington as deputy, Chaplain Trower had already brought Chaplain Murray Voth, an extremely talented guy, to the staff. Chaplain Voth had the G-1 shop, education and training of chaplains. He had commenced work on the development of a Chaplain Corps Resource Board, and it came into being. Chaplain Harry McCall was the first director of the Chaplain Resource Board, followed by Chaplain Lecke, Chaplain Kirk--Chaplain Boyette, I guess, is there now.

Because I had had experience on the training desk and because I had some strong feelings about the Chaplain Resource Board, Chaplain Trower signaled me to get with Chaplain Voth and run in the direction I wanted to run. The first thing I wanted to do, because of my previous experiences with the planning group of years gone by, was to get to the Chaplain Resource Board to understand that they work on what the Chief of Chaplains tasks them to do. Without a letter of tasking, they were to do nothing.

In other words, I did not want to invent another separate chain of influence. I wanted it clearly understood that anything that came from the Chaplain Resource Board had the imprimatur of the Chief of Chaplains on it. If somebody in the Chaplain Resource Board thought up a good idea, great. But don't just go working on it until you send up the paperwork to Washington for the Chief of Chaplains to say, "Execute." Or at least send us a "unodir" so that we could stop something that we wanted stopped.* We had precious resources, and we wanted them well used. I must also admit that I had some pet projects that I definitely wanted from the Chaplain Resource Board. [Chuckle]

Q: What were those projects?

Admiral Stevenson: I wanted a program planner calendar. That is, I wanted every chaplain in the Chaplain Corps to have a planning calendar in his hand that was the same as every other chaplain in the United States Navy. See, what I'm saying is, as I explained to the resource board in a long, two-day session when I first went down, you must give a diversified group as the faith groups of the United States Navy Chaplain Corps a unifying tool. (And that's what I call it--T-O-O-L, tool.) If all chaplains use the same planning

---

* "Unodir" is a Navy abbreviation meaning "unless otherwise directed." Typically, it is part of a message from a junior to a senior. The junior indicates that he or she is going to proceed with a certain course of action unless directed otherwise. This gives the senior the opportunity to step in and stop a course of action that he or she does not approve.

calendar, that's a unifying force. That's a real cohesion element within something as diversified as the Chaplain Corps. And, by golly, they worked on it and they came in with a winner. I still use the Chaplain Corps calendar for my appointments and things like that.

Q: Is it geared around the religious year?

Admiral Stevenson: It's geared around the religious year, entirely geared around the religious year. I wanted them to put out plan program budget books so that all command chaplains would have the same kinds of planning books from which to do the planning for their resources, etc. A commanding officer who has been an executive officer at one command and knows that the chaplains department puts together its programs in that fashion, is going to be more attuned to them when he's the CO at another command and the same tool is giving him the input.

We had them put out--again, practical--a thing called "Positive Reinforcements of Values Navy (PROVN). It was a whole series of positive things that could be put in plans of the day. You know, XOs and everybody are always looking for stuff to motivate the troops and put in the plan of the day. We also had them publish, in conjunction with the force chaplains, the force chaplains' handbooks so that every force chaplain could work with the CRB to develop a manual that would be applicable to the chaplains in that force. So SurfPac's handbook would not be the same as SurfLant's handbook because there are things that are different.

We decided that one of the things that might impact on Navy would be to put a poster series. We had a chaplain named Bob Williams on the board.[*] He was a talented artist who put out a series of posters for two or three years that were well received throughout the Navy. Again, you see, it's something you can put in the hand of the chaplain. The chaplain takes it to the XO and says, "Hey, XO, how do you like these posters?"

And the XO says, "Hey, that's got the right message. Put it down on the mess decks."

---

[*] Lieutenant Commander Robert H. Williams, CHC, USN.

What is the chaplain doing if the XO doesn't get a quarterly report, if he doesn't see the chaplain bringing in posters, if he doesn't see the chaplain involved with the troops? We wanted to give the chaplains the tools that would force him to see the XO and force him to get with the troops. I really did not want the Chaplains Resource Board working on a chaplains' manual. No way. Of course, a lot of them who were ordered there thought that's what they wanted to do, and so they weren't very happy till they saw that they were having a more positive impact than would come from an esoteric manual.

They surveyed the entire Chaplain Corps and came up with a book on prayers called "Occasional Ministries." Once again, if you have a good product for change of command, if you want to give guidance to other chaplains as to what is an appropriate prayer for a change of command, which is a pluralistic environment, why not put the tool in the guy's hand, hoping that he's got enough sense to use the good tool? A practical tool. And hopefully get away from the complaints of some commanding officers that the chaplain was insensitive to the pluralistic environment. You not only taught the chaplain at chaplain school, but you reinforced him by putting tools in front of him that would help him to do, hopefully, a better job.

Q: Did you get a complaint, on the other hand, that you were trying to standardize too much and discourage individuality?

Admiral Stevenson: I think some people probably felt that way, but, quite frankly, chaplains are so diversified and so individualistic that I don't think you've got to worry about that. I mean, if you've got some chaplains out there, after their years of education, training and ordination, and, also, naval service, who are that intimidated, you don't need them. [Laughter]

You have to assume the individual's a professional and, like any other professional, if you give him a tool that he does not find useful or does not find helpful, he's not going to use it. It's his prerogative not to use it. What he will likely have in its place is something that is strictly parochial to his faith group, that will make him less conscious of his institutional responsibilities. If he's a true professional, he's capable of making the decision.

Q: Were there any changes in the RP rating during your time as chief and deputy?

Admiral Stevenson: Yes. The school, which was first established at Keesler Air Force Base, was moved out from under the auspices of the Air Force and moved to Treasure Island.* The rating came less and less under direct Chaplain Corps sponsorship and Chaplain Corps supervision, to the point at which the RPs run the RP rating in the same manner that other ratings are run in the Navy.

Q: Has that been a good thing or a bad thing?

Admiral Stevenson: I think it's been a good thing. The master chiefs on the staff of the Chief of Chaplains were master chiefs who understood the difference between chain of command and chain of influence. They understood that on the Chief of Chaplains' staff, I have influence over the RP rating, but not command or control of the RP rating. All RPs are under their own command just as the RP school is under CNET. So I thought the RP rating came along.

Another practical factor we were working on was to train chaplains who had not been trained to supervise RPs, an enlisted rating, who had not been division officers, so they would know the kind of relationship they should have with RPs. We ran into a lot of uncomfortable situations in that regard that we tried to turn around. And, again, I probably came across as pretty hard-nosed. One of the things I ran into early on, for instance, was chapel situations in which the chaplain and the RP were in civilian attire on Sunday morning. Totally unacceptable, totally to the disadvantage of the chaplain and the RP, but more than that, to the disadvantage of the command.

What are you? You are a chaplain. What are you? You are an RP. Are you merely fulfilling your own religious obligation on Sunday morning? No. You're fulfilling a command function that you are tasked to perform as an employee of the institution which is

---

* Treasure Island is a man-made island in San Francisco Bay, located between San Francisco and Oakland. It served as the site of a world's fair in 1939-40, then was converted for use as a Navy base during and after World War II.

the United States Navy. And when you are performing naval service, you are to be in naval attire.

Now, do you put on vestments? Fine, put on vestments. Nobody is saying that you can't wear the vestments that are appropriate to your faith group. What we're saying is, when you get up in the morning, you need to know that you are working for the United States Navy, not just God. To some people, that's a very tough message to get across, because they think that you are attacking their conscience. You're not. You're simply saying, "As long as you're a naval officer and as long as you're an RP in the United States Navy, you need to be in the appropriate attire to perform your duties."

Q: Are RPs as a group more religious than sailors at large?

Admiral Stevenson: No. No. In my opinion, you don't want them to be.

Q: Why not?

Admiral Stevenson: Because being an RP is not the fulfillment of their religious role; it is the fulfillment of their Navy rating. The RP is to be as conscious as the chaplain is, in that sense that the RP is there not because he's a Catholic or a Presbyterian or Jewish; he's there because he's an RP. Now, if he's a devout member of his faith, wonderful. But his duty as a naval person is a duty to all other naval persons, just in the same sense that the RP is a combatant, not a noncombatant.

The Secretary of the Navy ruled correctly that an RP cannot be assigned to any command in which there is not a chaplain. I think that's a very good rule, because you could get a RP who is religious and ran off in the direction of their own. I think that would be a disaster. But the RP better know how to work all the equipment, better know how to set up the altar for all different religious groups, better know how to involve personnel in volunteer things like Sunday School teaching and teach them how to use audio-visual equipment--all those kinds of things. Nothing has improved the professionalism of the

<u>Chaplain Corps as much as the RP rating, because the enlisted rating demands appropriate leadership from its officers.</u>

Q: Why do you say that?

Admiral Stevenson: Because the RP, like the corpsman, in many cases makes the professional more accountable.

Q: In what ways does he do that?

Admiral Stevenson: He's a constant reminder that the chaplain is under naval authority.

Q: Is he sort of the chaplain's conscience?

Admiral Stevenson: Oh, I wouldn't say he's the chaplain's conscience, but he certainly is a very prominent reminder that it's the ship's library, it's not the chaplain's library. It's the command's religious program. The RP rating has meant an awful lot to the Chaplain Corps. Nobody could have brought it about except Chaplain O'Connor.

New subject--the manpower shop. I was very partial to the manpower planning people in the shop, because they have to think about 20 years ahead. I wish we could get the endorsing agents knowledgeable of the fact that when you make decisions, you've got to think what the implications are 20 years down the pike.

Q: That was why you got so concerned about that hump problem, for example.

Admiral Stevenson: Absolutely. You want to make sure that you have appropriate attrition, but you don't want to get to a RIF environment.[*] Avoid it as much as you can.

---

[*] RIF--reduction in force.

Q: What becomes of a chaplain who goes out through attrition because there's not a place for him in the Navy anymore?

Admiral Stevenson: Well, what happens to a dentist, what happens to a lawyer?

Q: He goes into the same line of work in civilian life, I guess.

Admiral Stevenson: You have the right to continue your profession as a private practice, or to get out of the profession. So I still think any clergy who came into the Navy for a tour duty and was attrited, would still be better off. I still think they would be professionally enhanced by that experience. Many of them go into the reserve program, maintain their federal years on that basis. My recommendation to the earliest ones being attrited, when I wrote to them or when I would talk to them, was that they should consider very seriously trying to make a connection with the Veterans Administration hospitals in order to maintain their years of federal service.

You know, the mentality that once somebody comes in the naval service, that the naval service is obligated to that person for the rest of their years is kind of a strange myth. The environment is that you come in, and you compete for a number of years. You may be one of the best chaplains in the world, but you may have run into the bad luck of having the wrong guy write your fitness report or something like that, and the next thing you know, you're on the list of being attrited. You stay on in the reserves or you don't. You go out and look for a parish like others do, or your bishop assigns you to one. It is like unto other people, and somewhere in there, Paul, there is a thing called the luck of the draw. I don't fathom that, but I know it's there.

Q: That works in a lot of businesses.

Admiral Stevenson: It works in all kinds of businesses. But I really feel, sincerely, that there isn't a clergyman in the land that cannot be enhanced in his profession, in the performance of his profession, by a tour of duty as a Navy chaplain.

Q: Well, he's likely to come out with a much broader world view.

Admiral Stevenson: Sure.

Q: Having been a roommate with this Catholic priest and found out he knew the Scriptures, and so forth.

Admiral Stevenson: Sure, and having found out what it's like to shower with the congregation. [Chuckle] You know, all of that, which is a break in on the ghetto of parochialism, I would think that the average church in the United States would be as interested in hiring somebody who had had that kind of experience as well as seminary experience and parish experience. Somewhat broadened in travel and so forth.

Q: You mentioned earlier a chaplain who had committed suicide. I heard of a terribly ironic case in which a chaplain wrote the suicide prevention manual and then committed suicide. Was that one of the items of concern in the Chaplain Corps, to minimize suicides?

Admiral Stevenson: Well, near the end of my tour, there were a couple of suicides in the Navy. And we had a very quick look at the suicide situation in the United States Navy, and, again, held some meetings in BuPers on suicide prevention. I'm not familiar with a manual that came out on the subject of suicide prevention. I mean, I know from my own experience, just from readings, that there are things to be alerted to in personalities and age groups. The thing that I remember the most was that when they looked at the statistics of the United States Navy and the statistics of the society in general, particularly in relationship to age groups, that the suicide rate in the United States Navy was not above that of the general population.

I think that in the Navy one has to be cautious to measure things against the general population of the United States. Over the years I've heard all kinds of things said about the divorce rate in the Navy because of sea duty, etc., etc., because of the immaturity of people who come in at 18 years of age getting married, and so forth. To the best of my knowledge, the Navy statistics related to age groups were not different from the general population. That may not be good news. You may want the Navy's statistics "better" than the general population because you're in a more controlled environment.

Q: But, as you pointed out before, there are unusual hardships that could put strains on a marriage.

Admiral Stevenson: True. It is interesting, when you've been a civilian pastor as I've been, to note that in the Navy you have the advantage of providing care for your personnel within the same command. The doctor, the lawyer, the chaplain were all part of the same command team, all headed in the same direction to try to provide some assistance to particular personnel. It's interesting to come out into the civilian world and, of course, the lawyer is over here, you don't know who he is and he's got his fee system. The doctor's over there, he's got his fee system. The clergy's over here doing his thing in connection with his parochial world.

Q: Well, let me make one other point in response to what you just said. In the Navy system, there isn't a fee to pay, either, and that probably makes an individual more likely to avail himself of these services.

Admiral Stevenson: I would hope so. That's probably true. The sign on the door just says, "Chaplain." [Chuckle] That door is open. You know, that's another thing that's very important about the RP rating. If a chaplain has a parish mentality and has not dealt on a daily basis with being an employee in an institutional environment, you can get into all kinds of problems with the use of the chapel. The chaplain can get a mentality that it's his or her parish. He will decide who can use it and who can't use it, rather than recognizing the fact that it's a government building. Between the chaplain and personnel is the RP, and the RP is the one who should be responsible for the chapel's use, in accordance with the command chapel usage instruction.

If I want to sign up for the chapel for a wedding and I'm not eligible to be married under the rites of the chaplain's church, the chaplain, in all honesty, has to say to me, "I'm sorry, I cannot officiate at your wedding because you're not eligible for the sacrament or the rites of my particular faith group." But the RP ought to schedule eligible personnel to use the chapel. Then it's just a matter of finding the right person, the qualified clergy or the willing judge, to perform the wedding.

Q: Did you have any programs in the Chaplain Corps about drug abuse?

Admiral Stevenson: We did have at different eras. We had in 1971, was it?--'71, '72, we had a whole professional development training courses on chaplains' awareness of drug usage.

Q: I guess that got elevated to a higher level in the Navy attention span.

Admiral Stevenson: An awful lot of that kind of training gets itself bogged down in pharmacology rather than ministry to people in drug programs. But we had chaplains assigned to the Navy drug rehab units at Jacksonville, San Diego, a variety of places. I don't know where any of that is today. Chaplain O'Connor in '76 put the Chaplain Corps through alcohol abuse professional development training.

Q: You said you could tell some stories about Admiral Watkins and terrorism.

Admiral Stevenson: When I was Chief of Chaplains, Admiral Watkins called me over with Chaplain McNamara. Admiral Watkins wanted to gather ethicists and moral theologians to deal with the subject of terrorism and response to terrorism. I had the feeling he wanted a sort of check-off list of responses. We had three separate sessions at the Naval War College. The Naval War College served as host. At each session we had 30-some ethicists and moral theologians, top-notch people in the United States. I would say 20 of them were at all three sessions. Some of them were not just in the moral and ethical field, but also in the terrorist field. For instance, we had people of the stature of Neil Livingston, who was a recognized expert in terrorism.

Q: What was the thrust of the program?

Admiral Stevenson: First of all, let me say that Chaplain Joe O'Donnell took the point on that program, did an outstanding job of getting the experts together, working with the war college to bring these sessions off. Even in the last seminar, we took advantage of the war-gaming capabilities of the war college. I was not overly comfortable with the assignment.

Q: Why not?

Admiral Stevenson: Well, Paul, once again my Vietnam experience in personal response, my Presbyterian background, which does not conform to the doctrine. (By the way, "natural law" was the basis on which a lot of Navy character education programs were built on back in the '50s.) I certainly said, "Aye, aye, sir," to Admiral Watkins. I appreciate that he is a devout Roman Catholic, extremely moral individual who was seeking what, I think, would be his expectations from the Chief of Chaplains in the realm of ethical, moral subjects. I used to annoy Admiral Watkins when I explained my theology was tied to Luther's adage to "Sin boldly."[*]

Nevertheless, they were successful, I think, in bringing together knowledgeable people to deal with the subject of the ethical response to terrorism. And we had Jewish, as well as Christian, as well as secular ethicists present, and we got a spectrum of findings. They were shared with the CNO.

Most of the ethicists were opposed to a policy of retaliation, but almost all of them were in favor of a policy of preemption. But then for command the question is, "How do you know your intelligence is good enough to preempt?" And if they're building the bomb in the local grade school, how do you preempt?" The terrorists aren't dummies.

---

[*] Martin Luther led the Protestant Reformation in the 16th century.

Q: What was the product of this effort--a set of guidelines?

Admiral Stevenson: The CNO, I think, wanted a more formalized set of guidelines than we were able to provide. I think he was somewhat disappointed. There's another observation that goes along with that for me, and that was that there were several debates at some Pentagon breakfasts and things in Washington over this whole subject. If I had come from a strong emphasis on Thomistic moral theology, I might have better fit and understood what the Chief of Naval Operations was looking for. But I don't, and I don't think the Constitution does either.

However, for what it's worth, Diane and I were dancing at a Navy ball two years ago, and we ran into Admiral Watkins and Mrs. Watkins. He grabbed me by the shoulder. He had just finished being the Chairman of the President's Commission on AIDS, in which he had made his outstanding findings public and indicated to the Congress that he did not want to get caught up in "a moral quagmire." He asked me how I thought it went, and I told him I was happy to hear him make that statement. And he said, well, he wanted to "sin boldly." So we had our own sense of humor about some of our debates.

Q: Do you have any other assessments of Admiral Watkins?

Admiral Stevenson: Oh, Admiral Watkins was brilliant and one of the most articulate naval officers. I was around him when he was the Chief of Naval Personnel as well as CNO. It's an American thing that we have sort of a mismatch. O'Connor or McNamara should have been his Chief of Chaplains. And at the same time, I'll bet you anything that all kinds of people in the Navy think that the Chief of Chaplains is CNO's handpicked guy. CNO is like all the rest of us. You get the team you get. You may get to pick a certain percentage of the team, but you don't get to pick the whole team.

Any leader must motivate. You've got to give your people a sense of vision, and then you've got to let them work the problems. You've got to make them accountable and let them work the problems. And you've got to keep--I would prefer to call it integrity-- you've got to keep that vision of integrity. As Admiral Watkins used to point out all the time, in spite of what the newspapers said, when it came to abuse of funds--expensive airplane toilet seats and things like that--it was the Navy that discovered these things and brought them to the fore.

Q: Do you have other items in your notes to discuss?

Admiral Stevenson: There's one thing I'd like to mention that I don't think a lot of people think of. It might be something somebody could use sometime. The fascinating thing about being a Navy chaplain is that when it comes to serving service personnel, and you think of where the chaplains' billets are located and if you've gone through any kind of a combat experience: the chaplain is one of the few positions in the United States Navy where you are with the troops in training, you're with the troops in deployment, you're with the troops and their families, in the chapel and other places, in a relationship that nobody else has. You're with the troops when they're hospitalized, and you're with the troops in a funeral. The chaplain is one of the few people who actually has the experience of being with people in the whole cycle of their lives--through all the rites of passage.

Q: In preparing for this interview, I heard from Chaplain Ferguson, who said you inspired a group known as the Deputy's Dogs. He wondered where that term came from.

Admiral Stevenson: The Deputy's Dogs gave themselves the name. There was a popular cartoon called Deputy Dawg. Anyway, the guys who were in the G-2 shop, planning and manpower, referred to themselves as the Deputy's Dogs. They were some of my favorites, because I used to just love to sit back and watch them go at something. I mean, they were tigers, and I think sometimes other people resented the fact that I got such a kick out of them. They worked like hell. They were highly motivated, and they didn't need much rudder. They produced things for the Chaplain Corps, and they had a degree of professionalism that bordered on arrogance. [Laughter] I guess three of the four are still on active duty in the Navy. They were Bill Gibson and Mel Ferguson and Vic Smith and Tom Hiers.

Neil M. Stevenson #7 - 334

If you take them out of bureaucracy and you turn them loose in a ship or in another command, they're going to get things done. And they're going to be available to sailors and Marines, and they're going to expect from others the kind of accountability that they themselves give. I think that all that stuff comes somewhat naturally. They include Southern Baptists, Pentecostals, and Christian Scientists, and that, to me, is another indication of pluralism. Where else in the world do you get that combination coming together and doing things the way they do them? You wouldn't get it outside of a military chaplain environment.

Q: Are there any specific achievements of the group that you want to mention?

Admiral Stevenson: Well, they were the ones mainly responsible for the integrated plan. They were the ones responsible for the long-range planning. They were largely responsible for the majority of the curriculum of the practical factors policies and practices, workbook and workshops. They put together the POM inputs for the 4100 community and RP rating. They did not have a lot of idle time. They were totally unsuccessful in challenging the rest of the staff in volleyball, as I recall, and maybe in tug-of-war. [Chuckle]

Q: So they were human, after all.

Admiral Stevenson: Yes, they were, somewhat. [Laughter] Anybody in any position of authority, a team like that, you've got to turn them loose.

Q: There's another question about an address you made to your staff on expectations and requirements when you took over as chief. What factors went into that talk that you made?

Admiral Stevenson: I wish I had a copy of it. [Chuckle] I'm told other people have a copy of it. What I did, Paul, was I had the privilege of observing Chaplain Kelly, Chaplain Garrett, Chaplain O'Connor, Chaplain Trower as Chiefs of Chaplains. I had had the privilege of watching Admiral Watkins as CNP and CNO, Admiral Hayward at PacFlt and in Washington. I had been writing down in my "if book" that if I became Chief of Chaplains, I wanted everybody from the beginning to know how I wanted the office to run. I compiled an outline of the things that I wanted them to know how I expected business to be carried out. Unbeknownst to me, I think it was Larry Martin who recorded the thing and then put it together on a piece of paper and brought it back to me and said, you know, "This is what you said."[*] That's a good thing to have in case people want to check on me.

Mostly it was standard stuff that you hear from other naval officers if you're around commands. You know, people on the staff have a right to say, "yes;" I'm the only one that has a right to say "no." If we're asked to do something, the response to the outside world is affirmative, unless you think it's disastrous, and then you come and you tell me that you recommend that I say no. And I get to say no, but I don't want anybody saying no on my behalf.

Probably one of the things I put down was that I didn't believe in sending out message traffic or letters that were not read by other people on the staff. I didn't need any entrepreneurs on the staff who just wrote things off in a corner somewhere without checking with other people on the staff and opening them up and saying, "Does this make sense to you? Does this read clearly? Does it communicate what I hope it communicates?" When it came to the major claimant staff chaplains, I wanted their positions recognized, and I wanted to deal directly with them. I mean, other members of the staff could deal with them, but I didn't want people calling claimant chaplains, senior O-6s, and telling them, "This is what the Chief said." I wanted to have a direct relationship with them, and when phone calls came in from them, I wanted to be available to them. I didn't want them waiting around. I don't know, a whole bunch of stuff like that. I probably emphasized what Chaplain Trower had always emphasized: that your chop is as good as your word, so don't chop anything unless you want to be accountable for it. All that kind of administrative, bureaucratic stuff. Someday, if somebody will give me a copy of it, I'll find out what I said. [Laughter] But I've lost my copy of it.

---

[*] Commander H. Lawrence Martin, CHC, USN, the individual who did much of the work on the Chaplain Corps oral history series.

Q: There's mention here of a professional training course on the chaplain as staff officer. Is that what you've been talking about as institutional ministry?

Admiral Stevenson: Yes, and that was the professional development training course that was put together on an in-house basis using chaplains of the corps as the resource persons. And, again, we could have blown up in our faces, but the people who planned and executed it did an outstanding job, and I think the chaplains who attended it appreciated getting practical factors. As you said, that's what line officers do.

Q: What specific distinctions can you draw in your functions between being Chief of Chaplains and Deputy Chief of Chaplains?

Admiral Stevenson: Well, I think that I would start by saying that the Chief of Chaplains is responsible for establishing the tone and the in-house policies of the Chaplain Corps. He has to see himself as the primary motivator for the doing of outstanding professional ministry. The deputy is in a position of totally supporting the Chief of Chaplains in that endeavor, in the direction that the Chief of Chaplains wants to take the Chaplain Corps.

You know, the chief is the skipper, the deputy is the chief engineer, and the guys in the Chief of Chaplains' office are the snipes. A lot of good ministry is done because the engines turn. It's the Chief of Chaplains that's got to be on the bridge with the sense of vision, but the deputy's got to make sure all machinery runs. If it has run well, he's also gained the vision that he takes to the bridge with him when he fleets up to be the Chief of Chaplains. He says to himself, "Okay, where do we go from here? How do we improve?"

I used an expression when I became the Chief of Chaplains that I would still use today, and I assume it's still valid: "The clergy of this nation who have the privilege of serving in the Navy Chaplain Corps are the best. Leading this community is a challenge held in common with all those in a position of leadership in our Navy, Marine Corps, and Coast Guard, namely, to make the best better."

That's the chief's job. How do you make the best better? And you can do that best, I think, only if you have been involved in the engine room of the Chaplain Corps. You've got to come up through the years with a sense of what ought to be done and how it might be done better. Then if you're fortunate enough to be given the opportunity, you've worked the mechanics, you've worked the engineering, you've become the Chief of Chaplains, and you say, "Okay, for a year or two it's my job to motivate the best to become even better." And there's always room for a ton of improvement. Isn't that what the rest of the Navy does? Doesn't CNO take all his experience and say, "Okay, now I'm here to take the best Navy in the United States and make it a better Navy"? Isn't that what somebody does when he becomes the principal of the school or pastor of a church? It's the same.

Q: What are the emotional satisfactions from reaching the peak of your profession?

Admiral Stevenson: You say, "Wow! I've got a chance to do it." A bunch of other guys could do it, too, but they weren't the ones selected, so you have at it. There are an awful lot of people who look on titles, and they see esteem. But those who have been in those titles see work, obligation, and responsibility.

I remember when I became Chief of Chaplains, I had something of the same anxiety I had when Frank Garrett made me head of the training department. It's the anxiety that says, "God, if I screw this thing up, I'm going to screw up a lot of chaplains." [Chuckle] You become Chief of Chaplains, you say the same thing to yourself. "God, if I screw this thing up, I'm going to screw up a lot of chaplains." If I screw up a lot of chaplains, I'm going to screw up a lot of people in the Navy. So, you know, there's pressure and there's anxiety and there's a lot of work.

When I was interviewed by Chaplain Apgar as a means of communicating to the Chaplain Corps, I got some negative feedback from chaplains who did not appreciate me referring to my position as a job.[*] What I was basically saying is that when you've been around and you've worked for other Chiefs of Chaplains, you realize that being a Chief of Chaplains is a job. And it's an interesting job, and it's a job that has both good days and bad days, you know, but it's a job. And it's a job that you've got to get done. You've got to get it done by a certain amount of time. You've got certain things you hope get done by that

---

[*] Lieutenant Ronald M. Apgar, CHC, USN. His interview is included as an appendix in this volume.

time, and you hope that you set a tone so that if they don't get done in the time you're there, that they will be so natural that other people will pick up on them and keep them going.

Another one of my pet peeves in those days was that to try to remind everybody, as I have to do in the parish, that decisions are made on the basis of the information known at the time the decision is made. You come in and tell me something new tomorrow, I might have to change my decision. That's what you've got to do when you're in any job. Design and decisions are mingled with contingencies.

Q: One of the effects Chaplain Ferguson pointed out in these notes of that huge hump of recruiting was that the Navy was confronted, all of a sudden, with a lot of inexperienced chaplains. How did you try to counteract that problem?

Admiral Stevenson: By ginning up the basic course at the chaplain school. Again, by having a professional development course that emphasized practical factors; by having the major claimant chaplains' conference focus on the claimant chaplain's job to train, train, train chaplains; by questioning chaplains when I traveled around as to how they were utilizing their force chaplain's handbook; to try to measure the difference between the new and young chaplain who had a grasp of the system that the old chaplain he was working for sometimes didn't have. [Laughter] And to try not to discourage respect for the senior chaplain, but at the same time, encourage the junior chaplain to understand the Navy system. We'd all been in that boat sometime in our careers.

Q: Did you get any feedback from commands that they were not satisfied with their inexperienced chaplains?

Admiral Stevenson: Yes, and some of that was environmentally induced. For instance, one of the most difficult environments for a chaplain to work in is the squadron environment. And, yet, because of rank requirements, you've got to put the junior chaplain in the squadron environment.

Q: What kind of squadron?

Admiral Stevenson: Destroyer squadron, amphibious squadron.

Q: Not aviation squadron?

Admiral Stevenson: No, not aviation squadron.

By ordering chaplains to desrons, you throw them into the briar patch, and they've got to learn real fast to survive. That's also the luck of the draw.

Q: There's also here a question about a chapel construction plan ashore and also setting up designated spaces on large ships. What was your initiative there?

Admiral Stevenson: Well, my initiative was really a follow-on to initiatives started by Chaplain O'Connor who challenged that the Navy had not prioritized, in any way, religious facilities in their construction plans. Chaplain O'Connor got that turned around. A young chaplain that I admired, Larry Shoberg, worked that problem at the NavMat level.[*] He did an outstanding job, even down to arrangements with architects for the most efficient and economic chapels. Then the natural progression of that thinking moved into planning ships' construction. In a growing 600-ship Navy the religious facilities would be in the basic planning, rather than an afterthought.

That's one of those things, again, that I've already illustrated where a chaplain like Chaplain O'Connor had the vision and the chutzpah. We've got to have people of this staff who are prodding the system and saying, "Yeah, but don't forget us, and we have our input." From what I saw, the input was always welcome. It's better that guys be in on the groundwork and tell us what the needs are of sailors, than coming around after the ship was constructed and saying, "Ah, I see you forgot about religion." At the same time, you've got to remind chaplains that ships are primarily for operational purposes.

---

[*] Commander Lawrence A. Shoberg, CHC, USN. NavMat--Naval Material Command.

Q: Not just as a place for them to hold services.

Admiral Stevenson: Right. It is because the First Amendment, it is because sailors have the right to the free exercise of religion, that you have a space dedicated to meet the needs of all. Not because there's a chaplain who needs to use the chapel. Because a citizen of the United States serving in that ship has the right to have his religious needs met. The chaplain is the person, who in the name of the command, provides, or facilitates, the meeting of that religious need. Very easy to get that thing backwards-forwards.

Q: You talked about the almost minute number of Jewish chaplains in the Chaplain Corps. Given this First Amendment right for providing for the needs of Jewish naval personnel, how did you go about doing that?

Admiral Stevenson: Again, it's provide and facilitate. If you're the chaplain in the ship, you know the high holy days of obligation in the Jewish faith. It is your responsibility to see that they are published in the plan of the day in adequate time to remind Jewish personnel of their obligation. It's the chaplain's task to speak to the supply officer about getting food that is applicable to Jewish personnel in those seasons. You know, this is all a requirement of pre-thought and planning. And then making sure the personnel in accompanying ships get the word. You may have to work with operations on lining up helo hops for Jewish personnel, get the space designated, put aside the ship's lounge or something that night, or the chapel, or whatever is appropriate. And if the rabbi is in your shoes, he does the same thing for your people. You know, cooperation without compromise--but, better yet, proactive ministry to provide for and facilitate to meet the religious needs of all.

Q: I'm sure that those holidays and requirements were all included in this standardized calendar that the Chaplain Resource Board came up with.

Admiral Stevenson: That's true. And, also, when I went to Washington, one of the things I wanted to put out in order to get attention was, from the OpNav level, wanted to put out a notice from either OpNav or SecNav level that listed in advance for all commands the religious holy days for each religious faith. That's the kind of thing I initiated and that needs to be done on a regular basis.

Q: This is SecNav Note 1730 of 27 December 1983. It lists holy days and days of religious observance for a variety of different faith groups for 1984, 1985, and 1986.

Admiral Stevenson: Well, again, the object, you see, was you don't send this out as an in-house piece of paper to chaplains.

Q: It comes with the force of the Secretary of the Navy.

Admiral Stevenson: It's the Chief of Chaplains' job to alert the Secretary of the Navy that a notice ought to go out, that it's helpful to all ships and stations. Because this is applicable to the supply officer, for example, as well as to the chaplain. Or the commanding officer whose ship is going into a certain place at a certain time and he looks it up, and his ops officers looks it up, and says, "You realize we're going into an Israeli port, or we're going into a Muslim-dominated nation, etc., at a high holy religious season?"

Q: Probably, otherwise, wouldn't be high on the list of the ops officer's concerns.

Admiral Stevenson: No, I don't think so. But it could turn into a high concern, and then somebody might say, "Why didn't the Chaplain Corps alert us to that?"

Q: How much relationship or interaction did you have with Secretary Lehman or Under Secretary Goodrich?[*]

Admiral Stevenson: I used to see Secretary Goodrich from time to time, since I had additional duty orders there, to answer any questions he had about the Chaplain Corps or

---

[*] James F. Goodrich served as Under Secretary of the Navy from 29 September 1981 to 6 August 1987.

for him to tell me about chaplains he had been impressed with as he traveled. The only time I was really around Secretary Lehman was at social functions and when I reported to him on several occasions as the president of a board.

Q: Any impressions of either one of them?

Admiral Stevenson: Well, I guess, the same impression everybody else had in Washington. Of course, Secretary Goodrich was one of the most personable people in Washington at the time. The Secretary of the Navy was very focused on the 600-ship Navy. What was his expression on playing Washington like the violin? [Chuckle] Some expression like that. He was focused on doing his thing and getting it done, and he did not seem to have any particular interest in the Chaplain Corps. He had an awful lot of interest for a period of time in the Medical Corps, Dental Corps, etc. I was happy that he had it there and not in the Chaplain Corps. [Laughter]

Q: The Medical Corps came to quite some grief during that period.*

Admiral Stevenson: Somebody in those days had a bumper sticker that said, "To hell with the whales, save the Dental Corps." [Laughter]

Q: You didn't exactly have a chain of command, and you've used, also, the term chain of influence. How would you characterize the nature of relationships you had with the fleet and force chaplains and with the major claimant chaplains?

Admiral Stevenson: Well, I tried to stay on a very close, personal level with them. I almost got to the place where I tried to log my calendar so that if I hadn't heard from a major claimant, talked personally on autovon or something to a major claimant staff chaplain in a

---

* During the mid-1980s the Navy's Medical Corps was beset by charges of negligence, incompetence, and malpractice. See Arthur M. Smith, "Are We Losing Confidence in Navy Medicine? U.S. Naval Institute Proceedings, May 1986, pages 120-131.

month, that my secretary was to alert me to call him. I wanted to keep that kind of contact, wanting to know what was going on, and so forth. That's just a desire not to be blindsided.

You have a particular problem in the Chaplain Corps when senior chaplains put themselves in the compromising position of being a pastor rather than a supervisor. You kind of have to alert them from time to time that that is to the disadvantage of chaplains and the Chaplain Corps. That if a chaplain has major problems that will impact on the naval community, the Chief of Chaplains better know about it pretty early on. The supervisory chaplain had best not contact the endorsing agent. It is the Chief of Chaplains' job to contact the endorsing agent. And, once again, for the protection of the chaplains, as well as for the Chief of Chaplains, not to be blindsided.

I know of a couple of cases in which the chaplains had put themselves into a compromising situation with chaplains whom they had allowed to come to them in the role of confession. [Chuckle] Well, then how do you supervise somebody with whom you have a confessional relationship? I mean, you're really putting yourself in a position of being manipulated.

Q: You made that point talking about your Orlando experience, I recall. In these suggestions that Chaplain Ferguson sent me, he said that those who served with you had the feeling that you quit way too soon. You've already discussed the reasons for why you retired when you did, but I think it's a worthy tribute that those who served with you would feel that way.

Admiral Stevenson: Well, nothing would make me feel happier than that, and I would like to do that all my life. That's what I call the "Ted Williams syndrome."[*] Ted Williams had no desire to stay in anything long enough to be a .200 hitter. And if you've had a successful career and you've been able to feel that you've made some kind of a contribution and if you've had a lot of young chaplains around you who are self-starters, like Ferguson, Gibson, Shoberg, and all the rest, that makes it easy to get out.

---

[*] Theodore S. Williams played outfield for the Boston Red Sox from 1939 to 1960, with time out for service as a Marine Corps aviator in World War II and the Korean War. Williams, a member of baseball's hall of fame, was the last player to have a batting average of more than .400 in a season.

And there's a time to get out. The United States Navy is built on attrition and terminal situations. You know, if you can be a flag officer in the United States Navy Chaplain Corps for five years, you're a very, very fortunate guy. CNO is only CNO for four years, you know. As I say, if I got a set of orders today, I would really not want to go back in the Navy as Chief of Chaplains. But I wouldn't mind having Diego Garcia or a something plush like a cruiser. But, you know, that's all wishful thinking.

My job right now is to face an afternoon of hospital calls, followed by a compulsory attendance at a Rotary dinner, followed by two meetings at the church. One is the board of deacons, and the other is a committee to decide whether or not we should have three services instead of two services on Sunday. That's reality.

Q: I don't want to hold you up too long from those obligations, but could you discuss briefly what you have done in the years since you have retired?

Admiral Stevenson: I retired with the idea that I would take six months off. I remember Diane and I talked a lot about what we were going to do in our six months between retirement and my getting a job. I had thought that I would get a church assignment in the Washington area since that was my presbytery. I also thought that it was important for me to go back and finish my career in the parish, sort of prove to myself, like Dick Hutcheson and others have done.

Q: There is life after the Navy?

Admiral Stevenson: Well, yes, that you not only can go from parish to institutional ministry, but you can go from institutional ministry to parish ministry. And, you know, I was only 54 years of age. Anyway, teasingly, Diane always said that she wanted to live in Annapolis; East Hampton, Long Island; Winter Park, Florida; or Williamsburg, Virginia. And, here and lo, they came and offered me a job at a church in Williamsburg, Virginia. So Diane made up her mind, and instead of taking six months off, I retired from the Chaplain

Corps on the first of September, and I went to work as pastor in Williamsburg on the first of October 1985.

The most difficult part of the transition, I think, for any naval officer going back into the civilian world, is camaraderie. The high degree of camaraderie that you take for granted in the Navy doesn't exist in the civilian world. It's because it's two different environments, and I think that's the hardest thing to adjust to. I don't hear a great deal about the Chaplain Corps today, and I think that's the way it ought to be.

Q: To kibitz, look over their shoulders?

Admiral Stevenson: I'm sure that whatever they're doing is the right thing at the right time. But I would still be convinced that the single biggest problem for chaplains is for a chaplain to comprehend institutional vice parish ministry. I still think that the most important thing they can do for training chaplains is practical factors. So I'm still on my hobby horse. [Chuckles]

Q: Could you discuss briefly your building program that you're working on here at the church?

Admiral Stevenson: Well, Williamsburg's a growing community, so the church is a growing church. It's a church that's increased in membership by about 450 members in the last four years. We have a hard time keeping up with it. I just finished elders' and deacons' retreat over the weekend, and the leadership of the church has said that the emphasis is on biblical orientation in worship and liturgy, increased staff to provide the kinds of Christian educational programs they want for all age groups.

I've been very fortunate to have two very fine associate pastors with me. The session wants to continue their ecumenical covenant with St. Bede's Roman Catholic Church. Father Zahn of St. Bede's was here for Ash Wednesday yesterday, and we did the imposition of ashes to the Presbyterians at noon and then I was with Father Zahn at St. Bede's at 7:30 Mass last night for the imposition of ashes there, and we'll be together for the

Stations of the Cross at St. Bede's on Good Friday. So that kind of thing is a little Navy-like in the civilian world. And, in addition to that, since the church has inadequate facilities, they commence on the 11th of March a formal capital funding campaign in the hopes of raising $4 million for the building of the new, improved master plan. And I would hope that when some of those things are accomplished, I can put a ribbon around this place and have an ecclesiastical change of office. [Laughter] And then my plans are to retire.*

Q: Well, I know that the Chaplain Corps and the U.S. Navy are better for you having exerted your influence on it in many ways, and grateful, also, for your spending the time and effort you have on this oral history. This will be another legacy that will be useful for many years in the future.

Admiral Stevenson: How could I turn you down when I get a stipend every month? Have you ever thought about the fact, Paul, that I and my associates are paid monthly to stay away from the United States Navy? [Laughter]

Q: We'll end on that glorious note. Thank you. I don't know if I've ever heard anybody else describe it that way. [Laughter]

Admiral Stevenson: That's the way I look at it. I tell them, "God, it's amazing what it costs the government to keep me away from the United States Navy." [Laughter]

Q: Less than it costs to keep you in.

---

* In editing the transcript in early 1997, Admiral Stevenson added the following postscript: "Neil M. Stevenson retired from the position of pastor of the Williamsburg Presbyterian Church on 15 September 1995. He is pleased that church's membership, staff, and facilities increased threefold during his ten years as pastor. It did so because (even though he firmly holds that parish and institutional ministry are worlds apart) he was able to apply what he had learned in the Navy to his pastoring. Neil and Diane live in Williamsburg, VA."

Index To

*Reminiscences of
Rear Admiral Neil M. Stevenson
Chaplain Corps
U.S. Navy (Retired)*

Air Force, U.S.
Navy destroyers were involved in a search for a downed Air Force plane in the Eastern Pacific in 1958, 48-49

Alcohol
Concern in the 1970s and 1980s about the use of alcohol by Navy chaplains, 215, 227-228, 231-232, 296

Altmann, Commander Richard G., USNR
Served in the mid-1960s as executive officer of Glenview Naval Air Station, 89-91, 285

Ammons, Lieutenant Commander James E., Jr., CHC, USN
Studied financial management at the Naval Postgraduate School in the late 1960s, then applied it in the office of the Chief of Chaplains in the early 1970s, 154-155, 157, 201, 229

Auel, Lieutenant Commander Carl A., CHC, USN
Detailing duty in the Chief of Chaplains' office in the mid-1960s, 81

Baseball
Stevenson played the sport while growing up in Brooklyn in the 1930s and 1940s, 4-5, 8; the Brooklyn Dodgers were a popular major league team in the 1940s and 1950s, 5-6

Begg, Commander Wendell R., CHC, USN
Set up press conferences for Rear Admiral James Kelly, Chief of Chaplains, in the late 1960s, 145

Below, Captain Ralph W., CHC, USN
Served as senior chaplain for the III Marine Amphibious Force in Vietnam in the late 1960s, 126, 138; ran the training desk in the Chief of Chaplains' office in the early 1970s, 138, 147-148, 150, 152, 156

Bigley, Vice Admiral Thomas J., USN (USNA, 1950)
Maintained an excellent relationship with the fleet chaplain while serving in the late 1970s as Deputy CinCPacFlt, 244

Blizzard, Sam
Professor who taught the sociology of religion at the Princeton Theological Seminary in the late 1960s, 104-112, 161; lectured at the Navy chaplains' school, 111

Boreczky, Captain John V., CHC, USN
Served on the staff of the Chief of Chaplains in the mid-1970s, 229, 233, 236

Brooklyn, New York
Neighborhood life and schools in the 1930s and 1940s, 1-13, 19-22; the New York Navy Yard as a local employer in World War II, 21-22

Budget--Navy
The Navy's Chaplain Corps switched from paternalism to planning and programming in the early 1970s as a way of receiving funding, 154-155, 157, 158-159; for the chaplains department at the Orlando Naval Training Center in the mid-1970s, 168, 171-172; Chief of Chaplains John J. O'Connor got the Chaplain Corps into the Navy POM in the mid-1970s, 194-210, 229; in Stevenson's view, the Navy's chapel program should be operated with appropriated funds, not offerings, 240-241

Bureau of Naval Personnel
As Chief of Naval Personnel in the mid-1970s, Vice Admiral James Watkins was helpful to Chief of Chaplains John J. O'Connor, 201-202; relationship with the Chaplain Corps, 203-210, 213, 306-307

Burke, Admiral Arleigh A., USN (Ret.) (USNA, 1923)
While hospitalized in the early 1980s, sent greetings to naval personnel deployed to the Indian Ocean, 267-268

Cambodia
Felt spill-over effects from the Vietnam War in the 1960s and 1970s, 143

Camp Lejeune, North Carolina
Site of a memorial service for Marines killed in Lebanon in October 1983, 308-309

Casualty Assistance Calls Officer
Role of naval officers in notifying Chicago-area families of the deaths or injuries of service members in the mid-1960s, 89-95, 285

Chambliss, Commander Carroll R., CHC, USN
As a chaplain at the Great Lakes Naval Training Center in the late 1950s, he was a hit with recruits, 32-33; objection in the early 1970s to being ordered to a certain billet because he is black, 220-221

Chaplain Corps, U.S. Navy
Indoctrination in 1957 at the Chaplain School in Newport, 27-29; few black Navy chaplains in the late 1950s, 33; tended to be more parochial about faith groups in the 1950s than in recent years, 36-37; value of sea duty in a chaplain's career, 38-39; the importance of military rank for U.S. Navy chaplains, 74; atmosphere in the Chief of Chaplains' office in the mid-1960s, 81; negotiations in the mid-1960s about admitting Latter Day Saints to the Chaplain Corps, 97-99; role of the Chaplain Corps Planning Group in Washington, D.C., in the late 1960s, 114-115, 118, 152; training in spirituality instituted by the Chief of Chaplains in the late 1960s, 147-153; the Chaplain Corps switched from paternalism to planning and programming in the early 1970s as a way of receiving funding, 154-155, 157, 158-159; Stevenson believes Navy chaplains

should do institutional ministry instead of parish ministry, 182-184, 244-247, 283-284, 329-330; Chief of Chaplains John J. O'Connor got the Chaplain Corps into the Navy POM in the mid-1970s, 194-210, 229; establishment of the religious program specialist (RP) enlisted rating in the mid-1970s, 201, 210-213; recruiting of minorities for the Chaplain Corps in the 1970s and 1980s, 202, 214-217, 285-286; working with the Bureau of Naval Personnel in the mid-1970s on billet justifications for chaplains, 203-210, 213; concern in the 1970s and 1980s about the use of alcohol by Navy chaplains, 215, 227-228, 231-232, 296; Stevenson's practices about detailing and treatment of minority chaplains in the mid-1980s, 216-221, 286-288; actions in the 1970s and 1980s in reducing the identity of Jewish chaplains as a separate category in the Chaplain Corps, 217-219, 288-289; creation of a Deputy Chief of Chaplains in 1980, 230-231, 262-264, 275; role of chaplains on medical ethics boards, 246-247, 277-278; some chaplains are more rank-conscious than others, 249-250; in the early 1980s the office of the Chief of Chaplains was staffed with talented officers, no longer a "house of representatives" of the Chaplain Corps, 272-273; establishment of a rotation of flag officers in the corps, 274-276; practices in detailing chaplains to various assignments in the early 1980s, 293-297; because of the increase in the number of billets under the POM system in the late 1970s, the Chaplain Corps was faced with a heavy recruiting requirement in subsequent years, 302-303; publication of a SecNav instruction on Chaplain Corps policy in December 1983, 311-314; maturation of the RP rating in the 1980s, 324-326

Chaplain Resource Board
In the early 1980s performed a number of tasks in support of the Chaplain Corps, 281-282, 320-322

Chaplain School, Newport, Rhode Island
Course of instruction in 1957 while training new Navy chaplains, 27-29; in the early 1970s the advanced course was designed to help individuals make the transition from chaplain to supervisor, 152, 160-162; emphasis under Chaplain Ross Trower in the mid-1970s, 215-216; role in the early 1980s, 319-320, 338

Claytor, W. Graham
As Secretary of the Navy in the late 1970s, directed that enlisted religious program specialists (RPs) would serve only with Navy chaplains, 212-213, 326

Cooke, Terence J.
Catholic archbishop of New York who visited South Vietnam in the late 1960s, 139

Cushman, Lieutenant General Robert E., Jr., USMC (USNA, 1935)
Served as commanding general of the III MAF in the late 1960s, 126-127, 138

Davis, Admiral Donald C., USN (USNA, 1944)
Qualities while serving as Commander in Chief Pacific Fleet in the late 1970s, 253

Day, Commander Richard T., CHC, USN
Role as chaplain in Hong Kong in the late 1970s in combating the drug problem, 248

Defense Officer Personnel Management Act (DOPMA)
Passed in 1981 after a long development period, 206-207, 230, 291, 302

Destroyer Force Atlantic Fleet
Captain Art McQuaid was the type command's hard-nosed senior chaplain in the late 1950s, but he also had a compassionate side, 52-56

Destroyer Squadron Ten
Role of the staff chaplain in the late 1950s, 39-50, 55-58, 69; Med deployment in 1958 turned into an around-the-world cruise, 42-44, 48-49, 59-60; Captain Robert Weeks was an excellent role model while serving as commodore in the late 1950s, 43-45, 50; trip to the Great Lakes in 1959, 47; search and rescue mission in 1958, 48-49; living conditions on board ships in the squadron, 58-59

Diego Garcia
Buildup of naval facilities on the island in the late 1970s, 260

Dimino, Captain Joseph T., CHC, USN
Served as senior chaplain in the aircraft carrier <u>Saratoga</u> (CVA-60) in the early 1960s, 81-82; on the staff of the Chief of Chaplains in the mid-1970s, 199-200, 229, 233

DOPMA
<u>See</u> Defense Officer Personnel Management Act (DOPMA)

Ecker, Captain Robert J., CHC, USN
Served as executive assistant to the Chief of Chaplains in the early 1980s, 265

Education
Public schools in Brooklyn in the 1930s and 1940s, 1-3, 8, 20; Stevenson's undergraduate years from 1949 to 1953 at Tarkio College in Missouri, 10-17, 22; Stevenson as a divinity student in the early 1950s at Pittsburgh-Xenia Theological Seminary, 16-23; Stevenson was a postgraduate student in 1967-68 at Princeton Theological Seminary, 103-113, 161; chaplains studied at the Naval Postgraduate School in the late 1960s, 154

Engineering Plants
Difficulties with 1,200-pound steam plants installed in new destroyer-type ships in the 1950s, 58-50

Enlisted Personnel
Low pay in the 1950s, 34, 51; networking among dependents in the 1950s, 52; establishment of the religious program specialist (RP) enlisted rating in the mid-1970s, 201, 210-213; maturation of the RP rating in the 1980s, 324-326

<u>See also</u> Recruit Training

Families of Servicemen
Financial difficulties for the families of low-paid enlisted personnel in the late 1950s, 51; networking among dependents in the 1950s, 52; support system for Diane Stevenson when her third child was born in 1960, 54-55; cases of spouse abuse at the Newport Naval Station in the early 1960s, 67-68; support for families of aviators lost from the aircraft carrier Saratoga (CVA-60) in the early 1960s, 72-73; stayed in Mayport, Florida, while the Saratoga went to sea to avoid a hurricane, 77; the Stevenson family at Glenview Naval Air Station in the mid-1960s, 82-83, 101; role of naval officers in notifying Chicago-area families of the deaths or injuries of service members in the mid-1960s, 89-95; Stevenson's family lived in Missouri while he was in Vietnam in the late 1960s, 119; the Stevensons lost money on a house they bought in Orlando, Florida, in the 1970s, 164, 198; Chief of Chaplains John J. O'Connor's view in the late 1970s of the role of chaplains' wives, 224-225

Ferguson, Lieutenant Commander Melvin R., CHC, USN
Personnel work on behalf of the Chaplain Corps, 204; work in the Chief of Chaplains office in the early 1980s, 282, 303, 333

Fires
Destroyed a multipurpose building at the Glenview Naval Air Station in the mid-1960s, 101; fires killed Rear Admiral Howard Yeager and Rear Admiral Richard Fowler in early 1967, 102

Fisher, Captain William G., Jr., USN (USNA, 1952)
Headed recruit training at the Orlando Naval Training Center in the mid-1970s, 186

Fitness Reports
Line officers are not always aware of the best way to write fitness reports for chaplains under their command, 250-252, 289

Forrest Royal, USS (DD-872)
Was a happy, hard-working ship in the late 1950s, 45; deployment to the Mediterranean in 1960, 55; depicted in a divine service painting that appeared on the cover of Proceedings in 1969, 57

Forrest Sherman, USS (DD-931)
Made a cruise to the Great Lakes in connection with the opening of the St. Lawrence Seaway in 1959, 47; involved in a search for a downed Air Force plane in the Eastern Pacific in 1958, 48-49; part of an around-the-world deployment in 1958, 50-51; site of Stevenson's swearing in as a regular Navy officer, 53

Fowler, Rear Admiral Richard L., USN (USNA, 1936)
Fine leader who served from 1965 to 1967 as Chief of Naval Air Reserve Training, 84; died when his quarters burned in January 1967, 102

Gallagher, Lieutenant (j.g.) Pete C., Jr., USNR
Served as navigator of the destroyer Hale (DD-642) in the late 1950s, 46

Garrett, Rear Admiral Francis, CHC, USN
Served as Chief of Chaplains in the early 1970s, 152-153, 156, 161, 182, 309

Gibson, Lieutenant Commander William H., CHC, USN
Duty as a Marine in Vietnam in the late 1960s, 136; personnel work on behalf of the Chaplain Corps, 204; work in the Chief of Chaplains office in the early 1980s, 282, 303, 311, 313, 333

Gilbert, Lieutenant Leroy, CHC, USNR
Worked on minority recruiting for the Chaplain Corps in the mid-1970s, 202, 216

Gillooly, Captain John F., USN (USNA, 1945)
Commanded the Orlando Naval Training Center in the early 1970s, 169, 186-187

Glenview, Illinois, Naval Air Station
Service in Naval Reserve training in the mid-1960s, 81-82; work of chaplains in serving both the air station and the Naval Air Reserve Training Command, 84-86, 102-103; role of naval officers in notifying Chicago-area families of the deaths or injuries of service members in the mid-1960s, 89-95; crash in the mid-1960s of an S-2 Tracker from a Naval Reserve squadron, 93-95; role of chaplains in officiating at funerals, 95-96; a fire in the mid-1960s destroyed a multipurpose building, 101; Rear Admiral Richard Fowler died when his quarters burned in January 1967, 102

Goodrich, James F.
Service as Under Secretary of the Navy from 1981 to 1987, 341-342

Graham, Billy
Popular television evangelist who visited Vietnam in the late 1960s, 137-138

Great Lakes, Illinois, Naval Training Center
Role of Captain Robert Schwyhart and his wife in indoctrinating junior chaplains and their families at the Great Lakes Naval Training Center in the late 1950s, 30-31; interaction between chaplains and recruit trainees, 32-36

Greenwood, Captain Charles L., CHC, USN (USNA, 1950)
At the Navy Chaplain School in the early 1970s, 182

Habitability
Living conditions on board ships of Destroyer Squadron Ten in the late 1950s, 58-59

Hale, USS (DD-642)
Med deployment in 1958 turned into an around-the-world cruise, 42-43, 50; the navigator annoyed the captain while doing star sights, 46; involved in a search for a downed Air Force plane in the Eastern Pacific in 1958, 48-49; damaged by a yard oiler in 1958, 50

Hauck, Captain Philip F., USN (USNA, 1935)
 Served as Commander Destroyer Squadron Ten in the late 1950s, 47-48, 53

Hayward, Admiral Thomas B., USN (USNA, 1948)
 Demonstrated great leadership while serving as Commander in Chief Pacific fleet in the late 1970s, 243, 255, 292; selected for CNO in 1978, 244, 253

Helicopters
 Role in shuttling chaplains between ships in the late 1950s, 40-41; a Marine Corps helicopter from Hawaii was lost during a rescue mission in the Eastern Pacific in 1958, 49; used in the late 1960s essentially to take South Vietnamese people into protective custody, 132-133

Hemphill, Captain Edward J., Jr., CHC, USN
 Served on the Chaplain Corps Planning Group in the late 1960s, 112, 114-117; started contemporary worship while at the Orlando Naval Training Center, 178

Hilferty, Commander Thomas J., CHC, USN
 Ran training for the Chief of Chaplains in the early 1970s, 153; as chaplain detailer in the mid-1970s, 191, 199-200, 207-208, 223

Hill Captain Rodger F., CHC, USN
 Served as senior chaplain at the Orlando Naval Training Center in the early 1970s, 163, 165-166

Homosexuality
 Clear-cut policy toward homosexuals in the service, 279; a few homosexual chaplains left the service in the 1980s, 293

Hong Kong
 Role of the Navy chaplain in Hong Kong in the late 1970s in combating the drug problem there, 248

Hutcheson, Captain Richard G., CHC, USN
 Headed Chaplain Corps training in the 1960s, 154

Indian Ocean
 Buildup of naval facilities on the island of Diego Garcia in the late 1970s, 260; visits by chaplains to deployed forces in the early 1980s, 266-270

Jensen, Commander Andrew F., Jr., CHC, USN
 In the early 1970s, while serving at Jacksonville, was court-martialed for adultery, acquitted, and reassigned, 155-156

Kelley, General Paul X., USMC
 Attended a memorial service at Camp Lejeune for Marines killed in Lebanon in October 1983, 308-309

Kelly, Rear Admiral James W., CHC, USN
As Chief of Chaplains in the late 1960s, instituted the Chaplain Corps Planning Group, 114, reaction to the Personal Response Program in Vietnam, 137, 144-145, 266; desires for chaplain training, 148-149, 151

Kennedy, President John F.
Visits to Newport, Rhode Island, in the early 1960s, 70-71; Stevenson, as a Navy chaplain, was asked to speak in civilian churches at the time of Kennedy's 1963 death, 80

Lake, Commander Julian S., USN
As executive officer of the aircraft carrier Saratoga (CVA-60) in the early 1960s, wanted to avoid the use of bribes during a yard period for the ship, 75; became upset in 1964 when he thought effervescent grape juice on board ship was champagne, 82

Lebanon
Memorial service at Camp Lejeune for Marines killed in Lebanon in October 1983, 308-309

Leyte, USS (CVS-32)
Hosted a number of high-level religious visitors for Christmas of 1958, 60

Lonergan, Captain Vincent J., CHC, USN
While serving in the late 1960s as staff chaplain for the Fleet Marine Force Pacific, tore up a letter addressed to the commanding general of the III Marine Amphibious Force, 126-128; talked about Vietnam with Stevenson, 137; headed the chaplains division in Washington in the early 1970s, 148, 221

Marine Corps, U.S.
A Marine Corps helicopter from Hawaii was lost during a rescue mission in the Eastern Pacific in 1958, 49; role of naval officers in the mid-1960s in notifying Chicago-area families of the deaths or injuries of Marines, 92; role of the Personal Response Program in the late 1960s in trying to win the hearts and minds of the Vietnamese people, 115-116, 118-140, 146; attributes of Marines, 120-121; memorial service at Camp Lejeune for Marines killed in Lebanon in October 1983, 308-309

Markos, Lieutenant Thomas, CHC, USNR
Naval reservist who said Mass at the Glenview Naval Air Station in the mid-1960s, 84-86

McNamara, Rear Admiral John R., CHC, USN
Served as Chief of Chaplains from 1985 to 1988, 275-276; as deputy prior to becoming chief, 307-308; involvement in a memorial service at Camp Lejeune for Marines killed in Lebanon in October 1983, 308-309

McQuaid, Captain Arthur F., CHC, USN
Hard-nosed individual who was the senior chaplain for Destroyer Force Atlantic Fleet in the late 1950s, but he also had a compassionate side, 52-56

Medical Problems
A tonsillectomy for the child of a Chaplain School student was an illustration that naval personnel are often separated from their families during emergencies, 28-29, problem in childbirth for Diane Stevenson in 1960, 54-55; in the late 1970s a chaplain in the Pacific Fleet was relieved of duty because of problems following his cancer surgery, 236-237; role of chaplains on medical ethics boards, 246-247, 277-278

Menges, Captain Harold F., CHC, USN
In the late 1960s ran the training desk in the Chief of Chaplains' office, 104, 106

Moore, Captain Frederick T., Jr., USN
Demonstrated great leadership qualities as commanding officer of the aircraft carrier Saratoga (CVA-60) in the early 1960s, 71-72; a kidney operation knocked him out of consideration for flag rank, 72

Murphy, Commander Pleasant L., USN
Commanded the destroyer Samuel B. Roberts (DD-823) during a Great Lakes cruise in 1959, 47

Music
Presentation of a Bach concert to recruits at the Orlando Naval Training Center in the mid-1970s, 180-181

Naval Academy, Annapolis, Maryland
Slow to develop religious pluralism in terms of chaplain assignments and worship style, 188, 282

Naval Air Reserve Training Command
Headquarters at Glenview, Illinois, in the mid-1960s, 82, 84; role of chaplains within the command, 84-89, 96-97, 99-101

Naval Logistics Command Pacific Fleet
Role in supporting the fleet religious program in the late 1970s, 234-239, 244-245, 247-249

Naval Reserve, U.S.
Role of the Glenview Naval Air Station in reserve training in the mid-1960s, 81-82; role of chaplains within the Naval Air Reserve Training Command, 84-89, 96-97, 99-101

Navigation
In the late 1950s, the navigator of the destroyer Hale (DD-642) annoyed the captain while doing star sights, 46

Navy Relief Society
Stevenson's view is that chaplains should not be involved in dispensing Navy Relief funds, 246

Newport, Rhode Island, Naval Station
Chapel program in the early 1960s, 61-71; social life available at the command and in the community, 62, 70; cases of spouse abuse among Newport naval personnel in the early 1960s, 67-68; role of the local YMCA in the lives of sailors, 69-70; visits by President Dwight Eisenhower and President John Kennedy, 70-71

New York Navy Yard, Brooklyn, New York
Was a prominent local employer during the World War II years, 21-22

Nickerson, Lieutenant General Herman, Jr., USMC
As commanding general in Vietnam in the late 1960s, was bothered by a non-regulation American flag, 133-134

Norfolk Naval Shipyard, Portsmouth, Virginia
Site of a yard period for the aircraft carrier Saratoga (CVA-60) in the early 1960s, 75

O'Connor, Rear Admiral John J., CHC, USN
Activist who served as Chief of Chaplains in the late 1970s, 155, 158; ordered Stevenson to Washington duty in 1976, 193-194, 197-198; advocate of the Vietnam War, 194; got the Chaplain Corps into the Navy POM in the mid-1970s, 194-210, 229; personality and working style of, 199, 222-229, 233, 316; pushed for the religious program specialist (RP) enlisted rating in the mid-1970s, 201, 210-213; views on minorities in the Navy, 214-215, 218; as Chief of Chaplains, paid visits to remote places, including Antarctica, 265-266, 271; assembled a top-notch staff in the chief's office, 273-274

Okinawa
Discussion in the late 1960s of cultural differences between people on the island, 128-129

Orlando, Florida, Naval Training Center
Stevenson formalized the planning and supervision process when he became senior chaplain in 1973, 164-167, 169-172, 174-175, 189-190; Stevenson's actions in tying in the chaplains department with the overall command, 167-168, 189-190; roles of chaplains department, 168-172; interaction between chaplains and recruits in the mid-1970s, 172-180; types of worship services, 178-188; Lieutenant Florence Dianna Pohlman, the Navy's first woman chaplain, served at the training center in the mid-1970s, 180-184; relationships among chaplains on the staff, 191-192

Pacific Fleet, U.S.
Role of the Naval Logistics Command Pacific Fleet in supporting the fleet religious program in the late 1970s, 234-239, 244-245, 247-249

Painting
A painting of a divine service on board the destroyer Forrest Royal (DD-872) appeared on the cover of Proceedings in 1969, 57

Pay and Allowances
Low pay for Navy enlisted personnel in the 1950s, 34, 51

Pearl Harbor, Hawaii, Naval Station
Construction of the submarine base chapel in World War II, 63; construction of a new chapel in the late 1970s, 228-229, 242; role of the old chapel at Makalapa in providing a program for Pacific Fleet personnel in the late 1970s, 235, 241-242; the closing of the old chapel after the new one was built brought some unhappy responses, 242-243; need for counseling sailors who cohabited without benefit of marriage, 256-258

Personal Response Program
Role of the program in the late 1960s in trying to win the hearts and minds of the Vietnamese people, 115-147

Pittsburgh-Xenia Theological Seminary, Pittsburgh, Pennsylvania
Education provided in the early 1950s to Presbyterian divinity students, 16-23

Planning
Stevenson formalized the planning process for chaplains at the Orlando Naval Training Center when he became senior chaplain in 1973, 164-165, 169-171, 174-175, 189-190; Chief of Chaplains John J. O'Connor got the Chaplain Corps into the Navy POM in the mid-1970s, 194-210, 229

Plishker, Captain Richard Alan, CHC, USN
Did a fine job of recruiting chaplains in the early 1980s, 303

Pohlman, Lieutenant Florence Dianna, CHC, USNR
As the Navy's first woman chaplain, served at the Orlando Naval Training Center in the mid-1970s, 180-184

Princeton Theological Seminary, Princeton, New Jersey
Dr. Sam Blizzard taught the sociology of religion in the late 1960s, 104-112, 161

Racial Integration
Minority recruiting for the Chaplain Corps in the 1970s and 1980s, 202, 214-216, 285-286; Stevenson's practices about detailing and treatment of minority chaplains in the mid-1980s, 216-221, 286-288, 298-299; in the early 1970s Commander Carroll Chambliss objected to being ordered to a certain billet because he is black, 220-221

Radcliffe, Captain Robert W., CHC, USN
While in the Chief of Chaplains' office in the mid-1960s was involved in negotiations for bringing Latter Day Saints into the Chaplain Corps, 98-99

Rauch, Captain Charles F., Jr., USN (USNA, 1948)
Was involved in human relations factors while serving in Vietnam in the late 1960s, 139-141

Reagan, President Ronald
Attended a memorial service at Camp Lejeune for Marines killed in Lebanon in October 1983, 308-309

Recruiting
Recruiting of minorities for the Chaplain Corps in the 1970s and 1980s, 202, 214-217, 285-286; because of the increase in the number of billets under the POM system in the late 1970s, the Chaplain Corps was faced with a heavy recruiting requirement in subsequent years, 302-303; dropoff in the availability of Catholic priests, 304-305

Recruit Training
Interaction between chaplains and recruits at the Great Lakes naval training center in the late 1950s, 32-36; interaction between chaplains and recruits at the Orlando Naval Training Center in the mid-1970s, 172-180

Reilly, Commander Thomas H., CHC, USN
Gruff, intimidating individual who served as senior chaplain at the Newport Naval Station in the early 1960s, 62-65

Religion
Catholics and Protestants were closely associated while Stevenson was growing up in Brooklyn in the 1930s and 1940s, 4-5, 7-9; affiliation in the 1940s and 1950s between various faith groups and colleges, 9, 13-14, 16, 18, 20; Navy chaplains should rise above faith group identities, 36-38; search for local Catholic priests to say Mass in U.S. Navy ships in the Mediterranean in the late 1950s, 41, 57, 239; meeting individual religious needs in the aircraft carrier Saratoga (CVA-60) in the early 1960s, 78; role of Protestant chaplains in the Chicago area in the committal of deceased Catholic service members in the mid-1960s, 95-96; negotiations in the mid-1960s about admitting Latter Day Saints to the Navy Chaplain Corps, 97-99; reflections of church philosophy in the late 1960s, 117; spirituality training for members of the Navy's Chaplain Corps in the late 1960s and early 1970s, 147-153; some chaplains don't realize that their individual beliefs should not be propagated in a pluralistic setting, 187-188; actions in the 1970s and 1980s in reducing the identity of Jewish chaplains as a separate category in the Chaplain Corps, 217-219; role of chaplains on medical ethics boards that deal with individuals of various faith groups, 246-247, 277-278; selection and retention of chaplains for promotion should be based on ability and potential, not on faith group, 251-252, 289, 299; providing for the needs of Jewish personnel in various commands, 340

Rosso, Rear Admiral George A., CHC, USN
While serving in the office of the Chief of Chaplains in 1957, advised Stevenson on executing orders to Chaplain School, 26-27

S-2 Tracker
 And aircraft from a reserve squadron based at Glenview Naval Air Station crashed during a training mission in the mid-1960s, 93-95

Saigon, South Vietnam
 During the late 1960s the atmosphere in this capital city seemed sort of other-worldly, different from the rest of the nation, 139-141

St. Lawrence Seaway
 Ships of Destroyer Squadron Ten made a cruise to the Great Lakes in 1959 in conjunction with the opening of the seaway, 47

Samuel B. Roberts, USS (DD-823)
 Made a cruise to the Great Lakes in connection with the opening of the St. Lawrence Seaway in 1959, 47

Saratoga, USS (CVA-60)
 Support system among crew member and air group families living in Mayport-Jacksonville, Florida, in the early 1960s, 72-73; role of the ship's chaplains in the early 1960s, 72-74, 77-78; yard period in Norfolk in the early 1960s, 75; novelist Herman Wouk visited the ship in St. Thomas, 76; went to sea to avoid a hurricane, 77; Stevenson was asked to speak in civilian churches at the time of President John Kennedy's death in 1963, 80; Stevenson's departure in 1964, 82

Sargent, Captain Gerald H., CHC, USN
 In the mid-1970s headed the Chaplains Division in the office of the Chief of Chaplains, 193, 196-198, 228

Schneider, Commander Otto, CHC, USN
 Was involved in the Personal Response Program in South Vietnam in the late 1960s, 126, 128, 134

Schwyhart, Captain Robert M., CHC, USN
 As command senior chaplain, joined his wife in indoctrinating junior chaplains and their families at the Great Lakes Naval Training Center in the late 1950s, 30-31

Search and Rescue
 Navy destroyers were involved in a search for a downed Air Force plane in the Eastern Pacific in 1958, 48-49

Selection Boards
 Selection and retention of chaplains for promotion should be based on ability and potential, not on faith group, 251-252, 289, 299; Stevenson's selection for flag rank in 1980 disappointed some who thought other candidates should have been picked instead, 261-262

Senieur, Commander Jude R., CHC, USNR
Served on the training desk of the staff of the Chief of Chaplains in the early 1970s, 111, 148, 150-153, 220

Shoberg, Commander Lawrence A., CHC, USN
Work in the early 1980s on facilities development, designing chapels, 339

Sixth Fleet, U.S.
Search for local Catholic priests to say Mass in U.S. Navy ships in the Mediterranean in the late 1950s, 41, 57, 239

Smith, Captain Roderic Lee, CHC, USN
Chaplain who provided comfort to Stevenson in May 1960, when Mrs. Stevenson was having childbirth problems, 54-55

Stevenson, Georgia Diane
Grew up on a farm in Missouri in the 1930s and 1940s, 6, 14-15; as a student at Tarkio College in the early 1950s, 13-15, 18, 224-225; work as teacher and marriage in 1953, 19, 21-24; homes with her husband during their marriage, 25, 30, 63, 65, 70, 72, 82-83, 136, 198; children of, 3, 25, 54-55, 82-83, 101, 105, 119, 136, 193, 198, 203, 233, 254, 258, 332; lived in Missouri while her husband was in Vietnam in the late 1960s, 119; to Hawaii for R&R while her husband was in Vietnam, 137; reaction to her husband's promotion to captain in 1973, 164-165; reaction on leaving Washington in 1977, 233; reaction to her husband's selection for flag rank in 1980, 259; as president of the Naval Officers Wives in the early 1980s, 267; reaction to her husband's retirement, 276, 344

Stevenson, Rear Admiral Neil M., CHC, USN (Ret.)
Boyhood in Brooklyn, New York, in the 1930s and 1940s, 1-13, 19-22; parents of, 1-12, 21-22; education of, 1-3, 8, 10-19, 103-116; children of, 3, 25, 54-55, 82-83, 101, 119, 136, 193, 198, 203, 233, 254, 258; wife of, 6, 13-15, 18-19, 21-24, 30, 54-55, 63, 70, 72, 101, 105, 119, 136-137, 164-165, 193, 198, 224-225, 233, 259, 264, 267, 276, 332, 344; from 1949 to 1952 attended Tarkio College in Missouri, 10-18, 22, 24; attended Pittsburgh-Xenia Theological Seminary, 1952-55, 16-23; process of joining the Navy in 1955-57, 23-27; brief stint preaching at a church in Nebraska, 24-25; as a student in 1957 at Chaplain School in Newport, Rhode Island, 27-29; as a junior chaplain in 1957-58 at the Great Lakes Naval Training Center, 30-38; duty in 1958-60 with Destroyer Squadron Ten, 38-60, 69; served 1960-62 as chaplain at Naval Station Newport, 61-71; as junior chaplain in 1962-64 on board the aircraft carrier <u>Saratoga</u> (CVA-60), 71-80; duty from 1964 to 1967 at Glenview, Illinois, Naval Air Station, 80-103; as a postgraduate student in 1967-68 at Princeton Theological Seminary, 103-113, 161; involvement in the Personal Response Program in South Vietnam in the late 1960s, 115-147; served 1969-72 in the training division on the staff of the Chief of Chaplains, 147-160; as a student in 1972-73 in the Chaplain School advanced course, 160-162; served from 1973 to 1976 as senior chaplain, Naval Training Center, Orlando, Florida, 163-192; promotion to captain in 1973, 163-164; duty in 1976-77 on the staff of John O'Connor, Chief of Chaplains, 193-233; served 1977-1980 as Fleet

Chaplain, Pacific Fleet/Chaplain, Naval Logistics Command Pacific Fleet, 233-262; selection for flag rank in 1980, 259, 261-262; served 1980-83 as Deputy Chief of Chaplains, 261-307; retirement from active duty in 1985, 275-276, 343-344; as Chief of Chaplains, 1983-85, 307-344; post-retirement years as a civilian pastor, 344-346

Takesian, Lieutenant Commander Eli, CHC, USN
Risked his life while serving with Marines in the Vietnam War, 146

Tarkio College, Tarkio, Missouri
Education provided in the late 1940s and early 1950s by this small liberal arts school, 10-17

Terrorism
As Chief of Naval Operations in the early 1980s, Admiral James Watkins was concerned about appropriate responses to terrorism, 330-332

Training
Course of instruction at the Chaplain School in 1957, 27-28; interaction between chaplains and recruits at the Great Lakes naval training center in the late 1950s, 32-36; physical training for Marines going to Vietnam in the late 1960s, 119-120; work of the training division on the staff of the Chief of Chaplains in the early 1970s, 147-153; in the early 1970s the Chaplain School advanced course was designed to help individuals make the transition from chaplain to supervisor, 152, 160-162; interaction between chaplains and recruits at the Orlando Naval Training Center in the mid-1970s, 172-180; professional development training courses for chaplains in the 1980s, 314-319, 336

Trost, Vice Admiral Carlisle A. H., USN (USNA, 1953)
Demonstrated brilliance while serving as Deputy CinCPacFlt in the late 1970s, 253-254

Trower, Captain Ross H., CHC, USN
Served in the office of the Chief of Chaplains in the early 1970s, 211; headed the chaplain school in the mid-1970s, 215; as Chief of Chaplains in the early 1980s, 219, 264-266, 294, 321; personality and working style, 264-265, 274, 280-281, 283, 335; assembled an outstanding staff as Chief of Chaplains, 273, 305-306; meetings with endorsing agents for the various faith groups, 301

Urbano, Commander Francis J., CHC, USN
Was present when Stevenson was promoted to captain in 1973, 163-164

Vietnam, South
Role of the Personal Response Program in the late 1960s in trying to win the hearts and minds of the South Vietnamese people, 115-147; the atmosphere in Saigon seemed sort of other-worldly, different from the rest of the nation, 139-141

Vietnam War
The U.S. Navy had an element of sloppiness about it during the war, then became much more professional later, 78-79; role of naval officers in the mid-1960s in notifying

Chicago-area families of the deaths or injuries of service members, 92; disruption to American civil life in the late 1960s, 107-109, 117; debates over the wisdom of the U.S. policy toward Vietnam, 108-110, 119, 146-147; role of the Personal Response Program in the late 1960s in trying to win the hearts and minds of the South Vietnamese people, 115-147; Chaplain John J. O'Connor was an advocate of the war, 194

Voth, Captain Murray H., CHC, USN
Directed education and training of chaplains while on the staff of the Chief of Chaplains in the early 1980s, 320-321

Walsh, Captain William J., CHC, USN
Served as a fine role model for Stevenson in the 1960s, 66-67; service in the Chicago area in the mid-1960s, 95-96, 104

Watkins, Admiral James D., USN (USNA, 1949)
As Chief of Naval Personnel in the mid-1970s, was helpful to Chief of Chaplains John J. O'Connor, 201-202, 229; as Commander in Chief Pacific Fleet in the early 1980s, he was unhappy when he learned that the old Makalapa Chapel near Pearl Harbor, Hawaii, had been closed, 243; as CNO in the early 1980s was concerned about the response to terrorism, 330-332; Stevenson's assessment of, 332-333

Weeks, Captain Robert H., USN (USNA, 1932)
Was an excellent role model while serving as Commander Destroyer Squadron Ten in the late 1950s, 43-45, 50

White, Rear Admiral David E., CHC, USN
Duty in the office of the Chief of Chaplains in the mid-1970s, later Chief of Chaplains in the 1990s, 202, 207-208, 216, 233

Williams, Lieutenant Commander Robert H., CHC, USN
Talented artist who in the 1980s put together a series of posters supporting the work of the Chaplain Corps, 322-323

Williamsburg, Virginia
Following his retirement from the Navy in 1985, Stevenson became pastor of Williamsburg Presbyterian Church, 344-346

Willis A. Lee, USS (DL-4)
Was ridiculed for engineering problems in the 1950s, 58-59

Witting, Lieutenant Martin J., CHC, USNR
Naval reservist who said Mass at the Glenview Naval Air Station in the mid-1960s, 84-86

Women
   Lieutenant Florence Dianna Pohlman, the Navy's first woman chaplain, served at the Orlando Naval Training Center in the mid-1970s, 180-184

World War I
   Stevenson's father served in the British Army during the war, 5, 21

Wouk, Herman
   This famous novelist, author of The Caine Mutiny, visited the aircraft carrier Saratoga (CVA-60) at St. Thomas in the early 1960s, 76

Young, Captain Merle N., CHC, USN
   Served as director of the Chaplain School in Newport, Rhode Island, when Stevenson reported for instruction in 1957, 27; as chaplain at the Naval Academy in the early 1950s, 188

Zumwalt, Admiral Elmo R., Jr., USN (USNA, 1943)
   Involvement with the Personal Response Program while serving as Commander U.S. Naval Forces Vietnam in the late 1960s, 139-141

Appendices to the Oral History of Rear Admiral Neil M. Stevenson, CHC, USN (Ret.)

Stevenson's End of Tour Report, dated 30 July 1969 after completing duty in Vietnam in connection with the Personal Response Program

Stevenson's letter to fellow chaplains on the occasion of taking over as Chief of Chaplains on 1 August 1983

Stevenson's remarks at his first staff conference as Chief of Chaplains, held at the Navy Annex, 1 August 1983

Stevenson's letter of 1 October 1983 to all active duty captain chaplains

Stevenson's interview with Chaplain Ron Apgar in 1983 on the occasion of taking over as Chief of Chaplains

Your Chaplain and the Command Religious Program

Secretary of the Navy Instruction 1730.7 of 14 December 1983: "Religious Ministries Within the Department of the Navy"

O-6 Minutes from the Office of the Chief of Chaplains, 15 December 1983

Secretary of the Navy Notice 1730 of 27 December 1983: "Holy Days and Religious Observance"

Stevenson's letter of 9 January 1984 to claimant chaplains

OpNav Instruction 1730.1A of 5 November 1984: "Religious Ministries in the Navy"

Stevenson's letter of 30 April 1984 to fellow chaplains

Stevenson's letter of 15 February 1985 to major claimant chaplains

Stevenson's letter of 1 July 1985 to chaplain endorsing agents

Stevenson's letter of 31 January to the Chief of Naval Operations on the subject of Christmas visits to deployed units and isolated areas

Stevenson's letter of 26 August 1985 to fellow chaplains on the subject of his retirement from the office of Chief of Chaplains

HEADQUARTERS
III Marine Amphibious Force
Military Assistance Command, Vietnam
FPO, San Francisco 96602

260
30 July 1969

From: Commander Neil M. STEVENSON, CHC, USN
To: Chief of Chaplains

Subj: End of Tour Report

Ref: (a) Unit Leaders Personal Response Handbook, NAVMC 2616
(b) I Corps Coordinators Instruction 1560.1, dtd 16 Jun 1968
(c) Memorandum for Chief of Chaplains, P1730/690 CPG: WWN:lp, dtd 4 Jun 1969
(d) III MAF, Operations Order 201, Annex H
(e) Force Bulletin 1560, dtd 20 Feb 1969

1. At the conclusion of a tour as the Personal Response Officer in III Marine Amphibious Force it is fitting and proper that I forward to the Chief of Chaplains an overview report reflecting the views that reason and conscience demand and expressing the concerns gained from a position of internal responsibility in the program. Since quarterly and monthly reports concerning the progress of the Personal Response Program in I Corps have been forwarded to the Chief of Chaplains throughout the year, these end of tour thoughts and observations will be presented in the form of five comments:

   a. Several goals established at the beginning of the tour came into fruition during the year. A systematic quarterly means of training instructors was instituted with the founding of ther Personal Response Instructors School. This method for training trainers presents an opportunity for confronting the personnel holding primary or collateral duties in Personal Response with the basic principles and materials of the program. They are thereby forced to think through the philosophy and didactic techniques they will utilize and not merely mimic the III MAF team.

   The 1969 Attitude Survey, reference (e) was completed and forwarded to the Marine Corps Education and Development Center, Quantico, Va. This 10% sampling of opinion among marines in I Corps should produce valid research materials. The data collection procedures adhered to in the conducting of the survey were beyond my expectations and I am grateful for the responsible manner in which reference (a) was carried out under arduous circumstances. It is unfortunate that as of this time none of the programmed read-outs of the survey have been made available to those in the field. In the present environment of re-deployment, turnover, etc, the information would be most beneficial.

With the submission and acceptance of a Personal Response section to the Standard Operation Procedures (SOP) for III MAF the program is assured a broader acceptance in the operational considerations of the Force. The publication earlier of reference (d) adds some permanence to Personal Response activities. It is the only reference at the present time that offers a continuance to the program in operational enviornments outside of Vietnam.

There is also a sense of accomplishment in looking back at the daily duties involved in the personal instruction of about 10,000 personnel, the indirect training of thousands of others, and in observing the positive effects of the program on numerous Junior Officers.

b. The majority of frustrations in the Personal Response area can be traced to its lack of structure. At each turn or attempted innovation, the officer in the field is confronted by the absence of any reference from higher authority. There are no Force Orders or Directives from Headquarters Marine Corps, or Fleet Marine Force-Pacific and the letter from the Bureau of Naval Personnel to the individual officer involved does not carry weight in a Marine Command. This void of direction from high echelons also limits the program geographically to Vietnam. An example of this porblem is readily available in the redeployment of the 9th Regiment to Okinawa. Once the unit is chopped out of III MAF, references (b) and (d) no longer apply. Therefore, Personal Response billets, training and efforts cease in that command.

It is in this non-structured area that the Chaplains participation is placed in acute jeopardy. What is his mission, task, function? As will be pointed out later, non-structured organizational inertia contributes to the program becoming more and more involved with ideological warfare (which is what Dr. R. L. HUMPHREY correctly calls his materials and what the commands are interested in) than with humanitarian concerns or any form of reconciliation ministry. Commands will interpret Personal Response in relationship to their pragmatic needs to exploit tactical situations. This is perfectly legitimate from a military standpoint, but questionable in ministry.

Attention is drawn to reference (c). There is no doubt that the line may well utilize the Organization/Manpower recommendations set forth in this memorandum. The important question for the Chaplain Corps is what will restrict the line from misusing the chaplains assigned? What authority will govern assigned tasks and who will bear the brunt of the work load? Who will appear before the public eye in the role of ideological specialist? Experience has shown that a Line Officer with "dual responsibilities" gives little time to the Personal Response aspects of His work. The selection and control of line personnel presently working in Personal Response is untenable under the best of "personal" relations and in a broader program without a structured base it would be unbearable.

c. Of primary concern to one who has lived in the paradoxical state of a Chaplain serving as Personal Response Officer is the danger that the continuation of the program in its present format threatens the success of both its military mission and humanitarian concern. There is ample evidence that our military needs the weapon of Personal Response in order to perform its tactical missions in intercultural environments. But by utilizing chaplains to administer the program, we are truncating the military's acceptance of the effort and at the same time placing our Chaplain Corps in a precarious position. The acceptance of Personal Response as a tactical tool is well noted in reference (a) p. VII, and in reference (b) para. 4. Attitude Surveys clearly demonstrate that our personnel know more about what they are fighting against than what they are fighting for. Counterinsurgency warfare or "stay time" factors for our military forces on foreign shores is of strategic import. Yet, the Line generally looks upon Personal Response as a Chaplains' program of "goodness" and they grant it low priority. At the same time there is no area of Chaplains' activity that places our Corps in more direct danger of criticism for over stepping the bounds of separation between church and state.

During this tour I have purposely avoided any interviews with members of the news media. It is true that Personal Response is a "good work" but it is also extremely manipulative. Subject to all manner of interpretation by an absence of structure, it opens the Chaplain Corps to both ecclesiastical and legislative disapproval. In the hands of a General Edwin WALKER, USA, it could be disastrous!! Again, where does the direction come from as to what will be emphasized in research and instruction or how it will be utilized? What structure does it have? It is interesting that the PsyOps personnel never wanted to be openly associated with the program. They considered it ideological warfare and claimed, but never could reference the fact that they were forbidden by law to PsyOp our own troops.

Personal Response endeavors might well be questioned by church authorities who have been concerned that a chaplain "not bear arms" or even serve on a cripto board. Yet, in a counterinsurgency war we have him assigned to a G-3 type billet working in the area of intercultural relations with the functional goals of providing our military with increased security, additional intelligence as well as reduction in potential casualties or the task to "increase mission effectiveness without turning neutrals...into enemies". (REf:c).

Again, I stress that I am personally in accord with the aims of Personal Response in producing harmonious relations, but not as a Chaplain's responsibility, duty, or primary assignment. The program meets national needs and military expediencies but in order to be truly effective it must go through a process of bifurcation in which Chaplains come to play a very minor role (merely supportive roles) in its division of labor. Because of the Line's unfamiliarity with the behavorial sciences they are slow to grasp the strategic significance and force dynamics of Personal Response as a weapon. When they do grasp it, as there are indications the next generation of senior officers will, it will be of deep concern to the American people to predict how far they will run with it. Operation Camelot is South American and the U.S. Legislature's reaction to it must be considered.

Personal Response has acceleration and shows signs of gaining more momentum, but no governor or steering mechanism. Is it to be limited to travelogue materials of religions and customs that won't do the job or shall it continue on an ideological frame of tactical significance without controls? Where does our Chaplain Corps fit? I am well aware of the good it can do, but even more respectful of its power. The military of the U.S. is under civilian authority and forbidden to influence the National population. What are its obligations, restrictions, in influencing the indigenous citizens of another government?

   d. The attitudes of our personnel are more negative now than in 1967. Despite any statistical information other than hand read-outs of the 1969 Survey and the feedback from Orientation Surveys, it is clear to this officer that the animosity level in I Corps is a least twice as high as in 1967. There are numerous reasons for this condition or milieu. Basic racism reinforced by second and third tours (especially among those in positions of leadership), cultural shock, inbreed negative attitudes fostered in the training process (in-coming personnel often don't distinguish between VC and Vietnamese) segregation from the indigenous citizens, the length of the conflict and its ethos, and the fact that the cultural gap between the "people of the moon" and the "people of the earth" grows wider every day, etc.

   A socioligist might well diagnose the destructive activities in the social milieu in terms of anomie. To a chaplain arrogance is our ill. As Dr. Lloyd AVERILL defined it in the 18 June 1969 issue of the Christian Century, "Arrogance is that opportunism of the self (for "self" read "age group","interest group", "race", "nation", etc.) which confidently assumes the inherent superiority, and perhaps the exclusive legitimacy, of one's own causes and claims. On its obverse side, arrogance is the utter freedom to ignore the causes and claims of others, or to recognize them only in order to demean, deny or misappropriate them". A measure of the inter-cultural atmosphere is best noted in the monocultural rigidity of this war's popular hits--"Detroit City" or "I Got to Get Out of This Place" or in that expression which symbolizes so well our ethos-- "the world". Nurtured and overwhelmed by the realities of complex society ("the world") our men are largely immune to the social distress of the "other world". Thus prophetic ministry demands, as it always has, men sensitive to the plight of their fellow man--the scriptures are most applicable and in Vietname Jonah and the other prophets become even more profound.

   e. There has not been for me any deep sense of joy concerning this tour in Vietnam. Thnakfulness for friendships made, admiration for the endeavors of many and even satisfaction in the personal tasks accomplished, but the overall feeling is an acknowledgement of despair. The climate of this struggle only unmasks the ugly realities of being less than we ought to be. Racism on all sides provides one with a Camus "shock of recognition" that prompts the hope that man has _not_ come of age.

   The yoke will always remain for me the symbol of the Vietnamese people-- they are the heavy laden. They move slowly but have their burdens in balance. It may be interpreted by some as the calm of ignorance or the natural outgrowth of centuries of despair, yet these members of simple society live from day to day related to "existence". This is not to romanticize primary cultures ala Margaret MEAD but tragic indeed is the man who hasn't been able to observe the quality of Vietnamese life that reflects peasants around the globe. How could we be so blind to their courage in adversity and their ability to endure privation and hardship? The tenacity and resiliance that the Vietnamese show in daily life displays the ingenuity that has maintained their identity and cohesion even as refugees. It is little wonder that so many officers observing the phenomena of the mixing of simple and complex societies are easily drawn to quoting Kipling:

"Now it is not good for the Christian's health to hustle the
   Aryan brown,
For the Christian riles and the Aryan smiles and he weareth
   the Christian down;
And athe end of the fight is a tombstone white with the name
   of the late deceased,
And the epitaph drear: "A fool lies here who tried to hustle
   the East."

                    Kipling   or   (*The Naulahka* chapter 5)

"Though I've belted you and flayed you,
 By the livin' Gawd that made you,
 You're a better man than I am, Gunga Din!"

While others are repelled, confused and disgusted by it.

   Is it any wonder that departing troops no longer yell cat-calls and poke fun at the incoming personnel getting offtther "freedom bird;" that when the plane departs the stewardess wonders why the men no longer shout when she announces "we have departed Vietnam." Everyone departs--very few will ever leave.

   2. During the past year I have had the strange advantage, if it be bhat, of seeing many of our Chaplains from a non-esoteric perspective. It is perhaps appropriate that I speak of my admiration for them and the professional manner in which they conducted their ministries in the most trying conditions. If they suffered from any fraility, it was something of an over-identification with those with whom they served. But is this not a necessity, as well as a weakness, if you so judge, of all true pastors?

CHIEF OF CHAPLAINS

1 August 1983

Dear Chaplain,

It is important to me that my first official act in this tour of duty be to communicate with you and share some of my views, expectations and observations about our Corps. This is a personal letter and I ask you to keep its contents within our community. I don't think you'll be surprised by my thoughts since they are largely concepts we share; in my case tempered by my experiences in our sea services in general and assignments on this staff in particular.

At the change of office ceremony last Friday I said, "The clergy of this nation who have the privilege of serving in our Navy Chaplain Corps are the best. Leading this community is a challenge held in common with all those in positions of leadership in our Navy, Marine Corps and Coast Guard today - namely, to make the best better."

Chaplain, we are the best. This is so because the ecclesiastical standards demanded for ordination and endorsement, combined with the government's requirements for commissioning, result in our Navy having chaplains of the highest competence. We are also the best since our predecessors established and maintained criteria of excellence. Their dedication to ministry in war and peace, at sea and ashore, and their expertise in working the system, set the foundation on which we continue to build. Therefore, because of who we are and what we have inherited, and because of the challenges before us, it is essential that we, the best, work to be better. "From everyone to whom much is given, much will be required; and to whom men commit much they will demand the more."

Our goal is to meet the requirements for ministry imposed by the circumstances of the 1980's. For our Corps it is a fascinating time, a time in which our ministry must be more inclusive and in which we must make our professional expertise more visible and available to a wider spectrum of service people and their families. It might be illustrated as similar to the transition that occurs when the department of religion in a small college changes to meet the needs of a university student body.

In June, I met with Chaplain Emmett Floyd (Director of Reserve Chaplains) and Chaplain John McNamara (Deputy Chief of Chaplains) for three days. Our purpose was to determine what needs to be done to make the best better in providing ministry for the sea services in the Total Force. Our intent was to establish practical objectives that would directly impact on the ministry of chaplains. Our deliberations were based on the sizable amount of information available to us such as the sea services' on-going heavy operational tempo, the climate of religious need in the society in general and the sea services in particular, the impact of current statutes (e.g., DOPMA and ROPMA) and directives, the ever essential present and future demographics of the Chaplains Corps, etc.

We concluded that the organizational goals of the next few years commencing with fiscal year 1984 would be:

- <u>A Restatement of Policy</u> - To provide a clear, concise directive to increase the chaplain's awareness of the environment in which he or she serves and to make commands more conscious of the requirements of the chaplain's ministry.

- <u>A Reemphasis of Accountability</u> - To provide a structured method for communicating, identifying, measuring and reporting requirements and accomplishments through the chain of command.

- <u>A Reassertion of Practical Factors</u> - To provide impetus to the networking of professional expertise and to encourage on the job training (OJT) to the benefit of all clergy practicing this "specialized" field of ministry called chaplaincy.

The procedures for accomplishing each goal have to be worked through with the claimant chaplains. The Major Claimant Staff Chaplain meeting is scheduled for 12-16 September. I can assure you that in due course "road maps" will appear so that we can measure progress, and that each objective will be aimed at enhancing our ability to better minister to sea service people and their families. I know that as I travel throughout our Corps you'll provide me opportunity to brief you on the progress.

Having addressed organizational goals, let me concentrate on a personal hope, one that I'm certain all my predecessors in this office shared. I would like to complete my tour without a self-inflicted tragedy overcoming anyone of us. Therefore, I must be straight forward with you and stress the standards that we have accepted by our calling as clergy and by our commissioning as officers in the Navy. Ministry imposes on its practitioners the burden of the dual standard. It always has and always will. It is reality, because in choosing our profession we were given the right and responsibility to represent more than self in this life. If we do not deport ourselves in a manner worthy of the institutions we are honored to represent, then both our institutions and ministries suffer.

A portion of my job description, like yours, is to advise and so I sincerely offer the following:

- Your ecclesiastical endorsement from your faith group is just as the directive states, "an essential element of a chaplain's professional qualifications. A chaplain whose endorsement is withdrawn is no longer professionally qualified to serve...." It represents, in fact, the confidence that your religious supervisors, who educated and ordained you, have in your faithfulness. I advise you to maintain it with all integrity.

- Your commission to serve the people of this nation is an honor of trust and makes you subject to military justice. Chaplains have not been and will not be excused from codes of conduct, security regulations, moral standards, directives, etc. I advise you to be as conscientious of this fact as you are of the uniform you wear.

All occupations have hazards and the prevention of accidents is initiated by establishing proper safety measures. For us this largely means practicing what we preach. Chaplain, maintain your devotional life and stay in tune with your own spirituality. This usually means practicing the basic disciplines of one's faith and knowing and communicating with one's pastor. The old rule of thumb used by one of my senior chaplains has stood the test of time - "if you notice a chaplain avoiding the conducting of divine services you have become aware of a chaplain with a problem."

Chaplain, I have also observed that the over consumption of alcohol has played a part in just about every disciplinary tragedy of which I've been aware in our Corps. You know me well enough to know this is not "a little liquor lecture" as we called them in seminary. It's an open plea in the hope that these words may help some chaplain avoid the abuse of alcohol and the bad decisions that often follow. The sad words, "I didn't know what I was doing, because I was drunk," are the most devastating I've heard, because the sobered chaplain couldn't undo the deed nor the legal consequences.

On a different, but sometimes related subject, you should know that my attitude and approach to alcoholism is identical with our Navy policy. Alcoholism is a disease and must be treated for the sake of the person who is ill. If you have a problem with alcohol, please seek help and get on the program to recovery. If you have a brother or sister in our Corps who needs to be helped, please remind him or her that help is available.

Experience testifies that the vehicle for the elevation of praise and the resolution of problems is the chain of command. The chain of command is an orderly and clear line for all of us. It has been my experience and I trust yours, that "chains of care and concern" as well as "chains of leadership and influence" parallel the chain of command. One of my objectives is to see that chaplains understand the elements of this traditional dynamic. It is essential that chaplains in the chain of command respect and responsibly use the chain of command.

In similar terms, every chaplain has the availability of his or her faith group's support system. It should be used and relied upon more in today's world of rapid communications than ever before. Every chaplain should be engaged in maintaining a good relationship with the pastor of his or her faith group.

You and I know that the practice of ministry in the sea services is not like "the parish back home." That's exactly why we are needed as chaplains. When our fellow citizens in the sea services have needs, including those of our faith, those not of our faith, and those who do not adhere to any faith, they can and do call on us as their chaplains. It takes clergy of special commitment to practice ministry in this environment. It takes clergy secure in their personal identities and comfortable in their professional roles to meet the demands of service life. I'm proud of the fact that we perform our ministry well. I pray to the Lord God of Hosts that we can even be better at what we do, for today's world demands more than ever that we be carriers of faith, communicators of hope and positive reinforcers of values.

Chaplain, know the territory, be with the people, work the problems, speak the good word in and out of season, and pray for yourself and all of us in this ministry.

With warmest regards.

Sincerely,

NEIL M. STEVENSON
Rear Admiral, CHC, USN
Chief of Chaplains

REMARKS OF

REAR ADMIRAL NEIL M. STEVENSON, CHC, USN

CHIEF OF CHAPLAINS, U. S. NAVY

AT HIS FIRST STAFF CONFERENCE

1 AUGUST 1983

HELD AT THE NAVY ANNEX

WASHINGTON, D. C.

You have all had this experience before, I would hope, so there will be nothing unusual about the time we spend together this afternoon. You have all gone to a change of command aboard ship and then sat down in the wardroom that afternoon with the new CO and talked about a few things that he might do a little differently than past procedures and then you have all sat around and said, "What the heck, if he wants the top of the bullets to be blue and the bottom to be green, we'll paint them that way." So that's the kind of meeting this is.

I attended the change of command ceremony this morning for Admiral Williams, Chief of Naval Material, who was relieved by Admiral White, four stars, and I would tell you all that you did exceedingly better than the Material Command was able to do in their change of command. Our change of office went smoothly and everything was done correctly. I am glad that everything went over so well. So I thank you for what you have done during the past weeks, getting ready for the party and getting ready for the change of command. I know that Chaplain Trower really appreciates it, and I certainly appreciate it. It is easier with you guys helping to have a change of office than it is to have a wedding, so . . . [One of Chaplain Stevenson's daughters was married the day after his change of office.]

Let me get down to some details now about doing business, and if you have any questions, raise them. There is a letter from me that went out today to every chaplain in the Corps. I worked on the letter with our Admin people and with Chaplain McNamara and Chaplain Floyd and I do not know of anything startling in the letter. If others find anything startling in it, that is good, for it will keep them awake. But please feel free to discuss the letter with me and with other members of the staff. If you should be asked about the letter, I believe you will be able to give answers that are appropriate.

I hope we can continue to have a good wardroom environment among ourselves. Some little guidance for all of you in regards to me. I am sure most of you have heard this before. Please give me the privilege of saying no. Your responses are either "yes" or "we will certainly try to do it" or "I have to find out." But allow me or the deputy to say no, particularly if a request comes from higher authority. One of the things that we lose sight of sometimes in the Chaplain Corps is "who is higher authority?" Let me give you an illustration.

Claimant chaplains are very important to me, in fact, I want the claimant chaplains to realize how important they are. If a claimant chaplain understands his job, he speaks to our office for the claimant. It is not old Joe Blitz who is calling, but the claimant chaplain who is calling and speaking for the claimant. I would dare say you will run into situations when the claimant chaplain is not aware of that, or perhaps he would not be saying what he is saying; but he ought to be aware of the fact that he is taking upon himself the responsibility of speaking for that claimant, and in the same manner he ought to be aware of the fact that when he is speaking to the claimant, he is speaking for the Chief of Chaplains. Anything you can do to remind claimant chaplains of that I am in favor of. I am certainly going to be reminding them of it. And you might have to ask the question, "Now is this Joe Blitz's opinion, or if the Chief goes back to the CINC on this, is this really what the claimant wants?" If we have to say no, let's remember to whom we are saying no. We are not saying no to Eli Takesian; we are saying no to the Commandant of the Marine Corps. Or Carroll Chambliss, to Naval Material; or Murray Voth, to CINCPACFLT. If they suddenly realize that that is how we are doing business, they might want to back off on some things and rethink them and make sure that they are speaking for whom they have authority to speak, and whether or not they have that authority.

As far as I am concerned, completed staff work is not easily done. I would urge you all to come in with completed staff work. Completed staff work also means that you come in with the solution, not just the problem. Come prepared to say, "Our division recommends that we do such and such because that is at least a possible solution to the problem."

Now let me run through the staff a little bit. One of the changes that I want you all to take note of is that I am going to overwork the deputy. There are some areas of responsibility that the deputy has not been involved in, so let me explain my philosophy concerning the deputy. The deputy will always be called the deputy, and that is all that will appear in anything official, but you should all know that in my mind it is deputy/ chief of staff. The deputy from now on is the Chief of Chaplains when I am not in the office. That is what a deputy is. We agreed in our meeting down at Quantico that as much as possible one of us will be in the office, and Chaplain McNamara can make decisions. If he makes a decision that I am not happy about, it is for him and me to sit down and discuss; but when he makes a decision, as far as I am concerned, the Chief of Chaplain's decision is made. We feel very good about the way we know each other and the way we each think about things and we do not see that this will be any problem whatsoever. All fitness reports, for instance, prepared by the division directors go through the deputy on their way to me. I want the deputy to be involved with all sensitive decisions in regard to individual chaplains or boards. I think it is important for the deputy to know everything that is going on. If he does, there is no reason why he cannot act when I am out of the office.

When somebody is running a fever, would you please stay home and get well and not play martyr and share bugs? I am really quite serious. When you have days like that, just call the office and say, "There is no way I am going to make it in today and be of any good for anybody." Get better and come back. Drink your gatorade and have your aspirin and come back.

The next subject I have is the divisions, and basically I am thinking of five divisions, including administative. I am a great believer in accountability, and the only way in which we can practive accountability is by practicing division integrity. Personnel is G3. If there is a personnel problem, it is G3's problem. He is stuck with it. He is the one who can't sleep at night for worrying about it. It is a difficult thing to do, because at the same time I believe in as much cross fertilization and communication among the staff as at all possible. So it means that you are not only required to have division integrity as to who has the responsibility for some things, but you also have to be aware of who else may be involved. For instance, if we have a personnel problem, G3 has the con because it is a personnel problem. The personnel problem may impact on billets, or may require policy, and that is G2's ball game. And the personnel problem may impact on an ecclestiastical relationship and that is G4's problem. And the way we work our way out of it may have something do say with the way in which we do professional development with some people, and so G1 gets in on the act. And so there is hardly anything that does not impact on everyone, but I want to know who is the lead, who is the point person on the problem, and sometimes that calls for buying and selling. There will be a point at which personnel will say, "Look, I have had the lead on this thing, but personnelwise it is resolved; it remains a problem for this guy's endorsing agent, so I am now selling it to G4. The negotiator and the decision maker on the buying and selling is the deputy.

In the same way, we have a habit of everybody getting involved in policy. G2 is policy. And policy is written policy. Opinion is opinion; policy is policy. Opinions do become policies, but they are not policies until they are written and have the authority of directives. I would hope that the Chief of Chaplains has strong opinions regarding certain things in the Corps, but I think we have to watch out also that we do not mix up opinions and policy. You know me well enough to know that I will not be hesitant about giving my opinion about something. The difference regarding policy is that the written policy authorizes us to really hold someone to it in the Chaplain Corps. Written policy means that it is a part of the chain of command requirement. The Chief of Chaplain's opinion can be overridden by a multitude of people who have command authority over chaplains. If we need to talk more about that kind of thing, we should do so among ourselves.

Everybody knows that I am the last one in the world to keep people from talking to each other; in fact, the more you talk to each other on the staff, the more you share the things you have written, and the more you get critiques from one another the better I like it.

Don't change anything that is on the schedule now, but for working within the office, where possible, please give me all the desk time you can in the morning. If we are to have a meeting or a briefing I would rather we had it in the afternoon. That is a personal wish and a work habit on my part. I like to come in in the morning and go to work and get at those things I have been thinking about at night.

Again, I want you to read the letter. No matter where you go, you will be asked to interpret the decisions we have made in the office. One of the reasons we have a staff meeting every week is to get those kinds of things out on the table. There are very few secrets in the United States Navy Chaplain Corps, as far as I am concerned, aside from personnel matters that impact upon people's private lives. I don't think we have any secret documents and stuff like that. So when you travel around, you have the burden of interpreting what we are doing and what we are trying to do in regard to chaplains. Don't hesitate to do it, but please have the story correct; and the way to do that is to talk it up. If you do not all see it the same way, check with me or with Chaplain McNamara.

Let me talk to you for a minute about O-6s. They have a couple of things on their label that you should be aware of. One says "shake well before using." Another is "handle with care." I have always felt that O-6s in the Chaplain Corps have reached the position, because of our Corps, that is somewhat synonymous with O-7s in the line. Once again, it is a two-edged sword. I really think we should get a lot more out of the O-6s than we are. I will be candid with you and tell you that I think an awful lot of O-6s are forgetting that the O-6 is a position not only of authority, but one of burden and of work. It should be a burden in my estimation. There are a lot of things that an O-6 should do that are not enjoyable. O-6s should be selected because of their potential to be a leader, with a capital "l." That doesn't always mean just placating everybody around you; it means shaking them up and moving them out and making them go many times where they do not want to go. I would like to set up an atmosphere in which I treat the O-6s in the same way in which I have seen Navy leadership treat 07s. Some of our 07 and 08 admiral types, if they were here, would start laughing, because they are not sure they are treated too well. But I will give personal concern to where O-6s are detailed with very specific things in mind as to what I want the individuals to accomplish in the environment we are ordering them to. And I will be corresponding with people along those lines. Newly selected O-6s will largely be given shaft jobs as they are in the line. By that I mean jobs that they are fighting to get, jobs that put them in the forefront of leading the troops. I think we have a reverse motivation going in the Chaplain Corps at times. The guy that is selected for O-7 is the guy who is saying, "Good, give me an assignment that throws me in the briar brush." That is the way I think about O-6s, particularly those who have just made O-6. I would imagine that they want a hot job that they can run and prove their stuff with. So again, if you are doing any interpreting and so forth, I do not expect O-6s to earn the salaries they make by sitting on the Autovon all day long, but I expect us to see results from what they do and I expect them to take charge of people of the areas in which they have responsibility. I'm preaching to the choir here this afternoon, and I know that, but the O-6 is the guy who sets the example. In the Navy and the Marine Corps, he is the one who goes out and leads the troops. The O-6 should be the first one to come up with an innovative idea and the first one to walk it through the mine field.

Let me talk a little bit about decisions, and I am not talking about this staff so much as I am talking about things we need to do for our Corps. There is an awful lot of thinking in the Corps that the office of the Chief of Chaplains exists to serve chaplains, and I think we all understand that. But I think we are trapped sometimes by that kind of thinking throughout the Chaplain Corps. We all exist to serve Navy, Marine Corps, and Coast Guard personnel. We do not exist in this office as an organization just to serve chaplains. We are supposed to be doing those things which make ministry most effective and available to personnel. That is a little bit of a jump and if you can help to put that across to our brothers and sisters in the Corps, fine. We are not a retired officers' association that meets the needs of our constituency. Our constituency is every member of the Navy, Marine Corps, and Coast Guard. It is true that if we meet certain needs for chaplains the end product is that they are able to do a better job for service personnel, and that is what it is all about. That's fine. But our whole intent is not just to take care of chaplains.

Along that line the rule of Admiral Zech and others is, and the more you can push this for our brethren, the more they will like it--I'll be pushing it--decisions are made at a specific time. The decision that is made is totally dependent upon the information that is available. So the more information we have, hopefully the better decision we can make. If there is a claimant chaplain out there who has information that he has not shared with this office, then he has to realize that he contributed to whatever decision was made by not sharing his information. We do not need anyone telling us that we sent the wrong guy to Diego Garcia, and we say "why?" and he says, "Well, don't you know. . .?" No. The next question is, "If you knew, why did you not make us aware of it? Why did you put us in the position of making a bad decision because you held back information?" If there is information regarding chaplains and the Chaplain Corps, the office of the Chief of Chaplains ought to know about it. If there is information in any of the divisions in the office of the Chief of Chaplains that needs to be known, again that is why we have the staff conference, if it is public information. If it is extremely private information, the detailer is in the office and that kind of information needs to be shared with him. We get all the information we can before making a decision. We work against the delaying of the making of decisions. We must make them promptly in order to stay up with bureaucracy. And then after we have made a decision, we support it. If it's really a bad decision, we'll just have to change it.

The news media. I am not interested in any publicity whatsoever. Now each of you is in a position where you may be called upon by the news media at some time or other regarding the making of a statement. Please know that my basic view toward the news media is that there is absolutely no advantage whatsoever to the Chaplain Corps from the news media. We might get a call tomorrow from the Presbyterian Church saying, "We now have a Chief of Chaplains who is a Presbyterian. Why don't we do a nice big article on him?" The answer to that is not to argue with them, not to debate with them, but simply to say that Neil Stevenson is rather ugly and chooses not to be interviewed. I really haven't got the time and I haven't read anything in the last ten years that in my opinion helped the Chaplain Corps. If it were the best article possible, putting the Chaplain Corps in best light possible, you still have done nothing except wave a flag before a bunch of people who had forgotten about the Chaplain Corps, and are now reminded, and who say, "Yes, that's a part of the military establishment and let's get rid of that darn thing too." And so what advantage is it to the Chaplain Corps? The Chaplain Corps has a thousand and fifty chaplains on active duty every day ministering to people, giving them the sacraments, preaching the Word, calling on them in the hospital. That's all being done without any help from the news media. My personal view is that I just don't see any need for it.

I had a warning from a friend this morning who knows bureaucracy rather well and he said, "Watch out for the news media." He said, "This coming election is going to be a feast day for everything in government. So stand by." I believe in the old adage that if you say to the news media, "No comment," you look like a dummy for one day; if you say anything past "no comment" you look like a dummy for a month, so I would just as soon look like a dummy for a day. (laughter)

About internal publicity. The Chief of Chaplain showed up at Camp Lejeune and so they want to put something in the newspaper at Camp Lejeune. Fine.

I also have no desire ever, and I would hope most chaplains have no desire ever, to comment on the internal policies of a faith group. Their internal policies are their business, not the business of the Chief of Chaplains. If the Presbyterian Church decides to send an army to the aid of the rebels in El Salvador, that is the Presbyterian Church's business, and I will say what I want to say on the floor of the Presbytery, not outside the Presbytery.

Now in regard to any of these things that I have talked about, I would urge you to talk to me about them now or to talk with me privately over the next week or so. As you can see, I've done some thinking about these things and I have made up my mind. I just want every member of the staff to know where my thinking and feeling are on a lot of these things.

To people who have been for a long time on the staff and those who are new to the staff, a couple of words of warning. Chaplains are used to trying to help people as much as possible. The Army has itself involved in a constitutional dispute because Army chaplains who were working in the office of the Army Chief of Chaplains thought they should help somebody who asked for help. So, as you well know, the Army gave away the store and ended up being sued. So be very careful whom you talk to, and what you say to them on the phone. I'm not trying to scare anybody, but I feel like I'm talking to my relief when my relief got to Vietnam. There are just some things that you have to tell somebody about the new territory. If somebody calls and says, "Yes, but I have a deadline; I must have this information right away," you think about it. The answer might still be, "Fine, you write to us requesting the information, and we will provide it." "But I must have it right away!" "Then you call Neil Stevenson. He's the one who told me to get it in writing." We get very anxious about being quick to help people and we find that we get right behind the eight ball. This is particularly true in regard to somebody trying to find out something about somebody. Don't respond very quickly to giving away the family secrets, or any information.

There is information that we do not have and we do not want. At least we do not want it in the next year or so; I will tell you that. The Air Force is bragging that the computer system is going to make it possible for them to add up rather quickly the cost of all their religious programs. I hope we will never have that kind of information, because we have saved the day a multitude of times because we do not have that information. We do not have any idea what religion costs the United States Navy. We don't have any inclination to add it up. We would just get ourselves in a bind.

It takes a while to become acclimated to this kind of an environment, and I don't want to turn you all paranoid or to make you suspicious, but in this environment in particular business is business and you must do it in a business-like fashion.

As I've said, as far as I am concerned, the majority of information we have is open information, but when we do have something that you think may have some confidentiality about it, I naturally expect that there will be no leaks. Chaplain O'Donnell is well versed to give you a briefing on how to handle the Freedom of Information Act, and what the requirements are for the Privacy Act, so please don't fall into any of those traps. In many cases, when people want information it is available to them so long as they are willing to pay the price, and we go to the proper authorities in the government and then go back to them and tell them how much it would cost to get that much information.

When we have our staff meetings, please keep in mind that it is just as important, in fact more important, to talk about what is about to take place in the future as what has happened in the past. It's when we talk about the future that the ears of our associates perk up and they begin to realize that they are a part of that action. That is the time that they can remind us that we might have left them out of the thinking as we make that approach to a situation.

Also, I hope that there is a spirit that meetings are for guidance, not just for concurrence. You don't have to go to

Chaplain McNamara just to get an approval, you go to Chaplain McNamara or to Neil Stevenson to say, "Have you ever dealt with this before?" or "Which way do you think we ought to go?" A pet concern of mine--and this will probably cause some problems for folks--I would like to have all correspondence serialized. I've been in enough binds trying to find a piece of paper here and there, and we have had several sections where we are not serialized. For me also, Mary Martha, let's serialize all the Chief of Chaplain's correspondence unless it is one of those rare pieces of paper that deals with a very sensitive private matter. For that reason, I have asked that all correspondence coming into the office be tickled and that the action officers be the division directors and the division directors can hand out the correspondence, assigning it to whomever they desire, but then I know to what division it went, but if the division directors want to buy and sell that is all right with me too, as long as the division director gets back to Admin and tells Admin, "I sold this to G4" or "I sold this to G3." But when we want to know what response we made to somebody, we have it all going out from Admin where it will be serialized, not in the divisions but by Admin, so we have a track on it there.

Tell your friends that if they are writing to you personally, to put "personal" on the envelope and then it will go to you. We have tried ever since Cy Rotrige to convince chaplains that you should write to an office by the title of the office, not to the individual person. And I would say that the Chief of Chaplains is as guilty of that as any one place I know. I would urge you that when you write to the PACFLT chaplain you would address the envelope to the PACFLT chaplain, not to Murray Voth; when you write to the LANTFLT chaplain that you write to the LANTFLT chaplain, not to Larry Keefe. I used to get so ticked off as a fleet chaplain when I would come back to find a pile of mail that no one would open because it said Neil Stevenson.

As far as I'm concerned, stuff that comes into the office is work. Admin will open it, assign it to one of the divisions, and if you have a friend out there in the Corps who is writing to you about working a deal with Walt Hiskett to get him a special set of orders, tell him to be wise enough to write "personal" on the envelope or Admin is apt to open it up and say that it's a detail problem and send it direct to G3 for action. And then the guy ends up more behind the eight ball than he was ever before in his life. (laughter)

I'm just trying to move paper work, and I feel that coming in and going out, it will work a lot better that way.

Please don't fall into denominational traps. What do I mean by that? I mean that because you are the "duty Presbyterian" on the staff you get a call from the Presbyterians. That is not the way the Navy Chaplain Corps works. You are not on this staff because of your denomination. This is not, as Chaplain Trower has said many times, "the house of representatives." (chuckles) It is the staff of the Chief of Chaplains. It has to be played that way because you can get into all kinds of hassles where someone is calling and asking, "Who is the duty Latter Day Saint?" "Who is the duty Seventh Day Adventist?" "Who is the duty rabbi?" Crazy. We have to respond to everybody. They all belong to us. They are all part of the Chaplain Corps. We might think that that is rather unique, but I have heard Admiral Zech on many occasions remind people that he is not the submarine warfare officer of the Navy--that he is the air warfare officer, the surface warfare officer, and the submarine warfare officer. So in case you get into a rough time with somebody, you have my permission to repeat my remarks to them and also to tell them that I am professional development, that I am policy, programs and budget, that I am the detailer, and that I am ecclesiastical relations and recruiting. Most of the fuss comes with detailing, from my experience, the E. F. Hutton syndrome of the Chaplain Corps; and many, many times people have talked as though they did not realize that they were talking to the detailer. I have heard chaplains say that the detailer is a dummy, and this is an insult to the Chief of Chaplains, who is the detailer. And so it goes with policy and everything else.

I am not a good proofreader, and I will rely on everybody else, division directors and Admin, to do proofreading for me. Letters are supposed to be brief and I know that to many of you that will be a big laugh, particularly when you open my first letter that is four pages long. (laughter)

I think that one of the things that we ought to remember is that the Chaplain Corps should not be different from the Navy. I think it is a very, very bad thing when we allow our chaplains to kind of get the feeling that the Navy is one thing and the Chaplain Corps is another. The way in which the Navy does business should be the way in which the Chaplain Corps does business. And in the long run that makes the chaplains better able to serve the people in the Navy. It's the old story that forty guys whose wives overspent from the checkbook could not come back from the Indian Ocean, because that is not an excuse under the Navy system for somebody to get emergency leave. But a chaplain can come back on emergency leave because his wife did. It's ridiculous! Fifty guys on a deployment cannot come home because their wives are having a baby, but the chaplain comes home. All those things are just ludicrous, the way we do business.

Now, a few items that you probably already know about, but I mention them just to know that I have mentioned them. We shall be picking up as a staff for the major claimant meeting 12-16 September. It will be a meeting in which we will be dealing largely with Chaplain Corps policy. We will spend a lot of time talking about the practices and procedures of the way things should be done in a thousand plus active duty Chaplain Corps. Talking a lot about what claimant chaplains should be doing and what we expect of them and the high regard in which we hold them. When the meeting is over, I will be traveling around with Chaplain Koeneman and Chaplain Wright to half a dozen or more spots throughout CONUS to spend an entire day with 0-6 chaplains to explain to them in detail the same things in kind of a one-day claimant meeting. Chaplain Wright will explain some of the complications of detailing so they as 0-6s can be leaders and get out and explain some of the problems to people, not just sit and hold hands with people. Chaplain Koeneman will explain the manpower and policy business to them, and then I shall answer any questions and square them away on some of the things we expect in the way of leadership from 0-6s.

On the second of October we shall have the service at the Mother Seton Shrine. To those of you who haven't been to it, I haven't talked to anyone yet who hasn't received a blessing out of seeing the shrine and participating in the service. If you can at all make that afternoon available to you and to your family to attend that service, I would recommend it.

We have a Service for the Navy on the sixteenth of October at the National Cathedral that is somewhat similar. The service at the Seton Shrine is sponsored and conducted by the Shrine; the service at the Cathedral is sponsored and conducted by the Cathedral, but we become participants and active in it and the Navy expects us to be active in both services.

I have asked this year that after the Cathedral service there be. . . Let me give you a bit of history. Years ago we used to have a Chaplain Corps anniversary in this town in which we invited the CNO and the Commandant of the Marine Corps and others, and I can personally verify for you ten years in which it was a total disaster. Mary Martha can verify twenty years in which it was a disaster. We are the only outfit I know of that so insulted the Secretary of the Navy that he walked out of the dinner. You really have to go far in order to have that kind of record in this town. And the Chief of Chaplain's staff got tied up in running the thing, which was also a pain in the neck. Now we have a nice system in which the chaplains in the area take turns. This year it is at Quantico, and it will be on Saturday night, the third of December. Chaplain Kaiser has promised us a great evening of eating and dancing and enjoying ourselves in a real birthday party atmosphere, and for those who want to stay overnight in Quantico, he will even arrange BOQ space.

The time of the heads of the services is so precious, that we just lay a burden on them by inviting them and they try to be polite and to show up. And it has been a disaster. And so what we have been doing is having a sherry hour after the service at the Cathedral and we have invited all these folks to come and have cheese and sherry and fruit and so forth, and that is our Navy celebration and that doesn't obligate them for more than an hour after the service, and I think they feel more free about that. This year we shall have it in a larger space, and I want to be sure that all the chaplains in the area who are participating in the processional and in the service are invited.

I have really appreciated the willingness of this staff to attend the Navy Ball. I think everybody has made a good evening of it whether they are dancers or not. It is certainly the night in town to see all kinds of folks. I can tell you quite frankly that the Chaplain Corps has made a lot of nickels out of the willingness of members of this staff and chaplains in the Washington area to attend that ball. The large contingency of chaplains is looked upon with a great deal of favor.

Chaplain McNamara, do you have anything you want to say?

Chaplain McNamara: It occurred to me while you were speaking that probably given the leadership and talent that are here, the only way in which we could fail would be through some self-inflicted wound. I remember that before when I was here--I am not reflecting so much on the present--there were times when the tensions between the divisions were such that it became a little self defeating. I don't think that is anything to go into with any kind of detail, but just in terms of the overall picture as I hear you talking about total openness, which will require a complete spirit of teamwork. Although little tensions and rivalries are often constructive, the whole thing will work beautifully if there are no self-inflicted wounds such as too much rivalry. I hope that that is sufficiently clear.

Chaplain Stevenson: Buying and selling can be an annoyance. Some things come down in very narrow lines. "Why should our shop have to deal with that?" "Why don't you deal with it?" Sometimes you have to have someone resolve it.

Sometimes the person who has the con on something, like everywhere else in the Navy and the Marine Corps, is waiting for other people's inputs in order to make the complete package. But I hope we don't ever go back to those days that I have seen in the office that were so horrible that some persons stayed after work to read what was in everybody else's in-baskets and out-baskets.

I was very concerned that the cut of the cards was that the four division directors would leave, all at basically the same time. I told Diane last week that I thought that the staff that we have had during the past three years, in work and in relationships, really has been head and shoulders above anything we had in the sixties and seventies when I was here. As I was telling Diane last week, to me it's been a very comfortable thing to see four new division directors come in and take over, really take charge, recognizing the fact that they have it, and I feel very comfortable about it.

I think it's very helpful also to have a deputy who has been in one end of the business in which I was never involved--I was never trusted in the detailing shop! (laughter)

(Brief general discussion)[1]

I hope it's going to be an interesting cruise. The Commandant of the Coast Guard said some awfully nice things today, not only about the change of office ceremony, not just about chaplains in general, but very specific things about the twenty chaplains that he has, including Chaplain Moran--what they are doing and what he hopes to do, and I presented to him the package that you have all been involved in putting together. He seemed pleased that he got the package and that the Coast Guard is mentioned in the instruction. It was just a good test for me before I go to meet the VCNO tomorrow morning and the Commandant of the Marine Corps on Wednesday and get all these official calls out of the way.

Chaplain McNamara and I will be calling on a number of people around town in the month of August. We are also hoping to run up to New York one day and call on some endorsing agents. We also hope to spend one day in August seeing some endorsing agents in the Washington area. A lot of those calls are going to be more than courtesy calls. We will be talking to 02, 03, 04, and 05 about business.

Please don't let rumors get started in the Chaplain Corps. If you can get information out in the 0-6 Minutes and the Navy Chaplains Bulletin, please do so. Drown them in information.

Endorsing agents are very important. They do not, in large measure, understand the system. It is our job to help them understand and to be friendly with them. . . I intend to work with them closely.

(Renewed general discussion, with friendly banter)[1]

God bless. I really hope it will be a lot of fun. I have always hoped that the Chief of Chaplain's staff could accept and take upon itself all the burdens of the USS SARATOGA but at the same time have as much fun as the guys who serve in something like the SARATOGA. That's basically what it's all about. Thanks a lot.

---

[1]Notes from general discussion: (1) Compliment your staff members and others who do good work. It is often best to write letters to a person's senior with a copy being sent to him.

(2) The Chief of Chaplains prefers to talk personally with staff members about proposed matters of policy and guidance, and then have them written in appropriate format, rather than beginning with carefully worded background statements and statements of purpose.

(3) Staff meetings may be held when both the Chief of Chaplains and the Deputy Chief of Chaplains will be away (an infrequent occurrence). The senior officer present will preside.

(4) The Chief of Chaplains and the Deputy Chief of Chaplains will be glad to make personal calls upon those in other offices in situations that might be of benefit to the staff.

THIS LETTER WENT TO ALL CAPTAINS ON ACTIVE DUTY

OP-09G-mr
Ser 3270
1 October 1983

Dear Chaplain

This is an appropriate time for me to share my policy regarding the assignment of Captains in our Corps. I'm certain it is a subject of interest to you in both its personal and professional parameters. I am basically using the method by which Flag officers are detailed. Let me assure you it is an area of my responsibilities to which I devote considerable thought and effort. I recognize that the decisions made have a direct effect on the vitality of ministry in the present and become the foundation of the leadership of the Corps in the future.

Basically the assignment process is pragmatic. I am looking for the chaplain with the best qualifications for a given job weighing the requirements of the billet, its past and present significance, and future potential in relation to the Captain I consider most suited to get the job done.

This decision process is influenced by several administrative and technical requirements that I feel are essential for you to know:

- Provision for adequate flow through the system to prevent stagnation and maintain challenge as well as to provide incentive for less senior chaplains.

- Provision of specific supervision experience and particular work climates in order to make more candidates better equipped for future assignments.

1 October 1983

- Utilization of individual abilities and talents for unique assignments.

- Flexibility to respond to unanticipated assignment needs imposed by illness, unplanned retirement requests, etc.

- Compliance with the existing regulations regarding the detailing of officers, especially the status of PCS funds, etc.

- Acceptance for an assignment which by tradition and courtesy requires me to nominate a candidate for the position. (It can be appreciated that these procedures are in many cases time-consuming and occasionally the assignment is not revealed to the individual concerned until appropriate confirmation has been received.)

- Accommodation to personal and family problems as they arise. It is essential that I have current information prior to decision making. In this area I am particularly sensitive to the needs of members of the Chaplain Corps community as well as conscious of the policies regarding similar circumstances on all members of the naval service.

It is my sincere hope that this sharing of the practical aspects of the assignment process will encourage you to communicate with this office regarding your plans. Written correspondence in the form of the preference card and/or letter serves the individual chaplain better than the telephone as an instrument of communication.

1 October 1983

When I'm prepared to nominate you for orders I'll write to notify you of my intentions. As a leader of our Corps dedicated to ministry to God's people in the naval service you should have that courtesy.

Sincerely,

NEIL M. STEVENSON
Rear Admiral, CHC, USN

Captain Walter A. Hiskett, CHC, USN
Director, Distribution & Placement
 Division (OP-09G3)
Office of the Chief of Chaplains
Washington, DC 20350

AN INTERVIEW

WITH

THE NAVY CHIEF OF CHAPLAINS

Published and distributed by:
Chaplain Resource Board
6500 Hampton Boulevard
Norfolk, VA 23508

DEPARTMENT OF THE NAVY
OFFICE OF THE CHIEF OF NAVAL OPERATIONS
WASHINGTON, D.C. 20350

IN REPLY REFER TO

Chief of Chaplains

Dear Chaplain,

As I trust you are aware, the printing hassles imposed on the Washington scene this last year have been horrendous. You've seen the results of it, in spite of the hard work of the staff, in the Chaplains Bulletin June 1983 coming to you as an "historical piece" in January of 1984. By the way, it still has good stuff in it as well as O.B.E. data. Well, Chaplain Ron Apgar interviewed me, as it were, on your behalf, when I became Chief of Chaplains. The article was to be distributed in the September 1983 issue of the Chaplains Bulletin. The Chaplain Resource Board has rescued the interview from the printing quagmire because they think it has value to establish dialogue between us and our profession. I hope they are right, because I'd be pleased to discuss each item with you when we meet at table around the world.

Thanks CRB, for getting the article on the streets and I hope, Chaplain, you will discuss its contents with me when I see you.

Sincerely,

Neil

NEIL M. STEVENSON
Rear Admiral, CHC, USN

Reviewed and approved 9 December 1983
                        (Date)

Hugh J. Lecky Jr.
(Signature, Reviewing Official)

Published in accordance with
SECNAVINST 5430

Interview

Apgar – Would you comment on how you find the Washington scene as you enter the Chief's office?

Stevenson – Washington is an extremely demanding environment, which is nothing new to chaplains. It's just that the demands come in an entirely different context in D.C.; void, I might add, of the kinds of compensation that you get from working in a ship or a station with people. Washington is in many ways like Wall Street -- it moves from bearish to bullish and vice versa. The Chief of Chaplains' staff (the snipes keeping the turns on, as I refer to them) have to be responsive from day to day with the way the market's going. I hope that there is a great familiarity throughout the Corps now with the Washington scene, i.e., the fact that the detailer has to fight for PCS funds, that the G2 shop has the tedious responsibility of maintaining 410X and RP billets, budgets, MILCOM, etc.

Apgar – Could you tell us how you feel about being the Chief of Chaplains?

Stevenson – Well, it feels good. I feel it's a good time to get things done. Having worked for four Chiefs of Chaplains, Chaplains Kelly, Garrett, O'Connor and Trower, I know that it's an interesting job. Like all of the jobs in our Chaplains Corps, it has both good days and bad days. I just hope most of mine will be good days.

Apgar – I find it interesting that you use the word "job" to describe the position. Would you want to say anything about that?

Stevenson – I suppose you could call it an assignment or something other than "job" if you wish. Remember, any set of orders is a statement that higher authority is convinced that you can do the job. That goes for your orders, Ron, as well as mine.

Apgar – What is your impression of the Chaplain Corps?

Stevenson – I'm very proud of our Chaplain Corps. I'm convinced that across the board our chaplains are the best clergy in the United States. As I stated at the Change of Office, the task before us is to <u>make the best better</u>. Of course, it's my good fortune to go from the Office of the Deputy into the Office of the Chief. I've had three years to appreciate what chaplains are doing all around this global village and it's impressive. I wish our civilian peers could observe the ministry being done in ships or in Marine units, or in isolated duty stations. They'd be surprised at how professionally it's done, with what dedication it is pursued, and how grateful people are.

Apgar – How many years have you served as a Navy chaplain and what have you learned most about doing ministry within a military environment?

Stevenson – Using DOPMA calculations, I've been a Navy chaplain 27½ years and the most important thing I've learned in those years about ministry is the term you used, "military environment." We minister best anywhere when we are able to recognize where we are, who we serve and that we are accountable for ministering there to them. Let me put it another way, I'm not pastoring a Presbyterian Church in Fruit Jar Junction, or a Presbyterian Church in Brooklyn. I am ministering to people in the sea services (Navy, Marine Corps, Coast Guard, Merchant Marine) and their families. I'm available to a total spectrum of American citizens.

I'm the chaplain their parents told them about when they left home with the words, "If you have a problem, go see the chaplain." That's a rather special trust and confidence. The Chaplain Corps does not exist for chaplains but for service people.

Apgar – It's along these same lines of environmental observations that you remind chaplains that the uniform is identified with work in the Navy, isn't it?

Stevenson – Yes, it's good of you to remember that. I'm always aware of the increased emotional heartbeat of some chaplains when I get on that subject. Nevertheless, in the sea services the uniform is associated with duty (work), vestments with worship, and civilian attire with liberty. Those kinds of non-verbals remain constant and I think a chaplain is wise to recognize them. I guess I should say regarding vestments that Rabbis and Priests have an advantage, but the minister can help many of the chapel attendees by just wearing a robe or stole. It often is just a reassurance to pew sitters that a Navy chaplain is officiating. Maybe you should just repeat the statement I put in a previous O-6 minutes.

Apgar – Along this same line would you say something about days off?

Stevenson – Is that a personal plea, Ron? (Laughter). Well, who ever heard anyone in the Navy talk about a day off. Rope Yarn, yes – but day off, no. Day off is in my experience a seminary, parish, civilian clergy expression that we inappropriately carry into Navy circles. It is not understood or appreciated. In sea service environs, those who stand CDO watches don't get a day off; those who come to work before 0800 or stay long after 1630 don't get compensatory time off; those who take leave don't get to deduct weekends, etc. However, they might pull a rope yarn from time to time. Again, I really think we need to relate to the environment in which we minister and to beware we are not playing civilian in uniform.

Apgar – Any other environmental observations?

Stevenson – How about one more. Chapel councils have advantages but in many cases they limit the chaplain's ministry because the chaplain begins to act as though he/she is responsible for a civilian parish vice a command religious program. The council becomes synonymous with a church board which is "inner-oriented" and their recommendations are confined, as they should be, to the chapel program. The problem comes when the chaplain feels he/she is meeting his/her requirements by responding to the chapel council which is merely one part of the chaplain's responsibilities. It reminds me of a sea story. "A chaplain years ago was running a needs-analysis survey, but only distributed the instruments to chapel attendees. He automatically truncated his ministry to the people of that command."

Apgar – You often use the terms "institutional" vice "parish" ministry. Would you say something about your view of the distinction between these two?

Stevenson – In the parish you are more or less the shepherd of your own sheep, while in the institutional setting you are just as responsible for your own, but "other sheep have you also." Again, it's part of coming to grips with the environment -- the distinction is as much common sense as it is academic. Parish usually implies that the parishioners had something to do with selecting you to be there, that you exclusively serve the adherents of that particular faith group and that you act as a representative of that group. It can be best illustrated from a professional perspective as being in "private practice". Institutional ministry implies public practice in which the professional has chosen to place him or herself in a position of accountability to a larger public domain, under authorities other than just one's own faith group. For example, the institutional chaplain works for the president of a university, or the board of directors of a hospital, or in our case, a commanding officer. Institutional ministry also obligates the individual to be available to a larger spectrum of the society. The best illustration would be the sailor who does not have any religious affiliation whatsoever, but certainly has every right to see the chaplain about a problem.

Apgar – What personal characteristics are necessary for a chaplain to have a successful ministry within institutional ministry?

Stevenson – Well, many characteristics, but let me mention those that come quickly to mind. First, the chaplain exhibits the belief of ordination --he/she is a person of faith, a person who professes faith. Then, the chaplain must have a strong sense of personal identity. I think the Hebrew word for comfort has something to do with strength. Chaplains have to be comfortable with themselves and not be running around trying to find out who they are. The chaplain must be comfortable being a clergy person. I suppose, to put it in bold print, I would say that a chaplain does not have the luxury of either an identity crisis or role conflict. The institutional environment hires the person to do the job and expects that person to exhibit the requirements of the profession.

Apgar - But you're not saying that doctors never get sick are you?

Stevenson - Of course not! But when they get ill the wise doctor has another physician prescribe a cure, and the doctor is responsible to know who his/her physician is -- just as any clergy person should know who his/her pastor is. If I were a doctor and said I'm not certain about who I am, I'm questioning whether or not I should be a physician, which says, "I'm not comfortable with practicing medicine in this place." One would greatly doubt the advisability of the hospital having such a doctor on the staff. The expectations of the clients served by the institution are that the professional has the credentials and the obligation to do the job.

Apgar - You use the term "professional" a great deal - would you like to say anything about your use of that word?

Stevenson - Well, as you point out, I do use it alot because I think it's a very important concept. The term speaks to our own standing among our peers and the perception the military has regarding our qualifications and performance. I find clergy who express a kind of false humility and that implies that they are not professional -- you know, they are just good ole boys. Well, the real world's response to that is, "Who needs you?" Why pay you as a professional to do a professional job, if you are not a professional?" Another essential quality about being a professional in a profession, is that those who are members of the profession are eligible to debate and discuss things esoteric to their profession. They don't criticize each other in front of the uninitiated.

Apgar - Let's turn our conversation from clergy in general to one specific issue of the Chaplain Corps. You used to joke that when you were the Deputy that if you were selected as Chief, the first thing you would do is buy some wire clippers and cut the phones out of the detailing shop.

Stevenson - I guess that's the first campaign promise that I've broken (laughter). On the serious side, Ron, I have directed the detailers in the G3 shop (and I would make the same request to all chaplains) to reduce the phone calls, to reduce traffic in and out of that division. It's my view that the excessive availability of the phone has worked to the disadvantage of all. Detailers need time to battle for PCS funds, to work up constant resubmission of budgets, to spend time on policy issues, to develop long range detailing plans, and to investigate placement requirements. Besides, the phone is not a good communications tool - phone conversations are too subject to interpretation depending on what's happening when the phone rings. If you ever had to answer your kitchen phone when the soup is boiling over you know what I mean.

Apgar - Do you have any advice for chaplains in regard to detailing?

Stevenson - Yes, make sure that your preference card reflects <u>your preference</u>, and that you provide on that preference card all the professional and personal information that you want the detailer to know in the decision making process. Let me also say something specifically about being timely, since it's one of my major emphases on management. <u>Decisions are made on the basis of information known at the time the decision is made.</u> So it's essential to get all the data in prior to the time of decision. It's the same thing that I've heard Admiral Zech speak of many times and reflects the way in which the Navy does business. It's the business of everyone to provide all the information possible before the decision is made and to support the decision after it's made. There are two other things I want to say about the "E. F. Hutton" world. First, the priority will always be the needs of the Naval services. Second, all those receiving orders are subject to the luck of the draw. That means that a set of orders can lead you into a command where there is a congeniality or where there is a personality clash, where you feel comfortable from the outset or where you go through an agonizing period of culture shock. Those are part of the impositions of life that come with the territory. This, by the way, is true of all who serve in the military and we ought to be mindful of it in our ministry. The advantage of our vocation is that we ought to know more about it and how to handle it.

Apgar - You've said from time to time that you believe in a dual standard and expect more of chaplains than you do of others.

Stevenson - I plead guilty. Ordination places a burden on the recipient. It brings to mind an old illustration that was used by Dr. Russ Hutchinson, my college chaplain and a WWII Navy Chaplain. He talked about a ladder going up to a burning building where a civilian was climbing down and a fireman was climbing up. That represented the reality in life. It was the civilian's obligation to get out of the building; it was the fireman's obligation to get into the building. That's a dual or double standard. Occasionally, I hear someone say it wouldn't bother them if a non-chaplain did that, so why get upset if a chaplain does it. Well, for me the answer is that a non-chaplain might do it and not lose professional credibility, whereas a chaplain does. The good news is that the vast majority of chaplains carry the standard day in and day out, in an outstanding fashion.

Apgar - Everywhere you have served, planning books have been used. Every chaplain in the Corps has them since you came to Washington. Would you care to say a word about the purpose of planning books?

Stevenson – I don't see how anyone can get a job done without a plan. Program objectives must be defined and funding identified, whether it be $10.00 or $10,000.00. (By the way, contrary to the rumor I hear -- I'm not interested in how large the sum of money is. I'm interested in the results of the programming). Planning books provide reasonable means for chaplains to plan and evaluate their ministry. When effectively used, planning books allow the chaplain to chart a course for the Command Religious Program that communicates to the commanding officer: identifying the needs of the people, implementing a course of action, measuring the program and projecting the results. This approach is professional and gives the chaplain the means to both brief and advise with expertise. Yes, I will expect to see planning books being used and I will anticipate that Claimant Chaplains and Force Chaplains will be anxious to see them as the initial part of all the briefings they receive when they visit their chaplains.

Apgar – What is the relationship or role of the Claimant Chaplain?

Stevenson – Major Claimant Staff Chaplains are those key individuals who are primary advisors to the Chief of Chaplains; supervisors of all chaplains within their claimancy; managers of Chaplain Corps resources, i.e. the billets within the claimancy; inspectors of command religious programs within the claimancy and above all, the Claimants' chaplain. I could say a great deal more, but perhaps the most important thing to be said is that Force Chaplains and their equivalents are to the Claimant Chaplains what Claimant Chaplains are to the Chief of Chaplains. A great deal of consideration is given as to who will be put into claimant positions. The task is to assign a chaplain who by experience is capable of advising chaplains, by personality is capable of leading chaplains, by administrative knowledge is capable of executing organizational requirements and who frankly needs the opportunity to show his or her potential.

Apgar – Are there what you would call "Career Enhancing" Assignments?

Stevenson – If you deal with fact, rather than myth in relationship to those words, the answer is yes. Let me distinguish for you. If you deal with the fact that every assignment has the potential of being career enhancing depending on what the professional does with the job -- the answer is yes! If you're looking for some mythical formula that automatically leads to promotion by just getting detailed to the "right billet", then the answer would be no! I might also add that you cannot predict on what billet the spotlight will shine. Today it's on our chaplains who are doing a magnificent job in Lebanon. What unit with what chaplains it will hit tomorrow, I haven't the slightest. Really, it is within the luck of the draw. You can only give it all you've got where you are, which is what a pro does anyhow.

Apgar - When you are traveling and visiting chaplains, what kind of information do you hope to learn?

Stevenson - As you know, I don't believe in traveling without specific agenda. I expect local supervisory chaplains in conjunction with the Force or Major Claimant Chaplains to set the right agenda. The proper courtesy calls are to be made, briefings on the Command's Religious Program provided, and time allocated for me to brief chaplains on what is going on throughout the Washington arena and the Chaplain Corps.

Apgar - As someone who has served three tours in the Washington, D.C. area, what advice can you give chaplains about working within the Navy system?

Stevenson - (Laughter) Well, let me say two things. First of all, the Navy system _is_ the Navy. It's not esoteric to Washington, D.C. Secondly, what other _system_ is there? My answer is related to what I was discussing earlier about environment. It is as uncomplicated as looking in the mirror and seeing yourself in uniform. Every element of the United States Navy is expected to operate within the Navy's system and to be in tune with the changes and modifications within that system.

You know Ron, chaplains have to be three dimensional performers. We have to know how to call on command resources, personal strength and God's grace to meet the needs of those to whom we minister. To push that concept one step forward, it means to brief the command on the value of the program, to maintain your own spiritual disciplines and not hesitate to call on the name of the Lord for others and for yourself.

Apgar - Well, to be more specific, isn't it essential that all chaplains be familiar with PPBS (plan program budgeting system), etc.?

Stevenson - Of course, but I would hope that this would be so much the normal course of everyday business or such common tools that they are taken for granted as the necessary processes for getting the job done. The job is ministry.

Apgar - I came across a piece of correspondence sometime back signed by Chaplain (Bishop) O'Connor in which he listed some of his idiosyncrasies and asked members of the Chaplain Corps to allow the senior man the privilege of his idiosyncrasies. Do you have any idiosyncrasies?

Stevenson - Their name is legion - do you really want me to recite some?

Apgar - (Laughter). Yes, please do.

Stevenson - I don't enjoy head tables where there isn't anyone across the table to talk to. I get concerned about chaplains who call me Admiral and don't seem to know the privilege we share; namely, that at any rank we are referred to as Chaplain. I also want people who are in charge to take charge. I like leaders to lead. I don't believe in "in and out" baskets. Admin responsibilities should be shared by an entire chaplain department rather than one chaplain. Even better, the senior RP can be assigned the admin responsibility. I dislike chaplains incorrectly pronouncing Chaplain Corps as the Chaplain's Corps. We don't own it! I suppose a final one would be that I don't like poor preparations for divine services as evidenced by blowing in the mikes, or searching for hymnals, or looking for a Bible, or deciding where to be seated at the last minute. Are there any of my idiosyncrasies you would like to mention Ron?

Apgar - Well, I thought you might mention the fact that you don't like to travel or go sightseeing, but you do like to play tennis and dance (laughter).

Stevenson - Tennis and dancing for me, Ron, are not idiosyncrasies -- they're necessities!! Which reminds me that all chaplains should read ZORBA. It says a lot about ministry to sailors and marines.

Apgar - Let's close out on a serious note. What do you expect chaplains to be doing?

Stevenson - That's easy: consistently conduct divine services for their faith group whether anyone shows up or not; facilitate services for other major faith groups; be visible and available to everyone in your command and other commands in the area; train RPs properly and use them extensively; brief command on your plan and programs for the command religious program; know the chain of command and above all, enjoy our profession.

Apgar - Chaplain Stevenson, thank you for the interview.

Stevenson - Thank you, Ron. Now I hope chaplains will ask questions about these items we've discussed as I travel about the Corps.

YOUR CHAPLAIN

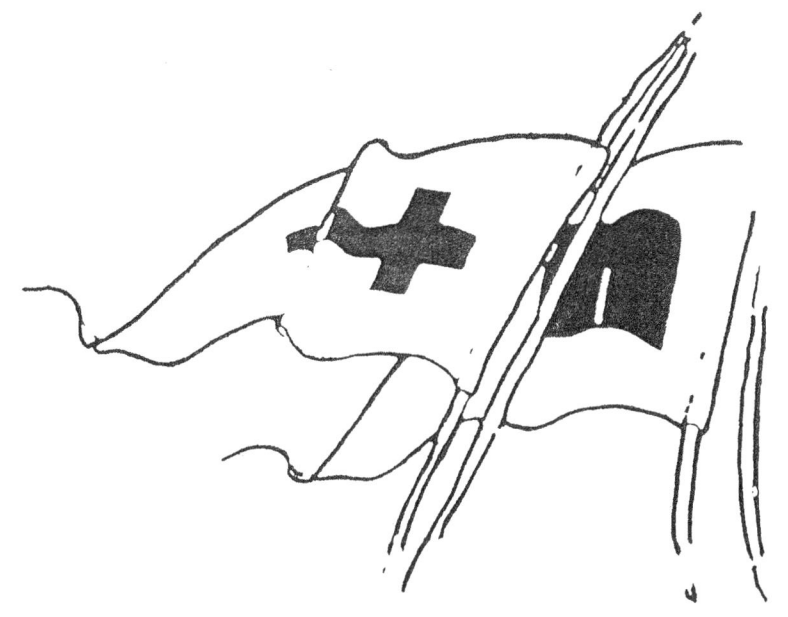

AND THE

COMMAND RELIGIOUS PROGRAM

Table of Contents

	PAGE NO.
INTRODUCTION	1
PROFESSIONAL QUALIFICATIONS	2
PROFESSIONAL REPRESENTATIVES	2
THE CHAPLAIN'S RELATIONSHIP TO THE COMMAND	3
THE COMMAND RELIGIOUS PROGRAM	3
EFFECTIVE UTILIZATION OF YOUR CHAPLAIN	4
DUTIES OF THE CHAPLAIN Collateral Duties	5

YOUR CHAPLAIN'S PROFESSIONAL DEVELOPMENT
    Duty Assignment
    Career Opportunities
    Training and Support Up-Date
    Fitness Reports
	6

ORGANIZATIONAL LEVELS OF ASSIGNMENT
    Chief of Chaplains
    Deputy Chief of Chaplains
    Office of the Chief of Chaplains
    Claimant Chaplain
    Supervisory Chaplain
	7

RELIGIOUS PROGRAM SPECIALISTS	9
PERTINENT DIRECTIVES	10

Introduction

Purpose of Booklet:

The purpose of the booklet is to acquaint commanding officers and executive officers with information pertinent to their chaplain(s) and the command religious program.

Responsibility for Religious Ministry:

The U. S. Navy has always recognized its responsibility to provide for religious ministries to meet the needs and rights of its personnel. Commanders and Commanding Officers are instructed by Navy Regulations to "use all proper means to foster high morale and strengthen the moral and spiritual well-being of the personnel under their command, and ensure that chaplains are provided the necessary logistic support for carrying out the command's religious program."[1]

Mission and Function of the Chaplain Corps:

"The Chaplain Corps is comprised of professionally qualified chaplains appointed from religious faith groups of the United States. Its purpose is to provide for the free exercise of religion for all members of the naval service, their dependents, and other authorized persons by providing ministries appropriate to their rights and needs and providing staff support to this end throughout the Department of the Navy."[2]

Since the days of the Continental Navy, chaplains have provided a religious ministry to the men and women of the Sea Services and their families. Representing some eighty faith groups of the one hundred and forty recognized by the Department of Defense, and embodying the motto of the Chaplain Corps, COOPERATION WITHOUT COMPROMISE, chaplains are committed to communicating to the people of the Navy, Marine Corps, Coast Guard, and Merchant Marine the timeless truths of the nature and relationship of God and mankind.

---

[1] U. S. NAVY REGULATIONS, 1973, Article 0727.

[2] SECNAV INSTRUCTION 1730.7

Professional Qualifications

To be appointed as a Navy chaplain, a person must possess an "ecclesiastical endorsement" from a religious body recognized by the Department of Defense.[3] Endorsement verifies that a chaplain is a fully ordained or qualified minister, priest, or rabbi -- spiritually, morally, intellectually, and emotionally qualified to represent that religious faith group in the Armed Forces Chaplaincy. It is possible for a chaplain to lose professional qualifications through removal of ecclesiastical endorsement by the Faith Group. In such cases, an active duty chaplain may be administratively separated from the Navy.[4]

Such a person must be a U. S. citizen, physically qualified, between 21 and 35 years of age at time of appointment to active duty, and able to complete 20 years active service by age 62 (waivers granted based on needs of the Service). He or she must possess 120 semester undergraduate credits (or equivalent) from an accredited college or university, and a Master of Divinity (or equivalent theological degree) or credit for completing 90 semester hours in theology or related subjects at an accredited theological school.[5]

The Navy chaplain of today enters the Navy as a highly educated and motivated professional. Ordinarily, he/she will have had parish or other clergy experience in a civilian milieu. The training of chaplains in Navy/Marine Corps practice and procedures and how to do ministry in the military setting begins with 7 weeks instruction at the Naval Chaplains School in Newport, RI and continues with on-the-job training in commands such as yours throughout their career.

Professional Representatives

Your chaplain performs liturgical, sacramental, and pastoral acts on the basis of ecclesiastical credentials. The mode and conditions of baptism, marriage or remarriage of divorced persons, serving and receiving of Holy Communion, etc. are determined by the regulations/canon law of a chaplain's faith group.[6] All official correspondence with a faith group, other than that of a chaplain with his or her own faith group, should be done in consultation with the Chief of Chaplains.

Endorsing Agents:

Each faith group has an officially recognized (DoD) Endorsing Agent entrusted with oversight of the chaplain's ministry. Some agents visit chaplains regularly to examine the ministry and well-being of the chaplain. Further, these agents interpret chaplaincy to their faith group. When such agents visit a chaplain, it is customary to schedule a courtesy call on the Commanding Officer (when clearances are necessary, this is done through the Department of Defense).

---

[3] DOD DIRECTIVE 1304.19 of 9 January 1980
[4] SECNAV INSTRUCTION 1900.10
[5] CNO ltr Ser: 114C31369190 dtd 19 May 1983 (NOTAL)
[6] 10 U. S. C., 6031 (a)

Relationship to Command

The Chaplain is ordered to the Commanding Officer. "As the principal advisor to the commanding officer on religious and moral matters, the chaplain will be assigned as a department head or principal staff officer directly under the executive officer or, as appropriate, the chief of staff."[7] When more than one chaplain is assigned, the senior chaplain supervises the command religious program and coordinates the ministry of all chaplains. Regardless of faith groups represented, there is only one senior chaplain.

The chaplain should communicate regularly with the Commanding Officer. Direct access to the commanding officer is guaranteed.[8] Also, the chaplain maintains daily contact with the executive officer/chief of staff and reports as any other department head or principal staff advisor.

The Command Religious Program

Planning, programming, and budgeting are a command responsibility. Expect your chaplain to present for your approval a plan for executing religious ministries within the command. This plan must be inclusive, designed to meet the needs of all faith groups. Commands will use local O & M funds for the support of the command religious program.[9] Command logistic support includes:

(1) Purchasing and providing consumable religious supplies and services such as religious literature, printing, liturgical accoutrements, transportation, and military band support.

(2) Providing nonconsumable support such as equipment, facilities, and furnishings.

(3) Contracting for musical and educational services such as organists, choir directors, directors of religious education, and other resource persons.

(4) Supporting the professional training of chaplains and the training of RP's in short-term training opportunities.

Note: Purchase of religious education material should utilize the Protestant, Catholic, and Jewish guides provided by the Chief of Chaplains. Procurement of ecclesiastical/religious education material is processed through normal Navy/Marine Corps channels.

Note: Contracting for clergy is done with the approval of the Chief of Chaplains.[10]

---

[7] SECNAV INSTRUCTION 1730.7
[8] NAVY REGULATIONS, 1973, Article 1107
[9] SECNAV INSTRUCTION 1730.7
[10] SECNAV INSTRUCTION 1730.3F

Effective Utilization of Your Chaplain

Ensure that your chaplain provides a full and complete command religious program, including: the provision of worship for his/her own faith group and the facilitation of worship opportunities for other faith groups; religious education; pre-marital and marital counseling; family enrichment programs; social awareness events on issues such as drug and alcohol abuse, ethnic and racial concerns; moral development, etc.

- Encourage your chaplain to become intimately involved in all command activities. He/she can provide valuable insight into the morale and well-being of command personnel.

- Include the chaplain as a resource person for training, professional development and orientation of personnel, both officer and enlisted.

- Encourage your chaplain to be visible to every echelon of the command - visiting work spaces, barracks, etc. on a regular basis.

- Encourage your chaplain to present his or her views on command practices, policies, judicial actions, morale, etc.

- Ensure that the chaplain is a full, active member of your staff. Include in staff/department head meetings, command planning of training, exercises, deployments, etc.

- Ensure that the chaplain is seen with you. Make sure that command personnel know you support the chaplain and the command religious program.

- Make sure your chaplain has a plan for ministry to all personnel and their families, not just during deployments, but at home or in port as well.

- Invite the chaplain occasionally to Captain's Mast or to Office Hours.

Remember: Information shared with a chaplain is "Privileged Communication". The Manual for Courts-Martial, United States says:

"A person has a privilege to refuse to disclose and to prevent another from disclosing a confidential communication by the person to a clergyman or to a clergyman's assistant, if such communication is made either as a formal act of religion or as a matter of conscience.

The privilege may be claimed by the person, by the guardian or conservator, or by a personal representative if the person is deceased. The clergyman or clergyman's assistant who received the communication may claim the privilege on behalf of the person. The authority of the clergyman or clergyman's assistant to do so is presumed in the absence of evidence to the contrary."[11]

---

[11]Manual for Courts-Martial, United States, 1969, Chapter XXVII, Rule 503.

Duties of the Chaplain

(1) Conduct divine services.

(2) Facilitate the free exercise of religion for all.

(3) Provide appropriate sacramental ministry and pastoral care.

(4) Organize voluntary programs of religious education.

(5) Visit the sick.

(6) At general quarters, report to a battle station to be available to minister to the wounded.

(7) At daily quarters, report his or her presence aboard to the Executive Officer.

(8) Visit personnel confined to brigs or correctional facilities.

(9) Maintain liaison with local religious groups in U. S. or foreign communities in order to develop public awareness of the religious activities in the Navy.

(10) Keep the public affairs officer informed of chaplains' activities of public interest.

(11) Report quarterly at the end of the quarter a summary of activities to the claimant chaplain.[12]

Collateral Duties:

In regard to the assignment of collateral duties to your chaplain, remember that the chaplain's primary duty is religious ministry. Duties which involve the following will not be assigned:

(1) Duties which violate the religious practices of the chaplain's faith group.

(2) Duties which violate the chaplain's noncombatant status.

(3) Serving as director or treasurer of fund drives.

(4) Serving in any capacity relating to the solicitation, collection, or disbursement of any monies, except as custodian of a Religious Offering Fund.

(5) Serving on a court martial or rendering judgement in disciplinary cases, except as required by Article 0845 of Navy Regulations, 1973.

(6) Standing watches other than that of duty chaplain.[13]

---

[12] SECNAV INSTRUCTION 1730.7
[13] SECNAV INSTRUCTION 1730.7

Your Chaplain's Professional Development

Duty Assignment:

A chaplain's assignment is determined by: (1) needs of the service; (2) career needs; and (3) desires of the chaplain. Assignment and distribution is made by the Chief of Naval Personnel. The Chief of Chaplains exercises final nomination authority for all assignments of active duty chaplains. Tour lengths are as follows:

LT's and below for FMF and first sea duty are at least 24 months.
LT's and below for shore duty normally 24 months but could be less.
2nd and subsequent sea tours for LT's are at least 27 months.
LCDR's and above are 36 months shore and at least 27 months sea duty.
Foreign shore tours vary depending upon DoD lengths for the location.

Career Opportunities:

To comply with congressionally mandated end-strengths and DOPMA limitations, the Chaplain Corps can retain 75% of officers whose initial Obligated Service Agreement (OSA) agreement expires. A Board is convened by CNMPC to consider chaplains for indefinite extension beyond their OSA. The Board meets in March of the fiscal year prior to the fiscal year the OSA expires. Chaplains follow the same procedures as other reserve officers for augmentation consideration.

Training and Support Update:

As a professional in religious ministry, your chaplain has particular needs and requirements. Opportunities for professional development and support update are provided by the Chaplain Corps and the chaplain's faith group. Annually, the Chief of Chaplains sponsors Professional Development Training at which your chaplain's participation is strongly encouraged. Also, a limited number are selected each year to attend workshops on Ministry to Black Persons and Hispanics. Participation in these events will benefit the command religious program and contribute to the professional development of your chaplain.

Active duty chaplains may apply for the Navy sponsored Graduate Education Program. Also, a 12 month Pastoral Care Residency Program is available (these two programs involve PCS moves). Finally, all chaplains are urged to participate in spiritual retreats required by their faith groups.

Fitness Reports:

Report on your chaplain's effectiveness as a chaplain; do not rank or compare with other staff members. Comments should specifically reflect the marks assigned, and should provide specific references to incidents/examples which illustrate the basis for evaluation. Emphasis should be on the chaplain's effectiveness as a professional on your staff. Cite specific illustrations of loyalty and support of the command, and effectiveness as a chaplain in working with all members of the command. Involvement in special programs (drug/alcohol abuse, child/spouse abuse, marriage counseling, human relations, etc.) should be noted with evaluative comments. Efforts to establish/strengthen relationships between command-level and unit personnel, work with dependents, pre-deployment preparations, etc. are worth noting. Specific statements concerning willingness and ability to work with personnel from various religious, racial, and ethnic backgrounds are helpful. Finally, a specific statement concerning the depth of feeling in connection with the recommendation for promotion, and any statement felt appropriate regarding the chaplain's future duty assignment should be made.

Organizational Levels of Assignment

Chief of Chaplains:

The Chief of Chaplains directs a major staff office under the Chief of Naval Operations and has the responsibility for implementing religious ministries throughout the Naval Service.[14] Functions and duties include:

(1) The Chief of Chaplains/Director of Religious Ministries (OP-09G) serves as the principal advisor to the Chief of Naval Operations on religious matters.

(2) As an additional duty, in accordance with SECNAVINST 5430.93, the Chief of Chaplains/Senior Chaplain of the Department of the Navy serves as advisor to the Secretary of the Navy on religious matters.

(3) As an additional duty, the Chief of Chaplains serves as advisor to the Chief of Naval Personnel on religious matters affecting personnel management and the requirements for religious ministry in the naval service.

Deputy Chief of Chaplains:

A Deputy Chief of Chaplains is assigned to perform all duties of the office as directed by the Chief of Chaplains.

Office of the Chief of Chaplains:

Chaplains are assigned to the Office of the Chief of Chaplains to assist in the accomplishment of the mission, function, and responsibilities of the office.

Office of the Chief of Chaplains

Telephone:

Commercial: (202) 694-4043
Autovon: 224-4043

Location:

Navy Annex FOB #2
Columbia Pike, Rm G842
Arlington, Virginia

Mailing Address

Chief of Chaplains (OP-09G)
Office of the Chief of Naval Operations
Department of the Navy
Washington, D.C. 20350

---

[14] SECNAV INSTRUCTION 1730.7

Claimant Chaplain:

A claimant chaplain is the senior chaplain assigned to the staff of a major manpower claimant. Duties include:

(1) Advising the claimant on all matters relating to religion and religious ministries within the claimancy.
(2) Advising the Chief of Chaplains on matters requiring attention at that level.
(3) Monitoring billets and billet requirements for chaplains and Religious Program Specialists and advising the appropriate authority on the initiation of manpower authorization change requests.
(4) Monitoring the auxiliary and contract chaplain program on behalf of the Chief of Chaplains.
(5) Coordinating matters such as site plans, justification data, priorities, programming, and funding for chapel construction.
(6) Participating in the Naval Command Inspection Program to assist commands in enhancing the effectiveness of command religious programs.
(7) Facilitating the ministry of chaplains in the claimancy via command channels.
(8) Facilitating the development of ministry models to meet needs unique to a command.
(9) Maintaining communication and conducting conferences for all chaplains in the command.
(10) Providing orientation and continued training for all chaplains in the command.
(11) Identifying training needs to the Chief of Chaplains.
(12) Analyzing quarterly report data from chaplains within the claimancy and providing pertinent report data for the Chief of Chaplains.

Supervisory Chaplain:

A supervisory chaplain is the senior chaplain assigned to a force, staff, or unit to facilitate religious ministries. Duties include:

(1) Advising the commanding officer on all matters related to religious ministries within the command.
(2) Advising the claimant chaplain regarding necessary actions concerning programming of chaplain and RP billets and other support requirements.
(3) Administering the command religious program to meet the needs of all assigned personnel.
(4) Coordinating the ministry of all assigned chaplains with due respect to religious pluralism and functional diversity in professional qualifications.
(5) Facilitating the continued training and development of all personnel assigned to the command religious program.

Religious Program Specialists (RP's)

Religious Program Specialists assist the command and the chaplain in the administration of the command religious program. RP's are limited to performing functions that do not require ordination or pastoral counseling.[15]

Duties of RP's include:

(1) Support chaplains and religious activities for all faiths.

(2) Assist in management and development of religious programs and determination of resources.

(3) Maintain records of various funds, ecclesiastical documents, and references.

(4) Train personnel in support of religious programs.

(5) Maintain shipboard libraries.

(6) Coordinate programs of religious education.

(7) Assist in preparation of devotional and religious educational materials and audio-visual displays.

(8) Publicize religious activities.

(9) Coordinate volunteer religious activities.

(10) Requisition, maintain, and safeguard ecclesiastical equipment and supplies.

(11) Perform administrative and clerical duties.

Unlike chaplains, RP's <u>are combatants</u> and receive combat training when appropriate. They are taught the fundamentals of the rating through "A" school (eight weeks duration) or through on-the-job training. Advanced training ("C" school) is required during later stages of the RP's career. RP's usually spend fifty percent of their career with fleet units and fifty percent at shore stations.

Note: RP's should not be assigned as Lay Readers.[16]

---

[15] Manual of Navy Enlisted Manpower and Personnel Qualifications and Occupational Standards, NAVPERS 180069 Series.

[16] SECNAV INSTRUCTION 1730.7

Pertinent Directives

Your command religious program should be guided by the following directives:

U. S. CODE TITLE 10, Art. 6031: Authorizes chaplains to conduct worship according to the forms of his/her faith group; directs commanders to cause divine services to be held; and enjoins all naval persons to behave reverently during divine services.

U. S. NAVY REGULATIONS, 1973, Art. 0722: Provides guidance to commanders concerning the performance of work on Sunday, the conduct of divine services, etc.

U. S. NAVY REGULATIONS, 1973, Art. 0737(a): Directs commanders to develop and strengthen the moral and spiritual well-being of personnel and to provide chaplains with the necessary logistical support.

U. S. NAVY REGULATIONS, 1973, Art. 0845: Designates chaplains as Noncombatants.

SECNAV INSTRUCTION 1730.7: This directive promulgates policy and assigns responsibilities for religious ministries within the Department of the Navy. It directs that "the command religious program is an essential element of a command's total administration," and that "it is to be supported and managed as an integral part of a command's planning, programming, and budgeting activities." It also states the policy regarding observance of the Sabbath, religious holy days, the appointment of Lay Readers, etc.

SECNAV INSTRUCTIONS 7000.23 and 7043.5A: Give guidance on establishment and management of nonappropriated religious offering funds.

COMDINST M1730.3: Provides guidance for chaplains serving with the Coast Guard.

MARINE CORPS ORDER 1730.5A: Concerns policy and procedure for logistic support of religious programs.

MARINE CORPS ORDER 4400.154: Gives policy and management principles for the acquisition of material, supplies and equipment for the provision of religious ministry.

NAVAL MILITARY PERSONNEL COMMAND NAVPERS 15555: Provides guidance for burial at sea.

NMPCINST 1770.1, (Chg. (1) AUG 83): Provides guidance and procedures regarding the Navy Casualty Assistance Calls Program.

FLAGS, PENNANTS, AND CUSTOMS NTP 13, June 1977: Gives guidance concerning rigging for divine services.

NAVSO P-3520: Gives accounting procedures for nonappropriated funds.

DEPARTMENT OF THE NAVY
OFFICE OF THE SECRETARY
WASHINGTON, D.C. 20350

CH-1 of 8 June 1984

SECNAVINST 1730.7
Op-09G
14 December 1983

SECNAV INSTRUCTION 1730.7

From: Secretary of the Navy

Subj: RELIGIOUS MINISTRIES WITHIN THE DEPARTMENT OF THE NAVY

Ref: (a) Title 10, United States Code (NOTAL)
(b) U.S. Navy Regulations, 1973
(c) DoD Directive 1304.19 of 9 Jan 1980 (NOTAL)
(d) SECNAVINST 1730.3F
(e) SECNAVINST 7000.23
(f) SECNAVINST 7043.5A (NOTAL)
(g) NAVSO P-3520
(h) SECNAVINST 1301.4 (NOTAL)
(i) Defense Officer Personnel Management Act (DOPMA), Pub. L. No. 96-513, 94 Stat. 2835 (1980)
(j) SECNAVINST 1900.10
(k) SECNAVINST 5430.93 (NOTAL)
(l) DoD Directive 5120.8 of 24 Jul 1979 (NOTAL)
(m) USCG COMDTINST 1730.3 (NOTAL)

Encl: (1) Responsibilities for Religious Ministries
(2) Programming for Religious Ministries
(3) The Chaplain Corps

1. Purpose. To promulgate policy and assign responsibilities for religious ministries within the Department of the Navy.

2. Cancellation. SECNAVINST 1730.5.

3. Applicability. This instruction is applicable to all persons throughout the naval service who are responsible for the provision, facilitation, and support of religious ministries. (NOTE: The term "naval service" as used here encompasses the Navy, Marine Corps, Coast Guard, and Merchant Marine.)

4. Background. From its inception, the naval service has recognized its responsibility to provide for religious ministries to meet the needs and rights of its personnel. The second article of Navy Regulations adopted 28 November 1775, stated that, "The commanders of ships of the thirteen United Colonies, are to take care that divine services be performed . . ." The naval service has always recognized this obligation to make possible the practice of religion and to ensure that citizens serving in the naval service are not deprived of opportunities for the free exercise of their religion.

5. Policy

  a. In keeping with section 6031 of reference (a) and article 0722 of reference (b), it is Department of the Navy policy that commanders and

SECNAVINST 1730.7 CH-1
8 June 1984

R) commanding officers shall provide for the free exercise of religion by all personnel of their commands as specified in enclosure (1).

   b. Commands are to provide programs of ministry in support of the free exercise of religion. The command religious program is an essential element of a command's total administration. It is to be supported and managed as an integral part of a command's planning, programming, and budgeting activities.

   c. The Navy appoints chaplains from the clergy of religious faith groups of the United States in accordance with reference (c). Navy chaplains exist to provide ministry throughout the naval service through the development and execution of command religious programs.

   d. Policy and procedures for implementing religious ministries within the Department of the Navy are set forth in enclosures (1) through (3) in accordance with references (d) through (m).

6. Action. The Chief of Naval Operations and the Commandant of the Marine Corps are assigned responsibility for implementing the policies and procedures in this instruction.

   a. The Chief of Naval Operations will:

      (1) Issue appropriate directives to implement these policies and procedures throughout the Navy.

      (2) Initiate appropriate action with the Commandant of the Coast Guard and the Director of the Merchant Marine to implement these policies and practices in those elements of their respective services which receive Navy support for religious ministry.

   b. The Commandant of the Marine Corps will issue appropriate directives to implement these policies and procedures throughout the Marine Corps.

James F. Goodrich
Under Secretary of the Navy

Distribution:
SNDL A3   (Chief of Naval Operations)
     A6   (CMC)

SECNAVINST 1730.7
14 December 1983

Copy to:
SNDL A1   (Immediate Office of the Secretary (SO, SO-1, SO-2, SO-5))
     A2   (Department of the Navy Staff Offices)
     A5   (Bureaus)
     B5   (U.S. Coast Guard)
     21A   (Fleet Commanders in Chief)
     FE1   (COMNAVSECGRU)
     FG1   (COMNAVTELCOM)
     FH1   (COMNAVMEDCOM)
     FKA1A   (COMNAVAIRSYSCOM)
     FKA1C   (COMNAVFACENGCOM)
     FKA1G   (COMNAVSEASYSCOM)
     FR1   (CNAVRES)
     FT1   (CNET)
     FT2   (CNATRA)
     FT5   (CNTECHTRA)
     FT72   (DPTNAVSCI USMERMARCAD, only)

Stocked:
CO, NAVPUBFORMCEN
5801 Tabor Ave.
Phila., PA 19120 (500 copies)

SECNAVINST 1730.7 CH-1
8 June 1984

RESPONSIBILITIES FOR RELIGIOUS MINISTRIES

1. General

   a. Authority. Section 6031(b) of reference (a) provides that, "The commanders of vessels and naval activities to which chaplains are attached shall cause divine service to be performed on Sunday, whenever the weather and other circumstances allow it to be done ...."

   b. Policy

   (1) In keeping with the cited provision of reference (a) and Department of the Navy policy, commanders snd commanding officers shall provide for the free exercise of religion for all members of the naval service, their dependents, and other authorized persons.

   (2) Chaplains appointed in accordance with Navy policy shall provide ministry and facilitate the free exercise of religion for all members of the naval service, their dependents, and other authorized persons through the Command Religious Program.

2. Command

   a. Command responsibilities. Commanders and commanding officers:

   (1) Comply with the provisions of article 0845 of reference (b) which designates chaplains as non-combatants in accordance with the Geneva Convention of August 12, 1949.

   (2) "Use all proper means to foster high morale, and to develop and strengthen the moral snd spiritual well-being of the personnel under his/her command, and ensure that chaplains are provided the necessary logistic support for carrying out the command's religious program" as cited in article 0727 of reference (b).

   (3) Comply with the stipulations of article 0722 of reference (b) in the conduct of divine services.

      (a) The Sabbath shall be observed on Sunday, except by members of the naval service whose religious convictions require them to observe some day other than Sunday as their day of worship. Those whose day of worship is other than Sunday are entitled to respect for their religious convictions and practices. Except by reason of necessity, personnel who celebrate the Sabbath on a (R
day other than Sunday will be afforded the opportunity to observe the requirements of their religious principles. Where excused from duty on a day other than Sunday, the workweek of such individuals should not be less than that of any other individual and may include work on Sunday. Determination of necessity (R
rests entirely with the commanding officer.

      (b) Consistent with the exigencies of the service, commanding officers are encouraged to give favorable consideration of applications for

Enclosure (1)

SECNAVINST 1730.7 CH-1
8 June 1984

leave from those who may desire to observe significant holy days of their faith with their families. This is particularly important where appropriate services are unavailable in the local areas.

R)   (4) In addition to the requirements set forth in 2a(3), above, relating to religious services, commanding officers shall not restrict the free exercise of religion by personnel in the naval service unless there is a military requirement to do so. Such requirements may exist in directives from higher authority or as otherwise determined by the commanding officer.

(5) Support of the Command Religious Program, including personnel, funding and logistics, is an essential element of a command's total operation. These matters will be managed as an integral part of the command's planning, programming, and budgeting activities as governed by current directives. Additional guidance is provided in enclosure (2).

   b. <u>Chaplain's Position in the Command</u>

(1) As the principal advisor to the commanding officer on religious and moral matters, the chaplain will be assigned as a department head or principal staff officer directly under the executive officer or, as appropriate, the chief of staff.

(2) As a principal advisor to the commanding officer, the chaplain shall have direct access to the commanding officer as provided in article 1107 of reference (b).

   c. <u>Religious Program Specialists (RP's)</u>

(1) Religious Program Specialists (RP's) assist the command, and specifically the chaplain, in the administration and coordination of programs in support of the Command Religious Program. The programming of RP billets within a command is an integral element in command manpower authorization actions.

(2) In keeping with their principal function, RP's are assigned primary duties only in support of chaplains. RP's are assigned only to units which have a chaplain assigned. The Chief of Naval Personnel establishes occupational standards for the RP rating in the Manual of Navy Enlisted Manpower and Personnel Classifications and Occupational Standards, NAVPERS 180068 Series. RP duties in support of religious ministries within the command must be given appropriate consideration when assigning collateral duties.

(3) To facilitate their work with lay readers of all religious faith groups, RP's should not be assigned as a lay reader of any particular religious faith group.

   d. <u>Lay Readers</u>. Commanders or commanding officers may assign a lay reader to serve for a period of time to meet the religious needs of a particular religious faith group. The commander or commanding officer may seek the advice of the command's chaplain or chaplain attached to a higher echelon regarding the selection of an appropriate lay reader.

Enclosure (1)

SECNAVINST 1730.7
14 December 1983

PROGRAMMING FOR RELIGIOUS MINISTRIES

1. <u>General</u>. Planning, programming, and budgeting activities are a command responsibility.

2. <u>Manpower and Personnel</u>

   a. <u>Manpower</u>

   (1) Planning, programming, and budgeting of Chaplain Corps manpower is an essential element of support for Command Religious Programs throughout the naval service. Major manpower claimants of the naval service will plan, program, and budget for Chaplain Corps manpower as an integral part of force structure to the level of service-wide standards established in accordance with Department of the Navy policy and procedures.

   (2) The Chief of Chaplains/Director of Religious Ministries manages chaplain (4100) and Religious Program Specialist (RP) program authorized billets through DCNO (MPT) and cognizant major manpower claimants. Claimant staff chaplains (CSC) advise and assist Navy, Marine Corps, and other major manpower claimants in planning and programming Chaplain Corps manpower and report to the Chief of Chaplains on all matters pertaining to 4100/RP manpower.

   b. <u>Personnel</u>. The Chief of Chaplains/Director of Religious Ministries, through interaction with the Commander, Navy Recruiting Command and Commander, Naval Military Personnel Command, recommends personnel for appointment, accession, distribution and placement by the Chief of Naval Personnel in designated active duty or reserve chaplain billets or in other forms of official status in the reserves or on the retired lists.

3. <u>Logistics</u>

   a. <u>Command Support</u>

   (1) Commands and units of the Navy and Marine Corps will use local operation and maintenance funds for the support of religious ministries within the command.

   (2) Command logistic support of religious ministries is interpreted to include, but is not limited to:

   (a) Purchasing and providing consumable religious supplies and services such as religious literature, printing, liturgical accoutrements, transportation, and military band support.

   (b) Providing nonconsumable support essential to religious ministries, such as equipment, furnishings and facilities.

   (c) Contracting for musical and educational services such as organists, choir directors, directors of religious education and resource persons.

Enclosure (2)

SECNAVINST 1730.7
14 December 1983

        (d) Supporting the professional training of chaplains and the training of RP's in short-term training opportunities.

    (3) Procurement of ecclesiastical material in support of religious ministries is processed through normal Navy and Marine Corps supply channels.

    (4) To meet the religious needs of personnel in areas where military chaplains are not available or to provide additional professional personnel necessary to supplement existing religious ministry, commanders and commanding officers may obtain the services of appropriately endorsed civilian clergy as auxiliary or contract chaplains. Appointments of auxiliary chaplains by the commander or commanding officer and awards of contracts by the contracting officer shall be made with the approval of the Chief of Chaplains. Procedures governing employment and payment of auxiliary and contract chaplains are outlined in reference (d).

  b. _Other Funds_. Religious Offerings Funds are non-appropriated funds established by and administered under the authority of the commander or commanding officer. References (e), (f) and (g) provide information and guidance on the establishment and management of non-appropriated funds. These funds will be used only for projects of religious benevolence beyond the limits of the Command Religious Program, not as an alternative to support for the Command Religious Program.

  c. _Fees_. No fees or gratuities will be charged or received for the use of government facilities in the performance of any religious act, sacrament or rite. No fees or gratuities will be charged or received by a chaplain for any religious act, sacrament or rite performed on government-owned property or for persons entitled to receive such services by authorization of the Department of the Navy. Nor will any RP be paid any fees for services performed on government property in support of any religious act, sacrament or rite, or for persons entitled to receive such services by authorization of the Department of the Navy.

Enclosure (2)

SECNAVINST 1730.7
14 December 1983

THE CHAPLAIN CORPS

1. <u>General</u>

    a. <u>Establishment</u>. The Chaplain Corps is established as a Staff Corps of the Navy under the provisions of reference (h), pursuant to the authority contained in reference (i).

    b. <u>Mission</u>. The Chaplain Corps is comprised of professionally qualified chaplains appointed from religious faith groups of the United States. Its purpose is to provide for the free exercise of religion for all members of the naval service, their dependents, and other authorized persons by providing ministries appropriate to their rights and needs and providing staff support to this end throughout the Department of the Navy.

2. <u>Chaplains</u>

    a. <u>Endorsement</u>. Chaplains are clergy persons endorsed by their ecclesiastical endorsing agency in accordance with reference (c). The maintenance of this endorsement is the responsibility of the chaplain and is an essential element of his/her professional qualification as a Navy chaplain. Loss of ecclesiastical endorsement requires administrative processing under the provisions of reference (j).

    b. <u>Responsibility</u>. Chaplains are assigned or attached to a specific unit or station for the primary purpose of providing and facilitating religious ministries within that unit or station. Chaplains have responsibilities to the commander or commanding officer of the unit or station to which assigned and to the appropriate supervisory chaplain at the next higher echelon in the command organization.

    c. <u>Address</u>. As commissioned officers, chaplains are addressed in oral or written communication in accordance with article 0810 of reference (b). Traditionally, chaplains are addressed as "Chaplain" regardless of rank.

    d. <u>Uniforms</u>. Navy Chaplain Corps officers assigned to Marine Corps or Coast Guard organizations may wear the appropriate service or field uniform prescribed for Marine Corps or Coast Guard officers respectively.

    e. <u>Functions</u>

        (1) Advising the commander or commanding officer on all matters related to religious ministries within the command.

        (2) Administering the Command Religious Program by conducting divine services, administering sacraments and ordinances, performing rites and ceremonies in accordance with the manner and forms of the chaplain's particular faith group and facilitating the provision of religious ministries for personnel of other faith groups.

        (3) Developing plans, programs, and budgets to execute religious ministries within the command.

Enclosure (3)

SECNAVINST 1730.7
14 December 1983

(4) Advising supervisory chaplains of the unit, or the command to which the unit is attached, of necessary actions concerning programming of chaplain and RP billets and other support requirements.

f. <u>General Duties</u>. With the approval of the commanding officer, a chaplain attached to a ship or station shall perform the following general duties:

(1) Conduct divine services.

(2) Facilitate the free exercise of religion for all.

(3) Provide appropriate sacramental ministry and pastoral care.

(4) Organize voluntary programs of religious education.

(5) Visit the sick.

(6) At general quarters, report to a battle station to be available to minister to the wounded.

(7) At daily quarters, report his or her presence aboard to the executive officer.

(8) Visit personnel confined to brigs or correctional facilities.

(9) Maintain liaison with local religious groups in U.S. or foreign communities in order to develop public awareness of the religious activities in the Navy.

(10) Keep the public affairs officer informed of chaplains' activities of public interest.

(11) Report quarterly at the end of the quarter a summary of activities to the claimant chaplain.

g. <u>Collateral Duties</u>

(1) When assigning collateral duties to the chaplain, the governing factor for commanders and commanding officers shall be the recognition of the primacy of the chaplain's duty of religious ministry as provided in article 0845 of reference (b).

(2) Chaplains will not be assigned collateral duties which involve:

(a) Actions in violation of the religious practices of the Chaplain's ecclesiastical authority.

(b) Violation of noncombatant status.

(c) Serving as director or treasurer of fund drives.

Enclosure (3)

SECNAVINST 1730.7
14 December 1983

(d) Serving in any capacity relating to the solicitation, collection, or disbursing of any monies, except as custodian of a Religious Offerings Fund.

(e) Serving on a court-martial or rendering judgment in disciplinary cases, except as required by Article 0845 of reference (b).

(f) Standing watches other than that of duty chaplain.

3. <u>Chief of Chaplains/Director of Religious Ministries/Senior Chaplain of the Department of the Navy</u>

   a. <u>Position in the Organization</u>. Section 5142 of reference (a) places the office of the Chief of Chaplains within the executive part of the Department of the Navy. The Chief of Chaplains/Director of Religious Ministries/Senior Chaplain of the Department of the Navy (hereafter referred to as "Chief of Chaplains") directs a major staff office under the Chief of Naval Operations with responsibility for implementing religious ministries throughout the naval service.

   b. <u>Mission</u>

   (1) The Chief of Chaplains, as the Director of Religious Ministries, directs, administers and manages the Navy Chaplain Corps and implements religious ministries to meet the needs of personnel in the naval service and their dependents in their pursuit of the free exercise of religion.

   (2) In accordance with reference (k), the Chief of Chaplains, as the Senior Chaplain of the Department of the Navy, serves as an advisor to the Secretary of the Navy on religious, spiritual, and moral and ethical implications of policies and action of the Department of the Navy. In these matters, the Chief of Chaplains shall provide such advice and counsel to the Secretary, the Civilian Executive Assistants, the Chief of Naval Operations, the Commandant of the Marine Corps, the Commandant of the Coast Guard and officials of the Merchant Marine on any issue they may direct. Additionally, the Chief of Chaplains may volunteer such advice and counsel to these same officials upon any matter that should be brought to their attention.

   c. <u>Functions</u>

   (1) The Chief of Chaplains/Director of Religious Ministries as the principal advisor to the Chief of Naval Operations on religious matters:

   (a) Advises the Chief of Naval Operations and the chain of command on religious, moral and ethical concerns and needs of personnel of the naval service and members of their families, and ensures consideration of these factors in all policy development.

   (b) Supports the Chief of Naval Operations, the Commandant of the Marine Corps, the Commandant of the Coast Guard and officials of the Merchant Marine in meeting the religious, moral and ethical needs of members of the naval service.

Enclosure (3)

(c) Develops and monitors plans, policies and programs of religious ministry in the naval service.

(d) Represents the Navy to religious faith groups in all matters pertaining to the ecclesiastical endorsement of clergy as Navy chaplains.

(e) Functions as technical sponsor for the acquisition, operation and maintenance of religious facilities and collateral equipment, both ashore and afloat.

(f) Coordinates and administers Chaplain Corps participation in command inspection programs for the naval service in those areas related to religious ministry, morale and quality of life.

(g) Monitors and manages the Auxiliary and Contract Chaplain Program in accordance with reference (d).

(2) As an additional duty, in accordance with reference (k), the Chief of Chaplains/Senior Chaplain of the Department of the Navy as advisor to the Secretary of the Navy on religious matters:

(a) Reports regularly on the religious, moral and ethical implications of the Department of the Navy policies and actions which impact upon the personnel of the naval service, their dependents and upon the nation's religious faith groups.

(b) Advises the Secretary of the Navy, the Chief of Naval Operations, the Commandant of the Marine Corps, the Commandant of the Coast Guard and officials of the Merchant Marine on meeting the religious, moral and ethical needs of members of the naval service.

(c) Informs the Secretary of the Navy on the policies, programs, and positions of religious faith groups of the United States.

(d) Represents the Department of the Navy on the Armed Forces Chaplains Board and maintains liaison with other boards, committees and agencies in matters pertaining to religious activities.

(e) Represents the Department of the Navy in meeting with the Chiefs of Chaplains/Senior Chaplains of the navies of other nations and in international forums affecting religious ministry and the well-being of persons in the naval service.

(3) As an additional duty, the Chief of Chaplains as advisor to the Chief of Naval Personnel on religious matters affecting personnel management and the requirements for religious ministry in the naval service:

(a) Identifies the requirements to support religious ministries in the naval service for sponsorship in the planning, programming, budgeting systems and manpower management.

(b) Develops, plans and establishes policies and programs governing the accession, professional development and distribution of chaplains.

SECNAVINST 1730.7
14 December 1983

(c) Establishes Chaplain Corps officer plans, policies and procurement requirements for the Commander, Navy Recruiting Command.

(d) Serves as technical and program sponsor of training for the Chaplain Corps.

(e) Serves as primary advisor and program sponsor for the Religious Program Specialist (RP) rating.

4. Organizational Levels of Assignment

   a. Office of the Chief of Chaplains

   (1) A Deputy Chief of Chaplains/Deputy Director of Religious Ministries/Deputy Senior Chaplain of the Department of the Navy is assigned to perform all duties of the office as directed by the Chief of Chaplains.

   (2) Chaplains are assigned to the office of the Chief of Chaplains to assist in the accomplishment of the mission function and responsibilities of the office.

   b. Claimant Chaplains

   (1) A claimant chaplain is the senior chaplain assigned to the staff of a manpower claimant, e.g., Chief of Naval Operations, Commandant of the Marine Corps, the Commander in Chief of the U.S. Atlantic Fleet, the Commander in Chief of the U.S. Pacific Fleet. Claimant chaplains, in the execution of their functional responsibilities, are particularly influential in assisting in the administration of religious ministries within the Department of the Navy.

   (2) Within the U.S. Coast Guard, the ecclesiastical and military activities of all chaplains, and any other clergy providing ministry to the Coast Guard, are coordinated snd supervised by The Chaplain, USCG.

   (3) Functions of claimant chaplains include:

      (a) Advising the major manpower claimant on all matters relating to religion and religious ministries within the claimancy.

      (b) Advising the Chief of Chaplains on matters concerning religious ministries within the claimancy which require the attention of the Chief of Chaplains.

      (c) Monitoring billets and billet requirements for chaplains and for Religious Program Specialists (RP's) in all units of the fleet, force, or command and advising the appropriate authority on the initiation of manpower authorization change requests.

      (d) Monitoring the Auxiliary and Contract Chaplain Program on behalf of the Chief of Chaplains in accordance with reference (d).

      (e) Coordinating matters such as site plans, justification data,

SECNAVINST 1730.7
14 December 1983

priorities, programming and funding for construction of religious facilities.

    (f) Participating in the naval command inspection program for the purpose of evaluating the effectiveness of command religious programs.

    (g) Facilitating the ministry of chaplains via command channels.

    (h) Facilitating development of ministry models to meet the unique needs of the command.

    (i) Maintaining communications and conducting conferences for chaplains, as required.

    (j) Providing orientation and continued training for all chaplains and Religious Program Specialists (RP's) in the command.

    (k) Identifying training needs of chaplains and Religious Program Specialists (RP's) to the Chief of Chaplains.

    (l) Reporting quarterly one month after the end of the quarter a summary of chaplain activities to the Chief of Chaplains (Op-09G).

  c. <u>Supervisory Chaplains</u>

    (1) A supervisory chaplain is the senior chaplain assigned to a force, staff, or unit. Supervisory chaplains are department heads or principal staff officers with responsibility to the commander or commanding officer through the executive officer or the chief of staff for administering, supervising and facilitating religious ministries and chaplain activities. This responsibility includes the professional supervision of chaplains, assigned enlisted and civilian personnel, and of chaplains in subordinate commands, as appropriate.

    (2) Functions of supervisory chaplains include:

    (a) Advising the commander or commanding officer on all matters related to religious ministries within the command.

    (b) Advising the claimant chaplain of the command to which the unit is attached, via the appropriate Force Chaplain, of necessary actions concerning programming of chaplain and RP billets and other support requirements.

    (c) Developing plans, programs and budgets to execute religious ministries within the command.

    (d) Administering the commander's or commanding officer's program for religious ministries to meet the religious needs of all personnel of the command.

    (e) Coordinating the ministries of all assigned chaplains with respect to religious faith and functional diversity in professional qualifications to meet the needs of personnel.

    (f) Supervising the activities of all assigned enlisted personnel

Enclosure (3)

SECNAVINST 1730.7
14 December 1983

and civilian employees.

    (g) Facilitating the continued training and professional development of all personnel within the command religious programs.

5. Interservice Relationships

  a. Armed Forces Chaplains Board

    (1) The Chiefs of Chaplains and Deputy Chiefs of Chaplains of the military services comprise the Armed Forces Chaplains Board.

    (2) The Armed Forces Chaplains Board advises the Secretary of Defense through the Assistant Secretary for Manpower, Reserve Affairs and Logistics, on religious and ecclesiastical matters and coordinates activities and policies among the chaplaincies of the three services in accordance with reference (l).

  b. Assignment with Other Armed Forces

    (1) Navy chaplains provide religious ministries under a variety of operational and administrative conditions. They may be assigned routinely to duty throughout the naval service, serve on joint staffs, or be assigned to naval activities which are tenants on Army or Air Force bases.

    (2) Information concerning Navy chaplains serving in the Coast Guard is provided in reference (m).

**OFFICE OF THE
CHIEF OF NAVAL OPERATIONS
DEPARTMENT OF THE NAVY**

BUPERS/NMPC DUTY
OFFICER...(AV)224-2768

OP-09G CODE-A-PHONE...
(AV)224-4326
(202)694-4326

*Memorandum from the
Chief of Chaplains*

15 DEC 1983

O-6 Minutes (27-83)

Dear Chaplain,

Season's Greetings to you and yours, especially those of you (one hundred and one, if my calculations are correct) who are ministering to men and women in deployed fleet units or at isolated stations. May the meaning of our religious observances lift the hearts of those we serve and may you be blessed to approach the New Year with an added sense of dedication and enthusiasm.

The first of January means I've been in the job for five months and that's a good time to share with you some observations the Deputy and I have made and what has been accomplished in regard to the goals set forth in my 1 August letter.

First of all let me tell you how very proud I am of the professional manner in which you have been and are performing your ministry. It is indeed sad that the tragedy of 23 October had to be - but it produced evidence of the Chaplain Corps' (Total Force) ability to meet the test. It was as though the words were being passed from one end of our Corps to the other - "This is not a drill, This is not a drill."

When Father John and I came to the office early on that initial Sunday morning to see what we could do - to let people know we were standing by - we talked about those things that would be required of chaplains. We knew you would all do what is required of you. Our confidence on that very rainy Washington day was correct; the whole of the Corps is greater than the sum of its parts.

Chaplains Pucciarelli, Wheeler and Resnicoff were on the scene and by now you are somewhat aware of their suffering and ministry. On 9 November when I made an all too brief visit to the site of the explosion with Chaplain Bob Riley I was in awe of what they had endured and how magnificently they responded. I have had the privilege of nominating all three of them for the Stan Parris Award given by the Chapel of the Four Chaplains in Philadelphia. The award will be presented on 2 Feb 1984.

As the entire family of the Navy - Marine Corps team felt the shock wave of hurt, you responded with appropriate ministry to meet the needs present at your station of duty. Immediately, chaplains from the ships off Beirut came ashore to help. Chaplains in duty stations like Naples prepared to minister to the wounded. Active and reserve chaplains around the world made themselves available to assist with casualty assistance calls. At Camp Lejeune, in particular, they organized themselves into around-the-clock teams. Chaplains there and in other locations prepared for and participated in memorial services including those at Dover AFB in Delaware, Camp Lejeune and in the multitude of commands. Our people needed a time to worship God and honor those who were killed while serving as peacekeepers. Still other chaplains worked to provide those special scriptures or to compose the right words to officiate at the funerals and the grave site committals of "our brothers departed."

You proved that all parts are related to the whole in the doing of ministry. It was faith and inter-faith as required - Jewish, Orthodox, Catholic, Protestant. It was 410X - USN, USNR, USNR-R, as needed. It was the clergy of the Corps of Chaplains ministering. B.Z.

Enclosure (1) is self-explanatory and I'm certain that you recognize the efforts to establish relationships, explain policies, set procedures, etc. Please note in it the fact that I'm most fortunate to have an outstanding staff and I enjoy a complete reliance on our Claimant Chaplains.

John and Emmett join me in thanking you for all the good birthday parties this year. Each one is unique, except when we three tell the same stories - Amazing Grace! - and we thank you for your glorious hospitality. We are also grateful for the anniversary celebrations we are not able to attend because we know all the parties show that we are proud of the CHC, pleased to entertain those who host us, and more than willing to have a good time.

I identified for you in my 1 August letter the organizational goals - Restatement of Policy, Reemphasis of Accountability and Reassertion of Practical Factors. The cornerstone of a clear, concise directive from which to build in these areas was acquired yesterday when the Secretary of Navy signed off on SECNAVINST 1730.7. The new instruction is the product of years of work by numerous chaplains and staff members of other naval communities who consistently help us in the practice of ministry in this vast system. An advanced copy of it will come to you in <u>0-6 Minutes</u> so you'll have an opportunity to study it before the regular distribution comes to your command. Of course, it's just the beginning. At all levels implementing instructions, orders, modifications in custodial letters, etc. will have to take place - the Claimant Chaplains will provide you with directions in these and other areas. For the present I just share with you that the policy climate is now set for us to all work together, as we are wont to do, to improve our individual and corporate ministry in service to God's people.

Since I've shared a major accomplishment with you let me also address a continuing frustration which proves <u>KAFKA LIVES</u>. As you know we had to combine <u>Items of Interest</u> and the

Chaplains Bulletin into one publication over a year ago. Well, with that problem resolved our editors produced the new Chaplains Bulletin on time. Then the world's greatest printing hassels commenced; actually, budget matters were beyond our control. "Long story, short" means you'll be getting the June 1983 Chaplains Bulletin one of these days. I decided that it should be forwarded in spite of O.B.E. items because the editors and contributors did a great job. So enjoy the Bulletin and join me in having a laugh. In the meantime, back at the staff, the lads have regrouped to see if we can eventually win the battle of printing via the C.R.B. Tune in next time.

I enter the new calendar year with excitement and concern. I am grateful for the ministry that has been performed this past year, often amid the most difficult conditions. I know well the quality of sharing God's life and love that all of us can bring to our service men and women. I am also aware of the difficult tenor of the times. The challenges for our service personnel are many and sustained. They are performing admirably. We can do no less.

My wish for us in this New Year is for Peace. May our lives continually reach for this goal.

Sincerely,

Neil

NEIL M. STEVENSON
Rear Admiral, CHC, USN
Chief of Chaplains

DEPARTMENT OF THE NAVY
Office of the Secretary
Washington, D.C. 20350

Canc: Dec 84

SECNAVNOTE 1730
OP-09G
27 December 1983

SECNAV NOTICE 1730

From: Secretary of the Navy
To: All Ships and Stations

Subj: Holy Days and Days of Religious Observance

Ref: (a) U.S. Navy Regulations, 1973, Article 0722
(b) NAVMILPERSMAN, Articles 5810110 and 3030100
(c) Marine Corps Manual, Paragraph 2816 (NOTAL)

Encl: (1) List of Calendar 1984-1986 Holy Days and Days of Religious Observance

1. Purpose. To provide commands with information concerning holy days and days of religious observance in order to facilitate planning for these events.

2. Discussion. References (a) through (c) set forth policies pertaining to religious observances. Enclosure (1) will assist activities to prepare timely publicity and proper menus for these observances as well as arrange for appropriate divine services.

CHAPMAN B. COX
Acting

Distribution:
SNDL 1 and 2
MARCORPS Codes H and I

SECNAVNOTE 1730
27 DEC 1983

OBSERVANCE	FAITH	1984	1985	1986
Shavuot	J	05-07 ~~JAN~~ JUN	25-27 MAY	12-14 JUN
Feast of Pentecost	EO	10 JUN	02 JUN	22 JUN
1 Ramadan (Note 6)	M	01 JUN	21 MAY	10 MAY
Idul-Fitr (Note 6)	M	30 JUN	20 JUN	09 JUN
Transfiguration of Our Lord	EO	06 AUG	06 AUG	06 AUG
Assumption of Mary (for EO, Dormition of the Virgin Mary)	RC, EO	15 AUG	15 AUG	15 AUG
Rosh Hashanah	J	26-28 SEP	15-17 SEP	03-05 OCT
Yom Kippur	J	05-06 ~~SEP~~ OCT	24-25 SEP	12-13 OCT
Idul-Adha (Feast of Sacrifice)	M	06 SEP	27 AUG	16 AUG
World Communion Sunday	P	07 OCT	06 OCT	05 OCT
Sukkot-Simchat Torah Period	J	10-19 OCT	29 SEP-08 OCT	17-26 OCT
All Saints Day	RC	01 NOV	01 NOV	01 NOV
Advent Begins	EO	15 NOV	15 NOV	15 NOV
Presentation of the Virgin Mary	EO	21 NOV	21 NOV	21 NOV
Immaculate Conception	RC	08 DEC	08 DEC	08 DEC
Hanukkah	J	18-26 DEC	07-15 DEC	26 DEC-03 JAN
Christmas	RC, P, EO	25 DEC	25 DEC	25 DEC

LEGEND: RC - Roman Catholic
J - Jewish
P - Protestant
EO - Eastern Orthodox
M - Muslim

NOTES:

1. Days of obligation include Sundays, Solemnity of the Mother of God, Ascension of Our Lord, Assumption of Mary, All Saints Day, Immaculate Conception and Christmas.

2. Many faith groups have memorial services on Martin Luther King's Birthday. This special day will become a National Holiday in 1986.

Enclosure (1)

CHIEF OF CHAPLAINS (G) AND DEPUTY CHIEF OF CHAPLAINS (GB) SCHEDULE, 1 AUGUST 1983 - 31 DECEMBER 1983

1-20 AUG	(G/GB)	OFFICIAL CALLS ON - UNDER SECRETARY OF THE NAVY - Honorable J. F. Goodrich; CNO - Admiral Watkins; CMC - General Kelley; COMCOGARD - Admiral Gracey; ASSISTANT SECRETARY OF THE NAVY (MANPOWER) - Honorable Chapman B. Cox; OP-01 - VADM Zech; OP-02 - VADM Thunman; OP-03 - VADM Walters; OP-04 - VADM Hughes; CHINFO - COMO Garrow; Army COC - Chaplain Hessian; Air Force COC - Chaplain Collins; OP-05 - VADM Schoultz; NDW - COMO Disher; NAVSEC - RADM McDowell; VCNO - Admiral Hayes; NAVSEASYSCOM - Admiral McKee; NAVMEDCOM - RADM McDermott; OP-11 - COMO Primeau; OP-12 - RADM Klein; OP-13 - RADM Herberger
12 AUG	(G/GB)	Endorsing agents in New York City area
25-26 AUG	(G)	Training Conference at AFSC, Norfolk, VA
29 AUG	(G/GB)	Endorsing agents in Washington, DC area
12-16 SEP	(G/GB)	Major Claimant Staff Chaplains Meeting, Washington, DC
19 SEP	(G)	06 Meeting NDW
21 SEP	(G)	06 Meeting Norfolk area
22 SEP	(G)	06 Meeting Camp Lejeune area
23 SEP	(G)	06 Meeting Charleston area
26 SEP	(G)	06 Meeting Jacksonville area
2 OCT	(G/GB)	Seton Shrine
3 OCT	(G)	Endorsing Agent, Salt Lake City
4 OCT	(G)	06 Meeting San Francisco/Seattle area
6 OCT	(G)	06 Meeting San Diego area

Enclosure (1)

11 OCT	(G/GB)	Armed Forces Chaplains Board - Pentagon
16 OCT	(G/GB)	Navy Sunday, Washington Cathedral
16-21 OCT	(GB)	PDTC Validation, Newport, RI
18 OCT	(G/GB)	German Protestant Bishop's Visit - Bishop Lehming
18-19 OCT	(G)	Basic Course, Chaplains School, Newport, RI
25 OCT	(G)	SUBLANT Chaplains Conference, Norfolk, VA
25-26 OCT	(G/GB)	National Conference on Ministry to Armed Forces (NCMAF)
28 OCT	(G/GB)	Navy Ball
29 OCT	(G)	Memorial Service at Dover Air Force Base
3 NOV	(GB)	REDCOM Meeting, Charleston, SC
4 NOV	(G/GB)	Memorial Service at Camp Lejeune
6 NOV	(G/GB)	Marine Corps Sunday, Washington Cathedral
7-16 NOV	(G)	Visit chaplains and commands - Gaeta, Naples, Beirut, USS IWO JIMA, USS AUSTIN, USS EL PASO, USS HARLAN COUNTY, USS PORTLAND, USS KENNEDY, NEA MAKRI, SIGONELLA, COMSIXTHFLT
9 NOV	(GB)	PAC/LANT Reserve Chaplains, Norfolk, VA
15-20 NOV	(GB)	CHC Anniversaries, Yuma, San Francisco, Seattle
17-23 NOV	(G)	CHC Anniversaries, Orlando, Jacksonville, Norfolk, Newport
27-29 NOV	(G)	CHC Anniversaries, Camp Lejeune, Cherry Point
11-13 DEC	(G/GB)	Naval War College Program, Newport, RI
14 DEC	(GB)	Commence Indian Ocean Trip w/Assistant LANTFLT Chaplain

OP-09G-mr
Ser 78
9 January 1984

Dear (Name of Claimant Chap),

Happy New Year! In the spirit of 1984 and 1730.7 let me share some items with you for your information and/or action.

<u>Letters to 0-6 Chaplains concerning their proposed PCS orders</u> - In the future I will share a blind copy of those letters with you for chaplains in your claimancy or for those who will be reporting to commands in your claimancy. This is a sensitive matter, so let me emphasize the rules of the road I expect in sharing blind copies with you:

- a) The proposal is to be held in the strictest privacy and the initiation for disclosing the information is with the individual concerned not the Claimant Chaplains.

- b) I expect absolute support in the decision from the Claimant Chaplain. This means that if you think my nominee is not qualified you should inform me, and me only, privately.

<u>Collation of Quarterly Reports</u> - The staff is developing methods for deriving information from the collated data you submit from the quarterly reports for my 1 February report to CNO, CNP and SECNAV. You know the importance for our Corps of my reporting to these offices statistical and narrative data in a timely fashion. Please forward your report to me on time. Please don't delay your report because others are late getting theirs to you. If you wish, just list those not heard from -- that is a report in and of itself.

<u>Communications</u> - An endless subject and one we will always have to strive to improve. It was discouraging to receive word that some of our chaplains in CONUS did not get the word by AUTOVON of Chaplain John Bruggeman's death. Please do everything you can to smooth out the system. Chaplains in your network may need to be updated on the priorities for communicating with their chaplains. A good rule of thumb is to pass on the news in the same manner in which it is received - AUTOVON by AUTOVON; mail by mail; message by message.

<u>Chapel Usage</u> - Let us emphasize the fact that chapels are for people <u>versus</u> chaplains. The existence of the RP rating and a viable chapel usage instruction should allow chaplains to meet the needs of people. It also provides us the advantage to delineate the distinction between the use of the chapel and the

OP-09G-mr
Ser 78
9 January 1984

availability of the chaplain. Please indicate to your chaplains that their commands should have a chapel usage instruction (samples provided 15 February 1982) that <u>opens</u> the chapel doors for people.

<u>Physical Fitness</u> - Chaplains are looking good. Those who are in shape need to be complimented. Those who are slipping need to be urged to act before the command acts.

<u>Religious Education</u> - From my perspective this is an area in which we need improvement across the board. I'm convinced that there are three things that need to be done -- 1) place the responsibility for being <u>coordinators</u> of religious education programs on the RP's (i.e., under the supervision of the chaplain, to manage the administrative details, resources, and personnel, both military and volunteer, essential to the effective functioning of a Religious Education Program); 2) ensure that chaplains <u>supervise</u> the religious education program and have total responsibility for the content and <u>selection</u> of the curriculum materials; and 3) emphasize the use of the religious education materials set forth in the <u>cooperative curriculum guides</u>. I have observed that where all three of these elements exist religious education is meeting the needs of our people. Please place these high on the agenda for your visits. If you uncover problems (i.e., materials ordered from the official guides not arriving in a timely fashion) please provide me with documented data. The few situations we've examined of late clearly indicate the command did not order materials in a timely fashion.

<u>F.Y.I.</u> The staff continues to work the problems and high on the current list are:

- PCS funds are of great concern and G3 works the problems daily. It's as tough a year as I've ever seen. Please keep your chaplains informed that detailing is a check book activity with a priority for operational requirements.

- MILCON needs your interest. Each installation chaplain should be participating in the base master planning process and should know and correct if necessary their Facilities Requirements List. Since your input to the claimant's facilities planners has taken on such a great importance, it is essential that facilities deficiencies be identified, prioritized and defended at the claimant input level. Special care should be given to projects submitted to the FYDP so that pricing and requirements are accurate, and so that the projects are well justified to make it in the budget. Chapels are in competition for funds with operational requirements, and need strong support. Keep my G2 informed.

OP-09G-mr
Ser 78
9 January 1984

- <u>Recruiting</u>. We must have contacts, leads, referrals. The current <u>Chaplains</u> School basic class is an example of recruiting well done. They look young, fit, sharp, and eager for ministry with the troops. Please continue to motivate your chaplains to recruit quality clergy for our Corps. The facts are clear that we need help in locating Catholic and Jewish clergy!! G4 needs your input.

- <u>P.D.T.C</u> - I know you are urging your chaplains to be present and active in the course. (By the way, G1 would like your nominations for chaplains to attend other courses.)

- <u>Chief of Chaplains Fund</u> - Donations are needed. As you know the fund is used to provide appropriate charitable contributions as well as expressions of sympathy and concern. It does need regular transfusions and I ask that you pass that word to the custodians of religious offering funds.

- <u>Write up from weekly OP-09G Staff Meetings</u> - I'm asking the GA to forward copies of these write-ups to you for <u>you eyes only</u>. I know they will not be too useful to you, but they do highlight topics, names and issues for you.

- <u>COC Interview</u> has hit the streets thanks to CRB. I hope it's as helpful to you as I intended it to be.

- <u>Actions Regarding SECNAVINST 1730.7</u> - a letter is being prepared to give you guidance on the follow-on actions required. I know you join me in wanting the revision of all directives done in an orderly fashion starting with OPNAV. It's an exercise where we don't want folks to get ahead of or behind the curve on, so please hold for our G2 shop guidance.

In closing I ask you to continue to teach the fundamentals to all our chaplains wherever you go - I know it gets old sometimes but we are the coaches. Please keep in contact with me and the G directors. Conall, Al, Walt, Jim and Joe join John and me in sending best regards.

Sincerely,

NEIL M. STEVENSON
Rear Admiral, CHC, USN

(Name & Address of Claimant Chaps.)

Blind copy to:
Chap. Ecker
Chap. MacCall

DEPARTMENT OF THE NAVY
OFFICE OF THE CHIEF OF NAVAL OPERATIONS
WASHINGTON, DC 20350

IN REPLY REFER TO

OPNAVINST 1730.1A
Op-09G/4U301259
5 November 1984

OPNAV INSTRUCTION 1730.1A

From: Chief of Naval Operations
To: All Ships and Stations

Subj: RELIGIOUS MINISTRIES IN THE NAVY

Ref: (a) SECNAVINST 1730.7 (NOTAL)
(b) DoD Directive 1304.19 of 1 Jun 84 (NOTAL)
(c) U. S. Navy Regulations, 1973
(d) SECNAVINST 1730.3F
(e) SECNAVINST 5401.2 encloses DoD 1015.1 of 19 Aug 81 (NOTAL)
(f) NAVSO P-3520
(g) OPNAVINST 5312.22
(h) SECNAVINST 7000.23 encloses DoD 1330.2 of 17 Mar 78
(i) SECNAVINST 7043.5A encloses DoD 4105.67 of 2 Oct 81 (NOTAL)
(j) NAVCOMPT Manual 075260
(k) SECNAVINST 7000.22 (NOTAL)
(l) SECNAVINST P-5212.5B
(m) SECNAVINST 1301.4 (NOTAL)
(n) Defense Officer Personnel Management Act (DOPMA), Pub. L. No. 96-513, 94 Stat. 28835 (1980)
(o) SECNAVINST 1900.10
(p) SECNAVINST 5430.93 (NOTAL)

Encl: (1) Responsibilities for Religious Ministries
(2) Programming for Religious Ministries
(3) The Chaplain Corps

1. Purpose. To implement reference (a) and establish policy, responsibilities, and procedures for religious ministries in the Navy.

2. Cancellation. OPNAVINST 1730.1.

3. Applicability. This instruction is applicable to all persons in the Navy who are responsible for the provision, facilitation, and support of religious ministries.

4. Background. Throughout its history, the Navy has recognized its responsibility to provide for religious ministries to meet the needs and rights of its personnel. The Second article of Navy Regulations, adopted 28 November 1775, stated, "The Commanders of ships of the thirteen United Colonies, are to take care that divine services be performed . . ." The Navy has always recognized this obligation to make possible the practice of religion

OPNAVINST 1730.1A

and to ensure that citizens serving in the naval service are not deprived of opportunities for the free exercise of their religion.

5. Policy

    a. Commanders and commanding officers shall provide for the free exercise of religion by all personnel of their commands as specified in enclosure (1).

    b. Commands are to provide programs of ministry in support of the free exercise of religion. The command religious program is an essential element of a command's total administration to be supported and managed as an integral part of a command's planning, programming, and budgeting activities.

    c. The Navy appoints chaplains from the clergy of religious faith groups of the United States under reference (b). Navy chaplains provide ministry throughout the Navy through the development and execution of command religious programs.

    d. Policy and procedures for implementing religious ministries in the Navy are set forth in enclosures (1) through (3) under reference (a) and references (d) through (p).

6. Responsibilities. Commanders and commanding officers shall accomplish their responsibility of providing for the free exercise of religion by implementing the policy and following the procedures set forth in this instruction and its enclosures.

7. Report and Form

    a. The Active Duty Chaplain's Report, located in paragraph 2f(11) of enclosure (3), has been assigned symbol OPNAV 1730-1 and is approved for three years from the date of this directive.

    b. Form OPNAV 1730/3 (Rev. 6-83) is stocked in Chaplains Resource Board, Norfolk, Virginia.

Ronald J Hays

RONALD J. HAYS
ADMIRAL, U. S. NAVY
VICE CHIEF OF NAVAL OPERATIONS

Distribution:
SNDL Parts 1 and 2
MARCORPS CODE L72

OPNAVINST 1730.1A

Commander
Naval Data Automation Command
(Code 172)
Washington Navy Yard
Wash., DC 20374 (200 copies)

Stocked:
CO, NAVPUBFORMCEN
5801 Tabor Ave.
Phila., PA 19120 (500 copies)

OPNAVINST 1730.1A

RESPONSIBILITIES FOR RELIGIOUS MINISTRIES

1. General

    a. <u>Authority</u>. Reference (a) reiterates that, "The commanders of vessels and naval activities to which chaplains are attached shall cause divine services to be performed on Sunday, whenever the weather and other circumstances allow it to be done ..."

    b. <u>Policy</u>

        (1) In keeping with Department of the Navy policy, commanders and commanding officers shall provide for the free exercise of religion for all members of the naval service, their dependents, and other authorized persons.

        (2) Chaplains appointed under Navy policy shall provide ministry and facilitate the free exercise of religion for all members of the naval service, their dependents, and other authorized persons through the Command Religious Program.

2. Command

    a. <u>Command responsibilities</u>. Commanders and commanding officers:

        (1) Comply with the provisions of article 0845 of reference (c) which designates chaplains as non-combatants under the Geneva Convention of 12 August 1949.

        (2) "Use all proper means to foster high morale, and to develop and strengthen the moral and spiritual well-being of the personnel under his/her command, and ensure that chaplains are provided the necessary logistic support for carrying out the command's religious program" as cited in article 0727 of reference (c).

        (3) Comply with the stipulations of article 0722 of reference (c) in the conduct of divine services.

            (a) The Sabbath shall be observed on Sunday, except by members of the naval service whose religious convictions require them to observe some day other than Sunday as their day of worship. Those whose day of worship is other than Sunday are entitled to respect for their religious convictions and practices. Except by reason of necessity, personnel who celebrate the Sabbath on a day other than Sunday will be afforded the opportunity to observe the requirements of their religious principles. Where excused from duty on a day

Enclosure (1)

other than Sunday, the workweek of such individuals should not be less than that of any other individual and may include work on Sunday. Determination of necessity rests entirely with the commanding officer.

    (b) Consistent with the exigencies of the service, commanding officers are encouraged to give favorable consideration to applications for leave from those who may desire to observe significant holy days of their faith with their families.

    (4) In addition to the requirements set forth in 2a(3), above, relating to religious services, commanding officers shall not restrict the free exercise of religion by personnel in the naval service unless there is a military requirement to do so. Such requirements may exist in directives from higher authority or as otherwise determined by the commanding officer.

    (5) Support the Command Religious Program, including personnel, funding and logistics, as an essential element of a command's total operation. These matters will be managed as an integral part of the command's planning, programming, and budgeting activities as governed by existing directives.

  b. <u>Chaplain's Position in the Command</u>

    (1) As the principal advisor to the commander or commanding officer on religious and moral matters, the chaplain will be assigned as a department head or principal staff officer directly under the executive officer or, as appropriate, the chief staff officer.

    (2) As a principal advisor to the commanding officer, the chaplain shall have direct access to the commanding officer as provided in article 1107 of reference (c).

  c. <u>Religious Program Specialist (RP's)</u>

    (1) Religious Program Specialists (RP's) assist the command and specifically the chaplain in the administration and coordination of programs in support of the Command Religious Program. The programming of RP billets within a command is an integral element in command manpower authorization actions.

    (2) In keeping with their principal function, RP's are assigned only to units which have a chaplain assigned. RP's are assigned primary duties only in support of chaplains. RP duties in support of religious ministries within the command must be given appropriate consideration when assigning collateral duties. The Chief of Naval Personnel establishes occupational standards for the RP rating in the Manual of Navy Enlisted Manpower and Personnel Classifications and Occupational Standards, NAVPERS 18068D Series.

    (3) To facilitate their work with lay readers of all religious faith groups, RP's should not be assigned as a lay reader of any particular religious faith group.

OPNAVINST 1730.1A

   d. <u>Lay Readers</u>. Commanders or commanding officers may assign a lay reader to serve for a period of time to meet the religious needs of a particular religious faith group. The commander or commanding officer may seek the advice of the command's chaplain or chaplain attached to a higher echelon regarding the selection of an appropriate lay reader.

OPNAVINST 1730.1A

PROGRAMMING FOR RELIGIOUS MINISTRIES

1. **General**. Planning, programming, and budgeting activities are a command responsibility.

2. **Manpower and Personnel**

   a. **Manpower**

   (1) Planning, programming, and budgeting of Chaplain Corps manpower are essential elements of support for command religious programs throughout the naval service. Major manpower claimants of the Navy will plan, program, and budget for Chaplain Corps manpower as an integral part of force structure to the level of Service-wide standards established in accordance with Department of the Navy policy and procedures.

   (2) The Chief of Chaplains/Director of Religious Ministries manages chaplain (4100) and Religious Program Specialist (RP) program authorized billets through DCNO (MPT) and cognizant major manpower claimants. Claimant staff chaplains (CSC) advise and assist Navy, Marine Corps, and other major manpower claimants in planning and programming Chaplain Corps manpower and report to the Chief of Chaplains on all matters pertaining to 4100/RP manpower.

   b. **Personnel**. The Chief of Chaplains/Director of Religious Ministries, through interaction with the Commander, Navy Recruiting Command and Commander, Naval Military Personnel Command, recommends personnel for appointment, accession, distribution, and placement by the Chief of Naval Personnel in designated active duty or reserve chaplain billets or in other forms of official status in the Reserves or on the retired lists.

3. **Logistics**

   a. **Command Support**

   (1) Commands and units of the Navy will use local operation and maintenance funds for the support of religious ministries within the command.

   (2) Command logistic support of religious ministries is interpreted to include, but is not limited to:

   (a) Purchasing and providing consumable religious supplies and services such as religious literature, printing, liturgical accoutrements, transportation, and military band support.

   (b) Providing support essential to religious ministries, such as equipment, furnishings, and facilities. To the extent that other items are necessary for the conduct of the religious service, such items can be purchased with appropriated funds. Items solely of a decorative or personal nature are not to be purchased with appropriated funds.

(c) Contracting for musical and educational services such as organists, choir directors, directors of religious education, and resource persons.

(d) Supporting the professional training of chaplains and the training of RP's in short-term training opportunities.

(3) Procurement of ecclesiastical material in support of religious ministries is processed through normal Navy supply channels.

(4) To meet the religious needs of personnel in areas where military chaplains are not available or to provide additional professional personnel necessary to supplement existing religious ministry, commanders, and commanding officers may obtain the services of appropriately endorsed civilian clergy as auxiliary or contract chaplains. Appointments of auxiliary chaplains by the commander or commanding officer and awards of contracts by the contracting officer shall be made with the approval of the Chief of Chaplains. Procedures governing employment and payment of auxiliary and contract chaplains are outlined in reference (d).

b. Fees. No fees or gratuities will be charged or received for the use of government facilities in the performance of any religious act, sacrament, or rite. No fees or gratuities will be charged or received by a chaplain for any religious act, sacrament, or rite performed on government-owned property or for persons entitled to receive such services by authorization of the Department of the Navy. Nor will any RP be paid any fees for services performed on government property in support of any religious act, sacrament, or rite, or for persons entitled to receive such services by authorization of the Department of the Navy.

4. The Religious Offerings Fund (ROF)

a. General. Many faith groups provide the opportunity for voluntary contributions and benevolence as a part of their worship and religious life. A ROF may be established to serve the religious needs of the contributors by allowing for the collection and disbursement of offerings as an act of worship within the context of the Command Religious Program. Appropriate recipients of support from the ROF are organizations or individuals generally recognized as benevolent or service-oriented or religious bodies recommended by the contributors to the ROF.

b. Policy

(1) The Command Religious Program is a command function and is supported by appropriated funds. The ROF is a nonappropriated fund established by and administered under the authority of the commander or commanding officer. References (e) through (j) provide information and guidance on the establishment and management of non-appropriated funds. These funds will be used only for projects of religious benevolence beyond the limits of the Command Religious Program, not as an alternative to support for the Command Religious Program. The provisions of reference (a) and this paragraph do not preclude the

receipt and use of designated contributions to the ROF for items to enhance worship of a more general nature or heighten the importance of a special religious service or activity. Such designated offerings may be used for general purposes such as chapel fellowship activities, purchase of altar flowers, etc., and/or to provide non-general use items such as individual baptismal candles, first communion veils and other similar items as a benevolent expression from the religious faith group.

(2) Only one ROF will be established aboard any command. All funds collected in the context of the Command Religious Program will be deposited and accounted for in that command's ROF. No group will receive religious offerings apart from the ROF. Most commands will require at least a Roman Catholic and a Protestant sub-account, with others as needed.

(3) Disbursals from the ROF will be approved by the commanding officer and made in accordance with Department of the Navy policy. The commanding officer may delegate the authority to approve expenditures up to an appropriate limit to the ROF administrator.

(4) When a ROF or sub-account within that fund is dissolved for any reason, the commander or commanding officer will authorize disposition of the ROF property and liquidation of all outstanding indebtedness, under references (e) and (f). The Chief of Chaplains Fund is designated as the successor Nonappropriated Fund for the receipt of all remaining cash and proceeds from the sale of ROF-owned property. These funds along with reports required in reference (f) will be forwarded to the Chief of Chaplains (OP-09G).

c. Religious Offerings Fund Administrator and Custodian

(1) The senior chaplain of the command shall be appointed in writing by the commanding officer as the administrator of the ROF. The administrator is a direct representative of the commanding officer and exercises executive control over the ROF under reference (f). The administrator shall approve disbursements up to limits established by the commanding officer and in accordance with the intention of the donors. Disbursement requests above this limit will be submitted to the commanding officer for approval.

(2) One or more custodians may be appointed by the administrator subject to the approval of the commanding officer. It is expected that custodians will be appointed for at least the Roman Catholic, Protestant, and Jewish ROF sub-accounts in those commands where these sub-accounts are established. If deemed necessary by the administrator, custodians may be appointed for each of the religious offerings sub-accounts of groups contributing to the ROF. Custodians shall be members of the command and may be chaplains or Religious Program Specialists. Duties of the custodians shall be in accordance with the tasks and policies in reference (f). The responsibilities of the custodians may include, but are not limited to:

(a) Receiving the counted and verified offerings for the ROF sub-account.

(b) Safeguarding, depositing, and accounting for all ROF monies and other ROF assets;

(c) Preparing financial reports as required; and

(d) Making disbursements in accordance with paragraph 4b(3).

(3) When either the ROF administrator or custodian is expected to be absent from an activity for a prolonged period of time, the commanding officer may appoint an acting manager or custodian for the duration of the absence under reference (f).

d. Accounting

(1) Accounting will be under the general policy guidance of reference (f).

(2) Accounting records will be maintained for each religious faith group represented in the ROF with transactions and disbursements limited to available cash balances in each account.

(3) At the end of each quarter, a ROF Statement of Operations and Net Worth will be prepared at the direction of the ROF administrator and posted. A cumulative report will be prepared annually.

(4) An audit of ROF will be conducted:

(a) Annually, at the close of the fiscal year;

(b) When the ROF administrator is relieved;

(c) When a ROF custodian is relieved;

(d) When the ROF is dissolved; or

(e) When otherwise requested by the commander or commanding officer.

(5) The commander or the commanding officer will appoint an auditor to perform the ROF audit.

(6) The report of appropriated and nonappropriated resources expended in support of nonappropriated fund activities shall be made under reference (k) and guidance provided by the local Morale, Welfare, and Recreation coordinator.

(7) All documents will be retained for the time periods indicated in reference (l).

e. Chief of Chaplains Fund

(1) The Chief of Chaplains Fund is a special fund under this instruction that serves as a successor Nonappropriated Fund for all field activities and is funded by contributions from ROF and individuals. This fund allows the Chief of Chaplains to make benevolent contributions and extend expressions of concern, appreciation, and outreach.

(2) The administrator of the Chief of Chaplains Fund is a chaplain

OPNAVINST 1730.1A

appointed by the Chief of Chaplains and functions as the policy maker and implementor. The custodian, appointed by the Chief of Chaplains, is responsible for the day to day operations of the Chief of Chaplains Fund, including depositing receipts, writing checks, and preparing reports. Expenditures are made and obligations incurred by the Chief of Chaplains Fund at the direction of the Chief of Chaplains or his designated representative.

Planned Ministry Objectives (PMO). The command chaplain of each activity will develop a detailed PMO for the Command Religious Program for the budget year and out years and will forward it during the third quarter of the present year, via the chain of command, for guidance from the claimant staff chaplain. The PMO will be inclusive in scope in establishing objectives for ministry that meet the religious needs of personnel assigned using available resources fully. When practicable, the PMO will include, but not necessarily be limited to, the following:

a. Divine services (sabbath, daily);

b. Special religious services (weddings, memorials);

c. Seasonal religious services (Yom Kippur, Passover, Holy Days of Obligation, Advent, Lent);

d. Religious education classes (Sunday school, Confraternity of Christian Doctrine, adult religious education opportunities, sacramental preparation, bar/bat mitzvah preparation, etc.);

e. Pastoral Visitation (brig, work spaces, hospital);

f. Pastoral Counseling (including group sessions);

g. Other programs of religious ministry (retreats, music, marriage enrichment, films, special programs, etc.); and

h. Duty watches and availability plans (evening activities, weekends, crisis response, hospital sacramental ministry).

The PMO will be so drawn as to affect the most effective use of the individual ministries of all the chaplains assigned to the activity.

OPNAVINST 1730.1A

THE CHAPLAIN CORPS

1. General

    a. Establishment. The Chaplain Corps is established as a Staff Corps of the Navy under the provisions of reference (m), pursuant to the authority contained in reference (n).

    b. Mission. The Chaplain Corps is comprised of professionally qualified chaplains appointed from religious faith groups of the United States. Its purpose is to provide for the free exercise of religion for all members of the naval service, their dependents, and other authorized persons by providing ministries appropriate to their rights and needs and providing staff support to this end throughout the Department of the Navy.

2. Chaplains

    a. Endorsement. Chaplains are clergy persons endorsed by their ecclesiastical endorsing agency under reference (b). The maintenance of this endorsement is the responsibility of the chaplain and is an essential element of professional qualification as a Navy chaplain. Loss of ecclesiastical endorsement requires administrative processing under the provisions of reference (o).

    b. Responsibility. Chaplains are assigned or attached to a specific unit or station for the primary purpose of providing and facilitating religious ministries within that unit or station. Chaplains have responsibilities to the commander or commanding officer and to the appropriate supervisory chaplain at the next higher echelon in the command organization.

    c. Address. As commissioned officers, chaplains are addressed in oral or written communication under article 0810 of reference (c). As a form of address, use of the term "Chaplain" is always appropriate.

    d. Uniforms. Navy Chaplain Corps officers assigned to Marine Corps or Coast Guard organizations may wear the appropriate service or field uniform prescribed for Marine Corps or Coast Guard officers respectively.

    e. Functions

        (1) Advising the commander or commanding officer on all matters related to religious ministries within the command.

        (2) Administering the Command Religious Program by conducting divine services, administering sacraments and ordinances, performing rites and ceremonies in accordance with the manner and forms of the chaplain's particular faith group and facilitating the provision of religious ministries

for personnel of other faith groups.

   (3) Developing plans, programs, and budgets to execute religious ministries within the command.

   (4) Advising supervisory chaplains of the unit, or the command to which the unit is attached, of necessary actions concerning programming of chaplain and RP billets and other support requirements.

   f. *General Duties*. With the approval of the commanding officer, a chaplain attached to a ship or station shall perform the following general duties:

   (1) Conduct divine services.

   (2) Facilitate the free exercise of religion for all.

   (3) Provide appropriate sacramental ministry and pastoral care.

   (4) Organize voluntary programs of religious education.

   (5) Visit the sick.

   (6) At general quarters, report to a battle station to be available to minister to the wounded.

   (7) At daily quarters, report his or her presence aboard to the executive officer.

   (8) Visit personnel confined to brigs or correctional facilities.

   (9) Maintain liaison with local religious groups in U.S. or foreign communities in order to develop public awareness of the religious activities in the Navy.

   (10) Keep the public affairs officer informed of chaplains' activities of public interest.

   (11) Report quarterly a summary of activities to the claimant staff chaplain.

   (12) Ensure appropriate training and supervision of assigned enlisted and civilian personnel.

   g. Collateral Duties

   (1) When assigning collateral duties to the chaplain, the governing factor for commanders and commanding officers shall be the recognition of the primacy of the chaplain's duty of religious ministry as provided in article 0845 of reference (c).

   (2) Chaplains will not be assigned collateral duties which involve:

OPNAVINST 1730.1A

(a) Actions in violation of the religious practices of the chaplain's ecclesiastical authority.

(b) Violation of noncombatant status.

(c) Serving as director or treasurer of fund drives.

(d) Serving in any capacity relating to the solicitation, collection, or disbursing of any monies, except as administrator or custodian of a ROF.

(e) Serving on a court-martial or rendering judgment in disciplinary cases, except as required by article 0845 of reference (c).

(f) Standing watches other than that of duty chaplain.

3. <u>Chief of Chaplains/Director of Religious Ministries/Senior Chaplain of the Department of the Navy</u>

   a. <u>Position in the Organization</u>. The Chief of Chaplains/Director of Religious Ministries/Senior Chaplain of the Department of the Navy, hereafter referred to as "Chief of Chaplains," directs a major staff office under the Chief of Naval Operations with responsibility for implementing religious ministries throughout the naval service.

   b. <u>Mission</u>

   (1) The Chief of Chaplains, as the Director of Religious Ministries, directs, administers and manages the Navy Chaplain Corps and implements religious ministries to meet the needs of personnel in the naval service and their dependents in their pursuit of the free exercise of religion.

   (2) In accordance with reference (p), the Chief of Chaplains, as the Senior Chaplain of the Department of the Navy, serves as an advisor to the Secretary of the Navy on religious, spiritual, and moral and ethical implications of policies and action of the Department of the Navy. In these matters, the Chief of Chaplains shall provide such advice and counsel to the Secretary, the Civilian Executive Assistants, the Chief of Naval Operations, the Commandant of the Marine Corps, the Commandant of the Coast Guard, and officials of the Merchant Marine on any issue they may direct. Additionally, the Chief of Chaplains may volunteer such advice and counsel to these same officials upon any matter that should be brought to their attention.

   c. <u>Functions</u>

   (1) The Chief of Chaplains/Director of Religious Ministries as the principal advisor to the Chief of Naval Operations on religious matters:

   (a) Advises the Chief of Naval Operations and the chain of command on religious, moral and ethical concerns, needs of personnel of the naval service and members of their families, and ensures consideration of these factors in all policy development.

   (b) Supports the Chief of Naval Operations, the Commandant of the Marine Corps, the Commandant of the Coast Guard, and officials of the Merchant Marine in meeting the religious, moral and ethical needs of members of the naval service.

   (c) Develops and monitors plans, policies, and programs of religious ministry in the naval service.

   (d) Represents the Navy to religious faith groups in all matters pertaining to the ecclesiastical endorsement of clergy as Navy chaplains.

   (e) Functions as technical sponsor for the acquisition, operation, and maintenance of religious facilities and collateral equipment, both ashore and afloat.

   (f) Coordinates and administers Chaplain Corps participation in command inspection programs for the naval service in those areas related to religious ministry, morale and quality of life.

   (g) Monitors and manages the Auxiliary and Contract Chaplain Program under reference (d).

 (2) As an additional duty, under reference (p), the Chief of Chaplains/Senior Chaplain of the Department of the Navy as advisor to the Secretary of the Navy on religious matters:

   (a) Reports regularly on the religious, moral and ethical implications of the Department of the Navy policies and actions which impact upon the personnel of the naval service, their dependents, and upon the nation's religious faith groups.

   (b) Advises the Secretary of the Navy, the Chief of Naval Operations, the Commandant of the Marine Corps, the Commandant of the Coast Guard and officials of the Merchant Marine on meeting the religious, moral, and ethical needs of members of the sea services.

   (c) Informs the Secretary of the Navy on the policies, programs, and positions of religious faith groups of the United States.

   (d) Represents the Department of the Navy on the Armed Forces Chaplains Board and maintains liaison with other boards, committees, and agencies in matters pertaining to religious activities.

   (e) Represents the Department of the Navy in meeting with the Chiefs of Chaplains/Senior Chaplains of the navies of other nations and in international forums affecting religious ministry and the well-being of persons in the naval service.

 (3) As an additional duty, the Chief of Chaplains as advisor to the Chief of Naval Personnel on religious matters affecting personnel management

and the requirements for religious ministry in the naval service:

    (a) Identifies the requirements to support religious ministries in the naval service for sponsorship in the planning, programming, budgeting systems, and manpower management.

    (b) Develops, plans, and establishes policies and programs governing the accession, professional development, and distribution of chaplains.

    (c) Establishes Chaplain Corps officer plans, policies, and procurement requirements for the Commander, Navy Recruiting Command.

    (d) Serves as technical and program sponsor of training for the Chaplain Corps.

    (e) Serves as primary advisor and program sponsor for the Religious Program Specialist (RP) rating.

4. <u>Organizational Levels of Assignment</u>

  a. <u>Office of the Chief of Chaplains</u>

    (1) A Deputy Chief of Chaplains/Deputy Director of Religious Ministries/Deputy Senior Chaplain of the Department of the Navy is assigned to perform all duties of the office as directed by the Chief of Chaplains.

    (2) Chaplains are assigned to the office of the Chief of Chaplains to assist in the accomplishment of the mission function and responsibilities of the office.

  b. <u>Claimant Chaplains</u>

    (1) A claimant staff chaplain is the senior chaplain assigned to the staff of a manpower claimant; e.g., Chief of Naval Operations, the Commander in Chief of the U.S. Atlantic Fleet, the Commander in Chief of the U.S. Pacific Fleet. Claimant chaplains, in the execution of their functional responsibilities, are particularly influential in assisting in the administration of religious ministries within the Navy.

    (2) Functions of claimant staff chaplains include:

    (a) Advising the major manpower claimant on all matters relating to religion and religious ministries within the claimancy.

    (b) Advising the Chief of Chaplains on matters concerning religious ministries within the claimancy which require the attention of the Chief of Chaplains.

    (c) Monitoring billets and billet requirements for chaplains and for RP's in all units of the fleet, force, or command and advising the appropriate authority on the initiation of manpower authorization change requests.

  (d) Monitoring the Auxiliary and Contract Chaplain Program on behalf of the Chief of Chaplains under reference (d).

  (e) Coordinating matters such as site plans, justification data, priorities, programming, and funding for construction of religious facilities.

  (f) Participating in the naval command inspection program for the purpose of evaluating the effectiveness of command religious programs.

  (g) Facilitating the ministry of chaplains via command channels.

  (h) Facilitating development of ministry models to meet the unique needs of the commands in the claimancy.

  (i) Maintaining communications and conducting conferences for chaplains, as required.

  (j) Providing orientation and continued training for all chaplains and RP's in the claimancy.

  (k) Identifying training needs of chaplains and RP's to the Chief of Chaplains.

  (l) Reporting quarterly one month after the end of the quarter a summary of chaplain activities to the Chief of Chaplains (Op-09G).

c. <u>Supervisory Chaplains</u>

 (1) A supervisory chaplain is the senior chaplain assigned to the commander or commanding officer of a force, staff, or unit. Supervisory chaplains are department heads or principal staff officers with responsibility to the commander or commanding officer through the executive officer or the chief of staff for administering, supervising, and facilitating religious ministries and chaplain activities. This responsibility includes the professional supervision of chaplains, assigned enlisted and civilian personnel, and of chaplains in subordinate commands, as appropriate.

 (2) Functions of supervisory chaplains include:

  (a) Advising the commander or commanding officer on all matters related to religious ministries within the command.

  (b) Advising the claimant staff chaplain of the command to which the unit is attached, via the appropriate Force Chaplain, of necessary actions concerning programming of chaplain and RP billets and other support requirements.

  (c) Establishing and submitting Planned Ministry Objectives for religious ministries throughout the command.

(d) Developing plans, programs, and budgets to execute religious ministries within the command.

(e) Administering the commander's or commanding officer's program for religious ministries to meet the religious needs of all personnel of the command.

(f) Coordinating the ministries of all assigned chaplains with respect to religious faith and functional diversity in professional qualifications to meet the needs of personnel.

(g) Supervising the activities of all assigned enlisted personnel and civilian employees.

(h) Facilitating the continued training and professional development of all personnel within the Command Religious Program.

DEPARTMENT OF THE NAVY
OFFICE OF THE CHIEF OF NAVAL OPERATIONS
WASHINGTON, DC 20350

IN REPLY REFER TO

OP-09G-mr
Ser 1102
30 April 1984

Dear Chaplain,

Shepherds lead because they know the way. In this letter I want to emphasize the importance of chaplains fulfilling their leadership roles in relation to their Religious Program Specialists. This leadership responsibility is relatively new to chaplains and one that demands study of the basic references which identify levels of competence at the various rates; those which guide the quality and nature of the Chaplain/RP relationship; and those which set standards of performance and evaluation.

It is my expectation that all chaplains have available to them a complete inventory of the "charts" necessary to lead RP's and that chaplains study, reference and use them constantly. Starting with the Division Officers Guide as the basic text on Naval leadership the chaplain should also have:

- Navy Enlisted Occupational Standards (NAVPERS 18068D) which forms the basis upon which RP's are trained, advanced and distributed.

- Personnel Advancement Requirements (PAR's) is a listing of those skills and abilities which RP's must demonstrate and have validated as a prerequisite to recommendation for advancement.

- "Handbook for Chaplains, RP Personnel Management and On the Job Training" (NAVEDTRA 113).

- Religious Ministries within the Department of the Navy (SECNAVINST 1730.7).

- Navy Enlisted Performance Evaluation System (NMPCINST 1616.1A).

- Naval Military Personnel Manual, article 2210200 (Enlisted Pay Grades and Titles).

In many commands the supervisory chaplain has wisely drawn these texts together to make a one shelf library to the value of Chaplains and RP's. I'm pleased to note in some commands the

OP-09G-mr
Ser 1102
30 April 1984

practice of regular training sessions is a standard operating procedure either within the command or in cooperation with other chaplain departments. Many a junior chaplain will be grateful some day that his/her supervisory chaplain assigned him or her the task of learning through teaching from these basic texts.

RP's have expectations of their leaders. I've seen and heard them expressed in several ways, but I'll set them out as follows:

RP's expect their relationship with chaplains to be professional. Professionalism is not necessarily rigid and formal but neither is it casual and familiar. Forms of address should include rate and last name when addressing an RP. To do so extends to the RP the military respect he/she may rightfully expect from any officer, line or staff. Though use of first names is intended to be friendly and informal, in point of fact, it is paternalistic and condescending.

RP's expect chaplains to have professional expectations of them. They have a right for a chaplain to know the occupational standards for their rate and to be utilized accordingly. In addition, it is important for chaplains to keep clear the distinction between personal and professional expectations. There are no personal chaplain expectations in the occupational standards. In the performance of duty, RP's do perform errands on official business; they do not run chaplains' personal errands. RP's do prepare coffee for work stations/Chapel functions. They do not get coffee for chaplains. RP's are expected to serve as Duty Driver for official functions/Command sponsored programs. They are not expected to use their own vehicles for the performance of work or for Command sponsored programs. These are only samples of areas of distinction that need to be thought through and applied.

RP's expect to be led and challenged by the example and knowledge of their chaplain. They should not be excused from military requirements (i.e., not standing personnel inspection) because the chaplain doesn't want to meet the requirement. They should not be required to disregard a directive (i.e., Religious Offerings Fund stipulations in SECNAVINST 1730.7) because the chaplain finds it more convenient. There will also be times when they know more about a Navy procedure than their supervisor, and that is when the Chief Engineer (chaplain) says

OP-09G-mr
Ser 1102
30 April 1984

to his Machinist Mate (RP), "I buy your recommendation and I trust your skill. You have my permission to get the job done."

Our present cadre of RP's are motivated and enthusiastic about performing their duties and are "on board" with the Navy's focus on responsibility and accountability. The vast majority are superb examples of pride and professionalism. I'm very impressed with the loyalty they display when they discuss their chaplain(s) with me. They are eager to serve the Navy and the Chaplain Corps.

I have said before, "Navy chaplains are the best." Our goal is to make the best better. I feel the same way about RP's; they are the best - we recommended and selected them. Sound professional leadership practices from chaplains will help achieve our goal for them as well, to make the best better.

Sincerely,

NEIL M. STEVENSON
Rear Admiral, CHC, USN
Chief of Chaplains

(THIS LTR WAS SENT TO ALL MAJOR CLAIMANT STAFF CHAPLAINS)

15 February 1985

Dear Chaplain _____,

From the number of items before me that I wish to bring to your attention, it's evidently been too long since I last corresponded with you. I'll try to do better in the future.

Please take appropriate action within your claimancy regarding the following items:

A. Security. In these times when special precautions are required I request that you make it abundantly clear to chaplains that they cannot take lightly the recommendations they make to command regarding civilian clergy access to military installations. A review of all base pass privileges given to clergy, Sunday School buses, etc. is appropriate at this time. Chaplains need to deal seriously with whether or not those who have passes or are requesting passes truly need them. As we all know, it's not the kind of subject that should be decided on a "clergy discount" basis.

B. OFFICER PREFERENCE CARDS. The new Preference Cards are being received and with today's technology they are being entered into the Officer Assignment Information System (OAIS) very quickly. OAIS is a automated processing system for use by the Detailer. Please advise your Chaplains that it is most important for them to submit the new preference cards since the old cards can not be entered into the system. Chaplains also need to know of the necessity of submitting a complete and correct preference card and be alerted to the all-to-frequent errors being made as noted in enclosure (1).

C. RELIGIOUS OFFERING FUND (ROF). Chaplains still need on the job training (OJT) in regards to ROFs and OPNAVINST 1730.1A. Emphasize that ROFs are not to be used to pay for organists and choir directors or other support personnel. In situations where the command has not come up to speed on that requirement, the command chaplain should be presenting a plan for eliminating the use of the ROF for such expenses. Chaplains and RPs must also be aware that they are neither to be paid for services performed on government property nor to receive compensation anywhere else from persons entitled to receive such services.

D. <u>PERMISSIVE ORDERS</u>. This subject is <u>not</u> addressed in <u>OPNAVINST 1730.1A</u>. It is addressed in the Navy Military Personnel Manual 1810280 and BUPERSINST 1321.2H of 13 January 1976, paragraph 5b(1). Chaplains requesting permissive orders involving travel at no cost to the government should research and use the above for references.

E. <u>MILITARY CHAPLAINS ASSOCIATION</u>. Under the Presidency of ole shipmate, Smokey Seiders and the Executive Direction of Bill Emery, the MCA has targeted this year for a membership drive. I request that you support them by recommending two things within your chain of influence:

(1) That you recommend to all chaplains that they give very serious consideration to joining the Military Chaplains Association and supporting its local activities wherever our chaplains are homeported or assigned.

(2) That you urge your command chaplains to keep the local MCA leadership informed of events that they might wish to participate in such as clergy day, retreats, seminars, etc.

F. <u>SECNAVINST 1730.7, CHANGE TRANSMITTAL 1, DATED 8 JUNE 1984</u>. It is essential that you impress upon your Chaplains and RPs the importance of the change in SECNAVINST 1730.7 that is set forth in Change Transmittal 1. It's my observation that numerous chaplains' offices have not made the change and I would appreciate your communicating that it is of the <u>highest priority</u> that the change be made. I am also tasking the Chaplains Resource Board to provide every chaplain with a clear updated copy of SECNAVINST 1730.7 so all the old copies held both by chaplains offices and more importantly by command can be destroyed.

I am enclosing a copy of the Veterans Day Speech General Vessey gave in Birmingham, Alabama in November (enclosure (2)). As you know, the Chairman of the Joint Chiefs of Staff is a great supporter of chaplains and command religious programs. I personally enjoy hearing him tell chaplains to be more like sycamore trees--"something that people can climb up on to see the Lord."

In the last two months I have gotten to see most of you personally and that's something I truly enjoy. Thank you very much for the outstanding job you are doing in both ministry and in administering. You are setting standards, patterns and practical factors that will provide for ministry to sea service people into the twenty-first century.

With warmest regards.

Sincerely yours,

NEIL M. STEVENSON
Rear Admiral, CHC, USN

(NAME & ADDRESS)

Enclosures

1 Jul 1985

Dear (Endorsing Agent):

I will be relieved by John McNamara on 27 August, and I wish to express my sincere thanks for your help and assistance during my tenure as Chief of Chaplains. The chaplains you have endorsed have "made ministry happen" at sea and ashore throughout the world.

Ministry in the military happens in this nation, which rightly separates church and state, because of the wise accommodation established over one hundred years ago by demanding ecclesiastical endorsements for chaplains. My personal appreciation of that system came from my own faith group. My professional involvement with it commenced in 1969 when Chaplain Jude Senieur and I were on Chaplain Jim Kelly's staff and we volunteered to organize a Navy Chief of Chaplains Conference for endorsing agents. The relations of endorsers and Chief of Chaplains have traveled a long way since then. So, I'm grateful for the years of association with you and I continue to be concerned that the church and the state maintain the health of the endorsing process.

I have expressed to you my concern that the future of the military chaplaincy is perhaps more fragile than we would like to think. There are certainly those in the armed services who will do all they can to continue the military chaplaincy; but, only you who represent the faith groups can be proactive in protecting the military chaplaincy from reduction or loss from disinterest or non-advocacy. I urge you to be prepared.

From whence might the challenges come and how can we prepare? We owe a great debt to the U.S. Army and the Army Chief of Chaplains for the battle fought recently in the courts. I think there will be future judicial cases and it would be a comfort to know some group outside of government studies all such cases.

A legislative challenge might arise in our austere climate. It would be good if legislators were kept aware that the public wants ministry visible and available to their service personnel. Worthy programs are easily decremented if legislators are not kept informed of their value. Endorsing agents representing a constituency could provide regular communications that assured legislators that the folks back home want a vital military chaplaincy.

Lastly, as in most of history, the greatest threat may come from within. It may be in the form of an endorser who does not really have the authority to withdraw an endorsement. That thought can cause even a Chief of Chaplains to wake up at night. The government side of the endorsement coin is secure in DOPMA. The faith group side is worthy of self-examination. Is there a codified statement in accordance with the polity of the faith group that gives its endorsing agent the right to endorse? Even more importantly, is there a clear statement that authorizes the withdrawal of endorsement?

Well, you see I'm still Neil -- I'm still asking questions. I'm still concerned that ministry is provided or facilitated to sea service personnel wherever they are. I'm still grateful for what you have done and will do to make that ministry happen.

As you know, the Navy has ordered an outstanding relief for me in John McNamara. It's a great pleasure to have him "fleet up."

My thanks for your counsel, cooperation and prayers. God bless. With warmest regards.

                Sincerely,

                NEIL M. STEVENSON
                Rear Admiral, CHC, USN

Blind Copy to:
The Honorable Chapman B. Cox
Vice Chief of Naval Operations
Chief of Naval Personnel
Army Chief of Chaplains
Air Force Chief of Chaplains
Executive Director, Armed Forces Chaplains Board
Captain Jude Senieur, CHC, USNR-R (Ret)

DEPARTMENT OF THE NAVY
OFFICE OF THE CHIEF OF NAVAL OPERATIONS
WASHINGTON, DC 20350

IN REPLY REFER TO
5050/41
Ser 09G/386
31 Jan 1985

MEMORANDUM FOR THE CHIEF OF NAVAL OPERATIONS
Via: Vice Chief of Naval Operations

Subj: CHIEF OF CHAPLAINS' CHRISTMAS VISIT TO DEPLOYED UNITS AND ISOLATED AREAS

1. During the Christmas Season, Captain Robert Ecker, CHC, USN, Atlantic Fleet Chaplain and I visited commands listed in enclosure (1) and conveyed seasons greetings on behalf of the Chief of Naval Operations, Commander in Chief, Atlantic Fleet and Commander in Chief, Pacific Fleet. In most commands we conducted a songfest, celebrated divine services, toured spaces and conversed with as many personnel as possible throughout the ship or station. Contact was made with a high percentage of the personnel serving in all units and from this experience the following observations were made:

   A. <u>Divine Services</u>.

       (1) Worship services, ashore or afloat are better planned and executed than in years past.

       (2) Attendance is on the increase and Chaplains' quarterly reports substantiate increased attendance.

   B. <u>Religious Education</u>. Scripture study and confirmation classes continue to be a strong thread woven into the fabric of sea going life.

   C. <u>Religious Ministries Policy (SECNAVINST 1730.7 and OPNAVINST 1730.1A)</u>. Chaplains are adapting at a fast pace to the obligations we are stressing, i.e.:

       (1) Chaplains are to provide for their own faith group, to facilitate services for other faith groups and to care for all regardless of faith group.

       (2) The specificity of the new policy is taking strong root in command religious programs.

Subj: CHIEF OF CHAPLAINS' CHRISTMAS VISIT TO DEPLOYED UNITS AND ISOLATED AREAS

D. <u>RP Rating</u>. A major factor for the improvement and expansion of ministry must be credited to the RP rating. The rating provides a true accounting for the mechanical, technical and clerical aspects of ministry. This is providing positive results for all our people.

E. <u>Morale</u>. Morale is high. Sea service people show pride in themselves and in their units as evidenced in:

(1) their attitude toward work and their working relationships

(2) the way in which they maintain their uniforms, introduce their shipmates and decorate their spaces

(3) their expressed understanding of the requirement for them to be serving in isolated areas and with deployed units.

F. <u>Leadership</u>. It was apparent that the majority of commanding officers and executive officers are approachable and have the total loyalty of their crews. Respect rather than rigidity pervaded the ethos of commands. I am pleased to report that commanding officers, executive officers, and chaplains were not only known by members of ship's company but it was obvious that the, "shepherds knew their sheep by name."

G. <u>Cleanliness</u>. It is next to Godliness. I have not seen cleaner ships since my early years (1958) in DESRON TEN. I attribute the cleanliness to a multitude of factors including improved habitability and leadership, but also to the sailors attitude which considers the ship his habitat <u>vice</u> an alien environment.

H. <u>Concerns</u>.

(1) Personnel are mature and self-reliant. They exhibit the intentions of our recruiting policies and training requirements of recent years. They are grateful for what they have received in our Navy but are not dependent on it. They will freely explore opportunities for employment and self-improvement. I judge that their attitude regarding retention is conditional on maintaining opportunity for advancement and the continuation of benefits; not the least of which is the option of retirement at an early age.

Subj: CHIEF OF CHAPLAINS' CHRISTMAS VISIT TO DEPLOYED UNITS AND ISOLATED AREAS

(2) Personnel living or homeported in Guam continue to be concerned about acts of violence. Statistically their perception may be exaggerated when compared with areas in CONUS but nevertheless it is a concern that they verbalize. To deal with this difficulty our Navy could not have a leader more conscious of the situation than Commodore Hagen nor a more trusted ally than Archbishop Flores.

Very respectfully,

NEIL M. STEVENSON
Chief of Chaplains

Copy to:
CNP

LIST OF COMMANDS VISITED

Naval Air Station, Keflavik, Iceland
Administrative Support Unit, Bahrain
Commander Middle East Force
CTG SEVEN ZERO PT NINE
USS INDEPENDENCE
USS ROBISON
USS GEORGE PHILIP
USS JOHN HANCOCK
USS MCINERNEY
COMDESRON TWO SIX
USS NIAGARA FALLS
USS JOHN KING
USS PLATTE
USS MCCANDLESS
USS HAYLER
USS ESTOCIN
USS CARL VINSON
USS LEAHY
USS GRIDLEY
USS STERETT
Naval Support Facility, Diego Garcia
Naval Station, Subic Bay
Naval Air Station, Cubi Point
Naval Station, Agana, Guam
Naval Air Station, Guam.

Enclosure (1)

26 August 1985

Dear Chaplain,

The oar is on my shoulder and I'm prepared to execute Homer's advise:

> ...Thereafter go thy way, taking with thee a shapen oar, till thou shalt come to such men as know not the sea, neither eat meat savoured with salt; yea, nor have they knowledge of ships of purple cheek, nor shapen oars which serve for wings to ships. And I will give thee a most manifest token, which cannot escape thee. In the day when another wayfarer shall meet thee and say that thou hast a winnowing fan on thy stout shoulder, even then make fast thy shapen oar in the earth and do goodly sacrifice to the Lord....
>
> <u>Odyssey</u>, book Xl

These Navy years have flown by compared to the memories of some very long days in which I experienced frustrations, programmatic failures and homesickness. Ministry in the Naval service is made up of painful days and joyous years. It has been a great honor to have been a Navy Chaplain and to have served in a Chaplain Corps comprised of professionals.

I thank you for your being professional in your practice of ministry. A friend recently handed me a copy of the following article from Martin E. Marty's <u>CONTEXT</u> of 15 June 1982. It is an excerpt from <u>U.S. CATHOLIC</u> by Mary O'Connell and my socio eye enjoyed it:

Father Philip Murnion of the National Conference of Catholic Bishops' Parish Project has identified several "operating styles" in parish ministry, and it is useful to think about them.

1) ORGANIZATIONAL STYLE. This style approaches ministry as many things to be organized; the parish calendar is the key thing.

2) HOSPITALITY STYLE. Here the pastor and staff are not the ones generating things; they tend to be more laid back, open, trying to listen and figure out what the people want..

3) TEACHING AND EVANGELISTIC STYLE. This puts the emphasis on questions of faith and response. The liturgy is the key. The pastor devotes much attention to homilies, etc.

4) SOCIAL ACTION. Enough said.

5) SERVICE/THERAPY. The key here is the accessibility of the staff to individuals and their needs. There is a lot of interest in counseling, in finding out what people's needs and hurts are and trying to help.

6) SACRAMENTAL SERVICE. You find this in churches in business areas that have no residents, as well as in a few other places where people have deliberately chosen to be isolated and don't want to be involved in anything; reliability of service is the only issue.

7) CHURCH AS CULTURE CARRIER. Classically these are the ethnic parishes; the staff support the culture of the people by celebrating their holidays and attending their feasts.

My friend then asked me, which "operating style" do chaplains use? My response was that, "Navy Chaplains are Professionals and therefore their operating style is to provide for all the above." I believe that; I've seen you do it, including the esoteric things which might be called "sea service ethnic." Your capability emulates the old chaplain's prayer, "O Lord, not my needs but their needs be met. Amen." You are second to none in the profession of ministry, chaplain, because you do care for all, facilitate for others and provide for your own. As Father Bill Walsh, of blessed memory, taught - the word Nave means ship and we have a duty to everyone in ships company.

Let me also express my appreciation to "the snipes," the C.R.B., and the RPs as follows:

- Snipes (CHC Snipes are chaplains ordered to duty on the staff of the C.O.C., as Claimant Chaplains, and as faculty of the Chaplains School) the 4100 community has been most fortunate and I have been greatly blessed these last five years to have chaplains of your talent and dedication in "engineering." You've kept the CHC on a true course and never lost the load. Thank you for making it possible for the rest of us to do ministry in the operational sphere where we all want to be.

- C.R.B., you've placed the finest tools of ministry in the institutional environment in general and Navy world in particular in our hands. Thank you, the highest compliment I can pay you is to tell you that we all take your products and quality for granted.

- RPs, you have truly matured. Thank you for being highly motivated and skilled people who want to provide outstanding services for shipmates and advance in all the parameters of your Navy careers. What a fantastic contribution you have made in such a short period of time. What potential you offer to all of us to provide better ministry for sea service personnel and their families. How did we ever get things done without you? We didn't! I'm pleased that every RP retained squares the man-years of experience necessary to best get ministry done in the institutions of the sea service.

I trust that you'll continue to enjoy your duty, Chaplain, and that you'll find the challenges of ministry and Navy duty exciting.

I regret that Chaplain McNamara becomes Chief of Chaplains in bearish (my term for austere) <u>vice</u> bullish times. This means that the justification for billets and budgets, etc. gets closer to the point of action - the local command - than the places of bureaucracy, like D.C. That's also why quarterly reports and P.M.O. are so very important for making commanding officers aware of the vital (don't be too humble) role chaplains and RPs play and of the value the command religious program offers to all.

Chaplain John McNamara has been a superb Deputy and he will be a great Chief of Chaplains. Chaplain Al Koeneman will serve well in fulfilling the multitude of requirements that are demanded of that one sentence job description of the Deputy. God bless them both.

The Lord be with you, Chaplain, in your practice of ministry. With warmest regards.

Sincerely,

NEIL M. STEVENSON
Rear Admiral, CHC, USN

P.S. I've enclosed portions of the Change of Office program and Pre-change of Office Prayer Service so you may join in wherever you are doing ministry.

www.ingramcontent.com/pod-product-compliance
Lightning Source LLC
Chambersburg PA
CBHW080625170426
43209CB00007B/1518